Total   0
YTD   0
LY   0
LCO   N/A

The Business of Sustainability

Volume I: Global Challenges and Opportunities
Volume II: The Global Supply Web
Volume III: The Road to Sustainability

The Business of Sustainability

Trends, Policies, Practices, and Stories of Success

VOLUME II: THE GLOBAL SUPPLY WEB

James C. Hershauer, George Basile, and Scott G. McNall

PRAEGER

AN IMPRINT OF ABC-CLIO, LLC
Santa Barbara, California • Denver, Colorado • Oxford, England

Library of Congress Cataloging-in-Publication Data

The business of sustainability: trends, policies, practices, and stories of success / [edited by] Scott G. McNall, James C. Hershauer, and George Basile.
v. cm.
ISBN 978-0-313-38494-3 (hardback) – ISBN 978-0-313-38495-0 (ebook)
1. Social responsibility of business. 2. Sustainability. 3. Business enterprises–Environmental aspects. 4. Sustainable development. I. McNall, Scott G. II. Hershauer, James C. III. Basile, George.
HD60.B8847 2011
658.4′08–dc23

2011028288

ISBN: 978-0-313-38494-3
EISBN: 978-0-313-38495-0

15 14 13 12 11   1 2 3 4 5

This book is also available on the World Wide Web as an eBook.
Visit www.abc-clio.com for details.

Praeger

An Imprint of ABC-CLIO, LLC
130 Cremona Drive, P.O. Box 1911
Santa Barbara, California 93116-1911

This book is printed on acid-free paper ∞
Manufactured in the United States of America

Contents

Introduction to Volume II

James C. Hershauer, George Basile, and Scott G. McNall

Global supply chains are all about global sustainability practices, and global sustainability practices are all about global supply chains. What we have learned during the first 50 years of slow growth of sustainability practices by some businesses all of the time and all businesses some of the time is that the business issues are driven by a complex web of intercompany and interindustry relationships. Volume 1 in this set clearly established the breadth and complexity of the economic, environmental, political, and human issues that must be considered in trying to avoid destruction of the planet and its ecological systems that we rely on for resources.

Let us provide an overview of the parts in this volume to learn how managing for sustainability requires understanding and strategically managing an entanglement of global supply webs. The chapters in part 1 illustrate that heretical and systemic innovations are required in both products and entire industries. Design must be done for entire product life cycles and for all related supply chains, demand chains, and waste chains. The chapters in part 1 will lead you through the staged thinking required to understand the new systemic sustainability approach needed for creating products and services. The chapters in part 2 provide the managerial concepts and demonstrate some tools needed to make the strategic, tactical, and operational decisions to achieve sustainable business practices in your organization. The chapters in part 3 emphasize the need for making supply web decisions based on metrics that provide transparency for all stakeholders. The chapters also provide the conceptual and knowledge foundation necessary to create appropriate metrics to drive sustainable business practices throughout the global supply webs of products and services.

Where Are We Now?

The Industrial Revolution has gone through a number of phases, as depicted in table 1. In a word, they have each focused on (1) extraction, (2) manufacture, (3) assembly, (4) engineer, (5) design and (6) need. Similar phases for use of ecological system resources by industry have been (1) opportunism, (2) efficiency, (3) conservation, (4) control, (5) reuse and (6) management. Similar phases for social equity in business have been (1) slavery, (2) working poor, (3) no child labor, (4) humane and safe conditions at the original equipment manufacturer (OEM), (5) humane and safe conditions upstream, and (6) humane and safe conditions throughout the life-cycle supply web.

One could hope that many industries are currently in phase 6 for all three; however, society and business have not been able to take the necessary set of actions to accomplish this state. Agriculture in the United States is probably the best example of an industry that

TABLE I

Phases in the Industrial Revolution: Sustainability Impact

Industrial Revolution Phases	Use of Ecological System Resources by Industry	Phases for Social Equity in Business
1. Extract, process, make, and transport	1. Pillage and plunder	1. Slavery
2. Make or buy, manufacture and sell	2. Extract efficiently	2. Working poor including children
3. Source, assemble, and deliver	3. Conserve and hoard	3. No forced child labor
4. Engineer, coordinate, and customize	4. Store and control	4. Humane and safe working conditions at OEM
5. Design, engineer, build, and use	5. Reduce and reuse	5. No child labor and humane and safe working conditions upstream from OEM
6. Understand need, design, engineer, source, build, sell, transport, customize, assemble, sell, deliver, use, and recycle	6. Manage cradle to cradle	6. Fair and humane treatment of all adult workers (no children allowed) throughout the entire supply web for the product life cycle

has achieved a great deal and might be close to phase 6 in all three areas (with the exception of migrant worker families paid per unit of harvested product). But sustainability problems are pervasive even for agriculture. In volume 3 of this series, Mark Edwards warns of the possible collapse of industrialized agriculture as we know it. In "Food Security in an Era of Climate Change," he states: "Our food supply depends on stable climate and cheap and available fossil resources including fertile soils, freshwater, fossil fuels, fossil fertilizers, and fossil agricultural chemicals. . . . Fossil agriculture is doomed because many of these nonrenewable resources will run out within 30 years and be unaffordable to farmers in 20 years." In volume 1, Simus and Workman even suggest that "water-stressed supply chains" could even cause us to move back into the early industrial revolution phases with a general lack of collaboration among supply web members. On a positive note, both Edwards and Simus and Workman offer hope through opportunities for solutions that are attainable (you will need to check out volumes 1 and 3 for the rest of the story).

With the sustainability revolution that we are in, we are now attempting to enter into a coordinated phase 7 for all three.

Key features of phase 7 (2010–2050) will be

- Information sharing on equity and ecology

- Interfirm tracking on equity and ecology

- Integrated life cycle analysis (LCA) on equity and ecology

- Industry-level environmental and labor standards

- Supplier and industry codes of conduct

- Environmental supply loops (cradle-to-cradle thinking)

- Engineering and design using design for the environment (DfE) and design for sustainability (DfS)

- Integration of e-business and ecological businesses such as carbon trading

- Ecology and equity and economics as an integrated whole for strategic thinking

Part I: Designing Sustainable Global Supply Webs

In "Being Strategic about Sustainability: A Pragmatic Guide," George Basile outlines a systems-based approach to strategic sustainability that has been developed and used by many companies in the last decade. The chapter by Basile provides a foundation for the whole volume. It provides a pragmatic framework for actually attacking the complexities of global supply webs with a rational approach to strategic decision making for both the long-term implications and the more immediate needs that any business must monitor. It flows from the larger idea of "what is strategy when talking about business and sustainability" and moves into very pragmatic and field-tested, albeit fairly high-level, planning tools. Mind you, while high level, these tools can be used at any scale from a global business to a mom-and-pop shop.

The methodology and tools described can help to integrate other strategic approaches and tools (this is described more in the volume 1 chapter by Basile, Broman, and Robèrt). This is a critical point since so many people believe that sustainability is so "soft" an idea as to have no bounds; therefore, there is no way to be rigorous about pragmatically and strategically addressing sustainability. The remaining chapters in this first part of volume 2 all speak to both this challenge and various ways to approach it. We are starting to see the power of the synergies and integration provided by these various approaches. Last, but not least, Basile's chapter clearly defines sustainability not only as a socio-eco-enviro challenge but as a "decision" challenge (see the chapters by Mittelstaedt, McNall, and Cortese in volume 1 for more on the decision challenge). This redefines sustainability then as a strategic "decision and design" challenge (which is very empowering for pragmatic and can-do folks in the supply web). This fits perfectly with the other chapters in volume 2 that discuss what kinds of decision challenges we face, what the implications are, where we have inherent gaps and uncertainty, and, finally, what this means for taking strategic action as part of the global supply web. Part 2 of the volume focuses more on tactical and operational issues, and chapters in part 3 of the volume explore the tough questions surrounding metrics.

In "'Heretical' Innovation: Tough Questions to Create New Value," Andrew Winston provides a window to heretical questions that we must ask about all of our products and services to dramatically reinvent our global supply webs. For example, why do we have tens of thousands of branch banks when we can handle all of the business with small locations in big box stores, with technology, or both? Given our current communication and computer technologies, the huge ecological footprint of the tens of thousands of branch banks seems completely unnecessary for delivery of the financial services received. The current system is a wasteful artifact from the historical development of our financial institutions.

In "Design for a Sustainable Future," Terry Irwin makes the point that all design problems are now wicked design problems. According to Irwin, their "solution can only be realized through a new type of design—holistic design. . . . Holistic design processes, based upon living system principles, can serve to situate business propositions within larger, more appropriate contexts and leverage the power of the interrelated and interdependent nature of complex, open systems that form this context." In "Redesigning the Bottom Line: How Design Thinking Can Help Business Become Sustainable," Phil Hamlett and Barbara Sudick continue this line of design-based thinking and state that "there is a fundamental shift in how 21st-century businesses characterize what constitutes success. A broader spectrum of more holistic and integrated considerations are being used to account for companies, brands, products, services as well as how they represent themselves in the marketplace."

The recognition that sustainability needs to be less of a metaphor and more a set of rational guidelines for analysis and action is driven home by Brad Allenby in "Sustainable Engineering and Industrial Ecology." Allenby provides a comprehensive overview of what to consider in engineering new products and services; however, he also provides a humbling dose of reality when he states,

> If it has not already become apparent to those reading this volume, the intersecting domains of sustainability, industrial management and performance, and relevant scientific and technical disciplines are complicated, ill-defined, and for the most part uncharted. This chapter will not attempt to bring order to this creative chaos; indeed, such an effort would probably be premature. There is something to be said for knowing when to be definitive, and when to employ constructive confusion. Thus, while I will initially position industrial ecology and sustainable engineering within a corporate social responsibility framework, which in turn nestles in a sustainability

approach to industrial and technological systems, I will not make too much effort to be categorical and specific. Rather, I will spend most of my time exploring the challenges of implementing sustainable engineering in an industrial environment, and industrial ecology as one way of doing so. While focused, this discussion will also be an excellent way of addressing broader issues involving the implementation of corporate social responsibility, and sustainability, in the firm.

Allenby argues that there are guidelines that can be derived from the field of industrial ecology to help business leaders navigate what he calls the minefield of sustainability, which is, among other things, made up of social preferences and value conflicts. Modern corporations face public, though differential, scrutiny for their environmental practices, treatment of employees, lack of corruption, practices of stewardship, even the pay of their executives. Allenby takes it as a given that managing for the triple bottom line requires a commitment to social responsibility as well as the knowledge, capacity, metrics, and managerial tools to do so. It is simply rational and makes good business sense to design for the environment, to think about how a product can be reused, renewed, and recycled. It makes sense to minimize the use of energy, eliminate toxics, and use fewer resources in processing and packaging.

Sustainable management, then, requires the management of complexity to allow for real-world, pragmatic design and management decisions at the level of the individual firm. This means, as we said at the outset, that to manage for a sustainable future requires that we consider simultaneously the real world and our visions rather than the mythic, environmental, social, and economic challenges a business faces in a carbon-constrained world. In the context of Schumpeter's original entrepreneurship definition (see McCraw 2007) of "creative destruction," "Creating Sustainable Entrepreneurship" by Bradley D. Parrish and Fiona Tilley then provides a conceptual framework for how this systemic and holistic approach to innovative design and engineering for wicked problems that leads to heretical innovations can be called "sustainability entrepreneurship." Sustainability entrepreneurship may be considered a process of heretical innovation to meet current perceived needs of our global society while conserving the planet's resources, health, and ecological systems for future generations of all peoples and creatures. By definition, an entrepreneur is someone who accepts risk. Parrish and Tilley ask what is actually required for entrepreneurs to create organizations that are sustainable economically, environmentally, and socially. Most entrepreneurs, as they point out, often define sustainability in terms of profitability, which is not irrelevant but causes a business to be managed differently than if sustainability was the goal. It also causes environmental and social issues to become compartmentalized within the organization because they are seen as silver bullet solutions for a specific environmental problem. For a business to be truly sustainable, it must be driven by a set of core values committed to a sustainable future, and it must be managed from a systems perspective, a point emphasized in volume 1. For example, shared core values for individual firms in a product supply web are central to an ability to eliminate toxic materials and toxic wastes from entire supply webs. In "Business Leadership in Advancing Safer Chemicals and Products in Supply Chains," Joel Tickner and Melissa Coffin state: "In response to growing scientific and public concern about chemicals in products, negative product safety attention, and increased government attention to and regulation of toxic substances in products, many leading-edge businesses are instituting efforts to screen, prioritize, and substitute chemicals of high concern in their products. Yet firms face a number of barriers to advancing safer chemicals in their products, including missing formulation and toxicity information. . . . Firms are beginning to work together within and across sectors to remove technological, market, information, and economic barriers to safer products." This leads us to the chapters in part 2 of volume 2 that deal with how to actually manage responsible global supply networks.

Part 2: Managing Responsible Global Supply Networks

In "Designing Socially Responsible Supply Networks: Creating an Environmental Management System Design," Dan L. Shunk states: "Companies do not compete with companies any more—supply networks compete with supply networks. This recognition has led us to begin to conceive the design of a global environmental management system (EMS) that meets the needs and requirements for global supply network transparency as well as certification through the International Standards Organization's ISO 14000 series." Shunk provides numerous procedures and guides for actually achieving the needed certifications to be able to participate in ecologically and socially responsible supply networks as one business entity in a larger supply web. As you learned from Allenby in part 1 of this volume, the journey to achieve successful supply web sustainability practice is not an easy one.

In "Green Purchasing Policy Development and Implementation by Higher Education," Brian K. Yeoman provides the intriguing story of the ongoing efforts by colleges and universities through numerous associations and groups to move universities to a leadership position in the practice of "green purchasing." The journey experienced by the National Association of Educational Procurement, as experienced and described by Yeoman, provides a roadmap to the pitfalls, difficulties, and successes that can be experienced as a united front is sought among a group of purchasing decision makers for a significant buying sector of the total economy. The key role that procurement plays in creating sustainable global supply webs is further emphasized in "The Role of the Chief Purchasing/Supply Office in Sustainable Business Practice" by Phillip L. Carter and James C. Hershauer. Unfortunately, the sustainability efforts of many firms to become both environmentally and socially responsible may simply transfer the problems to other geographic locations and other peoples. In the last 50 years, we have often seen the use of child labor and high-polluting plants simply shifted to other parts of the world; however, this practice has led to numerous public relations disasters for many firms as such practices upstream in the supply chain have been routinely discovered and then reported to the public. We continue to read and hear about these upstream problems on almost a daily basis. Carter and Hershauer point to the pivotal role played by chief purchasing officers in creating socially and ecologically responsible supply networks. They write, "Because organizations spend up to 80 percent of their cost of goods sold with suppliers, many of their sustainability initiatives, if they are to have a significant impact, must be directed at the supply base and the internal customers for the goods and services purchased from the supply base." This chapter provides a guide for how to achieve sustainable business practice in purchasing and an update on some current practice in industry.

It is also critical that organizations realize that they cannot simply look upstream to suppliers. They must also look downstream to buyers, product and service users, and the waste streams from the products or services. Proctor and Gamble, Unilever, Henkel-Dial, and numerous other companies now recognize that the major portion of the environmental footprint of many products and services is downstream in the use and disposal of the product or service. As one of the editors (Hershauer) found in his personal work with many corporations in the late 1990s, those firms doing the most in terms of their environmental practices made the least noise in marketing that fact. As one executive told Hershauer, "understanding the systemic and supply web complexity of sustainability makes you realize that you probably are not really doing much in the area and that perhaps you should just be quiet about your limited success." Conversely, we have now reached a critical mass of consumers that insist on knowing something about the sustainability of products and services. In addition, all consumers are now aware that it is at least an issue to consider, even if it is the third factor after price and quality. Although it might be the third trigger for buying, it is often one of the top issues when determining if a company is a good neighbor company. This can have significant brand consequences—all the way down to whether a company can keep its social license to operate

It is no longer possible not to consider sustainability in marketing decisions and advertising. In "Sustainable Marketing and Marketing Sustainability," Eric J. Arnould and Melea Press provide guidance to those responsible for making strategic marketing decisions in the context of sustainability. We are clearly in the early stages in this area of organizational actions related to sustainability. The visibility of entire product life cycles and upstream and downstream stakeholders makes marketing decisions particularly troublesome and risky. Arnould and Press state: "This chapter provides a basic understanding of the nascent relationship between marketing and sustainability. . . . Specifically, we discuss sustainable marketing, marketing sustainability, the sustainable marketing organization, and sustainable consumer behavior."

In "Aligning Consumer Decisions and Sustainable Energy Objectives: Energy Efficiency in the Residential Retrofit Market," Charlie Wilson and Hadi Dowlatabadi provide an excellent example of the complex relationships among the many stakeholders involved in consumer decisions related to sustainability. Because energy is a central issue in sustainability and because buildings account for more than one-third of the greenhouse gas emissions in the United States, it seems particularly appropriate to consider the role of the government, suppliers, and consumers in the residential retrofit market. According to Wilson and Dowlatabadi,

Making existing homes more energy efficient is an important challenge for sustainability. . . . The policy and business communities try to induce and influence these decisions through an 'inform, incentivize, and assure' approach. This approach has had only limited success in stimulating energy retrofits over the last 30 years. . . . This stands in stark contrast to the ever-growing popularity of amenity retrofits. . . . An investigation of home owners' retrofit decisions helps explains why: amenity retrofits are motivated by emotional, aesthetic, and social signaling characteristics. . . . This points to an unexploited potential for an alternative piggybacking approach to promoting energy efficiency in the home. Such an approach would reduce the effort, cost, and inconvenience of distinct energy retrofit decisions by packaging energy efficiency measures into amenity retrofits. As well as allowing businesses in the amenities supply chain to differentiate their service offering, this piggybacking approach would also help align policymakers' objectives with home owners' retrofit decisions.

Continuing with an emphasis on achieving energy efficiency in buildings, it is important to achieve efficient energy use in office, commercial, and manufacturing buildings as well. Most of our aging buildings were designed using energy technology from the early 20th century. In "Making It Happen: A Practical Guide to Achieving Energy Sustainability and Self-Sufficiency," Thomas E. Kiser points out that

America's path to energy sustainability and self-sufficiency is much easier to tread than most people realize. It lies straight through buildings. The energy-consumption goliath that buildings represent is a growing problem. We must start thinking of buildings as part of the supply chain that both gulps energy and is a major contributor to the threat of global warming. New buildings are designed primarily to meet maximum energy load demands—not generally to optimize energy performance. Existing buildings have not been retrofitted to employ even the most basic and affordable energy-efficiency strategies.

Kiser goes on to provide a very practical and doable approach for dramatic changes in the energy consumption of buildings, the concurrent benefit of greenhouse gas reduction, and the tremendous economic and political benefits of freeing the United States from dependence on foreign oil.

Taking a leap into the future of energy allows one to contemplate a possible source for energy that might eliminate much of the use of fossil fuels. In "Sustainable, Clean, Carbon-Neutral Bioenergy while Cleaning Air and Water," Mark Edwards explores the pitfalls of subsidizing corn ethanol and explores the promise of algal biofuels. Edwards stresses that "Algal biomass provides a sustainable and clean feedstock for liquid transportation fuel that does not compete with food crops for fossil resources. Algal biofuel production can include remediation of wastewater, recovery and recycle of waste nutrients, and carbon dioxide (CO_2) capture and sequestration from smoke plumes and other waste sources. Algal biofuels hold promise to provide economically sustainable, socially positive, and environmentally friendly production of liquid transportation fuels."

Part 3: Metrics and Supply Chain Transparency

An old and wise management adage is that "People manage to the measures." In the introduction to volume 1 in this set, we stated: "In a 1970 essay, Milton Friedman, one of America's best-known proponents of the free market system, said, 'There is one and only one social responsibility of business—to use its resources and engage in activities designed to increase profits.'" One could argue that the only reason that Friedman made that statement in 1970 is that we did not have any other accepted metrics to do otherwise in 1970. The chapters in this part of volume 2 not only provide other metrics, they provide a compelling case for using the expanded set of metrics to evaluate the performance of firms and supply webs. This also speaks to a slow redefinition of what "profit" is—the blended value concept Jed Emerson speaks to in volume 1, including an increased breadth of what being a fiduciary means. In other words, "Yes, Milton, but how does one actually measure profit?"

In "Making Greenhouse Gas Management Practical for Business," Christopher L. Weber, Andreas Vogel, and H. Scott Matthews provide comprehensive coverage of current efforts to make greenhouse gases an important part of the set of metrics for evaluating firms, industries, and supply chains. Supply chain risk management is a key aspect to monitor. They state:

> Managing greenhouse gas emissions throughout supply chains is an increasingly important skill for businesses to learn. We outline the

current state of greenhouse gas management (GHGM) tools, particularly life cycle assessment (LCA), and discuss their potential to help businesses become more environmentally sustainable. In its current state, such tools take considerable effort in upfront learning and data gathering, and we focus on how these tools can increasingly be made more practical for business. . . . We illustrate these thoughts with a case study in managing supply chain greenhouse gases in the soft drink industry.

An emphases on the use of LCA is continued in "Wind Power, Energy Technology, and Environmental Impact Assessment" by Hannes M. Hapke, Zhaohui Wu, Karl R. Haapala, and Ted K. A. Brekken. They state: "Wind power provides a mature electricity-generating technology that has the potential to substitute a share of the traditional thermal electricity generation. . . . The concept of environmental life cycle assessment (LCA) is introduced, and a case study of an Oregon wind power plant is presented. The results of the case study show a short energy payback time from the wind power plant." This point is reinforced in Gene Keluche's chapter in volume 3, which deals with the potential of wind power on tribal lands in the United States.

In "Metrics-Driven Sustainability," James Niemann provides a map for creating and using sustainability metrics for any organization or supply chain. According to Niemann, "Creating a flexible business and system architecture to support your sustainability vision will allow the corporation to make swift decisions to take advantage of unforeseen opportunities in the future. Making the right investments in implementing software and metrics will be the difference between winners and losers in the future marketplace. . . . Ultimately, keeping internal and external stakeholders informed of the benefits of sustainability will make the program legitimate and enable a dramatic culture change."

In "Regulatory Compliance, Sustainability, and Transparency in the Supply Chain," Robert Johnson provides a nice conclusion for the material in this volume when he states:

Industry-leading businesses are incorporating sustainability processes into their daily operations, signaling a paradigm shift in manufacturing that transcends traditional methods of doing business. . . . The supply chain is the sequence of steps, often done in different firms or locations, that results in the production of a final good from primary factors. . . . Businesses must closely monitor and manage their manufacturing processes and those of their suppliers and partners to ensure compliance with regulatory compliance requirements and voluntary sustainability commitments. New operating models may be required as companies respond to a regulatory landscape that poses increased risk and complexity in manufacturing and product design. . . . Today, organizations must understand and track in minute detail the chemicals, materials, designs, processes, and operations used to build and deliver their products, and to manage inputs from external partners, suppliers, and customers. Information is no longer a tactical necessity. It is a strategic requirement for organizations that expect to be at the leading edge of the global business environment.

Reference

McCraw, Thomas K. 2007. *Prophet of Innovation: Joseph Schumpeter and Creative Destruction.* Cambridge, Mass.: Belknap Press of Harvard University Press.

PART I

Designing Sustainable
Global Supply Webs

CHAPTER I

Being Strategic about Sustainability

A Pragmatic Guide

George Basile

Increasingly, businesses must face complex sustainability challenges and opportunities that cannot be addressed by ad hoc or purely reactive actions. As a result, systems-based approaches to strategic sustainability are being explored, refined, and applied in multiple business contexts, including at a number of Fortune 100 businesses. Here we describe the application of one field-tested, strategic approach to sustainable development and a number of supporting planning tools and process steps, including sustainability perspectives on systems mapping, gap analysis, vision setting, and strategic-action platforms. Examples described include the Home Depot and Interface Inc.

The Need for Strategy in Sustainability

For businesses, sustainability presents a number of challenges. While a widely used and broad definition of sustainability came from the Brundtland Commission—that is, sustainable development is development that meets the needs of the present without compromising the ability of future generations to meet their own needs (WECD 1987), that definition does little to point to specific strategic direction or actions. Businesses are also under short-term and "local" pressures that typically differ from the longer-term and larger-scale issues emergent in the sustainability arena (e.g., climate change, biodiversity loss, global poverty, or global health challenges). Sustainability challenges themselves are complex and often have few linear or direct cause-and-effect chains of aspects and impacts. In addition, the challenges are often fraught with inherent uncertainties—that fall into a class of "wicked" problems—that do not yield to increased computational modeling power, more intensive data collection and analysis, or traditional predictive forecasting methods (Rittel and Webber 1973; Allenby 2007).

For a business, this might seem to present a "wicked" challenge best met by sticking to strong and time-worn business drivers, such as gauging direct market forces and current policy contexts, and addressing sustainability as best fits within a near-term business context. Not unexpectedly then, this has often been the case. Making the "business case" for sustainability remains an ongoing discussion and an effort that must often pass a classic business bar (Margolis, Elfenbein, and Walsh 2007). Making the business case for nonsustainability is less often debated on a day-to-day basis.

However businesses are growing and now exist on global scales, linking individual decision makers to global realities. Supply chains have become supply webs and stretch across the globe, grabbing resources on one continent to serve needs on another. Individual businesses rival many national economies. Efficiencies of production of goods and services have multiplied to such an extent that the historic challenge of human capital has been replaced in many cases by the limits of natural capital (Hawken, Lovins, and Lovins 1999). Within this, individuals within businesses find themselves effectively "scaled up" where their short-term and local decisions can have long-term and global implications. At the same time, global realities bear down in often unexpected and unforeseen ways on business. In fact, the scale and pace of production has become so grand that even Mattel, a business that is exceptional at protecting its clients, could not stop the delivery of millions of lead-tainted toys to multiple nations even after it became aware of the problem (Kavilanz 2009). This is not simply a matter of poor quality control; Mattel has an outstanding safety record. This is a reflection of the combination of scale, speed, and momentum inherent within today's business systems.

A number of responses are evolving and pushing businesses to act. Policy in the European Union and Asia are leaning to force product liability on producers, no matter whether the product or service has been "sold" or not. Policies such as the Registration, Evaluation, and Authorization of Chemicals (REACH) chemical accords and Waste Electric and Electronic Equipment Directive (WEEE) electronic product waste guides put long-term environmental responsibility squarely in the bailiwick of producers.

As global economies expand, increasing cost and availability exposure to such basic materials as aluminum and oil have created potential limits to growth for a number of global businesses—or at least a growing concern. Increased transparency in communications and the rapid flow of news on a global, socially networked scale is making it difficult to argue strategically that misdeeds can be held back for long. Emerging global issues, such as climate change, ocean acidification, biodiversity loss, and contagious global health challenges, are increasingly brought to the public's eye and connected to the key roles that businesses play.

Increasingly, businesses have little choice but to act, no matter what scale a business works on. However, none of the pressures creates strategic pathways forward.

Strategic Sustainability

For more than a decade, a number of businesses, academics, and governmental and nongovernmental organizations have helped to develop a strategic method for sustainable development. While a brief overview will be provided here, a deeper exposé on the concept is provided in "A Systems-based Strategic Approach to Sustainable Enterprise: Requirements, Utility, and Limits" by George Basile, Göran Broman, and Karl-Henrik Robèrt in volume 1 of this set.

The approach combines a five-level model for planning in complex systems, backcasting from basic principles for sustainability, and the integration of any number of existing sustainability (and general planning) methods and tools (Basile and Rosenblum 2000; Broman, Holmberg, and Robèrt 2000; Holmberg and Robèrt 2000; Robèrt et al. 2002). We will highlight a specific selection of tools that have been used in case applications. The levels of the model include:

- Level 1: System level. This level identifies key constitutional aspects of the system in question. An appropriate analogy would be the rules in chess.

- Level 2: Success level. This level identifies the specific principles for success; for example, the definition of checkmate (i.e., the king cannot stay where he is and survive, nor can he move and survive). These principles must, as a group, be necessary, sufficient, and pragmatic enough to describe success.

- Level 3: Strategic level. This level describes general strategic principles that are useful or even necessary to lead to success within the system, (e.g., taking an opponent's most powerful players or getting coaching and training).

- Level 4: Action level. This level contains infinite numbers of actions, but whose probability of being useful for overall success is enhanced or directed by linking to levels 1 to 3.

- Level 5: Tool level. This level is for tools that can be created and applied in the effort to take actions at level 4, informed by levels 2 and 3, and lead to sustainability, in this case, in level 1.

In addition to these five levels, when undertaking strategic planning for sustainable development, four sustainability principles at level 2 have been identified that can be used as strategic guides. The sustainability principles support the maintenance of required biophysically based, life-supporting services on the planet and the need to deliver on a broad spectrum of human needs served by business and human enterprise in general. In the sustainable society, nature is not subject to systematically increasing

- Concentrations of substances extracted from the Earth's crust (such as fossil carbon or metals),

- Concentrations of substances produced by society (such as nitrogen compounds, chlorofluorocarbons, and endocrine disrupters),

- Degradation by physical means (such as systemic clear-cutting of forests and overfishing).

Moreover, in such a (sustainable) society, people are not subject to conditions that systematically

- Undermine their capacity to meet their needs (such as from the abuse of political and economic power).

The four principles were derived by asking and exploring by what primary mechanisms, upstream at the level of first approximation in chains of causality, do human activities set off downstream social and ecological impacts that will destroy this system? The answer revealed how myriads of impacts are rooted in a few systemic upstream errors of societal design and operation. Systematically avoiding these actions is critical to sustainable development.

Strategic Sustainability Approach

The application of strategic sustainability can be broken down into four basic steps: new awareness (or education), creating a vision that includes sustainability principles as guideposts, developing a baseline of where one is today, and, finally, developing flexible actions to move toward the vision of success (see figure 1). These steps combine to form an integrated systems approach that links sustainability principles and requirements with existing business drivers and context.

Step 1: Awareness of Sustainability Challenges

Step 1 is to develop a basic awareness of sustainability challenges within the business (or within the planning group, at least initially) and to reframe sustainable development and sustainable business as decision challenges and opportunities. It is critical that some baseline awareness is generated so that sustainability is not an abstract concept for those engaging in strategic

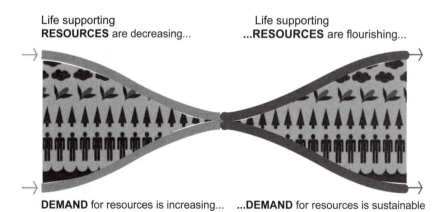

Life supporting
RESOURCES are decreasing...

Life supporting
...RESOURCES are flourishing...

DEMAND for resources is increasing...   **...DEMAND** for resources is sustainable

Figure 1   Highlights both the challenge and opportunity of sustainability, i.e., increasing cumulative impacts on global biophysical systems and the need to reverse this, and four key steps in strategic sustainability, i.e., (A) awareness, (B) vision setting, (C) baseline analysis and (D) backcasting from vision to move step-wise from baseline to success.

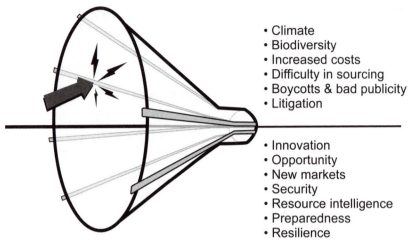

- Climate
- Biodiversity
- Increased costs
- Difficulty in sourcing
- Boycotts & bad publicity
- Litigation

- Innovation
- Opportunity
- New markets
- Security
- Resource intelligence
- Preparedness
- Resilience

Figure 2   A metaphorical decision-making funnel where room to maneuver is increasingly limited by unsustainable activities and cumulative impacts within our increasingly coupled human–natural global systems. Opportunity is also highlighted for moving through and beyond "the funnel."

planning. To have a command of the emerging global business space, strategic business planners need to understand that businesses are in an increasingly narrow global "decision space" when it comes to the life-supporting biophysical services provided by local and global ecosystems (e.g., climate stability, biodiversity, top soil stability). The narrowing decision space can be represented as a "decision funnel" (figure 2). The decreased room to maneuver has real-world implications for businesses. Large global businesses and nations—and all the businesses associated with them—are increasingly "hitting the walls" of this funnel through policy impacts (e.g., changing policies in Europe such as the REACH producer/product responsibility accords), the inability to source key natural resource–based products (e.g. clear-heart redwood at Home Depot), or consumer awareness (e.g., child labor issues at Nike and other clothing producers and retailers). Understanding the nature of and reasons for this decision funnel are required to inform strategy, drive innovation, and reduce risk.

Step 2: Setting a Vision

Step 2 requires setting a vision regarding what a sustainable business looks like for your company. Given an understanding of the emerging reality of sustainability challenges, it becomes possible to ask internal questions regarding what a business looks like when moving toward sustainability. At a basic level this means working within the design guides created by the sustainability principles. On a broader scale, this means thinking and planning about your business using longer-term and larger-scale perspectives to inform near-term strategic challenges. For Volvo Europe, this meant thinking about themselves less as a truck company and more as a transportation company that takes responsibility for the whole "value web" of transportation. The perspective shift increased their potential market by focusing on providing the best transportation solutions by any sustainable means.

Step 3: Setting a Baseline

Step 3 involves setting a baseline to move from or, in other words, asking what a business actually does today using a systems perspective and sustainability principles as a guide. The process of mapping a business against sustainability dimensions at each of the five levels of the strategic sustainability model lets a business discover what its physical impacts on the planet are, as well as on critical stakeholders and community members beyond a traditional customer or shareholder base. The mapping provides a method to understand what the business does at a more fundamental level than typically asked. For example, Interface Carpets, now a global leader in sustainability and business, discovered that their primary physical product was waste (both in terms of production waste streams and that 100 percent of their products ended up in landfills). These same business processes across the industry positioned Interface to uniquely differentiate themselves in both existing and new markets (more on that in the following) (Anderson 1999).

Step 4: Moving to Action

After exploring what success looks like and developing a baseline of where the business is today relative to where it wants to go, action steps can be generated and prioritized. Unlike forecasting based on past problems, the notion of "backcasting" from success using strategic sustainability principles as design guides lets a business design pathways to head where it wants to go, versus simply running from where it has been (Holmberg and Robèrt 2000). By asking how each action can help to create flexible platforms for continued progress (versus one-off dead ends) that fit within sustainability principles and other business success principles and will provide suitable return on investment (i.e., accrue the required resources to succeed), a business can create strategic, flexible, and forward-looking plans for sustainable development. Even incomplete attempts have helped such businesses as McDonalds to reframe their supply chain relations, for example, to better address sustainability challenges; Home Depot to generate new green product categories and address potential negative trade-offs when developing new products; and Electrolux to develop entirely new "climate aware" white-good product lines that are delivering unique access to markets such as China and India.

Applying Tools from a Pragmatic Toolbox for Action

Understanding what any business does from a biophysical, social, and economic systems perspective is critical to creating the planning context for strategic sustainability. Similarly, understanding how the business currently positions itself—consciously or not—within each of the five levels of the model provides a platform for understanding both gaps and synergies with sustainability challenges, opportunities, and action pathways. Thus, two "mapping" processes can provide critical insight for baseline setting and backcasting from sustainability principles and overall business success.

Strategic Planning Tool 1: Mapping Your Business against the Systems Model and against Planetary Systems Using Principles for Sustainability

Putting aside sustainability for the moment, consider your business at each level from system level to tools. What is the typical system that your business considers when it thinks about either strategic planning or the everyday activities that make up the effective strategic plan?

Consider the retail do-it-yourself (DIY) and home improvement store Home Depot, which shares many traits with businesses already facing significant sustainability challenges and opportunities. Without being exhaustive, like many large businesses, the system this business operates in when taking strategic actions includes its customer, its supply web, its shareholders, and, increasingly, a subset of vocal stakeholders. The system also includes the larger policy space that the business operates in, which can vary across markets and regions. And, depending on the make-up of the planning group or decision-makers involved, "the system" may be held as large as Home Depot's international efforts or as small as a single one of the more than 50,000 products sold. At the second level of the model, success, like any modern business, they might single out overall growth, profitability, and increased shareholder and customer value as core success principles. However, the business may also have a set of internal values and priorities that augment traditional growth metrics, at least in theory (Collins and Porras 1996). For Home Depot, this includes enabling their customers to build the places they want to live and to provide the best service in this pursuit. At the third level, or strategic principles, one often finds concepts and efforts that can be confused with overall success. For a business such as Home Depot, this can include a focus on associate retention and satisfaction, year-to-year growth at the store level, clear communications between the corporate home office and semiautonomous store managers and merchants, and many others. Each of these strategic principles provides general mechanisms to attain success within the business's overall system. The level of action will be populated with the enormous array of activities that feed off of and into the strategic means that Home Depot, in this case, undertakes every day. The tool level, while last, is not least. Understanding what tools are employed by a business—from standard accounting tools to novel sets of metrics, management, and communications tools—all give insight into what is currently being organized, tracked, prioritized, and acted on—or not acted on—by the business every day.

The next step is to undertake the same five-level mapping exercise but from the perspective of sustainability, and use this for comparison and gap analysis against the previous five-level map (undertaken without sustainability in mind) (see figure 3). At the systems level (level 1), sustainability demands a planet-scale perspective. At the success level (level 2), sustainability principles come into play. At the strategic principles level (level 3), a number of strategic platforms have been identified that improve overall planning for strategic development. At the actions level (level 4) and tool level (level 5), one can assess whether a business is already using tools and undertaking actions that fit the general strategic sustainability context.

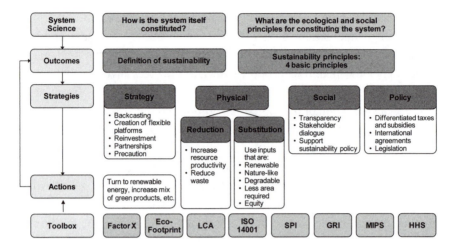

Figure 3   A compilation of strategic sustainability aspects are shown at each different planning level.

For a business such as Home Depot, a number of overlaps are apparent. At the system level, the business is focusing strategically on a global business model, which fits well with the global dimensions of sustainability. Additionally, Home Depot sources many products on a global scale, directly or via global supply webs. The latter foreshadows that global issues will increasingly be of strategic importance even for local Home Depot stores. At the success level, Home Depot has a number of direct overlaps with sustainability principles. For example, a core product of the business is wood and wood products. Thus, sustainability principles dealing with sustainable management of renewable resources is directly relevant to business success. Similarly, as a retailer of numerous man-made compounds and metal objects—from paint to plastic decking, and hardware to appliances—sustainability principles related to persistent compounds and mined resources also directly apply. And, as a provider of DIY home lighting, heating and cooling systems, and energy-efficiency products, for example, sustainability principles dealing with fossil-fuel reliance and supporting basic human needs highlight a pressing and growing market opportunity around renewable energy and energy efficiency. Indeed, in each of the challenge areas highlighted by sustainability principles, businesses such as Home Depot have the opportunity to provide new and sustainable solutions that better meet their markets' needs in both the near and long terms—and mesh with the business's core success values.

At the strategic principle level, a primary overlap comes, for example, at the key strategic principle of providing effective means "under one roof" for their customers to modify their homes and business. Why not do this sustainably? For example, the correlation with sustainability principles for sourcing renewable materials from sustainably managed sources and Home Depot's key profit center of lumber and wood-containing products highlights the potential for failure of the business if it does not act strategically and systemically to protect the very forests that its wood products come from. Home Depot, in partnership with the Forest Stewardship Council and the World Resources Institute, became an industry leader in setting and accepting guidelines for the purchasing, assessing, and selling of wood from more sustainably managed forests and of not purchasing wood from old-growth forests (Halweil and Mastny 2004, 131–32). Finally, at the action and tool levels, one can ask and find any number of actions and tools that may already being undertaken. This may vary from store-based recycling efforts to life cycle–based purchasing and product design. As described here, a comparison of the two systems maps—with and without sustainability taken into consideration—provides a first systemic view of synergies, gaps, and challenges for a business undertaking strategic sustainable development.

Strategic Planning Tool 2: Mapping Your Business System against the Biosphere, Lithosphere, and a Broad Stakeholder Community

A second type of mapping exercise that provides insight into what a business physically does as related to strategic planning for sustainability is mapping the business against the biosphere, the lithosphere, and community extending beyond traditional shareholders, customers, and employees. Pioneered by Interface Carpets and their chief executive officer, Ray Anderson, this method creates a combined qualitative–quantitative diagram of the flows of resources into and out of the business—now with sustainability in mind. Interface itself provides possibly the best example of this. A powerful visual planning tool can be generated by placing a business within a global context and mapping the business in terms of its internal activities in the form of people, value, and processes, and its suppliers and the markets and communities it serves and is served by (Anderson 1999).

Interface used this approach to develop two high-level strategic maps. The first describes a typical 20th-century business (figure 4). It becomes

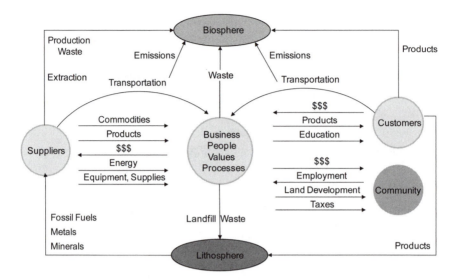

Figure 4   Traditional 20th-century production business. Note strong but not strategic linkages to both global ecological and social systems. Positive and negative benefits with respect to sustainability are ad hoc.

clear that resources flow into the business from the biosphere and lithosphere while waste flows back into each. In addition, a number of other economic and social flows are represented.

In the Interface model of a 21st-century business, features that do not align with sustainability principles have been removed (figure 5). Since 1994, Interface has worked diligently at moving away from the previous map and toward the latter by using basic sustainability principles and strategic principles to avoid making uninformed trade-offs and building flexible action platforms. As a result, Interface has achieved, in absolute magnitude, a 43 percent decrease in greenhouse gasses and 44 percent decrease in energy use, all while growing 27 percent in net sales. They have done this with direct cost savings of about $430 million. Additionally, Interface has developed new carpet technologies and designs that have allowed them to be market leaders and enter into new markets, such as the private home.[1]

Strategic Planning Tool 3: Gap Analysis

With these synergistic maps filled in, a business is armed with two key outputs: knowledge of what they actually, physically do (including a broader

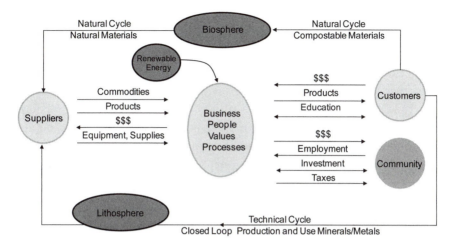

Figure 5 Interface's model for a 21st-century business. In this model linkages to the global biosphere are strategic and cyclical. Energy input is renewable. Linkages to social systems extend beyond simple financial dimensions and include a focus on larger community needs and services.

knowledge of how they make money and what sustainability dimensions their business is reliant on) and a direct mapping of what their current goals, strategies, and actions are vis-à-vis what may be required for a strategic, flexible, and successful approach to sustainability. Gap analysis often provides business leaders and senior managers with their first strategic view of what is happening at their business from a sustainability perspective. It can help address questions regarding ongoing "green" or corporate social responsibility (CSR) efforts and how they do or do not fit into overall business strategy. Prioritizing current green and CSR actions and developing new overall strategic action platforms must be undertaken within the context of the mapping knowledge. Efforts via mapping current context and context with sustainability principles and planetary systems included provides a solid context on which to step back into creating a realistic and galvanizing vision of sustainable success.

Strategic Planning Tool 4: Creating a Vision of Success at the Right Level and Backcasting from Principles for Sustainability

One of the challenges faced by businesses when considering sustainability and sustainable development is developing a vision of success that uses sustainability as a driver of innovation and increases confidence that individual actions are aggregating into overall success. This is a general challenge regardless of sustainable development. In a series of studies, Collins and Porras (1996) provide insight into core features of a robust strategic vision. Studying a suite of businesses that have either successfully withstood the tests of time and changing markets or have moved from a relatively even market position to consistently outdistancing the market overall (or both), two dimensions were uncovered as key to developing a robust vision: shared core values and core purpose. Core values are the values that underlie the business. They sit above exactly what a business does, or even why. These are operating values that a business will follow regardless of market pressures. As such, they flavor everything the business does. These have been captured in well-known examples such as the "HP way," a set of values that are the central tenets of Hewlett Packard since its founding (Packard 1995). The second dimension is core purpose. Similar to asking what a business actually does, core purpose is the reason the business exists. The business may serve this purpose in an almost infinite number of ways—all operating within the context of the core values. The combination of values and purpose provides a great flexibility of actions. If, in uncovering what a business actually does, it is noted that the business's actions do not serve the core purpose or mesh with core values, Collins and Porras's work indicates that failure looms in the future.

For strategic sustainability, Collins and Porras's work, when combined with the five-level planning model and basic principles for sustainability, highlight that the best level for setting a vision for strategic sustainable development planning is at level 2, i.e., purpose and success. For sustainability, principles for sustainability must sit side by side and integrate with existing core values and core purpose. For Interface Carpets, this meant restating what success looks like in terms of becoming a fully sustainable business. For others, such as Home Depot, it meant adding sustainability into their core purpose of helping DIYers build better and sustainable places. With a vision at this level, it then becomes possible to backcast from the vision of success (meaning to head toward success versus only away from past failure, e.g., forecasting), including core values, core purpose, and sustainability principles to guide the strategic plan and action agenda (Basile and Rosenblum 2000; Broman Holmberg, and Robèrt, 2000; Holmberg and Robèrt 2000).

Strategic Planning Tool 5: Developing an Integrated Action Approach by Taking Advantage of Multiple Existing Approaches and Using Backcasting to Generate Flexible Action Platforms

The five-level framework has been used to highlight the focal points and strengths of number of sustainability approaches, methods, and tools (Robèrt et al. 2002). Each of these approaches is useful on its own but can be integrated for a more robust strategic effort and to highlight, prioritize, and address specific needs. While it is beyond the scope of this chapter to describe how numerous combinations of sustainability approaches and tools can be mixed and integrated with more traditional business strategy approaches, the general utility of covering key challenge areas with appropriate concepts, methods, and tools is clear. This highlights two key questions for increasingly complete strategic efforts: Does your effort consider all five levels of the model? Have you chosen the most useful and appropriate approaches at each level?

For many businesses, the ability to more robustly integrate overarching sustainability success and strategic approaches has informed everything from the development of sustainability management systems to clear means to systematically address customer needs in more sustainable ways and communicate actions to key community stakeholders or policymakers. At Interface Carpets, this led to a vision of moving toward a 21st-century business by working in parallel across seven broad strategic fronts, including

- Eliminate waste

- Benign emissions

- Renewable energy

- Closing the loop

- Resource efficient transportation

- Sensitizing stakeholders

- Redesign commerce

Given this overarching strategy, informed by principles for success and systems mapping against both business and sustainability requirements,

Interface has brought a number of methods and tools to bear. For example, in order to effectively eliminate waste, a full life-cycle perspective is applied (i.e., from origination of raw materials to final end-of-life of products). Interface has taken this as far as to "own" the responsibility for their past creation of solid waste (an example of extending life-cycle perspective to multiple generations of products) and have developed new ways to recycle older carpet fiber types. Recognizing that their need to close loops, eliminate waste, and produce only benign emissions is to a great extent defined and informed by biophysical and human health dimensions. Interface has taken advantage of such classic environmental impact concepts as toxicity (pushed beyond human health to include health of ecosystems) and added new ideas such as biomimicry, an approach that uses natural systems as design models (Benyus 1997). The ideas and actions of sensitizing stakeholders and redefining commerce speak in turn to the understanding that individual perception and overarching policy both play key roles in sustainability efforts and success. As such, Interface is reaching across each of the levels of the strategic sustainability framework to create an increasingly robust approach to strategic planning for sustainable development.

Strategic Planning Tool 6: Measuring Efforts at All Five System Levels

Having understood where a business fits within the larger planetary system, as demanded by sustainability, and having developed a vision of success, a current baseline, and an evolving series of action platforms that can integrate numerous approaches, it is critical to apply this knowledge to the tools selected for aiding progress. While a number of tools, such as life cycle analysis, system maps, and gap analyses, have been mentioned, a critical tool set is the measurement of success.

The five levels of strategic sustainability highlight specific dimensions at which a business should assess itself in terms of its overall progress (see figure 6). Systems indicators reflect progress and impacts within the overall system a business operates within, both from business and sustainability contexts. Guidepost indicators are measures that assess how well specific strategies and actions are aligning with overarching principles for success, be they sustainability principles or a business's core values and purposes. Strategic indicators assess a business's efforts in two related

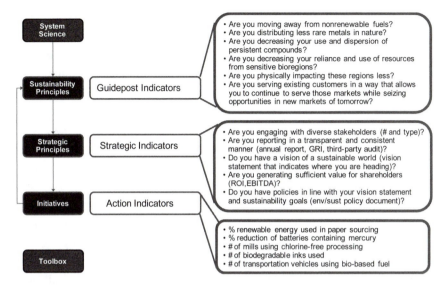

Figure 6 Shown are three general classes of assessment metrics that should be considered when assessing a business's overall progress against strategic sustainability. Shown is an example drawn from the paper and copying industry.

dimensions. First, by assessing whether a business is acting across the broad number of strategic principles that have been identified for robust sustainability efforts, a business can sense whether it is headed toward more complete and robust overall strategic efforts or maintaining significant gaps (e.g., is a business setting a clear vision and policies, identifying and communicating with key stakeholders, undertaking effective resource reduction and substitution efforts). Second, by assessing how well a business is doing within each strategic area across the business, businesses can monitor whether strategic principles are being acted on sufficiently (e.g., how many communications and by how many units; how many resource issues have been addressed). Finally, action indicators should be linked to overall success and strategic platforms.

Both Electrolux and Interface provide excellent examples of this systems approach. Interface's sustainability effort cuts across all five levels of the planning model. As such, they track specific action metrics such as carbon reduction and energy and water use across the life cycle of their products. In addition, they monitor, for example, how well they are communicating sustainability knowledge to their employees and broader stakeholder community, thereby providing assessment at the larger strategic level. Electrolux used their system-based assessment methods to push them into entirely new product lines. Beginning with system indicators (e.g., climate impacts) and guidepost indicators (e.g., sustainability principles, in this case), Electrolux decided to avoid chlorofluorocarbon and hydrochlorofluorocarbon use in a new line of commercial refrigerators (thereby avoiding unforeseen business issues with greenhouse gasses or otherwise arising from large-scale use of these persistent compounds). They then applied a series of life-cycle based action metrics to minimize overall resources in production, delivery, use, and end-of-life. Having identified China as a potential market for these new resource-efficient products, Electrolux then set up internal strategic guides that focus on effective communication and linkage to emerging water- and energy-efficiency policies in China. The latter provided a significant marketing advantage to their new class of products. For Electrolux, the systems approach to design, action, and marketing has led them to their largest growing new line of goods (Electrolux 2009).

Conclusion

The reality of sustainability is that it is an evolving and complex arena. However, that does not mean that there are not emerging methods that embrace uncertainties and enable businesses to take increasingly robust strategic actions. Strategic sustainability begins with the end in mind— "success"—and works backward from where a business is today to creating flexible strategic platforms for moving toward success. By defining the appropriate levels of knowledge, action, and tools needed to move directionally in a complex arena such as sustainability, strategic sustainability changes discussions from "where are we going" to "how do we get there." It also reframes trade-offs from a choice among evils to evolving discussions of what pathway is best aligned with overall goals and has the flexibility to be built on and adapted to an unforeseeable and changing future. A growing number of businesses are exploring approaches such as this. While many challenges remain, attempts at strategic sustainability provide both pragmatic stepping-stones for moving ahead and remind each of us that novel approaches will be required to succeed. Current planning methods are insufficient. However, one thing is certain: the future can no longer be built simply by looking back to the past.

References

Allenby, B. R. 2007. "Earth Systems Engineering and Management: A Manifesto." *Environmental Science & Technology* 41, no. 23:7960–65.

Anderson, R. 1999. *Mid-course Correction.* White River Junction, Vt.: Chelsea Green Peregrinzilla Press.

Basile, G., and J. Rosenblum. 2000. "Designing with the World in Mind." *Forum for Applied Research and Public Policy* 15:29–35.

Benyus, J. 1997. *Biomimicry: Innovation Inspired by Nature.* New York: Perennial.

Broman, G., J. Holmberg, and K.-H. Robèrt. 2000. "Simplicity without Reduction: Thinking Upstream towards the Sustainable Society." *Interfaces* 30:13–25.

Collins, J., and J. Porras. 1996. "Building Your Company's Vision." *Harvard Business Review.* 74:65–77.

Electrolux. (2009). *Sustainability Report 2009.* http://group.electrolux.com/en/sustainability-report-2009-595/.

Halweil, B., and L. Mastny. 2004. *State of the World 2004.* New York: W. W. Norton.

Hawken, P., A. Lovins, and H. Lovins. 1999. *Natural Capitalism.* Boston: Little, Brown.

Holmberg, J., and K-H. Robèrt. 2000. "Backcasting: A Framework for Strategic Planning." *International Journal of Sustainable Development and World Ecology* 7:291–308.

Kavilanz, Parija B. 2009. "Mattel Fined $2.3 Million over Lead in Toys." *CNNMoney.com.* June 5. http://money.cnn.com/2009/06/05/news/companies/cpsc/.

Margolis, J. D., H. A. Elfenbein, and J. P. Walsh. 2007. "Do Well by Doing Good? Don't Count on It." *Harvard Business Review* 86:19.

Packard, D. *The HP Way: How Bill Hewlett and I Built Our Company.* New York: Harper Business, 1995.

Rittel, H. W. J., and M. Webber. 1973. "Dilemma in a General Theory of Planning." *Policy Sciences* 2:155–69.

Robèrt, K.-H., B. Schmidt-Bleek, J. Aloisi de Larderel, G. Basile, J. Jansen, R. Kuehr, P. Price Thomas, M. Suzuki, P. Hawken, and M. Wackernagel. 2002. "Strategic Sustainable Development: Selection, Design and Synergies of Applied Tools." *Journal of Cleaner Production* 10:197–214.

WECD (World Commission on Environment and Development, the Brundtland Commission). 1987. *Our Common Future.* Oxford: Oxford University Press

Note

1 For the latest progress, see "Interface Progress to Zero," www.interface global.com/Sustainability/Progress-to-Zero.aspx

CHAPTER 2

"Heretical" Innovation

Tough Questions to Create New Value

Andrew Winston

Sustainability is no longer a side issue for business—it is quickly becoming a strategic imperative. The forces driving business down the green path are varied, powerful, and relentless. These pressures include such thorny issues as climate change, water shortages, business customers greening their supply chains, employees looking for values in their workplaces, technology-driven transparency, and resource constraints driven by the rise of the consumer around the world. Working within these new realities will require businesses to rethink how they fundamentally operate. This chapter makes the case that the world needs companies to ask themselves deep questions that challenge their businesses to the core: Can we operate without fossil fuels? Can we help customers use less of our product to help reduce their footprint? What's our responsibility to workers in our supply chain? A new form of creativity, what I introduced in my book *Green Recovery* as "heretical innovation," is needed. This chapter offers seven key rules and guidelines for finding those heretical innovations—new processes, products, and services—that dramatically change a business or industry.

Introduction

Companies now face an enormous array of environmental and social pressures that make the pursuit of sustainability unavoidable. Put bluntly, managing your environmental and social impacts—and those of your suppliers and customers as well—is simply not optional anymore. Luckily for business, this new strategic path is not just mandatory; it is enormously profitable as well.

Finding opportunities to create sustainable value requires seeing the world and your business through a new lens. Solving the sustainability challenges of our species will require massive changes in how we live, eat, work, and play. These seismic shifts will force large-scale innovation but will also create multi-trillion-dollar business opportunities. Who is better positioned to lead that charge than the private sector, which has the resources, tools, and strategies to find market openings and exploit them?

The focus of this chapter is on the kind of thinking we will need to solve the thorniest problems—a new kind of thinking that I call "heretical" innovation (Winston 2009, 115–22; see also the foundational work on disruptive innovation from Christensen 1997). This brand of creativity forces companies and managers to ask very tough questions that challenge the nature of their businesses to the core. Heretical innovations may take the form of operational changes that shift how things have always been done, or they may fundamentally reshape an industry.

Envision a cleaning company asking whether its floor-scrubbing device could clean without any chemicals. Picture airlines and plane manufacturers wondering if they could fly without fossil fuels. Consider how well it might go over in the boardroom to suggest that a shipping company slow down to save fuel and money. Leading-edge companies of all sizes are entertaining and acting on these ideas and many others. The companies that ask and answer the toughest questions will create the greatest value and dominate their markets.

But before we dive into heretical innovation, let us take a quick look at the relentless forces coming to bear on companies, the ones driving the pursuit of sustainability as a crucial—and unavoidable—business strategy.

The New World for Business

Over the past few decades, the business world has seen the definition of what makes a good company shift dramatically. Forty years ago, beyond making money and providing jobs, corporate responsibilities extended (sometimes) to philanthropy and complying with new laws on such big-picture environmental and social issues as water pollution and child labor. The responsibilities were focused mainly on the primary operations of the business under direct control or within the proverbial "four walls."

But over time, and especially in the 2000s, the list of expectations for business has exploded to include everything from carbon emissions and water use to human rights and the labor practices of suppliers halfway around the world (see Savitz 2006, 41–63). A wider array of issues, all considered along the full value chain, are now fair game and count toward your footprint.

I see the forces driving this explosion of responsibility falling into three primary, interlocking buckets: sustainability drivers, tectonic shifts in how the world works, and stakeholder pressures. Of course, in each category a complete list would be very long. For example, Esty and Winston (2009, 97) offer a chart with 20 different stakeholders divided into 5 categories. The 5 categories of stakeholders are (1) rulemakers and watchdogs, such as regulators and politicians; (2) idea generators and opinion leaders, such as academia and think tanks; (3) business partners and competitors; (4) consumers and community; and (5) investors and risk assessors, such as banks and insurers.

At a more general level for sustainability drivers, tectonic shifts, and stakeholder pressures, figure 1 shows a simple schematic of these three circles of pressure. But the ones shown here are the most powerful forces, so let us look at each area briefly.

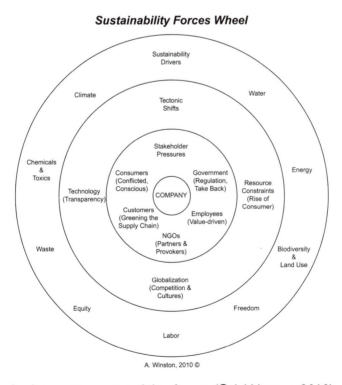

Figure 1   Interacting sustainability forces. (© A. Winston, 2010)

First, we face fundamental environmental and social challenges such as climate change, water quality and quantity, and toxic chemicals on the green side, and central issues of equity and freedom—to associate, from persecution, from forced labor, and so on—on the social side. Without these real and growing challenges, we would not be having the conversation at all.

Second, three big tectonic changes are changing business and society permanently.

- *Technology* is enabling a fast-moving shift toward transparency. Increasingly, customers and consumers expect access to information about what is in every product, its carbon footprint, who made it and where, and on and on. Governments are also mandating increased openness and data collection, on everything from greenhouse gas emissions to financial disclosure on the risks of climate change.

- *Resource constraints* are now a reality, driven largely by the appearance of hundreds of millions of new middle-class consumers, mainly in India and China. This explosion of consumption is changing demand patterns for everything that goes into our society. Supply of energy, materials, and food is very unlikely to keep up, so the cost of doing business will rise for those who do not get lean.

- *Globalization*, a big catch-all, is changing the nature of competition and exposing business to new cultural demands around the world. (For more on these forces, see Friedman 2008.)

Third, companies feel these pressures directly through the prism of key stakeholders. The range of stakeholders to deal with on sustainability issues is large. I highlight here just five key players and the larger trend they are a part of.

- *Governments* at all scales—and this is an important consideration since the activity is not just at the federal level—will continue to create regulations, on carbon in particular, but more generally to extend the responsibility companies have for their impacts up and down their value chains.

- *Nongovernmental organizations (NGOs)* continue their role as a check on the power of business but also increasingly work closely as valued partners of the private sector.

- *Business customers* are aggressively greening their supply chains, with Walmart taking the lead globally, but many others are also asking increasingly pointed questions of their partners.

- *Consumers* may not pay more for green products, but in general, they are conflicted and conscious of sustainability issues and will increasingly choose more sustainable products, all else being equal.

- And as generations shift in the workplace, *employees* are increasingly looking to work for companies that share their values.

Think of the strategic forces wheel in figure 1 as a tool for identifying key issues and opportunities. Imagine spinning each level to match up issues with tectonic shifts and key stakeholders. How, for example, will the convergence of customer demands, technologies to track supply chain data, and concerns about chemicals change the way companies make their products?

The combinations of pressures make for tough challenges and choices. Only the best companies, with leaders that take a new view on the role of business in society, will navigate these mazes. We will now explore the mindset companies will need to cultivate.

The New Mindset

Strategy gurus talk about paradigm shifts all the time, but truly significant changes come about rarely. The movement to assembly lines at the dawn of the Industrial Revolution, the development of management strategies for large organizations in the mid-20th century, the Information Revolution that is still brewing and changing business models—all of these shifts required dramatically new thinking. The sustainability wave is easily as profound, and it requires even more of a mental leap for corporate managers.

Out of necessity, the goal of business and society will be figuring out how to provide goods and services that use drastically less stuff. Given the gap that remains from where we are today to where we will need to be, only heretical innovation and a new mindset will get us there. Following are five critical ways of thinking that will enable the shift we require.

A Commitment from the Very Top Levels

The chief executive officer (CEO) needs to be involved, deeply, and needs to make clear statements to the organization regularly. Without that support, sustainability initiatives will not go very far.

A Broader View on Paybacks and Decision Making

Our current cost-benefit analyses are fundamentally broken. We do a poor job of taking into account longer-term benefits; in wonky terms, our discount values are high, making it appear that future profits are worthless. In addition, we do not know how to account for the intangibles that have value now. How much is a company's license to operate and grow worth? Or what is the value of maintaining the loyalty of customers and employees? These benefits are all pegged at zero in traditional financial models. The leading companies figure out a way around these systematic errors by, for example, lowering hurdle rates on sustainability initiatives or taking them out of the discussion for certain kinds of investments.

A Value-chain Perspective

For most companies, the majority of their impacts lie outside their direct control. The consumer products giant Unilever recently measured the carbon emissions throughout the life cycle of its products. The company discovered that only 2 to 3 percent of the total stemmed directly from its own operations—the rest of the footprint resided upstream with suppliers or downstream with customers (for example, laundry detergent requires a lot of energy to use in the washing machine). Identifying sustainability risks and opportunities up and down the value chain requires holistic, systematic, flexible thinking.

An Understanding That Resources Are Not Infinite

This idea sounds obvious at first, but it is not the way we have ever operated as a species. Global resources in minerals, energy, forest products, fish— you name it—seemed basically endless until recent times. While many executives will try to stay out of the debate on climate change, very few deny that resource issues are real. In a recent survey of European CEOs, four-fifths said they were using sustainability as a critical tool to battle shortages in such raw materials as oil and water (Barton 2010).

A Willingness to Break Through Normal Barriers ("No" Is Not an Option)

We need companies and leaders that push their organizations to take big leaps, to not accept the status quo, and to question everything. For example, energy entrepreneurs are not listening to the gospel that renewable energy costs more to produce than fossil fuel-based sources—they are creating new companies and technologies at a rapid pace to prove the naysayers wrong. Large companies may be less nimble, but they can challenge their industries as well. If they do not, they may find their markets have dried up. Consider the case of General Motor's Hummer brand. After energy prices rose in 2008 and consumer preferences shifted toward more energy-efficient vehicles, it only took two years for this once high-flying brand to disappear. At the same time, Toyota, Nissan, Ford, and even General Motors itself have developed (somewhat) affordable hybrid and electric vehicles instead. They have all challenged deep-seated views on what works in the auto industry.

With the right mindset, leaders can start to ask deeper, heretical questions. Let us look at a handful of examples of companies doing things very differently and see what lessons and themes we can draw.

Seven Rules for Heretical Innovation

Imagine you are a television or advertising executive in the middle of the 1990s, and someone in a meeting asks, "What if people stop watching commercials?" You would likely think that the question was inane. But TiVo and other digital video recorder companies created technologies that allowed viewers to skip advertisements entirely. The entertainment industry is still figuring out how to deal with the massive challenge to its business model. If just one new technology can force heretical questions and once-unthinkable outcomes, think about what global-scale sustainability pressures will do.

In the transportation sector, the prospect of declining fossil fuel availability raises an ugly specter for the aerospace industry. In response, Boeing has been working with a number of airlines (including Virgin Atlantic, Japan Airlines, Air New Zealand, and Continental) to test out biofuels made from such sources as algae (Wald 2009). On Earth Day 2010, the U.S. Navy tested an F/A-18 fighter jet dubbed the "Green Hornet" on a mix of conventional jet fuel and biofuels (Wright 2010). These companies are asking a new question: Can we fly without fossil fuels? The answer, it turns out, is "yes." The planes all work fine. But the idea must have seemed a bit out there to Boeing engineers and navy admirals at first.

These are examples of the kinds of heretical questions that challenge the core assumptions of a business or industry. Other questions are more general but just as provocative. What if there is no water available in a region, or if oil rises to $500 a barrel? What would these pressures do to your business? How would they impact your suppliers? What would they mean for your customers?

The companies that systematically ask and answer tough questions will create the most value. But where should companies look for innovative ideas and new ways to create sustainable value? I provide here a list of guidelines for identifying opportunities for green, heretical innovation. These ideas are listed roughly in order from the easiest for an organization to grab onto to the most challenging and heretical of all, completely rethinking a product or business model.

Look in All Parts of the Business for the "Fruit on the Ground"

Sometimes heresies are not big, overarching philosophical challenges to the status quo, but they tackle just one operational process. They seem like smaller ideas but can yield impressive savings. Many companies, spurred on by the recession that began in late 2008, have found new ways to get lean, saving both natural resources and money. These companies are not just grabbing the proverbial low-hanging fruit, they are picking up what energy guru Amory Lovins and others call "the fruit on the ground."

Five areas of operations hold particular promise for quick and significant savings: facilities (heating, cooling, and lighting), fleet and distribution, information technology, telework, and waste. Simple changes, such as moving from incandescent bulbs to compact fluorescents or LED lighting, can save money fast, often with paybacks in months, not years.

In the fleet arena, Walmart has improved the fuel efficiency of its trucks by 30 percent with a series of relatively simple changes. Wind skirts, which are basically pieces of plastic hanging from the side of a truck, make a vehicle more aerodynamic and save a percent or two. Adding auxiliary power units, which provide enough juice for heating or cooling the cab of the truck so drivers do not need to idle their engines for hours, improved Walmart's fleet efficiency by 8 percent.[1]

But the simplest cost-saving move in fleet operations is just slowing down. Conway, a large North American shipping company, reduced its maximum speed from 65 to 62 mph and is saving up to $10 million a year (Emily 2009). For a company that broke even in 2009 during the deep worldwide recession and netted $75 million in a more typical year in 2008, these savings are a big deal. Maersk, the Danish ocean shipper, has cut fuel use 30 percent on hundreds of its routes by working with customers that do not need their items immediately and can wait the extra week or two (Rosenthal 2010). For a freight company, slowing down is pretty heretical.

In another twist on fleet management, the international package giant UPS set a new policy of "no left turns" for its city deliveries. This catchy, simple idea masks a sophisticated system of GPS technology and routing software that maps new routes. By taking only right turns, drivers no longer wait to cross traffic, which wastes time, energy, and money. In total, UPS cut 28 million miles out of its routes and saved 3 million gallons of fuel per year (Lovell 2007). These are big numbers, but the real story here is about culture and heresy. Think about that first meeting when somebody asked, "Why don't we stop taking left turns?" It must have been seen as a very odd question. But the culture at UPS allowed for engineers to do the analysis and discover that a wacky idea was actually quite wise.

When it comes to our relationship with waste, a big movement is under way. Companies in a range of sectors are targeting "zero waste" as a goal (an important caveat: almost everyone uses this phrase to mean zero waste going to the landfill; waste is instead diverted to recycling centers or incinerated). In May 2004, the Subaru plant in Lafayette, Indiana, sent its last load of garbage to the dump. A concerted effort to reduce waste at its source, work with suppliers to reduce packaging, and sort literally everything has eliminated useless waste. The process has also slashed toxic emissions and carbon per car by 55 and 20 percent, respectively. The company has saved millions of dollars.[2]

Organizations dedicated to the waste-reduction mission, such as the Zero Waste Alliance, are collecting best practices and case studies from such companies as Xerox and HP, and from smaller firms such as Fetzer Vineyards of California.[3] Some companies find that what was once a cost center is now a profitable enterprise as they sell valuable waste streams rather than paying landfill tipping fees.

These companies and many more have started asking why waste cannot make money, or why they have to send anything to the landfill at all. Questions like these are changing how business is done and creating value inside companies. But the larger value may come from looking outward, up and down the value chain.

Reduce the Customer's Footprint (Think Value Chain)

A few years ago, Procter & Gamble (P&G) conducted life-cycle analyses on its key product lines. In the laundry category, the calculations revealed that neither manufacturing nor supplier operations used the most energy. The vast majority of energy usage was actually the washing of clothes in the home. And about 85 percent of that energy was spent heating the water, not running the washing machine.[4] P&G executives were quite surprised by this result, but they used the newfound perspective to formulate a different question: "Why can't people wash in cold water?" The company then developed Tide Coldwater to help customers save energy and money.

Minor heresies can lead to great new products but can also key up larger questions. It is worth asking what a deeper heresy would look like. For the laundry category, how about asking whether we can wash clothes with *no* water? Perhaps a new fiber or nontoxic coating would repel dirt and reduce the need for washing at all. These possibilities suggest new directions for innovation for P&G but more so for companies that may have never competed in apparel or laundry before. With heretical thinking, competition and new ideas can come from anywhere.

Look (Way) Outside the Category

Companies can get ideas from parallel industries or from much further afield. One of the most interesting trends in the product design world is the idea of "biomimicry," first popularized by green innovator Janine Benyus (1997). The idea is simple: nature has worked out some very efficient ways to do things over the course of five billion years of evolution. Want to develop a strong, flexible fiber? Well, spider silk is much stronger than steel, yet bends. How about adhesion properties? Many lizards can walk up sheer glass walls.

A few companies are copying nature directly. The famous Speedo "sharksuit" that swimmers wore in the 2008 Olympics—and that was subsequently banned from international competition—was modeled after the skin of a shark, which moves through the water with amazing efficiency. Or look at a stealth bomber and compare the shape to a stingray.

Calera, a new startup in Silicon Valley, is copying nature to discover new ways of making cement, one of the most energy-intensive products around. Cement production is responsible for up to 4 percent of worldwide greenhouse gas emissions; each ton produces about three-quarters of a ton of carbon dioxide (CO_2). Calera has developed a new way to make cement that mimics the way coral forms and actually *captures* a half a ton of CO_2 (Biello 2008). With new, heretical technologies, building a city could become a boon to society, not an environmental burden. Calera and a handful of other companies with new cement technologies are trying to change both an industry and how we view the built environment (Bradley 2010).

Look to the Bottom of the Pyramid

A branch of scholarship has cropped up in recent years, led originally by C. K. Prahalad (formerly of the University of Michigan) and Stuart Hart (Cornell University). The topic is how companies can serve and profit from the billion or so people near the bottom of the global income pyramid (the richest people represent the very small triangle at the top). For years now, companies such as P&G and Unilever have developed new products formulated for markets with low disposable income—the best known example being small detergent packets instead of normal, larger sizes.

But a new wave of interest in this bottom-of-the-pyramid market is centered on its role in driving innovation. Instead of just satisfying market demands for these billion new consumers, some companies are using the lessons learned—mainly about how to make things for dramatically less money—to rethink their products around the world. These products also reduce environmental impacts since they often have less material and fewer parts, or use less energy.

India in particular has become a testing ground for low-priced products, such as Tata Motors' $2,200 car, the Nano. In this case, the car is in no way a green innovation; if anything, the wide adoption of the cheap car would be an ecological disaster. But it is a great example of cost innovation. In a different sector, an Indian entrepreneur developed a new service where a company representative with a smartphone and fingerprint scanner provides basic banking services to villages—it is, in effect, a $200 bank branch.

And GE developed an electrocardiogram (ECG) machine that costs only $1,000, one-tenth the price of standard models sold in the West. As the *Wall Street Journal* put it, "GE hopes to sell the technology in the U.S.

eventually and elsewhere" (Bellman 2009). Without knowing the exact internal economics for GE, imagine this: if the company sells a $10,000 ECG in the United States, why couldn't it sell a higher-margin, modified version of the $1,000 machine for, say, $5,000?

For all of these products, the heretical questions are inherent. These companies asked: Why does a bank need a physical location? or, Why can't hi-tech medical care come at a lower price? Answering these questions requires new ways of thinking. Increasingly, innovation means bringing traditionally underrepresented people and perspectives to the innovation table, from within the company and without.

Open Up and Use the New Social Web

IBM has repeatedly held what it calls "innovation jams," online brainstorms that involve its employees in "far-reaching exploration and problem-solving."[5] The 2006 jam gathered 150,000 employees from 100 countries and resulted in 10 new businesses that garnered $100 million in corporate seed money. Throughout the jam, IBM-ers made it clear that going green was important to them. The "Big Green Innovations" business unit was born, and it established a philosophical precursor to the "Smarter Planet" global branding effort that IBM launched in 2009.

Picking the brains of people in 100 countries is only possible with the latest web and social media technologies. Increasingly, smart companies are using new methods to invite in different perspectives. Some are specifically looking for innovation and product ideas that they can take to market. P&G has opened up its innovation pipeline over the last few years to invite the world to create new products for them.

But in the green space, one of the most interesting developments is the drive by a handful of companies to open up their research and development (R&D) books and share innovations they think can help bring about sustainable development. In 2009, Nike, Yahoo!, Best Buy, and a few others formed the GreenXchange to share ideas and even patents.[6] For example, Nike has developed new ways to chemically bond rubber to plastic in footwear, slashing toxic chemical use in that process by more than 90 percent. The company is sharing the "green rubber" technology with Mountain Equipment Co-op, maker of outdoor gear, to help it reduce its chemical footprint.

Being completely—or even somewhat—open with your patents and innovations is at the very least uncomfortable and, for many, even heretical. Companies will need to find the right balance in sharing innovations that could provide competitive advantage versus ones that just provide an overall benefit to the industry. No matter where these companies end up on this, the path to innovation has just gotten a whole lot more interesting.

Rethink Your Products Entirely

Sometimes radical ideas come from the most unlikely places. Tennant is a quiet, 150-year-old company based in Minneapolis, Minnesota, that sells commercial cleaning machines such as the large floor-cleaning machines that custodians push around hard floors in malls and institutions. These machines have worked the same way for decades. Put a box of chemicals— legally hazardous chemicals—in the machine, add some water, and scrub the floor. But Tennant developed a new machine, ec-H2O, which uses only tap water. By oxidizing and ionizing the water, Tennant's machine bumps up the cleaning properties of plain H_2O. While the charged water will not scrub a crime scene (you will need some chemicals for that), for everyday cleaning, it works just fine.

This new product costs a bit more, but customers never have to buy the chemicals again. They can also avoid the hassle and legal exposure of training their employees on how to handle hazardous chemicals. The machine lowers operating costs, uses 70 percent less water, and is safer. Not surprisingly, this is the fastest growing product in Tennant's history.

The story is another one of culture change. The CEO, Chris Killingstad, arrived a few years before this development and changed the company's mission. From now on, he said, we are an environmental cleaning company. A couple of R&D scientists were in Japan soon thereafter and noticed that hospitals used ionized water to clean wounds. They wondered, Why can't we do that on the floor?"

But a deeper heretical question was at work here: Can we clean the floor with no chemicals? Nobody in the industry had really posed the question before. By asking tough questions about what a product really does—as in, what is the service it supplies—companies can really develop leapfrog innovations. People do not want chemicals on their floor, they just want it clean.[7] Increasingly, companies are exploring how to make their products into services and are challenging their own business models to the core.

Rethink Your Business Model (The "Use Less" Challenge)

For years, printer producers, such as Xerox, Hewlitt Packard (HP), and Canon, have sold many millions of printers and copiers. But markets are saturated, and in many companies, nearly every employee has his or her own printer. So Xerox has started to help customers reorganize their printing devices to save energy, paper, and money.

The company helped Dow Chemical move from using 16,000 printers and copiers to just 5,000 multifunction and centrally located devices. Dow will save $20 to $30 million over the course of a few years (Winston 2009, 61–62). It is a nice little eco-efficiency story for Dow. But the real innovation here is that Xerox is actually asking a customer to use less of its product. This approach may seem like it will cannibalize the core business, and it might. But as the CEO of Xerox, Ursula Burns, says, "someone else doing it is much worse" (ibid., 121). Xerox sees a future where customers are trying to reduce their impacts and use less of everything, including paper around the office. Xerox would rather enable that shift than lose its customers.

Other companies are challenging their core models as well. For years, Waste Management has had a good business hauling away garbage and getting paid by the ton. But with companies and municipalities setting zero-waste goals, the waste hauler's core business will most likely shrink. So the company is planning for this near future and evolving into a new company with a growing service business. When a major retailer approached Waste Management and asked for help reaching its zero-waste goal in a test store, they worked together to both reduce waste at the source and manage the recycling waste streams (or capture some for incineration in waste-to-energy power plants). In this case, Waste Management ended up making more money from the waste streams than it did just hauling the garbage. It was a win-win.

Both Xerox and Waste Management are asking the most heretical question of all: Can we help customers use less but still grow our business? In a resource-constrained world, consumption is going to get much smarter and more focused. The companies that can help customers meet their goals while using less stuff will win market share and loyalty.

Systematizing Your Green Innovation

It is easy to advise companies to look anew at their processes, products, and business models, but it is fair to wonder how to make all of that happen in an organization. The "how" is always harder than the "what." Doing all of the steps requires a new way of thinking, so there is a heavy quotient of culture change in this. While I have no quick and easy answer to culture questions (and whole books cover the topic), I suggest that companies need to make green innovation a regular process with real structure.

The first step is to make green innovation someone's job. Somebody should manage the heretical innovation process, and this role should not be the sole responsibility of the sustainability officer. A manager in this role should work to understand how environmental and social challenges affect the business and its products, seek perspectives from inside and out, and drive this thinking into the core innovation processes of the company. In essence, this person will need to build green into design and R&D, use technology to bring people together, set goals, and set aside time and funds.

Build Green into Design and R&D

Putting in place a design for environment (DfE) process will go a long way toward the goal of integrating green into innovation. A solid DfE system may not always foment completely disruptive thinking, but at least designers will know where the impacts lie and how their decisions affect sustainability metrics up and down the chain.

Use Technology to Bring People Together

As described earlier, new technologies allow for new ideas and thinking. Conduct "jams" and open innovation sessions, both for employees and for customers and other external stakeholders. Do it frequently.

Set Goals

GE has regularly established total revenue targets for its ecomagination products on the order of tens of billions of dollars. P&G set a goal of $50 billion in revenue over five years from what it calls Sustainable Innovation Products, which are defined carefully as those with a 10 percent improvement in life-cycle footprint on key metrics such as energy, water, or waste. Aspirational goals such as zero waste can drive new thinking.

Set Aside Time and Funds

Google and 3M are famous for mandating that their engineers and thinkers spend 10 to 20 percent of their time doing whatever they want. Imagine telling people they need to spend some portion of that time on green innovation. Ask them to think about climate change and water shortages and what they mean for the business. And of course, some dedicated R&D funds for sustainability would help people fund some wacky ideas.

As Albert Einstein (purportedly) once said, "The significant problems we have cannot be solved at the same level of thinking with which we created them." The problem of sustainability is the most challenging humanity has ever faced. Clearly we need new thinking.

The world is counting on the business community to come up with new, leaner, and smarter ways to provide a good quality of life for what will be nine billion people on the planet. These new methods and life-styles are not going to be incrementally different—they will need to be dramatically more efficient and sustainable.

We will need to systematically ask entirely new, heretical questions. We will need to cultivate the renegades in all our organizations and set them free to think big new thoughts. Only then will we find a truly sustainable path.

References

Barton, Heather. 2010. "81 Percent of European CEOs Focus on Sustainability," *Sustainable Life Media*, February 25. http://www.sustainablelifemedia.com/content/story/brands/81_percent_of_european_ceos_focus_on_sustainability.

Bellman, Eric. 2009. "Indian Firms Shift Focus to the Poor." *Wall Street Journal*, October 21.

Benyus, Janine. 1997. *Biomimicry: Innovation Inspired by Nature*. New York: William Morrow.

Biello, David. 2008. "Cement from CO_2: A Concrete Cure for Global Warming?" *Scientific American*, August 7.

Bradley, David. 2010. "TR10: Green Concrete." *MIT Technology Review*, May/June.

Christensen, Clayton M. 1997. *The Innovator's Dilemma*. Cambridge, Mass.: Harvard Business Press.

Emily (no last name). 2009. "American Truckers Lobby for 65 MPH Speed Limit." *Sustainable Life Media*, February 3. http://www.sustainablelife media.com/content/story/climate/american_truckers_lobby_for_65_ mph_speed_limit.

Esty, Daniel, and Andrew Winston. 2009. *Green to Gold*. Hoboken, N.J.: John Wiley & Sons.

Friedman, Thomas. 2008. *Hot, Flat, and Crowded*. New York: Farrar, Straus and Giroux.

Hawken, Paul, Amory Lovins, and L. Hunter Lovins. 1999. *Natural Capitalism*. Boston, Mass.: Little, Brown and Company.

Lovell, Joel. 2007. "Left-Hand-Turn Elimination." *New York Times*, December 9.

Rosenthal, Elizabeth. 2010. "Slow Trip across Sea Aids Profit and Environment." *New York Times*, February 16.

Savitz, Andrew. 2006. *The Triple Bottom Line*. San Francisco: John Wiley & Sons.

Wald, Matthew L. 2009. "A Move Toward Veggie Power Aloft." *New York Times*, January 6.

Winston, Andrew. 2009. *Green Recovery*. Cambridge, Mass.: Harvard Business Press.

Wright, Liz. 2010. "Navy Tests Biofuel-Powered 'Green Hornet.'" U.S. Navy Office of Information, April 22. http://www.navy.mil/search/display.asp?story_id=52768.

Notes

1 Elizabeth Fretheim, Mark Helms, and Kory Lundberg (Walmart). Conversation with author, February 6, 2009.

2 Tom Easterday, Presentation at the Southwest Michigan Sustainable Business Conference, November 13, 2008.

3 See http://www.zerowaste.org/

4 Len Sauers (P&G). Conversation with author, February 11, 2009.

5 IBM jam events page, https://www.collaborationjam.com/; and Paul Arnold, "Big Green Innovations," *Idea Connection*, http://www.ideaconnection.com/open-innovation-success/Big-Green-Innovations-00147.html

6 See http://www.greenxchange.cc/

7 See a foundational discussion on "servicizing" in Hawken, Lovins, and Lovins (1999, 134–43).

CHAPTER 3

Design for a Sustainable Future

Terry Irwin

Both design and business are implicated in the large, complex problems confrontingsociety in the 21st century (global warming, overpopulation, the global economic crisis, etc.). These can be seen as wicked design problems whose solution can only be realized through a new type of design—holistic design.

This chapter proposes that wicked design problems are always composed of triads of relationships between people, the environment, and the built world (design) that form as humans strive to satisfy their needs. These needs can be satisfied in either sustainable or unsustainable ways, and an understanding of genuine "needs" versus "desires" is fundamental to developing sustainable business propositions and designed artifacts. Holistic design processes, based upon living system principles, can serve to situate business propositions within larger, more appropriate contexts and leverage the power of the interrelated and interdependent nature of complex, open systems that form this context.

Introduction

Both design and business are implicated in myriad problems confronting society in the 21st century (Worldwatch Institute 2010) that threaten the possibility of a sustainable future. Understanding the complex, interdependent nature of these problems is fundamental to creating sustainable business models and design solutions.

Design is typically associated with the products, communications, and complex built environments that arise out of the business arena as the physical components of commerce and service offers, which links design in a subordinate position to business. This chapter proposes a separate, metalevel definition of design as a ubiquitous human activity that is an emergent property of people striving to satisfy their needs (Wheatley and Kellner-Rogers 1999, 67–69). Design can therefore be seen as the shaping of flows of energy and matter to meet human concerns (Orr 1994, 104). I argue that business propositions based upon the satisfaction of genuine human needs (as opposed to wants and desires) will create an imperative for more sustainable and appropriate design, and will, overall, be more sustainable. Three broad topics relevant to this argument are introduced in this chapter, along with references intended to facilitate additional research on the part of the reader.

Wicked Problems

The large problems confronting society, such as global warming, pollution, water shortages, the global economic crisis, poverty, and overconsumption, to name a few, are wicked problems (Rittel 1972, 392–96), a class of complex, systemic, and purportedly unsolvable problems composed of seemingly unrelated yet interdependent and interrelated elements, each of which manifest as problems in their own right, at multiple levels of scale. The design disciplines have identified and developed processes for addressing wicked problems but heretofore have not directed ongoing energy toward understanding their composition or behavior. Discoveries in mid-20th-century science such as chaos and complexity theories can provide keys for understanding the characteristics, anatomy, and dynamics of wicked problems that are fundamental to developing sustainable solutions at any scale.

Design and the Satisfaction of Needs

Wicked problems are composed of complex, interdependent webs of relationships at multiple levels of scale, which are formed as humans strive to meet their needs. Design can be seen as the emergent physical embodiment of this activity, which, because of its ubiquity, is implicated in wicked problems. Design also has the potential to contribute significantly to the solutions of wicked problems because needs can be satisfied in either sustainable or unsustainable ways. Unsustainable design is often linked to the satisfaction of a want or desire as opposed to a genuine need; conversely, satisfying a genuine need in a sustainable way will involve designed artifacts and processes that are themselves more sustainable. A better understanding of genuine human needs (versus wants or desires) can inform more sustainable business practices and design processes.

Systems Thinking

A more holistic design process, applied within a new business paradigm, aimed at the satisfaction of genuine needs has the potential to contribute significantly to the solution of wicked problems and the transition to a sustainable society. Such a process, based upon living systems principles (Capra 1996, 2002; Skyttner 2005; Meadows 2008; Wheatley and Kellner-Rogers 1999; Wheatley 2006; Augros and Stanciu 1987; Hayles 1991; Harman and Sahtouris 1998; Walker and Salt 2006; Laszlo 1996; Briggs and Peat 1989, 1999; Clayton and Radcliffe 1996), frames problems in larger, more appropriate contexts and involves highly collaborative, transdiciplinary teams of practitioners. New business and design paradigms based upon radical shifts in mindset and worldview (Kearney 1984, 109; Woodhouse 1996, 4–46; Berman 1981, 27–65) will place social and environmental values and ethics at the heart of business propositions and design solutions.

Wicked Problems and Unsustainability

Problems such as global warming, pollution of ground water, terrorism, and the increasing fragility of the global economy are both symptoms and drivers of our current unsustainable society and manifest along a continuum from global to local. The design disciplines have for decades termed large, complex, and seemingly unsolvable problems "wicked." Rittel and Webber (1973, 155–69) provided an excellent discussion of wicked problems nearly four decades ago. They established that wicked problems have no definite formulation, no ultimate test of a solution, no opportunity to learn by trial and error, and that they are unique, they are a symptom of another wicked problem, and they can be explained in numerous ways. Researchers have distinguished wicked problems from so-called tame problems that can purportedly be solved using traditional, linear design methodologies (Cross 1993). This chapter argues that the wickedness or tameness of a problem has more to do with context and understanding its sensitivity to initial conditions (Mitchell 2009, 20) than the problem itself. Framed within larger contexts that take into consideration social, environmental, and economic factors, most problems can be considered wicked through their connections to, and interdependencies with, larger more complex problems at higher levels of scale (holarchic structure) (Koestler 1967, 45–58). Once these connections are revealed, the business propositions and myriad of designed artifacts and processes that are embedded within them become visible. Acknowledging and attempting to understand these connections is critical to conceiving appropriate, sustainable solutions within the domains of design and business.

Practically any product or service can be analyzed in terms of its connection to larger wicked problems and issues of unsustainability. As an example, let us say that a soft drink manufacturer believes there is a larger share of the market to capture with the introduction of its own line of bottled water. From both design and business points of view, this presents a set of relatively simple problems to be solved, none of which would appear to be connected to the aforementioned wicked problems, as long as the problem is framed within a narrow context with profitability as the primary objective.

Marketing research can be undertaken to determine a sales strategy, distribution channels can be developed to serve the target markets, and designers can produce packaging, advertising campaigns, and other promotional materials to ensure the new product's success. The designer might also be charged with developing a package that satisfies a strategy to keep the unit cost below a particular amount, which would affect the choice of materials and the size and shape of the bottle, but it would still be seen as a tame problem. If however, the business objectives shift to embrace a triple bottom line model (Gray and Milne 2004, 70–79), the design problem must be framed within a larger context that addresses both social and environmental implications as well as economic ones. Once this happens, a very different landscape that calls for entirely different design solutions emerges.

A complex web of hypothetical relationships with connections and interdependencies at both larger and smaller levels of scale is formed once the social and environmental implications of this business proposition (and the design solutions that arise out of it) are considered. Issues related to the entire life cycle of the water bottle must be considered, including resource extraction, processing and manufacture, consumption and waste, which will involve the bottle's swift and benign or slow and toxic return to the nutrient pool (McDonough and Braungart 2002).[1] Analysis of one facet of the "ripples of consequence" that radiate out from the bottle of water reveals that the resource extraction involved in the manufacture of a typical, petroleum-based water bottle often contaminates the ground water in the region where the oil is extracted (Peterman, Thamke, and Futa 2010), which exacerbates the need for bottled water. Even more ironically, statistics since 1999 show that bottled water itself is often contaminated (Imhoff 2005, 30). To follow the connections further, the problem of polluted ground water is connected to the global water shortage, which in turn can be traced to the problem of resource exploitation in developing countries, which underpins the consumer-based lifestyle in developed ones (Sachs 1999, 1–3). The dominant, consumer-based lifestyle can be related to the politics of oil extraction in the Middle East, which in turn is directly connected to global terrorism. Thus, dots can be connected between the seemingly harmless water bottles and terrorism. An alternative business proposition and design brief based upon triple-bottom-line objectives might suggest locally sourced materials and more sustainable production processes in the manufacture of the bottle or might even call into question the business proposition itself if its sole objective is profit predicated upon social and environmental violations or costs.

The Anatomy and Dynamics of Wicked Problems

The webs of relationship described earlier resemble complex food webs (Polisand and Strong 1996, 813) found in ecosystems that are comprised of mutualistic interdependencies between species. This chapter proposes that wicked problems are comprised of similar webs of relationship at multiple levels of scale between people, the environment, and the things people make and do (design). These relationships can be either mutually beneficial (symbiotic) or unsustainable, and are always informed by mindset or worldview.

Unlike an ecosystem, in today's society, the relationships within this triad are most often not reciprocal. Tight feedback loops, which provide checks and balances within healthy ecosystems, are generally not present either. Wicked problems do, however, follow the same dynamics seen in living systems. Characteristics of living systems can be summarized as follows:

- Living systems are structurally closed and organizationally open.

- Living systems maintain themselves in a state far from equilibrium due to their constant exchange of energy and matter with their environment. This is a "region" where new physical and behavioral forms of order (emergent properties) often arise.

- Living systems are composed of decentralized, networked, interdependent, and often symbiotic relationships in a networked structure.

- Living systems are composed of systems nested within other systems (atoms, cells, organ systems, organisms, communities of organisms, etc.). As systems evolve, emergent forms of order often arise as new levels within the holarchic structure.

- Living systems are "self-making" and exhibit coherent behavior and generate spontaneous responses to internal changes and their environment. They are self-organizing and autopoetic.

- Living systems have emergent properties. Within open living systems, new physical and behavioral forms of order arise unpredictably and spontaneously as the system responds to internal changes and perturbations from its environment.

- This concept from chaos and complexity theories asserts that open, dynamic systems often display extreme sensitivity to initial conditions. Examples are global warming, weather patterns, and viral epidemics.

- Living systems maintain their ability to survive and adapt (flexibility and resilience) through the presence of multiple feedback loops that restore balance to the system after a large disturbance.

- Within living systems, single events are part of circular, cause-and-effect chains (feedback loops) that affect present and future functioning of the entire system.

- Open systems are composed of nonlinear relationships in which causes do not produce proportional effects.

- Living systems are comprised of semi-discreet "wholes" that exist at multiple levels of scale (whole and part).

- Living systems, particularly ecosystems, are interconnected via a vast network of mutually dependent relationships (yielding interdependence and cooperation).

- Diversity within a system refers to the multiplicity of relationships or variables found within it.[2]

Understanding these dynamics is essential to developing sustainable business offers and design solutions. Understanding the principles of emergence and sensitivity to initial conditions are especially important.

Chaos and complexity theories tell us that open, nonlinear systems (single organisms, communities of organisms, or even the planet) (Capra 1996, 2002; Briggs and Peat 1999; Lovelock 2000), which are in a constant exchange of energy and matter with their environment, are highly sensitive to small changes in initial conditions due to the potential for positive feedback (Capra 1996, 2002; Meadows 2008). This sensitivity causes changes or perturbations that have exponential ramifications throughout the system (global warming is an example of cumulative CO_2 emissions causing a change in the weather that has ramifications through the global weather system). Malcolm Gladwell refers to this principle with his well-known notion of tipping points (Gladwell 2000). Systems theorist Donella Meadows describes this principle of feedback as a powerful leverage point for change (Meadows 2008, 145–65), and her list of the dynamics of open systems can be directly applied to the wicked problems discussed here. In the case of our water bottle, as more oil is drilled around the planet and more landfills (overflowing with plastic bottles) leach harmful chemicals into the ground (Mor et al. 2006, 435–56), more regional water supplies become compromised and the need for pure, bottled water increases—a positive feedback loop within the complex wicked problem of the global water shortage (Shanahan 2005).[3]

The principle of emergence (Wheatley and Kellner-Rogers 1999, 66–75) is particularly relevant for designers because it posits that preconceived or designed change within open systems cannot be directed; the system can be perturbed, but the way in which it responds is self-determined. Therefore, designers cannot accurately predict how their design will "perturb" the system upon which it is imposed—they can only design as catalysts for change. Understanding the dynamics at work within these open, autopoetic systems (Capra 1996, 2002) is crucial to the design of effective perturbations (solutions). The classic example of this principle given by complexity theorists and introduced by anthropologist Gregory Bateson (2000) is to "kick a dog and try to predict the outcome" (Capra 1996, 2002). There are, of course, several possible outcomes, but it is impossible to predict which will manifest; a better understanding of context (the dog's history and conditions of its environment, etc.) would aid in predicting the most likely outcome. This example underscores the need for business people and designers to gain a thorough understanding of the contexts within which their work will reside and frame business offers and design problems within larger, more responsible contexts.

The introduction of a new business proposition or design solution into the marketplace can be seen as a similar perturbation to the system (its greater context), which is always social and environmental. The effects of these perturbations always move from local to global levels. Because the feedback is delayed (sometimes for years or even decades, in the cases of pollution in the environment or global warming), we do not connect action to effect until large patterns of change at higher levels of scale are already under way and difficult to reverse or rectify. The phenomenon of delayed feedback may account for the increasingly short horizons of time within which new business offers and design solutions are conceived and brought to market, and is in stark contrast to Native American cultures that made decisions based on their impact seven generations out (Meadows 2008, 182). Offers that are quickly conceived and realized, with profit as the primary objective, cannot help but be unsustainable in the long term because profit is often realized at the expense of social and environmental concerns.

The principles of emergence, feedback, and sensitivity to initial conditions tell us that the consequences of such hasty additions to these webs of relationship are likely to have unpredictable consequences throughout local, regional, and global systems. These principles, therefore, hold both a caution and a promise for business people and designers; when systems are perturbed in ignorance by business models and designed artifacts, sweeping unpredictable negative consequences can result. If, however, these principles are understood, they can be leveraged to create an equal degree of momentum for positive change.

Environmentalist and educator David Orr has said, "Where good design becomes part of the social fabric at all levels, unanticipated positive side effects (synergies) multiply. When people fail to design carefully, lovingly, and competently, unwanted side effects and disasters multiply" (1994, 105).

This chapter proposes that the conscious aim to create mutually beneficial relationships within this triad (which is similar in principle to the triple-bottom-line economic model) will, by default, be sustainable. This concept has been developed into a viable business model by the Zero Emissions

Research Initiative (ZERI), whose objective is "to view waste as resources and seek solutions using nature's design principles as inspiration," which can be distilled to the principle waste = food (McDonough and Braungart 2002, 92–117).[4] Within this model, commercial clusters configure in which the waste of one industry becomes the raw material or resource for another, and dense, mutualistic webs of relationship form a sustainable, commercial–industrial ecosystem.

If we evaluate the water bottle through the lens of the relationship triad or a ZERI cluster (a cluster of businesses related through the waste = food model), we can begin to see where it falls short of sustainability objectives: the relationship between the bottle and the environment is not symbiotic due to the resource extraction methods, the manufacturing processes, and the likelihood of a toxic return to the nutrient pool. The relationship between the bottle of water and the consumer may or may not be mutualistic. Certainly the water is successfully delivered; however, research is increasingly pointing to the possibility that, under certain conditions, harmful chemicals from plastics may leach into the contents causing health hazards.

The last relationship in the triad—that between people—is often the most difficult to evaluate because it involves interactions that take place in other locations that cannot be readily assessed (delayed feedback). The exploitation of workers in Gap's factories in six countries around the world (Lawrence 2002) and the common corporate practice of shipping electronic waste from North America to Asia, where families scavenge in toxic landfills for reusable parts (U.S. GAO 2008), are just two examples of social violations within this triad in other business models. Design for disassembly (Steffen 2005), a design strategy that considers the need to design products so that they can be disassembled for future repair, refurbishment, or recycling, is one example of a design process that can solve for this aspect of a larger, wicked problem. These examples underscore the need for transparency and ethical practices regarding the social and environmental implication of a product's creation and demise, both of which are determined within the business and design arenas at the point of conception (which is always influenced by mindset or worldview).

To summarize, wicked problems can be seen as complex ecosystems of relationship with dynamics that mimic those in living systems and form the greater context for most new business propositions and designed artifacts. Because wicked problems are by their nature unsustainable, an understanding of both their anatomy and dynamics should enable business people and designers to conceive sustainable solutions.

Design and the Satisfaction of Human Needs

Design is most often thought of in terms of the artifacts created by practitioners within such traditional areas of specialty as product, interaction, interior, and communication design, advertising and marketing, and architecture, to name a few. Buchanan (1995, 7–9) has developed a useful framework, or "placements for invention," for understanding design's scope and ubiquity within all facets of business offers. This chapter argues that design can be viewed as the ongoing and ubiquitous activity involved in satisfying human needs and can therefore be seen as the physical embodiment of needs satisfaction. Therefore, an understanding of genuine human needs must be central to any discussion of sustainable business practices and design solutions.

Development economist Manfred Max-Neef's theory of needs (1991) proposes (perhaps counterintuitively) that human needs are universal and finite; all people everywhere share the same relatively minimal set of needs regardless of their culture, period of history in which they live, and geographic location. Max-Neef proposes that the universal needs are subsistence, protection, affection, understanding, participation, idleness, creation, identity, and freedom (ibid., 30–37). However, the ways in which people satisfy those needs are limitless and historically, culturally, and geographically distinct. This chapter contends that these needs can be satisfied in either sustainable or unsustainable ways. For example, in the attempt to satisfy the most basic of subsistence needs, an individual may choose to drink water out of his tap or purchase a commercial bottle of water. We have already noted that bottled water has many connections to wicked problems and unsustainable practices at multiple levels of scale, yet because of all the reasons discussed earlier that have made bottled water popular—such as contaminated ground water—the choice to drink water from the tap is not a simple, sustainable alternative.

A common alternative to bottled water, which is also a business proposition, is a water purifier that affixes to the tap, which eliminates the need for bottled water. However, to determine its viability as a sustainable alternative, the same analysis performed on bottled water should now be applied to the water purifier. What raw materials were used in its fabrication, and what were the conditions under which workers manufactured it? How many miles did it travel on its distribution route to reach the store where it was purchased, and what will become of it once its useful life is at an end? What materials were used in its packaging, and what are the social and environmental ramifications associated with them? These questions form a hypothetical web of relationships that arise out of the simple question of how to best satisfy a subsistence need sustainably, through the comparison of two different business propositions: bottled water versus a water purifier. These two business models, based upon the satisfaction of a basic need, involve a myriad of designed artifacts (the bottle, the filter, packing, labeling, etc.) and processes (fabrication processes, distribution channels, marketing strategies, etc.). The satisfaction of needs in today's society happens almost exclusively within the commercial marketplace and is therefore directly tied to both the business and design domains and to sustainable solutions or unsustainable solutions connected to wicked problems.

Max-Neef (1991, 31–37) makes a further distinction between types of satisfiers: "synergistic satisfiers," "singular satisfiers," "pseudo satisfiers," "inhibiting satisfiers," and "violators or destroyers." He argues that "synergistic satisfiers" are the optimum choice, those satisfiers that fulfill more than one need at a time. For instance, a locally run community garden or co-op satisfies the needs for subsistence and participation. Breast-feeding simultaneously satisfies a baby's need for subsistence and affection. It is interesting to see how relationships to business and design come into play, when, for instance, a mother makes the decision to feed her baby with a bottle instead of breast-feeding. It could be argued that bottle-feeding is not as integrated a satisfier since the bodily contact provided by breast-feeding is absent, but it is interesting to note, within the context of the business and design domains, what happens with the introduction of the bottle.

When the designed and mass-produced artifact of the formula bottle is introduced, the satisfaction of this need is catapulted into the consumer marketplace, and entire industry sectors have arisen in response to the seemingly simple decision to bottle-feed. Dozens of different types of bottles are available in the marketplace, each with their own manufacturing and distribution system, distinct packaging, marketing materials, and websites. Often there are a host of complementary products developed such as breast pumps, coolers for carrying the pumped milk, bottle sterilizers, or even disposable liners. Typically, these are organized under a "parent brand" that represents a broader offering of products in an industry sector, in this case, baby care. Even a cursory look at this industry reveals a staggering array of products and services, all deriving from the satisfaction of this basic need. Since most are conceived and produced within the single-bottom-line business model, they are unsustainable and connected to larger wicked problems in the same way the water bottle is.

Most business models are embedded within the dominant single-bottom-line business–economic paradigm that is predicated upon credit, which can be classified within Max-Neef's framework as either a "pseudo" or "inhibiting" satisfier. For example, the credit card can be used to directly satisfy any number of genuine needs; however, if used without discretion and over the long term, it will ultimately annul the possibility of satisfying the need it was originally aimed at fulfilling. This chapter proposes that an alternative business model based upon the satisfaction (over the long term) of genuine needs, whose objective is to develop and market synergistic satisfiers will help to usher in a new, sustainable business–economic paradigm and will serve as both enabler of and imperative for sustainable design.

Systems Thinking as the Basis for Holistic Design Process

A design process based upon living systems principles and the systems dynamics discussed by Meadows can contribute to both new business and design paradigms. There has been a proliferation of sustainable product design processes and methodologies in the past decade (Tukker and Tischner 2006), such as life cycle analysis (Lewis and Gertsakis 2001, 42–57; McLennan 2004, 82–83), cradle-to-cradle design (McDonough and Braungart 2002), and biomimicry (Benyus 1997).

Life cycle analysis (LCA) looks at material impacts throughout all stages of the life cycle—resource extraction, construction and manufacturing, use, and refuse. The cradle-to-cradle approach is based on the ecological principle of waste = food and, similar to LCA, tracks impacts throughout the entire life cycle of a material, product, or building. In addition, materials such as metals, fibers, dyes, and so on are placed into two categories: "technical" and "biological" nutrients (the earth is seen as the nutrient pool out of which all man-made artifacts arise). Technical nutrients (waste) that are not toxic and harmful are used over and over as raw material for new artifacts. Biological (organic, nonsynthesized) nutrients can be disposed of in any natural environment to decompose naturally. Biomimicry is a design approach that looks to nature (its forms, processes, and systems) for inspiration and instruction for how to develop more sustainable products, processes, and built environments. All of these processes are based to greater or lesser extents upon living systems principles and can be used to develop more appropriate and sustainable designs; however, their effectiveness is directly tied to the mindset and context within which they are applied. Their effectiveness can be compared to the "leverage points" for change in a system that Meadows refers to.

In table 1, several sustainable product design processes and methodologies have been mapped along a continuum that corresponds to Meadows's systems leverage points (2008) to illustrate their effectiveness. This chapter argues that sustainable design processes that are not applied within larger contexts and are not based upon a new socioeconomic paradigm (with correspondingly different consumption patterns that result from a shift in mindset or worldview) will always fall short of their potential for change.

Ray Anderson, CEO of Interface carpets, is an illustration of the connection between an individual's worldview and transformative, sustainable business models. After reading Paul Hawken's *The Ecology of Commerce* (Hawken 1993), which outlines the environmentally destructive aspects upon which most business models are predicated, Anderson has famously transformed his own company and has influenced an entire industry to become more sustainable. Anderson has said: "I was running a company that was plundering the earth. . . . I thought, 'Damn, some day people like me will be put in jail!'. . . it was a spear in the chest" (quoted in Dean, 2007). Anderson's epiphany led him to set a 2020 target to become a "restorative enterprise," a sustainable operation that takes nothing from the earth that cannot be quickly recycled or regenerated and that does no social or environmental harm. Instead of profits plummeting and design going into decline, the company has saved more than $336 million since 1995 through their environmental efforts and higher employee retention rates, and their innovative designs have not only won awards but have created an entirely different way for consumers to think about flooring. Because the fundamental business model is based upon a triple-bottom-line objective, all design within the company shares a sustainability imperative—from the design of the product (materials, configurations, color, and motif) to its

TABLE 1

Changing Products, Consumption, and Lifestyles through Policy and Design

	9	8	7	6	5	4	3	2	1
	Designing for greater efficiency and less waste	Designing with biogradable, nontoxic materials	Redesigning the product/service mix	Measuring and loading back impacts into product design	Providing information in advertising and packaging	Leveraging relationships among government, business, consumers, and design	Designing products and messages that change aspirations and social norms	Designing to include user preferences and needs, including if socially inclusive	Designing products based upon sustainable lifestyle aspirations
	Can products be more efficient?	Will redesign make it more sustainable?	How can products become flows of services?	How is feedback incorporated?	How is information conveyed?	Who are the players included?	Can design help change "the rules"?	How can design be bottom up?	How can design create sustainable lifestyles?
Degrees of change	**Changing products**				**Changing consumption**			**Changing lifestyles**	
Examples of government policy	WEE*, ELVs**, Batteries, ROHS directives			IPP and EuP***	Product labeling schemes and standards		Sustainable procurement	Participatory design of public services and infrastructure	
Opportunities for design and designers	Product design to improve resource and energy	Redesigning products (e.g., new materials, durability,	Designing service and ownership solutions (e.g., design	Full life-cycle impacts feedback into product	Communication and packaging design to promote	Raising awareness of different constituent groups that	Branding and marketing design to influence social norms	Bottom-up design processes based on involving	Creative inputs into envisioning future scenarios for everyday life

(Continued)

54

	efficiency and reduce waste	design for durability)	for sharing or leasing)	redesign	sustainable products	influence product design	and lifestyle aspirations	users and consumers	
Examples of design approaches, methodologies, and principles	Hierarchy of waste management		Product service solutions (narrow)	Dynamic life cycle analysis				User-oriented design	Manzini's principles
	Factor X eco-efficiency		Bespoke product-services	Cradle to cradle					Biomimicry (extended)
									Product service systems (extended)

In this table, several popular ecological design approaches and government policies are mapped along a continuum of effectiveness that corresponds to Meadows (2008) "leverage points." The greatest potential for sustainable business propositions and design arises from a change in mindset or paradigm that is based upon lifestyle changes.

Source: Previously unpublished table by Terry Irwin, Julie Richardson, and Chris Sherwin

*Waste Electrical and Electronic Equipment Directive is the European community directive on waste and electronic equipment.

** End of Life Vehicle Solutions

*** Energy-using Products

messaging (corporate/brand/product identity, website, and communication design). Every aspect of design is aimed at creating mutually beneficial relationships between the three constituencies within the relationship triad: people, designed artifacts, and the environment.

Transforming a business model such as this is, at the highest level, a design problem that involves building bridges and facilitating collaboration across disciplines. A key step in Interface's transformation was the formation of an "Eco Dream Team" (Posner 2009, 49) that includes environmental thinkers, engineers, architects, authors, activists, scientists, entrepreneurs, and thought leaders who have worked together to help develop a "restorative" corporation. The same analysis applied to the bottle of water can be applied to a company; its products, processes, and social practices are often implicated in such larger wicked problems as pollution of the regional environment, manufacturing and distribution methods that involve nonrenewable energy resources, and conditions for employees that are judged to be far from optimum. Understanding the web of relationships that a company simultaneously creates and is embedded within is an essential first step toward the company's sustainable transformation and can only be achieved through transdisciplinary collaboration. Once identified and understood, these strands of relationship can be assessed and redesigned to become mutually beneficial or, as Anderson puts it, "restorative."

Conclusion

Design has a role to play at all levels of scale in the transition to a sustainable future; it serves as a transdisciplinary bridge and collaborative facilitator, it frames problems within appropriate contexts, and it performs the hands-on work of developing effective, sustainable products, services, processes, and built environments. Networking small, local solutions across different disciplines, commercial enterprises, and grassroots and governmental organizations will produce cumulative effects or tipping points for sweeping change (solutions) within wicked problems at higher levels of scale. New business models and design methodologies based upon living systems principles and an understanding of systems dynamics can inform new more sustainable solutions, but these must be applied from within a new, more holistic/ecological worldview in order for them to reach their potential for change.

References

Augros, Robert, and George Stanciu. 1987. *The New Biology*. Boston: New Science Library, Shambhala.

Bateson, Gregory. 2000. *Steps to an Ecology of Mind*. Chicago: University of Chicago Press.

Benyus, Janine. 1997. *Biomimicry: Innovation Inspired by Nature*. New York: William Morrow.

Berman, Morris. 1981. *The Reenchantment of the World*. Ithaca, N.Y.: Cornell University Press.

Briggs, John, and F. David Peat. 1989. *Turbulent Mirror*. New York: Harper & Row.

Briggs, John, and F. David Peat. 1999. *Seven Life Lessons of Chaos*. New York: Harper Collins.

Buchanan, Richard. 1995. "Wicked Problems in Design Thinking." In *The Idea of Design*, edited by Victor Margolin and Richard Buchanan. Cambridge, Mass.: MIT Press.

Capra, Fritjof. 1996. *The Web of Life*. London: Harper Collins.

Capra, Fritjof. 2002. *The Hidden Connections*. London: Harper Collins.

Clayton, Anthony M. H., and Nicholas J. Radcliffe. 1996. *Sustainability: A Systems Approach*. London: Earthscan Publications.

Cross, Nigel. 1993. "A History of Design Methodology." In *Design Methodology and Relationship Science*, NATO ASI Series, edited by M. J. De Vries, N. Cross, and D. P. Grant. Dordrecht: Kluwer Academic Publishers.

Dean, Cornelia. 2007. "Executive on a Mission: Saving the Planet." *The New York Times*, May 22. http://www.nytimes.com/2007/05/22/science/earth/22ander.html?scp=1&sq=Executive%20on%20a%20Mission&st=cse.

Gladwell, Malcolm. 2000. *The Tipping Point: How Little Things Can Make a Big Difference*. London: Abacus.

Gray, Rob, and Markus Milne. 2004. "Toward Reporting on the Triple Bottom Line: Mirages, Methods and Myths." In *The Triple Bottom Line, Does it All Add Up?* edited by Adrian Henriques and Julie Richardson. London: Earthscan.

Harman, Willis W., and Elisabet Sahtouris. 1998. *Biology Revisioned*. Berkeley, Calif.: North Atlantic Books, 1998.

Hawken, Paul. 1993. *The Ecology of Commerce*. London: Weidenfeld & Nicholson.

Hayles, N. Katherine. 1991. *Chaos and Order*. Chicago: University of Chicago Press.

Imhoff, Daniel. 2005. *Paper or Plastic*. San Francisco: Sierra Club Books.

Kearney, Michael. 1984. *World View*. Novato, Calif.: Chandler & Sharp Publishers.

Koestler, Arthur. 1967. *The Ghost in the Machine*. London: Pan Books.

Laszlo, Ervin. 1996. *The Systems View of the World*. Cresskill, N.J.: Hampton Press.

Lawrence, Felicity. 2002. "Sweatshop Campaigners Demand Gap Boycott." *Guardian*, November 22. http://www.guardian.co.uk/uk/2002/nov/22/clothes.globalisation.

Lewis, Helen, and John Gertsakis. 2001. *Design + Environment*. Sheffield, UK: Greenleaf Publishing.

Lovelock, James. 2000. *Gaia: A New Look at Life on Earth*. Oxford: Oxford University Press.

Max-Neef, Manfred. 1991. *Human Scale Development*. New York: Apex Press.

McDonough, William, and Michael Braungart. 2002. *Cradle to Cradle: Remaking the Way We Make Things*. New York: North Point Press.

McLennan, Jason F. 2004. *The Philosophy of Sustainable Design*. Kansas City, Mo.: Ecotone Publishing.

Meadows, Donella. 2008. *Thinking in Systems*. White River Junction, Vt.: Chelsea Green Publishing.

Mitchell, Melanie. 2009. *Complexity: A Guided Tour*. Oxford: Oxford University Press.

Mor, Suman, and Khaiwal Ravindra, R. P. Dahiya, and A. Chandra. 2006. "Leachate Characterization and Assessment of Groundwater Pollution Near Municipal Solid Waste Landfill Site." *Environmental Monitoring and Assessment* 118, no. 1–3 (December): 1–10.

Orr, David. 1994. *Earth in Mind*. Washington D.C.: Island Press.

Peterman, Zell E., Joanna Thamke, and Kiyoto Futa. 2010. "Use of Strontium Isotopes to Detect Produced-Water Contamination in Surface Water and Groundwater in the Williston Basin, Northeastern Montana." U.S. Geological Survey, Denver, Colo., Helena, Mont. Paper presented at the GEOCANADA 2010 conference, Calgary, Alberta, May 10–14. http://steppe.cr.usgs.gov/pdf/Peterman_et_al_GeoCanada_2010.pdf.

Polisand, Gary A., and Donald R. Strong. 1996. "Food Web Complexity and Community Dynamics." *The American Naturalist* 147, no. 5 (May): 813–46.

Posner, Bruce. 2009. "One CEO's Trip from Dismissive to Convinced." *MIT Sloan Management Review* 51, no. 1. http://sloanreview.mit.edu/the magazine/2009-fall/51114/one-ceo%E2%80%99s-trip-from-dismissive to-convinced/.

Rittel, Horst. 1972. "On the Planning Crisis: Systems Analysis of the 'First and Second Generations.'" *Bedrifts Okonomen* 8 (October): 390–96.

Rittel, Horst, and M. Webber. 1973. "Dilemmas in a General Theory of Planning." In *Policy Sciences*, vol. 4. Amsterdam: Elsevier Scientific Publishing Company.

Sachs, Wolfgang, ed. 1999. *The Development Dictionary*. London: Zed Books.

Shanahan, Mike. 2005. "Millions Face Water Shortages Due to Climate Change." *Science and Development Network*, November 17. http://www .scidev.net/en/news/millions-face-water-shortages-due-to-climate-change.html.

Skyttner, Lars. 2005. *General Systems Theory*. Singapore: World Scientific Publishing.

Steffen, Alex. 2005. "Design for Disassembly, Zero Waste and Sustainable Prosperity." *WorldChanging*, January 26. http://www.worldchanging .com/archives/002005.html.

Tukker, Arnold, and Ursula Tischner, eds. 2006. *New Business for Old Europe*. Sheffield, UK: Greenleaf Publishers.

U.S. GAO. 2008. "Electronic Waste: EPA Needs to Better Control Harmful U.S. Exports through Stronger Enforcement and More Comprehensive Regulation." Report to the Chairman, Committee on Foreign Affairs, House of Representatives. August. http://www.gao.gov/new .items/d081044.pdf.

Walker, Brian, and David Salt. 2006. *Resilience Thinking*. Washington D.C.: Island Press.

Wheatley, Margaret. 2006. *Leadership and the New Science*. San Francisco: Berrett-Koehler Publishers.

Wheatley, Margaret, and Myron Kellner-Rogers. 1999. *A Simpler Way.* San Francisco: Berrett-Koehler.

Woodhouse, Mark B. 1996. *Paradigm Wars.* Berkeley, Calif.: Frog, Ltd.

Worldwatch Institute. 2010. *2010 State of the World: Transforming Cultures.* Washington, D.C.: Worldwatch Institute.

Notes

1   For more on a product's life cycle, see *Lifecycle Assessment: Where Is It on Your Sustainability Agenda?* Deloitte, LLC, 2009, http://www.deloitte.com/assets/Dcom-UnitedStates/Local%20Assets/Documents/us_es_LifecycleAssessment.pdf

2   Based on Capra 1999, 2002; Skyttner 2005; Meadows 2008; Wheatley and Kellner-Rogers 1996; Wheatley 2006; Augros and Stanciu 1987; Hayles 1991; Harman and Sahtouris 1998; Walker and Salt 2006; Laszlo 1996; Briggs and Peat 1989, 1999; Clayton and Radcliffe 1996.

3   Water Encyclopedia: Science and Issues, "Landfills: Impact on Groundwater," http://www.waterencyclopedia.com/La-Mi/Landfills-Impact-on-Groundwater.html

4   Zero Emissions Research Initiative, http://www.zeri.org

CHAPTER 4

Redesigning the Bottom Line

*How Design Thinking Can Help Business
Become Sustainable*

Phil Hamlett and Barbara Sudick

Design has evolved from solving tactical problems by styling artifacts to collaborating with executives and solving strategic problems; and businesses are routinely called upon to explain their activities in social, ecological, and philanthropic terms rather than the financial ones to which they were accustomed. The most adept practitioners from each of these orientations understands that flexibility is important to adapt to these changing conditions, the most prevalent of which are often found lumped together under the umbrella term "sustainability."

Accordingly, there is a fundamental shift in how 21st-century businesses characterize what constitutes success. A broader spectrum of more holistic and integrated considerations are being used to account for companies, brands, products, and services as well as how they represent themselves in the marketplace. This chapter will examine those trends and demonstrate how design's role is growing more important in their continued development.

Introduction

Thomas Watson Jr. stated that "good design is good business." When he first uttered these words, he forged a relationship between the quintessential international corporation, IBM, and design. He believed in design as a "strong business success force." Watson also said, "If the organization looks the part with good design, people begin to think the company is going somewhere" (Watson 1975, 249–50). Good design meant making things look good—simple, attractive, and pleasing to the eye—and a reflection of the technological innovation embodied within its products. "Good design was not simply a veneer but an integral component of 'corporate culture,' which like any culture was comprised of symbols and icons" (Heller 1999, 148). The work of designers Paul Rand, Eliot Noyes, Charles Eames, Ray Eames, and Eero Saarinen branded IBM as a successful business leader in the late 20th century and set the standard for good design.

The relationship that Watson initiated has become an increasingly important strategy. Over time, companies as diverse as Nike, Coca-Cola, Target, and BMW have made similar commitments to design and have built formidable brands as a result. Along the way, the criteria for what constitutes good design has changed, as have the expectations of what constitutes a good business—and increased competition has put more pressure on each.

Sustainability is moving quickly into the mainstream, where it is now the stuff of headline news, campaign trail talking points, business value propositions, and brand promises. However, some still consider "sustainable" to be synonymous with "ecological"—confined to issues surrounding such natural resources as trees and water. In its broadest measure, sustainability is about viability; not just trees, but an institution's ability to persevere over time, providing ongoing sustenance to the widest possible definition of stakeholders. Business is coming to understand the importance of innovation and sustainability beyond simply environmental issues, as well as becoming sustainable and resilient itself in a constantly changing world. "Design means being good, not just looking good" (Mok 1996).

The Traditional Bottom Line

According to economist and Nobel laureate Milton Friedman (1970), "there is one and only one social responsibility of business—to use its resources and engage in activities designed to increase its profits." In the 1970s, profit was the principal measure of success for business, and allegiance to their shareholders was paramount. Companies had no formal obligation to society or the environment; goodwill existed primarily as a by-product of profits. Like Melville's Captain Ahab, executives' myopic pursuit of profit—their great white whale—took place at the expense of human capital, natural resources, and the environment. Short-term return on investment often trumped long-term planning, research, innovation, and humanitarian concerns.

Decades worth of management theory have subscribed to Freidman's doctrine that the sole responsibility of business is to increase profits, maximizing shareholder wealth—and indeed, profit motive remains a uniquely compelling force. However, most balance sheets do not fully account for the cost of conducting business. Externalities such as natural resources and health consequences are often taken for granted or ignored. Many of the costs associated with goods and services do not show up in the prices that are paid for them, resulting in an unbalanced economy that plays havoc with natural resources, human capital, health, and general well-being (consider the downstream pollution that kills fish and causes health problems, none of which show up in the price of whatever is being manufactured at the offending factory).

This dynamic is exacerbated by the way in which we typically describe economic well-being in the form of gross domestic product (GDP), which makes no distinction for environmental or social concerns. David Korten observes that "driving in a car contributes more to GDP than riding a bicycle. Turning on an air conditioner adds more than opening a window." If we extend this logic, "GDP, technically a measure of the rate at which money is flowing through the economy, might also be described as a measure of the rate at which we are turning resources into garbage" (Korten 2001, 44).

The sobering economic realities of the last few years have underscored the need to take a broader view of economic progress and prosperity, and to get more specific about how those two ideas relate to one another. They are not entirely the same thing—our current state of crisis has reminded us of this difference. A BBC report contends that "Britain is less happy than in the 1950s—despite the fact that we are three times richer. Polling data from Gallup throughout the 1950s shows happiness levels above what they are today, suggesting that our extra wealth has not brought extra well-being. In almost every developed country, happiness levels have remained largely static over the past 50 years—despite huge increases in income" (Easton 2006).

This dominant narrative of profit motive needs to be reexamined to more accurately reflect our current understanding of how the world works and our relatively new appreciation for the consequences of our actions. We must recognize "the economy is but one of the instruments of good living—not the purpose of human existence" (Korten 2001, 17), and we must reconfigure our expectations of business to deliver accordingly.

The Evolution of Brands and the Value of Design

Following World War II, the expansion of multinational corporations provided companies with much larger playing fields, making the development of cohesive brand identity more important than ever. The stakes got higher, and in the hands of large international branding firms and advertising agencies, brands evolved and became more sophisticated, from providing guarantees of consistency and quality to providing more intangible psychological assurances. Branding expert Debbie Millman of Sterling Brands charts the evolution of brand guarantees accordingly:

- Guarantee of consistency (Coca-Cola)

- Guarantee of quality (Morton Salt / Food and Drug Adminstraton era)

- Guarantee of social cachet (Levi's)

- Guarantee of emotional transformation (Starbucks)

- Guarantee of connection (Twitter)

In his book *The Brand Gap*, Marty Neumeier cites a similar shift in "the emphasis of marketing appeals":

- 1900—Features: "What it is"

- 1925—Benefits: "What it does"

- 1950—Experience: "What you'll feel"

- 2000—Identification: "Who you are"

So if "a brand is a person's gut feeling about a product, service or company" (Neumeier 2003, 2), then it follows that design's ability to "transmit ideas or emotions that words themselves cannot convey" (Pink 2005, 70) plays an important role. Given this intertwined relationship of branding and design, a corresponding development has been the increasing sophistication and wider application of design. Maturing as a profession, design has simultaneously enjoyed specialization and refinement yet continues to place a premium on holistic examination and lateral thinking. To deal with new business paradigms, Daniel Pink predicts the need for a "whole new mind" and singles out design as a "high-concept aptitude that . . . increasingly confers a competitive advantage in business" (ibid., 86).

With the help of their design consultants, IBM was able to "turn business strategy into social opportunity, and good design into good will." In a booklet about how corporate design can impact a company's bottom line, Rand described design as "a potent strategy tool that companies can use to gain a sustainable competitive advantage" (1987, 1). He believed that by collaborating with management, designers could make a significant contribution to corporate strategy, writing, "I believe that design quality is proportionately related to the distance that exists between the designer and the management at the top. The closer this relationship, the more likely chances are for a meaningful design" (ibid., 3).

In today's business environment, the power of design has become acknowledged and most businesses understand the price of not using good design. Increasing numbers of business journals and schools now include design training and prototyping, and they place an emphasis on innovation. In today's image-driven society, it is easier than ever to find examples of successful companies that have embraced design. Proctor & Gamble, Hermann Miller, and Apple Computer frequently acknowledge the role design plays in their strategic planning and brand development and have continued to build on the precedent Rand established with IBM.

The Growth of the Environmental Movement

While environmentalism can readily trace its historical lineage to the 19th century and the efforts of such towering figures as Henry Thoreau, John Muir, and Theodore Roosevelt, most people perceive of environmentalism as a relative recent phenomenon, perhaps citing the publication of Rachel Carson's classic *Silent Spring* in 1962 as its origin. Initially issued as a response to the widespread use of the highly toxic pesticide DDT, *Silent Spring* became the spiritual centerpiece of the nascent ecology movement that was the logical extension of 1960s activism.

It was against this backdrop that the Environmental Protection Agency was created and significant legislation (such as the Clean Air Act and Clean Water Act) was passed. In addition to the ecology movement, Earth Day was first celebrated within a few short years and the National Resources Defense Council was formed.

Battle lines were drawn as circumstances often pitted the forces of environmentalism against those of big business. Regulatory agencies assumed a watchdog position for industry transgressions. Many of these groups and much of these policies are still in place and protect us daily from a variety of unscrupulous actors who would otherwise do as they pleased. However, recently enlightened business leaders have realized that to truly play the part of corporate global citizen to which many of them aspire, they must actively participate as leaders. Accordingly, one prevalent characteristic of sustainability, as it is currently defined, is that much of it is being developed from an entrepreneurial vantage point within the world of business. Contemporary business leaders, such as Paul Hawken (Smith & Hawken), Yvon Choinard (Patagonia), Anita Roddick (Body Shop), Ray Anderson (Interface), and the architect/chemist team of William McDonough and Michael Braungart (MBDC) are among the most active and articulate proponents of sustainability.

This development is a key to the eventual success of sustainable thinking and practice. As corporations become more powerful, there is a growing acknowledgment that they must be reckoned with in order to effect meaningful change. To paraphrase former Sierra Club president Adam Werbach's defense of his consulting relationship with retail titan Walmart: "We cannot do it without them" (Werbach 2009).

In his books *The Ecology of Commerce* (1993) and *Natural Capitalism* (1999, with Amory Lovins and L. Hunter Lovins), Paul Hawken asserts that industrialists are largely responsible for the destruction of the Earth and are the only ones powerful enough to stop it. His more recent work celebrates the rapid proliferation of nonprofits that now shoulder much of this effort as well.

The Triple Bottom Line

These dynamics—the shifting nature of brands and design, enlarged expectations for business in public life, growing environmental concerns— have conspired to create new criteria for how companies account for their success. In the late 1980s and early 1990s, a new perspective emerged on the measures of business performance. The United Nation's Conference on Environment and Development in 1992, also known as the Earth Summit, brought attention to environmental and social crises, suggesting a link to capitalism and legitimizing sustainability.

A few years later John Elkington spoke out against business for its lack of social values and responsibilities, and scorned the idea that the only purpose of business is to maximize shareholder wealth. His remedy was to give them three-pronged forks—people, planet, and profit—expanding the range of the traditional bottom line by adding environmental protection and social equity to its economic prosperity metric. His acclaimed book poetically and pragmatically declared "sustainability as the new value" that society would demand of business in the 21st century (Elkington 1998).

This triple-bottom-line approach also acknowledged a company's social responsibility to its stakeholders, not just to its shareholders. Integrating the triple bottom line with corporate strategy required new ways of thinking and new values. Thinking sustainably meant using slow knowledge (Orr 1996) and making decisions based on considering their impact at least seven generations into the future, an idea that was inspired by the shared values of the Native American Iroquois. Design participated in shaping business strategies and producing innovative sustainable processes and products.

One tangible arena in which this shift can be observed is the transformation of corporate reporting. In addition to the traditional annual report—primarily a vehicle for economic results—many public companies have augmented their reporting strategies to include such things as corporate social responsibility reports and citizenship reports. The most prevalent model that has emerged to accommodate such other considerations is the triple bottom line, sometimes referred to colloquially as the three Ps: people, planet, and profit.

In business circles there are a variety of indices and reporting structures whose intent is to account for these considerations. Validity is expressed through participation, much of which is voluntary in nature:

- Global Reporting Initiative[1]
- SustainAbility[2]
- Ceres Coalition[3]
- Dow Jones Sustainability index[4]

Other business outlets track trends and management expectations:

- PriceWaterhouseCoopers[5]
- Businesses for Social Responsibility[6]
- Newsweek Green Rankings[7]

In the consumer marketplace, there are dizzying assortments of certifications that allow companies to wear their values on their sleeves, including no less than five forest-product management schemes. Some of these actually have teeth (e.g., "organic" as defined by the U.S. Department of Agriculture) but others less so (e.g., any use of the word "natural").

The Triple Top Line

In their groundbreaking book titled *Cradle to Cradle*, William McDonough and Michael Braungart (2002) articulated a new design perspective, the concept of the triple top line. Rather than focusing on limiting liabilities, designers should ask questions that allow for accountability for the well-being of culture and nature and that create economic value. By placing "filters on our brains, not on smokestacks," they described cost savings inherent in the design process.

Rather than constraining the "influence of one or the other of these value systems," they projected that triple-top-line thinkers would "discover opportunities in honoring the needs of all three." This way of thinking would introduce a "new standard of quality, adding ecological intelligence, social justice, and the celebration of creativity to the typical design criteria of cost, performance, and aesthetics" (McDonough and Braungart 2002, 154). These ideas—along with the delineation of ecological and industrial ecosystems—became the foundation of the cradle-to-cradle (C2C) ethos, a certification scheme for product and service design.

Hawken and other business leaders began to develop or contribute to a variety of models and frameworks to account for such considerations—namely that success is more complicated than the short-term gains expressed in quarterly results. Most of these frameworks are intended to be built upon; many of them rely on (or borrow from) one another and some have been adapted by designers.

- The Natural Step[8]

- The Sustainability Helix (Shedroff 2009, 93–97)

- The Sustainability Scorecard[9]

Many of these frameworks place a premium on the idea of "transparency" (in some cases referred to as "radical transparency"), which Dan Gray describes as "the process of making it simple for stakeholders to understand and fairly interpret an organization's decisions and conduct. (Note: it has nothing to do with the volume of information made available; it's about the usefulness of that information in forming reasonable judgments)" (2010, 64).

As companies continue racing to take ownership of externalities and anticipate legislative trends, the goalpost will continue to move and "today's standards will become tomorrow's eco-myopia" (Goleman 2009, 26). If businesses are to make sense of this jumble to their employees, customers, and partners, communication and design must be used effectively.

Cultural Considerations

At the beginning of the new millennium, Jon Hawkes proposed to expand the metrics for sustainability by adding a fourth pillar, cultural vitality. He suggested that "community creation of values, meaning and purpose in life" are "essential to a healthy and sustainable society" (2001, 25–26). His concern for cultural vitality reflected the notion of a global economy and respect for its growing number of stakeholders.

In 2003 David Throsby wrote about cultural sustainability, linking cultural systems to economic output. He articulated a set of six principles for the sustainable management of cultural capital:

- Material and nonmaterial well-being

- Intergenerational equity

- Intragenerational equity

- Maintenance of diversity

- Precautionary principle

- Maintenance of cultural systems and recognition of interdependence

The Hannover Principles, developed by McDonough and Braungart prior to writing *Cradle to Cradle*, were commissioned by the city of Hannover, Germany, which hosted the 2000 World's Fair. Intended as a set of sustainable design principles to guide development of a responsible future, this manifesto acknowledged the vital role of design in planning for a sustainable future.

In this living document, McDonough and Braungart wrote about the importance of human experience, foreshadowing the addition of cultural vitality as the fourth stream of sustainability. They framed the primary concerns of the environmental program, based on the elements that provided a structure for the ancient world, describing spirit saying that "this most ineffable of elements is also the most human. Concern for sustainability is more than a matter of compliance with industrial regulation or environmental impact analysis. It embraces a commitment to conceive of the work of design as part of a wider context in time and place. The design for EXPO 2000 must embody the form of the theme 'Humanity, Nature and Technology,' illustrating and fostering the sense of place essential to any human experience of the meaning of sustainability" (McDonough + Partners 1992, 12).

They also defined the process of sustainable design, stating that "designing for sustainability requires awareness of the full-, short-, and long-term consequences of any transformation of the environment. Sustainable design is the conception and realization of environmentally sensitive and responsible expression as a part of the evolving matrix of nature. . . . The Hannover Principles aim to provide a platform upon which designers can consider how to adapt their work toward sustainable ends. Designers include all those who change the environment with the inspiration of human creativity. Design implies the conception and realization of human needs and desires" (ibid., 4).

Business strategist Adam Werbach has advanced cultural considerations from the vantage point of advertising in recognition of that industry's pervasive nature and wide influence. From a commercial perspective, "corporate culture" could be considered "basic assumptions about an organization and the way it functions, typically shaped by shared values and learning experiences ('the way we do things around here')" (Gray 2010, 62). In a broader context, a community's vitality is closely related to the quality of its cultural engagement. By extension, "it is no exaggeration to say that designers are engaged in nothing less than the manufacture of contemporary reality. Today, we live and breathe design. . . . We have absorbed design so deeply into ourselves that we no longer recognize the myriad ways in which it prompts, cajoles, disturbs and excites us" (Poynor 1999).

A visual communication designer's contribution to culture is often responsible for the integrity of the language that is used, the veracity of what is said. In sustainable parlance, failure to do so often results in "greenwash"—a superficial or disingenuous attempt to present products or services as environmentally friendly (Gray 2010, 63). In our increasingly complex and interconnected world, designers owe it to themselves, their clients, and their audiences to more carefully consider the values and behaviors that our work promotes and encourages.

The Living Principles

Initially released in 2009 by AIGA—the professional organization for design—the Living Principles for Design distill the collective wisdom from decades of sustainability theories and bring them to life in a comprehensive framework for design. By integrating environmental protection, social equity, and economic health, these principles build upon the commonly accepted, triple-bottom-line framework. Significantly, they also incorporate cultural vitality as a fourth stream in recognition of its importance (AIGA 2009).

As a common focal point for designers and business people, the Living Principles provide a guide for purposeful action, celebrating and popularizing the efforts of those who endeavor to use design thinking to create positive cultural change. As a lens used to evaluate design-related decisions, the Living Principles facilitate critical discourse and provide a comparative model by which one can tackle the more ineffable (yet vitally important) dynamics required for sustainability to take hold in the collective imagination.

Communication design is uniquely responsible for the messages, artifacts, and experiences that pass through the hands, minds, and hearts of people everywhere. Responsible development of these things ensure that sustainability will be woven into the broader fabric of culture, thereby shifting lifestyle aspirations and consumption habits to a more sustainable basis for living.

Design's role is changing: formerly an ornamental consideration, it is now understood to play a more pivotal role in the way things behave and function. Many businesses are making stronger commitments to their communication strategies, product development, and brand identities, and are making more complicated requests of designers. In its "Designer of 2015" initiative, AIGA outlines what these dynamics potentially mean for the profession by identifying major trends and anticipating core competencies necessary to compete in an evolving field (many of which relate to the complexities inherent in grappling with sustainability). The trends and core competencies.

- Effectively combine traditional skills with a broader perspective on problem solving;

- Take many forms, including intangibles such as strategy and experiences;

- Address scale and complexity at the systems level;

- Anticipate problems and their solutions rather than solving known problems;

- Use cocreation platforms to encourage broader audience participation;

- Come to grips with the challenges of working in a world of limited resources; and

- Respond to audience contexts such as physical, cognitive, cultural, and social factors.

Design Thinking

It is worth noting the emergence of "design thinking" and examine its potential to unlock much of sustainability's promise and potential. Traditionally, analytical thinking has been used to solve most business problems. Edward de Bono refers to this approach as vertical thinking—making one logical step at a time, selecting the most promising pathway, and excluding all others. Design also uses this type of thinking but then balances it with what de Bono calls lateral thinking—probing in many different directions, following the less-likely paths. Lateral thinking is intuitive and generative—"the process of using information to bring about creativity and insight restructuring," which balances and complements vertical thinking (de Bono 1973, 7).

Businesses often regard intuition with suspicion, preferring outcomes that are reliable and predictable. Unfortunately, this process can inhibit imaginative breakthroughs. According to Rotman Business School dean Roger Martin, "organizations dominated by analytical thinking are built to operate as they always have . . . organizations dominated by intuitive thinking innovate fast and furiously" (Martin 2009, 6).

Tim Brown, CEO of design powerhouse IDEO, is often credited for coining the term "design thinking." He defined design thinking as "a discipline that uses the designer's sensibility and methods to match people's needs with what is technologically feasible and what a viable business strategy can convert into customer value and market opportunity" (Brown 2009, 86). The key to design thinking is abductive reasoning, a reconciliation of two opposing modes of logic into integrative thinking, a method of logical inference first introduced by Charles Sanders Pierce. When considering seemingly unrelated information, a designer uses experience and context to infer probable relationships. Roger Martin continues: "The most successful businesses in the years to come will balance analytical mastery and intuitive originality in a dynamic interplay. . . . Design thinking provides a long term business advantage with its focus on systems design" (Martin 2009, 6–7).

Design thinking is an integrative systems approach to creative problem solving—finding the dynamic equilibrium of contextualized abductive reasoning, analytical–vertical thinking and intuitive–lateral thinking. This makes it ideally suited to addressing sustainable concerns where developing holistic solutions and achieving balance are highly prized outcomes.

Balance is a universal principle of design, a point of equilibrium between opposing concepts. In business, balance often involves the comparison of assets and liabilities. Sustainability requires the balance of social equity, economic value, environmental protection, and cultural vitality. Rhode Island School of Design president John Maeda writes, "The best designers in the world all squint when they look at something. They squint to see the forest from the trees—to find the right balance" (Maeda 2006, 21). George Nelson states that "no design can exist in isolation. It is always related, sometimes in very complex ways, to an entire constellation of influencing situations and attitudes. What we call a good design is one which achieves integrity—that is, unity or wholeness—in balanced relation to its environment" (1965, 11). Obtaining balance in its broadest measure and incorporating sustainable design constitute complex ecological-systems subjects for both business and design that are sometime referred to as "wicked problems," a term bestowed upon overly complex dynamics that many designers relish attacking. Having extensive experience with the collaborative research and design of complex systems, Hugh Dubberly and Shelley Evenson suggest that "conversations about wicked problems especially benefit from—and may require—a variety of views," balancing vertical with lateral thinkers (2009, 1). Concerning collaborative environments, Tim Brown wrote, "a competent designer can always improve upon last year's new widget, but an inter-disciplinary team of skilled thinkers is in a position to tackle more complex problems" (Brown 2008, 7).

Connecting design thinking to innovation, Brown wrote: "as the center of economic activity in the developing world shifts inexorably from industrial manufacturing to knowledge creation and service delivery, innovation has become nothing less than a survival strategy" (2009, 7). Commenting on the human-centered tasks that designers do, Brown continued, "it is, moreover, no longer limited to the introduction of new physical products but includes new sorts of processes, services, interactions, entertainment forms, and ways of communicating and collaboration" (2009, 7–8).

Support for, and examples of, design thinking can be found regularly in business and mainstream publications such *Business Week*, *Fast Company*, *Newsweek*, *Dwell*, and *Good*. Design industry press such as *Communication Arts*, *Print*, *Metropolis*, and *Eye* also provide coverage. Professional organizations such as AIGA, Industrial Design Society of America, Design Management Institute, American Institute of Architects, the Designers Accord, and the UK Design Council offer a variety of support materials and community. In academia, many design programs and business schools have incorporated design thinking, innovation, and prototyping into their curriculum, and degree programs can be found at traditional institutions and new schools that are emerging to concentrate on sustainable curriculum.

Looking Ahead

Design educator Nathan Shedroff (2009) believes that "design is the problem" and asserts that if you aren't part of the problem, then you cannot legitimately claim to be part of the solution. So while the current state of affairs is not necessarily design's fault (the profession exists within a flawed context), it must be acknowledged that design has been complicit in creating or exacerbating certain problems, and that, to assume its proper role, design needs to divest itself of certain tendencies, including:

- Promoting overconsumption in general (serving as a lubricant for rampant commercialization);

- Exaggerating cycles of obsolescence;

- Using disingenuous language and/or outright deceit (consult Terrachoice's seven sins of greenwashing for elucidation); and

- Generating obfuscation (versus authenticity).

When considering how business might engage design—or employ design thinking—moving forward, it is useful to consider a three-stage path for advancing knowledge and capturing value devised by Roger Martin (2009), which he calls "the knowledge funnel." The initial stage requires identifying a mystery or question that confounds society. The next stage is the development of a heuristic, a way of understanding the mystery through a basic concept or approach. The final stage converts the heuristic to an algorithm, a formula. The business that can balance the exploitation of existing knowledge with their exploration for new knowledge will move more efficiently through the funnel, which will benefit all of their stakeholders. In short, companies derive value by solving the mysteries of our time and turning those mysteries into replicable formulas.

So the biggest mystery that currently confronts mankind is: "How do we continue to thrive and prosper on an increasingly crowded planet with fewer and fewer resources?" Who is going to figure that one out, and what kind of value will flow from it? We need to define how we are going to live our lives, then describe it in terms that people understand (and desire). Amid the drama of recent economic hardships, there exists an expectation that eventually things will return to "normal." To truly be at the forefront of innovation, business, design, and society need to recognize that "normal" is what got us into trouble in the first place, and we must develop healthier ways to conduct ourselves.

Society's dominant narrative needs to change. Profit motive has long served as the principal means by which we organize economic activity and construct our daily lives. We need to develop a broader, healthier, more compelling narrative, making certain that value is defined in its broadest sense, not just dollars and cents. And we need to make certain that value is clearly communicated to the widest possible spectrum of society. Business and design working in concert have the best possible chance of accomplishing this task.

Rest assured—change is afoot. Regardless of exactly what is to come, design will play an important role in the transformation of society and business into a vastly different paradigm than the one we inhabit today.

References

AIGA. 2009. "AIGA's 'Living Principles for Design' Introduce Quadruple Bottom Line for Design and Business." Press release, October 9. http://www.aiga.org/content.cfm/news-091009.

Brown, Tim, 2008. "Design Thinking." *Harvard Business Review*, June.

Brown, Tim, 2009. *Change by Design: How Design Thinking Transforms Organizations and Inspires Innovation*. New York: Harper-Collins.

Carson, Rachel. 1962. *Silent Spring*. Boston: Houghton Mifflin.

de Bono, Edward. 1973. *Lateral Thinking: Creativity Step by Step*. New York: Harper Colophon.

Dubberly, Hugh, and Shelley Evenson. 2009. *A Model of the Creative Process*. Calgary: Institute for the Creative Process. http://www .dubberly.com/concept-maps/creative-process.html.

Easton, Mark. 2006. "Britain's Happiness in Decline." *BBC*, May 2. http:// news.bbc.co.uk/2/hi/programmes/happiness_formula/4771908.stm.

Elkington, John. 1998. *Cannibals with Forks: Triple Bottom Line of 21st Century Business*. Mankato, Minn.: Capstone.

Friedman, Milton. 1970. "The Social Responsibility of Business Is to Increase Its Profits." *New York Times Magazine*, September 13.

Goleman, Daniel. 2009. *Ecological Intelligence: How Knowing the Hidden Impacts of What We Buy Can Change Everything*. New York: Crown Business.

Gray, Dan. 2010. *Live Long and Prosper: The 55-Minute Guide to Building Sustainable Brands*. Royston, Hertfordshire, UK: Verb Publishing.

Hawken, Paul. 1993. *The Ecology of Commerce: A Declaration of Sustainability*. New York: Harper Business.

Hawken, Paul, Amory Lovins, and L. Hunter Lovins. 1999. *Natural Capitalism: Creating the Next Industrial Revolution*. Boston: Little, Brown.

Hawkes, Jon. 2001. "The Fourth Pillar of Sustainability: Culture's Essential Role in Public Planning." *Cultural Development Network*. http:// community.culturaldevelopment.net.au//Downloads/HawkesJon%282 001%29TheFourthPillarOfSustainability.pdf.

Heller, Steven, 1999. *Paul Rand*. London: Phaidon Press.

Korten, David. 2001. *When Corporations Rule the World*. San Francisco: Berrett-Koehler.

Maeda, John. 2006. *The Laws of Simplicity*. Cambridge, Mass.: MIT Press.

Martin, Roger. 2009. *The Design of Business: Why Design Thinking Is the Next Competitive Advantage*. Boston: Harvard Business Press.

McDonough, William, and Michael Braungart. 2002. *Cradle to Cradle: Remaking the Way We Make Things*. New York: North Point Press.

McDonough, William, + Partners. 1992. "The Hannover Principles: Design for Sustainability." Prepared for EXPO 2000, The World's Fair, Hannover, Germany. http://www.mcdonough.com/principles.pdf.

Mok, Clement. 1996. *Designing Business*. San Jose: Adobe Press.

Nelson, George. 1965. *Problems of Design*. New York: Whitney.

Neumeier, Marty. 2003. *The Brand Gap: How to Bridge the Distance between Business Strategy and Design*. Indianapolis: New Riders.

Orr, David. 2006. "Slow Knowledge." In *Conservation Biology*. Hoboken, N.J.: Wiley-Blackwell.

Pink, Daniel H. 2005. *A Whole New Mind: Why Right-Brainers Will Rule the Future*. New York: Riverhead Books.

Poynor, Rick. 1999. "First Things First (Revisited)." *Emigre 51*. http://www.emigre.com/Editorial.php?sect=1&id=13.

Rand, Paul. 1987. *Good Design Is Good Will*. New Haven, Conn.: Yale University Press.

Shedroff, Nathan. 2009. *Design Is the Problem: The Future of Design Must Be Sustainable*, 1st ed. Brooklyn, N.Y.: Rosenfeld Media.

Throsby, David. 2003. "Cultural Sustainability." In *A Handbook of Cultural Economics*, edited by Ruth Towse. Cheltenham, UK: Edward Elgar Publishing.

Watson, Thomas J., Jr. 1975. "Good Design Is Good Business." In *The Uneasy Coalition: Design in Corporate America*. Philadelphia: University of Pennsylvania Press.

Werbach, Adam. 2009. *Strategy for Sustainability: A Business Manifesto*. Boston: Harvard Business Press.

Notes

1 http://www.globalreporting.org/Home
2 http://www.sustainability.com/
3 http://www.ceres.org/
4 http://www.sustainability-index.com/
5 http://www.corporatereporting.com/guidance-legislation.html
6 http://www.bsr.org/
7 http://www.newsweek.com/green
8 http://www.naturalstep.org/
9 http://www.celerydesign.com/eco-tools/

CHAPTER 5

Sustainable Engineering and Industrial Ecology

Brad Allenby

If it has not already become apparent to those reading this volume, the intersecting domains of sustainability, industrial management and performance, and relevant scientific and technical disciplines are complicated, ill-defined, and for the most part uncharted. This chapter will not attempt to bring order to this creative chaos; indeed, such an effort would probably be premature. There is something to be said for knowing when to be definitive, and when to employ constructive confusion. Thus, while I will initially position industrial ecology and sustainable engineering within a corporate social responsibility framework, which in turn nestles in a sustainability approach to industrial and technological systems, I will not make too much effort to be categorical and specific. Rather, I will spend most of my time exploring the challenges of implementing sustainable engineering in an industrial environment, and industrial ecology as one way of doing so. While focused, this discussion will also be an excellent way of addressing broader issues involving the implementation of corporate social responsibility, and sustainability, in the firm.

Grounding Sustainable Engineering and Industrial Ecology: Corporate Social Responsibility

"Corporate social responsibility," or CSR as it is known to its intimates, has been a hot corporate (and nongovernmental organization) buzzword for years now. Nonetheless, there is only a vague consensus on what the concept actually includes. In part, this reflects the fact that the term not only grows out of historical experience but also reflects a confluence of a number of new, previously independent trends.

The idea that institutions have responsibilities to the broader society within which they function is clearly neither new nor limited to any particular culture. Business activities have long been constrained by moral and religious dictates such as edicts against usury or limitations on days when business activity is appropriate (Epstein 1987). Moreover, that the idea of reciprocal privileges and duties would extend to corporations as they began to evolve in their modern form and to gain in power and social status compared to other institutions is not surprising. The charter corporations of European imperialism, as the medieval merchant and craft guilds before them, had to function within the assumptions and constraints of their cultures, just as before them the Islamic traders had done so for centuries. And even though the advent of general incorporation laws and subsequent legal structures such as the Uniform Commercial Code has established a structure where responsibility to shareholders is paramount, firms in virtually all countries continue to behave in ways that reflect a respect, if not an embrace, of broader social role (Allenby 1997).

There are, however, two modern themes that come together in CSR. The first is the sustainability movement, itself a combination of the older environmental and human rights movements, both of which saw significant growth beginning in the 1960s (Choucri 1993; Sassen 1996). Sustainability arises out of the effort to integrate environmental and economic development values popularized by the World Commission on Environment and Development (WCED 1987). But it has become much more complicated, in part because its normative content is interpreted differently in different cultures: in the United States, emphasis is on environmental quality because economic development and egalitarianism are less favored in that culture; in Europe, it is both, because sustainable development as initially presented by the WCED is essentially a restatement of northern European social democratic values; in developing countries, it is interpreted as a need for economic support for development, and sometimes for environmental reparations (Allenby 2005).

The second theme is the continuing reaction by civil society against perceived unethical behavior on the part of firms. Initially, this arose from antiwar and antiestablishment campaigns (against firms that manufactured napalm for use in Vietnam, for example); but with the collapse of Enron and MCI Worldcom from accounting and securities irregularities, this reaction subsequently extended to criminal mismanagement of large firms in the United States and Europe, and disparities in pay between top executives and workers. Most recently, of course, the behavior of banking executives who led their firms and the world economy into crisis but continued to pay themselves huge bonuses has been the most evident source of public reaction against firms (although, interestingly enough, this seems to have made the public annoyed at bankers but not at the capitalist system generally).

Firms have responded by supporting the idea of the "triple bottom line," which holds that firms should attempt to satisfice their performance not just economically but also socially and environmentally. Within this triple-bottom-line framework, both CSR and sustainable management and engineering can be framed, with CSR representing social demands on the firm and sustainable engineering and management reflecting more of the internal tools with which firms can respond to some of the issues raised in the much broader CSR space (figure 1). Some have critiqued this idea as being too narrow, arguing that a cultural dimension should also be included, while many have argued with the particular values that may or may not be included in the social domain. At least from a public relations perspective, however, the result is that many global firms now produce annual sustainability reports of varying quality. Interestingly

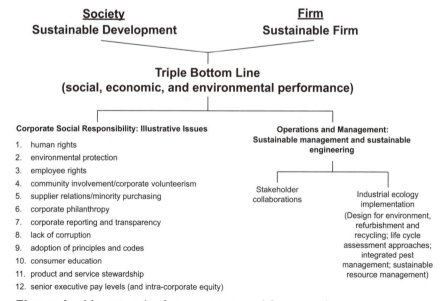

Figure 1 Managing the future: conceptual framework.

enough, there has been little discussion of the wisdom of firms becoming agents of sustainability—whether they are qualified to judge social issues, for example, or whether such authority should be vested in legally limited entities to begin with (Allenby 1997).

The development of CSR must also be seen against a broader background. It is apparent that firms face an environment of accelerating complexity that renders their operations and strategies far more contingent and difficult than in the past (Senge 1990). Thus, the effect of this "perfect storm" of discourses, issues, and communities and the rise of nongovernmental organizations (NGOs) as independent centers of perceived authority has profoundly changed the governance structure within which firms conduct their business (Mathews 1997). This renders the governance structure within which CSR must be implemented more ambiguous. This is especially true for the social dimensions of CSR. While it may be possible for parties to verify and agree on the validity of financial or environmental data, it is virtually impossible for all stakeholders to agree on what constitutes appropriate social goals. Because social goals are generally a matter of values, the question of whose values one must support remains open and contentious.

Thus, while one might identify issues that arise within a CSR context, such as selling minerals from war zones, the inherent normative nature of CSR remains a difficult challenge from an operational or managerial perspective. Civil society remains an uneven source of prioritization regarding CSR. Human rights and environmental NGOs continue to frequently and visibly campaign on various aspects of CSR, but the ad hoc and single-issue character of such organizations provides neither a comprehensive guide to CSR nor the assurance that all aspects of CSR will be equally weighted. Some business-oriented research organizations such as the Conference Board have been active in attempting to help companies understand the demands of the environment within which they are now operating, and there are limited but relatively stable socially responsible investment funds and investment indexes. Nonetheless, although somewhat dated, Friedman's comments are perhaps more true now than they were when he wrote them: "The discussions of the 'social responsibilities of business' are notable for their analytical looseness and lack of rigor .... The first step towards clarity in examining the doctrine of the social responsibility of business is to ask precisely what it implies for whom" (1970, 122). As we will see, this confusion is central to the contradictions at the heart of sustainable engineering as well as industrial ecology.

Framing Sustainable Engineering

Perhaps more than most professions, engineering because of its practical and applied focus reflects the immediate environment within which it operates. It is therefore not surprising, given the interest in sustainability, that the idea of "sustainable engineering" has arisen. This is both a powerful and a challenging cultural construct, offering interesting insights into both sustainability and engineering. To begin with, it recognizes that appropriately designed products, infrastructures, technology systems, and services are critical to better environmental and social performance across a globalizing economy. But it is one thing to appreciate the power of an abstract concept and entirely another to reduce it to a useful and rigorous framework, a toolbox of methods and metrics, and a set of practices that can be applied by professionals. Neither of these sets of tasks can be said to have been accomplished at this point.

It is not just societal interest in sustainability that is generating this interest, however. It is becoming clear that the Industrial Revolution and associated changes in human demographics, agricultural practices, technology systems, institutions, cultures, and economic systems have resulted in the evolution of an anthropogenic Earth, one in which the dynamics of major natural systems are increasingly impacted by human activity (Allenby 2005). This world is increasingly characterized by the integration of human, built, and natural systems into complex structures producing emergent behaviors that could not have been predicted—integration that often occurs as a result of, and reflects, engineering decisions. Failure to appreciate the complexity of these interacting systems has serious consequences. Arguably, this is one reason the climate change negotiation process has generally failed: climate change has been positioned as an environmental issue—which might, like ozone depletion, be handled through a bounded set of international agreements (such as the Montreal Protocol, in that case)—when in reality climate change arises from, cuts across, and involves numerous systems—including, importantly, foundational cultural systems, different value systems, established social and economic practices and systems, and technological frontiers. Such a complex system is not easily addressed by single-issue policies or indeed by a treaty process at all.

Or consider a more limited example within the climate-change policy framework that more clearly illustrates the complexities of these integrated

Earth systems: the dysfunctional U.S. policies that require the production and use of corn-based ethanol at large scale as a substitute for fossil fuels. There is nothing wrong with the basic technology that makes ethanol from corn; it works well and, at a small scale, is done where economics make it feasible. But the U.S. policy constituted a dramatic scale-up of this technology, pushing it far into a domain where the implications for other systems were highly nonlinear. Among the easily foreseeable but unanticipated results were much higher food prices, which in turn created significant suffering, especially among poor people affected by unpredicted shifts in global food market product availability and prices, and which in their turn caused political instability in many nations, creating security issues. This interpenetration of human systems and decisions, especially technology, with natural systems can no longer be ignored. As the journal *Nature* put it in a 2003 editorial, "Welcome to the Anthropocene," or, roughly translated, the Age of Humans.

Technology obviously plays a major role in such an anthropogenic world; it not only directly couples human, built, and natural domains, but as new technologies evolve, they also change Earth systems directly and significantly. Such technologies do not just have impacts on other technologies but also have profound impacts on economic, social, institutional, and other systems as well (Bijker, Hughes, and Pinch 1997). The development of the first deep-ocean European sailing ship, the caravel, by the Portuguese in the 1400s, for example, not only enabled European expansion and colonization but also led to globalized transportation activities that directly changed the biology of many previously inaccessible islands. Railroads had similar profound effects. As an integrated network requiring real-time coordination, railroads required a uniform, precise system of time and thus created "industrial time" and its associated culture; similarly, railroads created the need for, and coevolved with, the telegraph as the first national-scale communications system (Schivelbusch 1977). They also required unprecedented complexity and scale in the firms that were to operate them, thus creating modern managerial capitalism (modern accounting, planning, and administration systems) (Freeman and Louca 2001). Finally, the railroads were also environmentally transformative, transforming huge areas of land that previously could not economically support agriculture into breadbaskets (the American Midwest, for example) (Cronon 1991). This sort of institutional change is not limited to society as a whole; the shift from tubes to transistors on chips did in RCA, and AT&T

(in its old stand-alone state) was done in by the shift from telephone to Internet technology as the platform for voice services.

Such examples can be used to establish several important themes. Perhaps most importantly, they refute the idea, very common among sustainability gurus, that sustainability can be understood, studied, or indeed even conceptualized without understanding technology and technological systems. This of course puts a substantial burden on engineers, as well as on private firms, who in quasi-capitalist global economic systems are the principal generators of technology. It is also a serious indictment to those elements of the sustainability community that tend toward the technophobic. Equally important, it warns firms that they need to independently understand the implications of the sustainability dialog for their operations and stakeholder management activities; it is not sufficient simply to respond to the playing field as it has been defined by the sustainability discourse so far. That playing field is inadequate and highly normative and is dysfunctional when it comes to technology.

Additionally, these examples and many others that could be cited clearly demonstrate that technological change, especially when it involves fundamental systems, is profoundly destabilizing and unpredictable. Who would have predicted that railroads would create our modern sense of time? Or managerial capitalism? Or that corn-based ethanol would destabilize national governments far from the United States? Or that automotive technology would give rise to consumer credit? This is a particularly important theme right now, given that not just one foundational technology but five—nanotechnology, biotechnology, robotics, information and communication technology (ICT), and applied cognitive science—are undergoing rapid evolution. Facebook and social networking are less than ten years old, as are virtual realities such as Second Life, not to mention Google's displacement of memory from the brain to the Net. The implications of just these few technologies are yet to be understood, but the potential for massive social change is apparent. Some are pessimistic about the implications and some optimistic (Kurzweil 2005), but for the engineering community it is sufficient to recognize that these converging technologies, with their mutually reinforcing integration across technological frontiers, have become major earth systems in their own right. If there is to be sustainable engineering, it lies more in understanding these systems, and less in the ideological tussles that have characterized the sustainability discourse to date.

We can identify three major earth system impacts of technological evolution, which can also be framed as the challenges to which sustainable engineering must respond: social, technological, institutional, and economic destabilization; accelerating complexity; and radical contingency. Each affects engineering in different ways. The destabilizing effect of technology has already been discussed; let us turn then to complexity.

The complexity of the anthropogenic earth, and technological evolution as a factor of that development, is just beginning to be recognized. While there are a number of ways one could frame this complexity, for our purposes it is useful to understand it as appearing in four different guises. The first, and for most of us the most obvious, can be categorized as static complexity, a measure of what the system looks like at any point in time— the number of components, stakeholders, interactions among different infrastructure, and linkages among them, for example. Since these systems constantly evolve, dynamic complexity arises as components of a system interact over time. As chaos theory has indicated, dynamic complexity can be quite unpredictable even in systems that are fairly simple statically (birds in a flock or fish in a school, for example). A third form of complexity arises as systems include human components, as of course all technology systems do; "wicked" complexity arises as systems dynamics change to reflect the reflexivity and intentionality of human systems and institutions. Finally, as one moves to the level of earth systems, scale complexity also increases. Not only is the emergent behavior of these global scale systems different in complexity from the behavior of subunits, but the problem of understanding and managing multiscale phenomena becomes more problematic (Allenby 2007).

Put this way, complexity sounds simple, but we routinely mismanage it. Consider, for example, the economic crisis of 2008, which was in large part a reflection of unmanaged complexity that led to the inability to determine where financial risk really was, which in turn shut down the credit markets and almost led to a rerun of the Great Depression. Or consider a geopolitical example: Communism in the Soviet Union collapsed not from external conquest but because the centralized economic model adopted by large Marxist societies simply became incapable of managing the complexity inherent in a modern, postindustrial economy. Gosplan, the Soviet economic planning ministry, was not incompetent, but it made a category mistake: an effort to manage a complex adaptive system (the modern economy) using simple system tools (explicit planning and command-and-control mechanisms). As a final example, consider the climate-change negotiations that, in this perspective, are an effort to use a simple system solution (a binding treaty affecting nation-states) for a system perturbation—climate change forcing—that is not so much a problem to be solved by treaty but a condition arising from a world that now has some 7 billion people on it, all seeking a better life.

The third theme is radical contingency. There have clearly been powerful technology systems in the past that have had substantial and unpredictable social and institutional impacts, but today's technology palette adds several arguably unique features. First, as already mentioned, accelerating change in five foundational technology systems creates an environment of unprecedented change. More importantly, perhaps, the human has become a design space as well—in biological terms, with genetics and proteomics; in cognitive science and ICT terms, in the way people are integrating into information networks and grids, and downloading important elements of their cognition, such as memory, to the Net. These changes, which are accelerating geometrically in the case of many technologies, undermine the stability of the cultural and institutional frameworks within which engineers and others operate. Thus, the modern engineer faces a world where it is not just the professional discipline that has become far more complicated but also the environment within which it is practiced in ways that make even basic assumption questionable over relatively short time periods (Allenby and Sarewitz 2011).

Sustainability from an Engineering Perspective

It is one thing to enjoy the usual argument about the content of the cultural construct of "sustainability." It is entirely another thing to be tasked by clients, and society, with implementing it in real-world technology systems with no real guidance as to what it actually meant by the term. Understanding this dilemma from the perspective of an engineer or a manager requires some perspective on sustainability, which is ambiguous but not undefined, as well as a clear understanding of what engineers and managers do in the real world, which is the basis of the confusion about sustainability, sustainable engineering, and sustainable corporate behavior.

To begin with, one can establish the two basic components of sustainability by returning to the origin of the phrase "sustainable development" (SD). SD is a classic example of a large class of terms known as cultural constructs—symbols, ideas, or phrases by which societies create and transmit meaning (Allenby 2006). In this case, SD was intentionally designed and launched as a cultural construct by the popular book *Our Common Future* (WCED 1987). As with most deliberately created cultural constructs, it was intended to serve several important political purposes. First, it was in large part created to try to reduce conflict between two important communities and discourses—economic development, especially in developing countries, and environmental. These were particularly in conflict in developing countries, where economic development was seen as inimical to environmental values. Those who supported both values had difficulty finding common ground, much less convincing either the development or the environmental discourses of the importance of both. Additionally, the cultural construct provided a political base for SD, in that the favoring of egalitarian policies (relatively equal distribution of wealth among and across generations) over libertarian, individualistic policies meant that the SD concept was in some ways simply an objective rephrasing of social democratic values already dominant in northern Europe and, more broadly, in the European Union. This effort to create a new cultural construct was successful: in a little more than 20 years, the idea of "sustainability" has evolved into a major policy discourse. Especially at the beginning, "sustainability" or "sustainable development"—the two tend to be interchangeable in use—embodied two major themes: egalitarianism and redistribution of wealth within and among generations, and environmental preservation and protection (WCED 1987). But although this fairly clear, if normative, focus has significantly eroded over time and the attractiveness of sustainability does not appear to have suffered, as the increasing popularity of sustainable engineering itself suggests.

This has led some to suggest that the value and attractiveness of sustainability arises not from its particulars (Americans, for example, tend to dislike egalitarian policies, which leads them to focus on the environmental axis of sustainability). Rather, sustainability provides a modern, scientific-sounding foundational narrative that helps individuals make sense of a complex and unpredictable world—in other words, it is important not as pure cultural construct but as social myth.

This way of understanding sustainability is useful in explaining some of the metaphorical language that surrounds it, which in turn helps managers and engineers understand what is being demanded of them when stakeholders insist on sustainable engineering or sustainable firms. It is not at all unusual, for example, to hear people insist that "the planet is in danger," or even, as McKibben (1989, 180) puts it, is "suffering." This makes no sense to the typical manager, scientist, or engineer, because planets cannot suffer in any commonly understood sense of the word, nor is anything that engineering or private firms are currently doing in any way capable of endangering the Earth as a planetary body. Indeed, what appears to be suffering, if anything, is the idea of the planet that such commentators hold, rather than anything real. In mythic structures, however, it is notable that the suffering of nature, the individual, and society are frequently conflated. Sustainability, then, encourages a form of metaphor, not rational analysis—which is very important because managers, engineers, and technocrats tend toward rational analysis and are thus quite likely to misinterpret the sustainability concerns and comments of stakeholders. It is thus critical to understand that sustainability is, among other things, an objective façade over a normative and even mythic structure; otherwise it can significantly mislead those who attempt to apply what they believe is an objective set of criteria to industrial, technological, or engineering situations.

This is also the core of the problem that many firms and engineers have in coupling sustainability to their decision-making processes. For engineers, for example, it is the misunderstanding of sustainability as an objective function, rather than as a guiding myth, that perhaps causes the major conceptual problems regarding sustainable engineering. Engineers, like managers, are basically problem solvers; an engineer's primary responsibility is to produce a solution that works in the real world, with all its attendant economic, competitive, regulatory, and pragmatic constraints. Moreover, again like managers, engineers must appropriately consider other stakeholders, especially the public and workers. To enable solutions in such complicated spaces, managers and engineers both rely on methods and tools that are highly quantitative—accounting and business plan techniques, design methodologies. Thus, sustainability, a concept that to some extent is validated by its ambiguity, obviously poses substantial challenges because the luxury of constructive ambiguity does not exist for either managers or engineers. The business plan, the product launch, the engineered device or infrastructure—whatever managers and engineers create and build—has got to work in the real world.

But this analysis, which implies that managers and engineers should ignore sustainability challenges, is incomplete and partial for one obvious reason: the concern about sustainability is increasingly a part of the real world with which they must engage. Indeed, it has always been the case that firms, managers, and engineering change as society and technology change. Thus, the increasing interest in sustainability cannot be brushed off just because it is normative, or ambiguous, or mythic; engineers, managers, technologists, and the firms they work for are now generally being tasked with understanding the broader social, economic, and environmental implications of their work as well as the technical specifics, with an implication that they have some responsibility for those dimensions. Thus, for example, a firm building a road in a tropical rain forest might find itself responding to questions about how their road might change future settlement patterns in nearby sensitive locations, and the firm that introduces new genetically engineered crops finds itself responding to questions about the social and environmental impacts of the basic technology, rather than simple profit and loss questions that might have characterized past periods.

This is a subtle but nontrivial change that has significant implications for the engineering profession and for engineering education, as well as for firms and managers that deal with engineered systems. These implications include seriously increasing the complexity of the ethical dimensions of engineering activities and engineered systems, broadening engineering education, and teaching engineers about technology systems as well as about engineered systems. In this, of course, it also poses similar challenges for both firms and managers within those firms. Indeed, to the extent it suggests that managers and engineers must be cross-trained on a number of issues, it also implies fundamental changes not just in business and engineering education but also in the cultures of the disciplines, a shift that, frankly, neither community is ready for. It is thus helpful that there is a nascent area of study, industrial ecology, that offers some potential for incremental adjustment while more fundamental change can be encouraged.

Industrial Ecology: A Limited Response

To understand the strengths and weaknesses of industrial ecology in supporting both sustainable engineering and sustainable management, it is necessary to understand the history of this field.[1] To begin with, it is an extraordinarily young area of study; the term "industrial ecology" seems to have been first used in the title of a very limited-circulation journal in 1970, which promptly failed, probably because the environmental policy and management community was not yet mature enough for an approach that treated environmental issues as inherent in industrial systems rather than simply a by-product of improper operations. But the implicit suggestion of similar systems structure between industrial and biological systems, along with increasing interests in complex systems of all sorts, meant that initial failure was not forever; in 1972 the Japanese Ministry of Industry and International Trade began considering such an analogy as a model for structuring the Japanese industrial system. This preliminary effort also failed, probably as a result of the challenge of the 1973 energy crisis.

In 1989, however, a third, and ultimately successful, attempt to introduce industrial ecology began with a 1989 article by Frosch and Gallapoulos, both with General Motors at the time, which suggested that industrial systems could be more efficient if their material flows were modeled after natural ecosystems. This article led a few individuals at AT&T to initiate industrial ecology within the electronics industry, in particular by translating the general principles of industrial ecology, such as they were at the time, into specific design methodologies and recommendations. In particular, early proponents created design for environment (DfE) methods that provided a mechanism for driving environmental considerations and constraints into the product design process (Allenby 1991). More specifically, DfE was originally intended to be a subset of the existing product realization process then in use in the electronics industry, known as "Design for X" or DfX, where the "X" stands for a desired product characteristic such as testability, safety, manufacturability, or reliability (Gatenby and Foo 1990). This internal AT&T effort was augmented by formation of the Design for Environment Task Force at the American Electronics Association (AEA) in 1990, which began the process of developing DfE as an operative methodology for the electronics industry as a whole. An important step in this process was the production of ten AEA DfE white papers, which covered everything from materials recyclability, to design for refurbishment, to design for disassembly and recyclability, and thus introduced the broader electronics industry to the concepts of DfE.[2]

A major drawback of some of the early efforts is that they too often consisted of environmental professionals trying to prescribe to design and manufacturing teams, with poor results. It was thus noteworthy when the major professional organization of electrical and electronics engineers, the IEEE, developed a serious interest in industrial ecology. Indeed, the single greatest resource for following the progress of technical industrial ecology is probably the proceedings of the annual IEEE symposia on electronics and the environment, focusing on DfE, from 1993 to the present (renamed the International Symposium on Sustainable Systems and Technology in 2009, to reflect the expansion of interest from merely environmental to sustainability). The shift toward a more technically rigorous approach was not the only notable one. The 1990s also saw a migration of initiative in many industrial ecology projects from the United States to Europe, especially as European environmentalists and regulators became increasingly interested in product takeback, especially as applied to electronics. The Netherlands in particular took a broader approach that began to move away from a purely environmental focus and sought to define a sustainable society in one generation, publishing their first *National Environmental Policy Plan* in 1989 and the *National Environmental Policy Plan Plus* in 1990.

In retrospect, it is apparent that the history of industrial ecology to a large extent parallels the evolution of environmentalism. Initially, when the environmental focus was simply on air and water quality and waste flows of various kinds, there was little perceived need for a more systematic approach, and industrial ecology initiatives failed. However, when it became apparent that environmental perturbations were not just the results of mismanaged material flows but arose instead from the accumulated economic and technological activities of billions of people, and when the complex nature of such perturbations—in particular, the complex, systems-based nature of regional and global environmental perturbations such as ozone depletion, the regional and global spread of pollutants, the loss of biodiversity, and the inability of reductionist regulatory approaches to address such issues adequately—became obvious, so also did the inadequacy of traditional approaches. Increasing regulatory costs and responsibilities and the demands of stakeholders and customers encouraged new, more systemic ways of thinking about these issues in firms (environmentalists and regulators, it must be said, were far less quick to understand the systemic implications that led industry to develop industrial ecology).

This history explains several important limitations of industrial ecology as a framework for sustainable management or engineering. First, reflecting its origins, industrial ecology and many of its methodologies such as DfE remain focused to a large extent on environmental issues. This reflects the development of the field and the fact that many of the people involved in it come from environmental backgrounds because that is overwhelmingly where the activism and regulation continue to be focused.

Second, much of the early industrial ecology literature, and industrial ecology today to some extent, tends to focus on manufacturing sectors. The industrial ecology literature on services, especially on the importance and role of information and communication technology (ICT), is sparse and unsophisticated. This is partly because manufacturing firms were the ones most affected by environmental regulations and politics when the field was evolving, and because much environmental impact was seen as coming from manufacturing (a bias that still exists in environmental organizations and regulators). Because this approach combines an emphasis on traditional manufacturing with environmental interests, it tends to embed a focus on material and energy flow, making industrial ecology fairly poor at dealing with forward-looking questions of emerging technology systems. Finally, industrial ecology was developed in advanced economies to respond to environmental problems as perceived and valued in such countries, so it is not only not particularly effective or even useful in developing economies, but it tends to carry with it the developed country environmentalist bias against economic development in poorer countries. Thus, for example, it is more than mildly ironic that Europe can probably be considered the leader in industrial ecology just at the point when manufacturing has so strongly shifted away from Europe and the United States toward Asia.

In this light, then, what is "industrial ecology"? A leading textbook defines it thus:

> *Industrial ecology* is the means by which humanity can deliberately and rationally approach and maintain sustainability, given continued economic, cultural, and technological evolution. The concept requires that an industrial system be viewed not in isolation from its surrounding systems, but in concert with them. It is a systems view in which one seeks to optimize the total materials cycle from virgin material, to finished material, to component, to product, to obsolete product, and to ultimate disposal. Factors to be optimized include resources, energy, and capital. (Graedel and Allenby 2010, 32)

A second, somewhat contrasting definition was provided in an early IEEE white paper:[3]

> *Industrial ecology* is the objective, multidisciplinary study of industrial and economic systems and their linkages with

fundamental natural systems. It incorporates, among other things, research involving energy supply and use, new materials, new technologies and technological systems, basic sciences, economics, law, management, and social sciences. Although still in the development stage, it provides the theoretical scientific basis upon which understanding, and reasoned improvement, of current practices can be based. . . . It is important to emphasize that industrial ecology is an objective field of study based on existing scientific and technological disciplines, not a form of industrial policy or planning system. (IEEE 1995)

Both definitions emphasize several common themes. Both encourage a systemic approach, and both focus on industrial and economic activity as well as the ways in which they are coupled to natural systems. Both, however, reveal their environmental history in their emphasis on resources, especially materials and energy; information is not mentioned (a particularly interesting omission in the IEEE white paper). Finally, the last caution of the IEEE definition is important. Most obviously, it illustrates an effort to place industrial ecology in a nonpartisan mainstream, rather than as an extension of environmental policy implying an agenda of centralized industrial planning. Second and more subtly, it reflects the tension within the field itself between viewing industrial ecology as an adjunct to environmental and sustainability activism and viewing industrial ecology as a field of study committed to scientific values of discovery and disclosure.

The basic analogy of industrial ecology is that industrial systems should evolve to generate more efficient use of resources, just as ecosystems do. This is usually illustrated by the classic industrial ecology model given in figure 2. One begins with a Type I system, where a single type of organism eats what it finds and excretes waste back into the environment; this is not unlike many industrial systems where a material is used only once (fossil fuels in a car engine, for example). Then one develops limited cycling in a Type II system, where the waste from one organism is used by another as food; many industrial processes in the chemical industry do this sort of limited internal recycling. The ideal, of course, is a Type III system, where resources are heavily cycled within the community before eventually becoming waste. As indicated by the size of the spheres, each jump in function is accompanied by the ability to support a greater degree

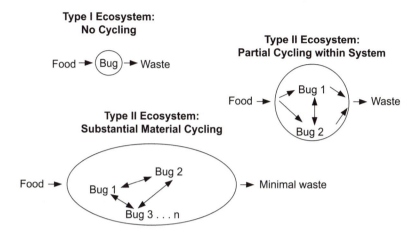

Figure 2 Industrial ecology conceptual model (based on figure 12.1 in Allenby [2011]).

of biomass with the same input of resources—or a higher level of human activity and population in an industrial ecology system. This is obviously a highly oversimplified version of both biology and economic activity— among other things, it overlooks the fact that material recycling usually carries an energy cost with it, which means that a heavily recycling system is an energy-intensive system, all things being equal—but it does present a clear and simple idea of the fundamental insight of industrial ecology. Figure 2 shows a highly simplified conceptual model of industrial ecology, with the ideal being a Type III system.

In addition to the environmental flavor and systems orientation of industrial ecology evident in the definitions, there are several additional important themes. In general, and reflecting its origin in private firms rather than nongovernmental organizations, industrial ecology analyses and methodologies tend to emphasize engineering and scientific approaches, rather than the more heavily normative and prescriptive approaches characteristic of the traditional environmental community. This is evident in the tools, such as DfE and mass flow analysis (MFA), that industrial ecologists tend to use. Moreover, industrial ecology tends to do studies at many different scales, from in-plant process studies, to facility-wide studies, to life-cycle studies of particular products, to broader studies of the context within which products may be used. This obviously raises a number of challenges because each level of such a system hierarchy has its own dynamics as well as its own economic and policy implications, and thus its own set of issues and considerations. Additionally, one must be sensitive to the way in which different levels may interact, and whether such interactions require consideration in a given situation. Using the automobile as an example, if one is working on an engine technology such as fuel injection that improves performance but has little impact beyond the engine, one need not worry much about higher levels of the system. But if one is proposing to shift from a gasoline internal combustion engine to a hydrogen internal combustion engine, one has a far different situation because the biggest challenge is not designing a hydrogen internal combustion engine, which is easily done with today's technology, but building a hydrogen fuel infrastructure—which is neither trivial nor achievable in the short term. Note also that the fuel injector technology is only loosely connected to other fundamental systems, and those are mainly technological in nature—developing an appropriate supply chain, for example. Conversely, the biggest barriers to building a hydrogen fuel distribution infrastructure are probably not technological—financing such a large construction project would be daunting, for example, and political opposition from the existing infrastructure owners, such as gas station proprietors, would be very potent and difficult to overcome.

As a final definitional exercise, it is instructive to look at some of the questions that industrial ecologists have raised about their field because they indicate where some of the future challenges for industrial ecology and sustainable engineering and management might lie. One question that has already been mentioned but that deserves further emphasis is the foundational question of whether industrial ecology, or any related field such as "green engineering" or "green chemistry," is intended as a normative exercise that is valid only to the extent it directly supports environmental and sustainability activism, or, rather, whether it is intended to be a more objective exercise that is intended to supply rigorous data to private and public decision makers but not to displace them. Obviously, how this is answered in practice will have a lot of implications for the ways in which firms, and governments, will use industrial ecology data. More basically, it is not surprising that a principle question that any integrative field, such as industrial ecology, will raise is one of boundaries: where are they and, equally pressing, to what extents are various social sciences included within the field. A related question is the degree to which biological ecology is a metaphor from which private firms can learn, as opposed to a model that private firms should (must?) follow. While any good manager or engineer seeks inspiration wherever it may lie, it is one thing to use biological systems, with their complex flows and transformations of energy and materials, as a useful guide; it is quite another to elevate it to a design mandate. In doing the latter, it often appears that some people perceive biological communities as being identical to industrial systems for all practical purposes, which amounts to a category error: no biological community has the equivalent of a rogue CEO, for example, or a brilliant savior of the firm, or the equivalent of a downgrade of one's corporate bonds by a rating firm.

It is also important to highlight the difficulties of the implied shift of industrial ecology, and for that matter sustainable management or engineering, from an environmental focus to a sustainability focus. This reflects a number of conditions, most obviously historical. In engineering, for example, the fields that contributed the most to industrial ecology and sustainable engineering—ranging from "green engineering" as developed in such places as Carnegie Mellon University, to industrial ecology, to pollution prevention, as well as the most familiar methodologies such as DfE, MFA, and life cycle assessment—almost always have arisen from exclusively environmental concerns. Accordingly, we know a lot more about environmental issues and how to identify and quantify them than we do social and cultural issues. It is not just that environmental issues, which can be more easily defined and unambiguously measured than social or cultural issues, are more tractable to engineering cultures and frameworks. It also reflects the opposite: social and cultural issues are not just less familiar; they are far more difficult to define with precision, are invariably normative, and are usually highly contested. Even business leaders, policymakers, and social scientists have trouble with them. Thus, even many of the stakeholders with self-declared interests in sustainable products or engineering actively oppose the few heuristics that do exist, such as regulatory compliance and consumer acceptance. A classic example of this is the Greenpeace report on the Apple iPhone, which criticized the device for containing certain chemicals, even though they are legal, as is the phone itself.[4] The phone shows no indication of being hazardous and, based on consumer response, obviously has a high social value. So who gets to decide what is socially preferable: consumers, stakeholders, or activist groups? This highlights a more subtle limitation on industrial ecology: the skills necessary to evaluate environmental concerns are accessible to the manager or technocrat; the skills necessary to navigate the minefield of social and cultural preferences and value conflicts are not.

Nonetheless, it is possible to generate some basic criteria from the industrial ecology experience that can inform sustainable engineering and management. For example, one textbook on sustainable engineering suggests the following list:[5]

- In design of manufacturing processes and products, minimize energy, material, and toxics use, as well as the number of separate processes.

- Include noneconomic stakeholder values in design objectives and constraints (environmental and social).

- Reduce energy and material consumption over the product life cycle. Reduced energy consumption not only benefits consumers because power sources last longer but it also reduces the flow of waste from used power sources as well.

- Reduce packaging over the life cycle. Many industrial ecology studies have shown that packaging tends to be overengineered, with consequent waste of packaging materials.

- Reduce use of toxics in all applications, including routine maintenance.

- Design products to take account of their roles in services, networks and infrastructure, and cultural patterns.

- Allow for technological evolution and concomitant efficiency gains. There is a trade-off between designing long-lasting artifacts and greater efficiency with new design. What would air quality be if 1960s muscle cars still filled the road today? (Allenby 2011)

Conclusion

Many engineering and managerial professionals and their firms are increasingly challenged by sustainability issues. Although inadequately recognized, the biggest conceptual barrier to rational management of such challenges is the contrast between the mythic nature of sustainability and the need for real-world, pragmatic design and management decisions at the level of the individual and the firm. Activists can be oversimplistic; professionals and firms are treated very roughly by markets and physical constraints if they take that route. That does not mean, however, that sustainability can be ignored or discounted; it is an independent fact in an increasingly complex world that must be managed. One can tell firms that are sophisticated in their management of sustainability issues by the skill with which they evaluate, manage, and operationally integrate conflicting stakeholder demands. Those that merely reflect ad hoc stakeholder demands into their processes are doing themselves no favors, for they are not understanding sustainability in its fundamental sense, and neither, in many cases, are they responsibly fulfilling their roles in society. Treating stakeholder demands regarding sustainability in rational and integrated internal processes that produce preferable designs and decisions as a result, however, can often enable individuals and firms to better manage a complicated and changing environment—and, frequently, to also develop more robust and competitive products and services. The complicated landscape of sustainability is indeed a challenge, but it can also be a significant source of strategic advantage as well—for the individual, for the firm, and, eventually, for society as a whole.

References

Allenby, B. R. 1991. "Design for Environment: A Tool Whose Time Has Come." *SSA Journal*, September, 5–9.

Allenby, B. R. 1997. "Environmental Constraints and the Evolution of the Private Firm." In *The Industrial Green Game: Implications for Environmental Design and Management*, edited by D. J. Richards. Washington, D.C.: National Academy Press, 101–16.

Allenby, B. R. 2005. *Reconstructing Nature.* Washington, D.C.: Island Press.

Allenby, B. R. 2006. "The *Real* Death of Environmentalism." *Environmental Quality Management* 16, no. 1: 1–10.

Allenby, B. R. 2007. "Earth Systems Engineering and Management: A Manifesto." *Environmental Science & Technology* 41, no. 23: 7960–65.

Allenby, B. R. 2011. *The Theory and Practice of Sustainable Engineering.* Upper Saddle River, N.J.: Pearson/Prentice Hall.

Allenby, B. R., and D. Sarewitz. 2011. *The Techno-Human Condition.* Cambridge, Mass.: MIT Press.

American Electronics Association (AEA). 1993. *Design for Environment.* Washington, D.C.: American Electronics Association.

Bijker, W. E., T. P. Hughes, and T. Pinch, eds. 1997. *The Social Construction of Technological Systems.* Cambridge, Mass.: MIT Press.

Choucri, N. 1993. *Global Accord: Environmental Challenges and International Responses.* Cambridge, Mass.: MIT Press.

Cronon, W. 1991. *Nature's Metropolis: Chicago and the Great West.* New York: W. W. Norton.

Epstein, E. M. 1987. "The Corporate Social Policy Process: Beyond Business Ethics, Corporate Social Responsibility and Corporate Social Responsiveness." *California Management Review* 29, no. 3: 99–114.

Freeman, C., and F. Louca. 2001. *As Time Goes By: From the Industrial Revolutions to the Information Revolution.* Oxford: Oxford University Press.

Friedman, M. 1970. "The Social Responsibility of Business Is to Increase Its Profits." *New York Times Magazine*, September 13, 122–126.

Gatenby, D. A., and G. Foo. 1990. "Design for X: Key to Competitive, Profitable Markets." *AT&T Technical Journal* 63, no. 3: 2–13.

Graedel, T. E., and B. R. Allenby. 2010. *Industrial Ecology and Sustainable Engineering.* Upper Saddle River, N.J.: Prentice-Hall.

Institute of Electrical and Electronic Engineers (IEEE). 1995. *White Paper on Sustainable Development and Industrial Ecology.* New Brunswick, N.J.: IEEE.

Kurzweil, R. 2005. *The Singularity Is Near.* New York: Viking.

Mathews, J. T. 1997. "Power Shift." *Foreign Affairs* 76, no. 1: 50–66.

McKibben, B. 1989. *The End of Nature.* New York: Random House.

Sassen, S. 1996. *Losing Control: Sovereignty in an Age of Globalization.* New York: Columbia University Press.

Schivelbusch, W. 1977. *The Railway Journey: The Industrialization of Time and Space in the 19th Century.* Berkeley: University of California Press.

Senge, P. M. 1990. *The Fifth Discipline.* New York: Doubleday.

WCED (World Commission on Environment and Development, the Brundtland Commission). 1987. *Our Common Future.* Oxford: Oxford University Press.

Notes

1 Much of this discussion is drawn from *The Theory and Practice of Sustainable Engineering* (Allenby 2011).

2 The ten white papers were (AEA 1993): "What Is Design for Environment?" (B. Allenby, AT&T); "DFE and Pollution Prevention" (B. Allenby, AT&T); "Design for Disassembly and Recyclability" (R. Grossman, IBM); "Design for Environmentally Sound Processing" (J. Sekutowski, AT&T); "Design for Materials Recyclability" (W. Rosenberg, COMPAQ, and B. Terry, Pitney-Bowes); "Cultural and Organizational Issues Related to DFE" (B. Allenby, AT&T); "Design for Maintainability" (E. Morehouse, USAF); "Design for Environmentally Responsible Packaging" (K. Rasmussen, General Electric); "Design for Refurbishment" (J. Azar, Xerox); and "Sustainable Development, Industrial Ecology, and Design for Environment" (B. Allenby, AT&T).

3 For purposes of full disclosure, the author wrote the IEEE white paper and contributed to the textbook definition. He is thus very familiar with the reasons why both are somewhat similar yet differ in important ways, reflecting their different audiences.

4 "Missed Call: The iPhone's Hazardous Chemicals," *Greenpeace*, October 15, 2007, www.greenpeace.org/usa/news/iphone-s-hazardous-chemicals

5 Note that the first five injunctions can be derived from industrial ecology as it is because they involve responses to environmental concerns, but the last two, which are broader, begin to suggest a path based on industrial ecology toward a more rigorous version of sustainable engineering and management, and perhaps even the development of a design for sustainability capability.

CHAPTER 6

Creating Sustainable Entrepreneurship

Bradley D. Parrish and Fiona Tilley

For sustainability entrepreneurship to ever be more than an occasional happy contingency in which profitable market opportunities happen to align with the contribution to an ecological or social good, such contributions must be integrated into the very purpose of an organization—integrated into the basic understanding about what it means to be an entrepreneur and into the continuous process of organizational becoming. By critically examining some prevailing assumptions about entrepreneurship, this chapter provides an alternative characterization of what sustainability entrepreneurship is and what it necessarily entails. We examine the "what" and the "how" of effective sustainability entrepreneurship to demonstrate how dualities that constrain approaches to organizing, such as "self/other," "human/nature," can be transcended in practice by a creative process that is transformative of people as well as organizations.

Entrepreneurs are organizers. Whether they are launching new ventures or transforming existing enterprises, whether they are creating radical new business models or replicating well-established ones, all are engaged in organizing people and resources to turn envisioned possibilities into concrete realities. The question before us is how these professional organizers who make their living by forming and reforming the organizational landscapes of our economy can effectively create organizations that sustain rather than undermine our social and ecological support systems.

Introduction

Much ink has been dedicated to rationalizing how actively pursuing sustainability within ventures is in an entrepreneur's immediate self-interest—it may lead to reduced operational costs, or competitive advantage in the marketplace, or there may be opportunities to profit from market failures or otherwise unmet environmental and basic quality of life needs, and so on. This essay serves a different purpose. Rather than focusing on the question of "why" pursue sustainability through entrepreneurship, we focus on the "what" and the "how" of it. What is actually required for entrepreneurs to create organizations that materially contribute to sustainability? And how can entrepreneurs pursue such an endeavor effectively? Curiously, though, in the end we find we cannot really detach these questions from the "why" question because it becomes clear that purpose is a central fulcrum on which pivots the trajectory of entrepreneurial practices.

Unfortunately, the answers to these questions have often been confused and muddied by authors writing on the basis of ingrained assumptions about what entrepreneurship and enterprise necessarily is and should be. These assumptions include the primacy of profit maximization as the motivation for entrepreneurial action; that organizational sustainability is synonymous with responsible stakeholder management; and that these are achieved by incorporating various environmental and social impact assessment tools to otherwise unmodified organizing practices. By critically examining these assumptions, this essay provides support for an alternative characterization of what sustainability entrepreneurship is and necessarily entails.

Before we proceed down this path, a note of caution is needed. Entrepreneurs are creative actors, and studying their craft of organization design is in many respects akin to studying the techniques of accomplished artists. Imagine a potter sitting at a spinning wheel. Although she is constrained by the physical properties of the clay with which she works, her creative expressions come to be through the imaginative interplay between her intentions and an intuitive and felt understanding of the possibilities of expression in constant emergence from the ever-changing form of clay cupped in her hands. Recognizing a similar interplay of intention, imagination, and the ever-changing concrete realities of specific times and places, studies of entrepreneurship cannot expect to develop prescriptive technical–rational rules for effective entrepreneurial action (Parrish 2010). Rather, researchers have increasingly come to focus on the "thinking–doing" connection that links ways of thinking to the practical action of organizing in diverse and evolving contexts (Mitchell et al. 2007). We see this thinking–doing nexus as an aspect of the ongoing process of being and becoming, in which organizational actors continuously reweave their "webs of beliefs and habits of actions to accommodate new experiences obtained through interaction" (Tsoukas and Chia 2002, 567). To understand sustainability entrepreneurship, our task is thus twofold: we must understand the concrete realities inherent in organizing for sustainability (the "what"), and we must understand the approaches to being and becoming that enable entrepreneurial intentions to be expressed in ways that are consistent with such concrete realities (the "how" and, inevitably, the "why"). To accomplish these tasks we begin by discussing some broad, guiding conceptual frameworks, then we will gradually get more concrete as we address specific practices that accord with these guiding frameworks.

Creative Realism: Survival and Sustainability

Creative acts entail foresight, imagination, and vision. As creative actors, entrepreneurs organize the emergence of new products, new business models, and even whole new markets. There is an aspect of idealism to the creative practices of entrepreneurship because entrepreneurs must see not only what is but also what is possible and what could be. But for entrepreneurs to succeed, theirs must be an idealism grounded in realism. In capitalist societies, this means creating organizations that can survive the rigors of a competitive market economy. The creative aspect of entrepreneurship is found in the diverse and innovative ways in which entrepreneurs accomplish this feat. A convention has developed to distinguish between innovative entrepreneurs, who are seen to bring something new to market, and imitative entrepreneurs, who are seen to merely replicate existing business models. While this distinction may be useful at a broad scale, a finer lens reveals that all entrepreneurial endeavors necessarily involve acts of innovation and novelty. Entrepreneurs are highly embedded in particular contexts of time and place, involving locally specific industry structures, institutions, customer dynamics, competing organizations, available resources, and so on. In fact, it does not seem a stretch to argue that the most significant expertise of successful entrepreneurs is in skillfully making use of their contextually embedded positions to build coalitions of support for organizations to survive and thrive in the day-to-day realities of unique operating environments. Thus, no two entrepreneurial endeavors can ever be the same. Given that the process of organizing in diverse contexts involves innovation and novelty, particular organization design outcomes cannot be prescribed. However, the results of entrepreneurial organizing, no matter how diverse, must all contend with some common requirements for survival in a market economy, and a century of organization research has yielded some useful insights about what these requirements are. It is therefore possible to identify what is required for organizations to survive over time while leaving the means of achieving this open to creative variation.

What this means for sustainability entrepreneurship is that organizing for sustainability does not exempt one from the very real requirements of organizational survival, but neither does it necessitate replicating entrepreneurship as usual. There is ample room for novel approaches to entrepreneurship founded on a different set of priorities that nonetheless satisfy the key organizational requirements for surviving and thriving in a market economy. But these strategies are not limited to the rather narrow approach of simply "making sustainability profitable." The key here is that sustainable development of the wider social–ecological system is in fact a priority for some entrepreneurs (e.g., Kuckertz and Wagner 2010; Schlange 2009). Indeed, empirical studies of entrepreneurship in practice demonstrate that some sustainability-driven entrepreneurs have a remarkable ability to balance the competing interests of self, other people, and nonhuman nature to the mutual benefit of all three (Schlange 2007; Parrish 2010). Doing so, therefore, requires designing organizations in which operational activities work to support wider social and ecological systems as they support the organization's own continued survival. Lessons from the areas of organization research and sustainability research provide a useful framework for understanding the requirements for doing so.

Considering first the requirements for enterprise survival, Barnard (1938), Simon (1957), and March and Simon (1967) have contributed a model that, with subsequent elaborations, continues to prove relevant. Based on their view of an enterprise as "a system of interrelated social behaviors of a number of persons" who they called participants, Barnard and Simon argued that enterprise survival involves balancing the contributions that participants make to the enterprise with the inducements the enterprise provides to participants (March and Simon 1967, 86). This model was extended through several different research domains and was significantly elaborated on and popularized by Freeman (1984) under the heading of the "stakeholder perspective." As Clarkson explains, "*Stakeholders* are persons or groups that have, or claim, ownership, rights, or interests in a corporation and its activities, past, present, or future," and a "*primary* stakeholder group is one without whose continuing participation the corporation cannot survive as a going concern" (Clarkson 1995, 106, emphasis in original). Thus, an important principle for enterprise survival is that the entrepreneur must first attract organizational participants to her venture and then continue to induce contributions to its ongoing operations. Clarkson (1995) provides multiple examples of enterprises that have dissolved due to the loss of support from an important stakeholder group.

Achieving ongoing stakeholder support requires that the enterprise adapt over time with its evolving operating environment (DiMaggio and Powell 1983; Hannan and Freeman 1977; Lewin and Volberda 1999; Nelson and Winter 1982). Thus, the need to continually adapt structures and operations to maintain a degree of efficiency and to satisfy other technical requirements provides a complementary principle of enterprise survival (Williamson 1991). Together, then, organization theory suggests that the principles of enterprise survival involve a continual process of enterprise design and redesign in concert with changes in the operating environment in order to maintain stakeholder contributions as a going concern. The strength of this framework is that it describes the universal tasks that must be accomplished for organizations to continue their existence without ascribing any predefined normative values or motives to organizational actors.

Turning our attention to sustainability, principles for organizations have only been recently considered. Due to the close association between stakeholder theory and corporate responsibility research (see Epstein and Roy 2001; Maignan, Hillebrand, and McAlister 2002; Roberts 1992; Warhurst 2005), several authors have looked to stakeholder theory for insights. For example, Tencati and Perrini defined a "sustainability-oriented company" as one that "develops over time by taking into consideration the economic, social and environmental dimensions of its processes and performance affecting the quality of stakeholder relationships" (2006, 95). Similarly, Dyllick and Hockerts defined corporate sustainability as "meeting the needs of a firm's direct and indirect stakeholders . . . without compromising its ability to meet the needs of future stakeholders as well" (2002, 131). The stakeholder approach to organizational sustainability has proven popular because it provides a way of making the somewhat vague notion of society more tangible and because it provides an obvious link with organizational survival. However, the stakeholder concept is a misleading basis for defining principles of organizational sustainability for at least two important reasons. The first is based on issues of scale, and the second is based on recognizing the importance of functional realities beyond ascribed stakeholder value assessments.

Regarding scale, Clarkson (1995) explains the importance of distinguishing between stakeholder issues and social issues, as each operate at a different level. As he explained, "The connotation of *social* is society, a level of analysis that is more inclusive, more ambiguous, and further up the ladder than a corporation itself" (Clarkson 1995, 102). Sustainable development is about the welfare of the whole of human society now and into the foreseeable future. While this certainly includes an enterprise's participants, they are neither the exclusive nor often the most critical concern for questions of sustainable development. Rather, sustainable development provides a vision of the future that couples the long-term survival of human society with a qualitative improvement in the experience of life on Earth, particularly the experience of society's most vulnerable. It is a macro-level concept, and the contribution of an enterprise to sustainability must be understood at that level (Atkinson 2000; Figge and Schaltegger 2000). Social and ecological issues are therefore clearly distinguishable from the issues of organizational participants or stakeholders. Although the two may contingently overlap at times, they also may conflict. For example, increased public safety (a social good) may decrease the need for private security firms, which, at one level, is clearly not in the immediate interest of those enterprises' employees, suppliers, or shareholders. Similarly, the importance of conserving a forested ecosystem for maintaining flows of socially and ecologically sustaining ecosystem services may be at odds with the immediate interests of the employees, owners, and local community stakeholders of an extractive enterprise.

It is important to distinguish between the functional realities of social–ecological systems and the ascribed value assessments of organizational stakeholders. "Functional value" describes the effects of an action while "ascribed value" describes a normative assessment of the goodness or badness of those effects. For example, a white-water rafting venture may affect land-cover changes to the riparian ecosystem in which it operates. If these land-cover changes result in an increase or decrease in erosion-preventing vegetation, the ecosystem functioning will be supported or undermined accordingly, regardless of what value the enterprise's stakeholders ascribe to it. To take another example, enterprises that set expectations for 80-hour workweeks undermine the capacity of their employees to contribute to the nurturing and caretaking functions of their families and communities, while those that make provisions for short commute times, flexible working hours, and extended paternity and maternity leaves support such social sustaining functions. Thus, for an enterprise to contribute to sustainable development it must support rather than undermine "the social and biophysical context within which it takes place" (O'Hara 1997, 142).

The relationship between an enterprise and its stakeholders therefore represents a partial but incomplete understanding of enterprise sustainability principles. To more fully appreciate the relationship between enterprise and sustainable development, an enterprise must be positioned between the micro concerns of its stakeholders and the macro functions of the social–ecological system (Parrish 2007). Positioning the enterprise in this way emphasizes that to contribute to sustainable development in a real, material way, enterprises must not only attend to their own stakeholders' needs and wishes but must also contribute to the sustaining services of the greater social–ecological system. In other words, the daily operational activities that ensure the enterprise's own capacity to survive and thrive must also contribute to the capacity of its stakeholders and the social–ecological system to do the same. Considering the way an enterprise supports or undermines the very real ecological and social sustaining functions that support society's continued existence and well-being provides a concrete way of thinking about an enterprise's contribution to sustainable development. How entrepreneurs will achieve this is as varied as their enterprises and the contexts in which they operate. Just as skillful entrepreneurs excel at crafting enterprises that can attract support within the contexts in which they are embedded, so too sustainability entrepreneurs must excel at crafting enterprises that concurrently support the social and ecological contexts within which they are embedded.

Creative Success = f(Intentionality, Performance)

Creation is an act of intention. New ventures do not sprout up accidentally but are the result of concrete practices of organizing driven by the aspirations (intention) of entrepreneurs and backed by careful and sustained thought (planned behavior). Within entrepreneurship research, the concepts of intention (Bird 1988) and planned behavior (Ajzen 1985) provide two of the clearest links between ways of thinking and doing that propel the ongoing process of organizational becoming. Of course this does not mean that entrepreneurial intentions and plans can directly predetermine outcomes. For example, empirical studies have found that expressed intentions to start a business predict actual new venture launches only about 50 percent of the time (Davidsson 1995; Krueger and Carsrud 1993). We must also give a nod to the role of situational factors, uncertainty, contingency, and surprise in contributing to their fair share of unintended consequences, whether for better or worse. In fact, the ubiquity of uncertainty in the entrepreneurial context has been singled out as a key contributor to the success of experienced entrepreneurs, although intentions still influence the way uncertainty is confronted (Sarasvathy 2001). And intentions and plans are not static but rather evolve over time.

Unfortunately, most of the research on entrepreneurial intentions has focused on the simple bivariate intention to start a business or not, rather than more qualitative explorations of the nature of the venture one intends to start and for what purpose. Economists ascribe profit seeking as the sole motivation of entrepreneurs not because it necessarily holds true for all entrepreneurs but because they believe that using simplified assumptions as if they were true allows them to model close approximations of actual economic activity. Entrepreneurship researchers heavily influenced by the characterizations developed by economists have adopted the assumption of profit-seeking motives to the extent that is has become one of the defining features of entrepreneurship (Mitchell et al. 2007). The introduction of social entrepreneurship as an accepted category of entrepreneurship has done surprisingly little to broaden this view and is instead used by many as a residual category in which to place those who do not fit the mold of the profit-seeking entrepreneur proper (e.g., Dean and McMullen 2007).

Adopting such narrow assumptions of the intentions and motives underlying entrepreneurial actions has significant consequences. One consequence is that it inhibits understanding of entrepreneurship in practice. Studies of entrepreneurial performance are directly influenced by these assumptions because they consistently use the criteria of survival or growth to measure performance. Survival understates the performance of an enterprise because survival is a minimum requirement but does not speak to how well the organization is fulfilling its intended purpose. A focus on organizational survival may also be misleading because it does not take into account that shutting down one formal organization may be a strategic move in a larger playing field, for example, in the successful career of a serial entrepreneur that spans more than one organization. The preoccupation with growth and growth rates as indicators of success is also misleading. As with any system, there are appropriate times for well-functioning organizations to grow and not to grow, and even important periods of consolidation. The peculiar Western preoccupation with perpetual growth, preferably as fast as possible, is a distorted view of reality that is confounding our understanding of effective organizations and, on a larger scale, of effective economies (Victor 2008).

Indirectly, even studies of qualitative aspects of entrepreneurship reflect the influence of this assumption in the criteria they adopt for selecting successful and unsuccessful cases for their studies. The inevitable result is that the stock of knowledge we have accumulated in entrepreneurship research pertains to only a subset of entrepreneurs: those that are driven predominantly by a profit-seeking and profit-maximizing motive. The unfortunate consequence of this is that well-meaning advice on effective entrepreneurial practices can be at a minimum misleading, and can be at the extreme actually detrimental to entrepreneurs who are guided by different or more wide-ranging motives, of which sustainability entrepreneurs are an important case (Parrish 2010).

Even more ominously, such assumptions promote the hegemony of these motives in the design of new markets, organizations, and products. As Feenberg (1998) argues, "centralized technical decision making, working to fulfill certain mandates such as profits or growth, generates strong pressure to narrow the range of concerns incorporated into design." More than a decade ago, Gladwin, Kennelly, and Krause (1995) discussed in their seminal article how our organization and management theories can act as barriers to integration in full community, meaning both our social and ecological communities. Reflecting this hegemony, the most usual approaches to sustainability entrepreneurship involve developing management tools that promise sustainable results without calling into question the more fundamental priorities underpinning organizational practices and structures. For example, traditional eco-efficiency and environmental and social impact assessment tools designed to be added-on to existing management practices (e.g., Robèrt et al., 2002) compartmentalize environmental and social performance, and position these as constraints on the activities of the organization. Even the opportunity-oriented approaches, such as "Bottom of the Pyramid" (Prahalad and Hart 2002) and "Strategic Sustainability" (Funk 2002), allow ecologically and socially beneficial actions only when they conform to an overriding profit motive. These approaches do not lead to a questioning, rethinking, or broadening of the very purpose for which organizations exist. Therefore, they are limited in their capacity to support sustainability entrepreneurship in practice.

The point of this critique is not for intellectual positioning or simply critique for critique's sake. The critical examination of these largely taken-for-granted assumptions points the way for an alternative characterization of what effective sustainability entrepreneurship is and necessarily entails. It should be clear from the discussion so far that for sustainability entrepreneurship to ever be more than an occasional happy contingency in which profitable market opportunities happen to align with the contribution to an ecological or social good, such contributions must be integrated into the very purpose of an organization—integrated into the basic understanding about what it means to be an entrepreneur, and into the continuous process of organizational becoming. Some exciting recent work in this field has begun to appreciate and explore the diversity and multidimensionality of motives that drive entrepreneurial actions. For example, Cohen, Smith, and Mitchell (2008) have begun exploring how environmental, social, and financial intentions may link to equally diverse performance outcomes, both separately and in combination. Their work represents an initial step into this underappreciated terrain, and further extensions of their ideas can contribute greatly to our understanding. In another important study, Schlange (2007) demonstrated entrepreneurs in practice effectively pursuing a tripartite motive of financial return and socioethical and environmental performance. Of significance is his finding that these entrepreneurs demonstrated unique capabilities for effectively balancing outcomes in all three of these domains.

Our own work on sustainability entrepreneurship in practice supports this finding and provides greater insight into exactly how such entrepreneurs are able to effectively balance concern for themselves, other people, and nonhuman nature (Parrish and Foxon 2009; Parrish and Tilley 2009; Tilley and Parrish 2009; Tilley and Young 2009). Recent results have emphasized the role of five cross-cutting principles of sustainability entrepreneurship that describe an alternative approach to being an entrepreneur (Parrish 2010): the principles of resource perpetuation, benefit stacking, strategic satisficing, qualitative management, and worthy contribution. Together they describe an approach to entrepreneurial thinking and doing termed "perpetual reasoning" that directly contradicts some of the general wisdom on entrepreneurship. The approach has proven effective in creating enterprises with a sustainable character that are also leaders in their respective

industries. The analysis of these principles demonstrates how they effectively reconcile conflicts between requirements for organizational survival
and sustainability. They do this by functioning not as a list of must or must
not items but as a more adaptable basis for reasoning through the wide
variety of situational contingencies that must be confronted in the process
of organizational becoming.

All entrepreneurs must contend with issues of operational efficiency,
unwelcome tradeoffs, evaluative criteria for their decisions, and the necessity of inducing ongoing contributions from organizational participants.
The principles of perpetual reasoning are manifestations of a different
understanding of what these issues mean to an enterprise and how they
are to be approached. The basis of these differences is the underlying purpose that the enterprise is meant to serve. Conventionally, enterprises are
thought to be created for the purpose of exploiting resources for one's own
advantage by maximizing financial gain in the shortest time as possible.
In contrast, entrepreneurs using perpetual reasoning created enterprises
to perpetuate human and nonhuman resources by using them in ways that
maintain or enhance the quality of their functioning for as long as possible.
By doing so, a range of benefits, financial and otherwise, could be accrued
to the entrepreneurs and other organizational participants. The critical
point about these principles of perpetual reasoning is that the entrepreneurs who embodied them developed modes of being an entrepreneur in
practice that were attuned to their foundational sustainability purpose for
pursuing entrepreneurship. And it worked.

While the five principles of perpetual reasoning can be adopted by any
entrepreneur, it is important that they not be used as yet another add-on tool
guaranteeing sustainability performance. To be effective, practices such as
perpetual reasoning must be an expression of the integration of sustainable development priorities into entrepreneurial intentions and practices.
But how can entrepreneurs and their organizations come to embody such
holistically integrated intentions, and how can practices such as perpetual
reasoning become genuine expressions of these intentions?

Creative Destruction: A Personal Transformation

The process of becoming sustainability entrepreneurs is in essence a journey into the unknown, something that is innovative and novel so as to be
intentionally life-sustaining within the context-specific circumstances the

entrepreneurs find themselves. For this to be fully embodied, it needs to be personally experienced. Whilst making every effort to provide an abstract description in conceptual form in order to more deeply appreciate how this may be personally manifested, it necessitates a personal involvement. In the world in which we live, the written word is often placed in higher regard than personal experience. Sustainability entrepreneurship requires participation; when this begins, the real transformational learning will start. While we will make every effort to refer to business literature for the language to be accessible, much of what we say is already known. It is ancient knowledge and in many ways is already within each and everyone of us, and yet for many it thus far remains invisible, unseen, and unknown.

Sustainability entrepreneurs will often refer to a strong inner sense of knowing what lies beyond the dominant rational, logical, and linear world view. In other words, they are referring to a process of being guided by their integrated self. Surfacing what is intuitively known within and placing the emphasis on relationships rather than objects or outcomes is described by Thomas Berry (1999) when he states, "The universe is a communion of subjects not a collection of objects." Sustainability entrepreneurs are seeking to reconnect themselves with all of nature to have a deeply personal appreciation and understanding of what sustainability means. From this perspective, it is possible to establish how to express this in organizational form. This personal reconnection is unavoidable. Taking a definition for sustainability off the shelf is not possible if you want it to have any practicable meaning. The ubiquity of the Bruntland definition is warning enough in this regard. It is acceptable to most if not all and operational by none.

In our contact and research with sustainability entrepreneurs, we have found some common elements that might guide others on a similar journey. Sustainability entrepreneurship is a balancing of the purpose of the enterprise (alignment) with due consideration to the provision of the necessary support for the well-being of the human and nonhuman life associated with the enterprise (attunement). Harrison (1984) brought into focus the emotional, nonrational, and intuitive aspects of organizational leadership alongside the more traditionally recognized logical, action-oriented decision-making functions. What tends to happen in unsustainable enterprises is the structure and functioning of the organization (alignment) is placed before the care of human and nonhuman life (attunement), resulting in high alignment and low attunement. Another way of understanding this is that there is not sufficient awareness and appreciation of the relational values intrinsic to the balanced functioning of the enterprise, thereby placing the survival of the enterprise at risk as well as the survival of life-sustaining social and ecological systems.

In an entrepreneurial context, balancing alignment and attunement requires each entrepreneur to discover their own sense of sustainability. Creating a new venture start-up embedded with these values is no easy task because no enterprise or entrepreneur is truly separate from the system in which they function. Any sense of sustainability and enterprise design resulting from these values is a cocreation. If only it was as easy as taking up the knowledge of chaos theory, complexity science, and systems theory as applied to the social sciences and bolting it onto existing business theory. The transition from the forms of entrepreneurship that objectify and compartmentalize the world resulting in trade-offs to a more integrated and relational understanding of the world in sustainability entrepreneurship is not simple, smooth, or straightforward. There are likely to be many bumps, much turbulence, and confusion along the way.

Knowing we live in a world of high alignment and low attunement does not mean that we will suddenly have sustainability entrepreneurship in action if entrepreneurs pay greater attention to valuing human and nonhuman life. The rebalancing of alignment and attunement will inevitably lead to a period of confusion and chaos as the currently established ways break down and disintegrate, yet it is out of this tumult that the novel and innovative entrepreneurial ideas can emerge.

Harrison's (1984) model is helpful because it recognizes the importance of the emotional, nonrational, and intuitive functions needed on the journey of sustainability entrepreneurship; however, it does set up a dichotomy. Scharmer's (2007) U Theory is a useful framework that transcends the dualistic thinking that too often dominates currently established ways of thinking and is helpful in guiding aspiring sustainability entrepreneurs toward sustainability entrepreneurship. It is so named because it visually illustrates the upside-down rollercoaster shape of the descent into the unknown, the letting go and surrendering that is necessary to open the mind, heart, and will of the entrepreneur to the possibility and potential presencing of their sustainability innovation or vision. It is this ability to listen to what you are called to do, observing all around with an open mind, and sensing connections to others with an open heart that allows the sustainability entrepreneur to connect with their deepest intention. This is in many ways beyond logic and rationalism and can therefore be blocked by your own or other voices of judgment, cynicism, and fear. This is especially true if what is discovered runs counter to societal norms, which is why this journey is particularly suited to the maverick entrepreneurial spirit and to those who do not seek to please, follow the crowd, or require external validation.

At the point of deepest connectivity, which is best learned through personal experience, your own personal sustainability can be revealed along with a sense of your contribution, which may be expressed in an entrepreneurial way. This presencing moment is at the lowest point of the U in this journey. From this place, U Theory describes a process of letting the ideas come so that a crystallization of intention can be made. The questions to be asked are

- What is it I do?

- What do I offer others in the cocreation of a sustainable planet?

- To whom do I make my offer?

With a clear idea or intention, the sustainability entrepreneur can begin to prototype. This is sometimes referred to as the rehearsal space (Olivier 2008) or integration of head, heart, and hand whereby the thought ideas are synthesized with the values/feelings and compassion of the heart and enacted through the hand by deed. Once the practice of prototyping is completed and the sustainability entrepreneur is ready to make his full offering, the experience is fully embodied and it is possible for the entrepreneur and his organization to fully enter and contribute to the community.

In our view, the right-hand side of U theory—the description of crystallizing an idea, prototyping, and then making a full offering—is very typical of much of the commentary associated with the classical entrepreneurial process of creative destruction observed by Schumpeter in the middle of the last century. It also mirrors the business-planning steps of idea generation, market research, product testing, and new venture start up. What makes U theory a useful model for reflecting on sustainability entrepreneurship is the all-important left-hand side of the U Theory process: the opening of mind, heart, and will in order to surrender judgment, cynicism, and fear to explore the mysterious and the unknown from which the new can emerge. Entrepreneurs are not about reinventing the wheel; they are about presencing and realizing the new. For those who feel drawn to sustainability entrepreneurship, it may help, although it is not essential, to find a good guide or mentor who will offer assist on the journey. There is no substitute for participation. We learn and discover most about ourselves and our potential by doing.

Summary

Sustainability entrepreneurship becomes about the practice of integrating multiple intentions—involving the active support of self, other people, and nonhuman nature—and effectively expressing these intentions in the structure, operations, and character of an enterprise. If we stop searching for a technical, predefined, universally applicable panacea and accept that, knowing what we know about entrepreneurship, the process is likely to be open, indeterminate, and messy and the outcomes diverse, context-specific, and particular, then we are better prepared to learn from the experiences of those entrepreneurs who have already begun to tread this path in practice. We are also better able to learn from ourselves about what sustainability means to each of us and therefore how we can offer our gifts in the communities in which we live. In summary, we suggest there is no substitute for participation as a process of learning to become a sustainability entrepreneur. That the journey sustainability entrepreneurs embark upon is nondualistic and emergent, by which we mean the conventional dualities that lead to compartmentalized activities, such as self and other, human and nature, are transcended by integrated intentions and organizing practices. Intentions may be known; however, the outcomes are unknowable, emerging from the inevitable cocreation that takes place in the act of becoming. We acknowledge in this essay that some very complex themes have had to be briefly expressed; we therefore encourage all to explore, read, participate, and experience in much greater depth the ideas we have shared.

References

Ajzen, I. 1985. "From Intentions to Actions: A Theory of Planned Behavior." In *Action Control: From Cognition to Behavior*, edited by J. Kuhl and J. Beckmann. New York: Springer.

Atkinson, G. 2000. "Measuring Corporate Sustainability." *Journal of Environmental Planning and Management* 43:235–52.

Barnard, C. I. 1938. *The Functions of the Executive*. Cambridge, Mass.: Harvard University Press.

Berry, T. 1999. *The Great Work: Our Way into the Future*. New York: Bell Tower.

Bird, B. 1988. "Implementing Entrepreneurial Ideas: The Case for Intention." *Academy of Management Review* 13:442–52.

Clarkson, M. B. E. 1995. "A Stakeholder Framework for Analyzing and Evaluating Corporate Social Performance." *Academy of Management Review* 20:92–117.

Cohen, B., B. Smith, and R. Mitchell. 2008. "Toward a Sustainable Conceptualization of Dependent Variables in Entrepreneurship Research." *Business Strategy and the Environment* 17, no. 2: 107–19.

Davidsson, P. 1995. "Determinants of Entrepreneurial Intentions." RENT IX Workshop in Entrepreneurship Research. Piacenza, Italy, November 23–24.

Dean, T., and J. S. McMullen. 2007. "Toward a Theory of Sustainable Entrepreneurship: Reducing Environmental Degradation through Entrepreneurial Action." *Journal of Business Venturing* 22, no. 1: 50–76.

DiMaggio, P. J., and W. W. Powell. 1983. "The Iron Cage Revisited: Institutional Isomorphism and Collective Rationality in Organizational Fields." *American Sociological Review* 48:147–60.

Dyllick, T., and K. Hockerts. 2002. "Beyond the Business Case for Corporate Sustainability." *Business Strategy and the Environment* 11, no. 2: 130–41.

Epstein, M. J., and M.-J. Roy. 2001. "Sustainability in Action: Identifying and Measuring the Key Performance Drivers." *Long Range Planning* 34:585–604.

Feenberg, A. 1998. "Escaping the Iron Cage, or, Subversive Rationalization and Democratic Theory" In *Democratising Technology: Ethics, Risk, and Public Debate*, edited by R. Schomberg. Tilburg, Neth.: International Centre for Human and Public Affairs. Available at http://www.sfu.ca/~andrewf/schom1.htm.

Figge, F., and S. Schaltegger. 2000. *What Is "Stakeholder Value"? Developing a Catchphrase into a Benchmarking Tool*. Paris: United Nations Development Programme (UNEP), Division of Technology, Industry, and Economics.

Freeman, R. E. 1984. *Strategic Management: A Stakeholder Approach*. Marshfield, Mass.: Pitman.

Funk, Karina. 2002. "Sustainability and Performance." *MIT Sloan Management Review* 44, no. 2: 65–70.

Gladwin, T. N., J. J. Kennelly, and T.-S. Krause. 1995. "Shifting Paradigms for Sustainable Development: Implications for Management Theory and Research." *Academy of Management Review* 20:874–907.

Hannan, M. T., and J. Freeman. 1977. "The Population Ecology of Organizations." *American Journal of Sociology* 82, no. 5: 929–64.

Harrison, R. 1984. "Strategies for a New Age." *Human Resource Management* 22, no. 3: 209–35.

Krueger, N. F., and A. Carsrud. 1993. "Entrepreneurial Intentions: Applying the Theory of Planned Behaviour." *Entrepreneurship and Regional Development* 5:316–23.

Kuckertz, A., and M. Wagner. 2010. "The Influence of Sustainability Orientation on Entrepreneurial Intentions: Investigating the Role of Business Experience." *Journal of Business Venturing* 25, no. 5: 524–39.

Lewin, A. Y., and H. W. Volberda. 1999. "Prolegomena on Coevolution: A Framework for Research on Strategy and New Organizational Forms." *Organization Science* 10, no. 5: 519–34.

Maignan, I., B. Hillebrand, and D. McAlister. 2002. "Managing Socially Responsible Buying: How to Integrate Non-economic Criteria into the Purchasing Process." *European Management Journal* 20:641–48.

March, J. G., and H. A. Simon. 1967. *Organizations*. New York: Wiley & Sons.

Mitchell, R. K., L. W. Busenitz, B. Bird, C. M. Gaglio, J. S. McMullen, E. A. Morse, and J. B. Smith. 2007. "The Central Question in Entrepreneurial Cognition Research." *Entrepreneurship Theory and Practice* 31, no. 1: 1–27.

Nelson, R. R., and S. G. Winter. 1982. *An Evolutionary Theory of Economic Change*. Cambridge, Mass.: Harvard University Press.

O'Hara, S. U. 1997. "Toward a Sustaining Production Theory." *Ecological Economics* 20:141–54.

Olivier, R. 2008. "Presentation on Sustainability Leadership." Schumacher College, UK, Schumacher College Short Course, October.

Parrish, B. D. 2007. "Designing the Sustainable Enterprise." *Futures* 39:846–60.

Parrish, B. D. 2010. "Sustainability-Driven Entrepreneurship: Principles or Organization Design." *Journal of Business Venturing* 25, no. 5: 510–23.

Parrish, B. D., and T. J. Foxon. 2009. "Sustainability Entrepreneurship and Equitable Transitions to a Low-Carbon Economy." *Greener Management International* 55:47–62.

Parrish, B. D., and F. Tilley. 2009. "Sustainability Entrepreneurship: Charting a Field in Emergence." In *Making Ecopreneurs: Developing Sustainable Entrepreneurship*, edited by M. Schaper. Aldershot, UK: Gower.

Prahalad, C. K., and S. L. Hart. 2002. "The Fortune at the Bottom of the Pyramid." *Strategy + Business* 26:54–67.

Robèrt, K.-H., B. Schmidt-Bleek, J. A. de Larderel, G. Basile, J. L. Jansen, R. Kuehr, T. P. Price, M. Suzuki, P. Hawken, and M. Wackernagel. 2002. "Strategic Sustainable Development: Selection, Design and Synergies of Applied Tools." *Journal of Cleaner Production* 10:197–214.

Roberts, R. W. 1992. "Determinants of Corporate Social Responsibility Disclosure: An Application of Stakeholder Theory." *Accounting, Organizations and Society* 17:595–612.

Sarasvathy, S. D. 2001. "Causation and Effectuation: Toward a Theoretical Shift from Economic Inevitability to Entrepreneurial Contingency." *Academy of Management Review* 26:243–63.

Scharmer, C. O. 2007. *Theory U: Leading from the Future as It Emerges.* Cambridge, Mass.: Society for Organizational Learning.

Schlange, L. E. 2007. "What Drives Sustainable Entrepreneurs?" *Indian Journal of Economics and Business*, Special Issue on ABEAI Conference, Kona, Hawaii (2006), September, 35–45.

Schlange, L. E. 2009. "Stakeholder Identification in Sustainability Entrepreneurship: The Role of Managerial and Organisational Cognition." *Greener Management International* 55:13–32.

Simon, H. A. 1957. *Administrative Behavior: A Study of Decision-making Process in Administrative Organization.* New York: Macmillan.

Tencati, A., and F. Perrini. 2006. "The Sustainability Perspective: A New Governance Model." In *Corporate Social Responsibility*, edited by A. Kakabadse and M. Morsing, 94–111. New York: Palgrave MacMillan.

Tilley, F., and B. D. Parrish. 2009. "Introduction to Sustainability Entrepreneurship Research." *Greener Management International* 55:5–12.

Tilley, F., and W. Young. 2009. "Sustainability Entrepreneurs: Could They Be the True Wealth Generators of the Future?" *Greener Management International* 55:79–92.

Tsoukas, H., and R. Chia. 2002. "On Organizational Becoming: Rethinking Organizational Change." *Organization Science* 13, no. 5: 567–82.

Victor, P. 2008. *Managing without Growth: Slower by Design, Not Disaster*. Northampton, Mass.: Edward Elger.

Warhurst, A. 2005. "Future Roles of Business in Society: The Expanding Boundaries of Corporate Responsibility and a Compelling Case for Partnership." *Futures* 37:151–68.

Williamson, O. E. 1991. "Strategizing, Economizing, and Economic Organization." *Strategic Management Journal* 12 (Winter): 75–94.

CHAPTER 7

Business Leadership in Advancing Safer Chemicals and Products in Supply Chains

Joel Tickner and Melissa Coffin

There is increasing evidence that toxic chemicals used in everyday products are building up in our environment and in our bodies, and may be contributing to health and ecosystem damage. In response to growing scientific and public concern about chemicals in products, negative product safety attention, and increased government attention to and regulation of toxic substances in products, many leading-edge businesses are instituting efforts to screen, prioritize, and substitute chemicals of high concern in their products. Yet firms face a number of barriers to advancing safer chemicals in their products, including missing formulation and toxicity information, higher costs for safer materials, and technological and performance challenges of substitutes. These challenges are consistent across sectors and levels of supply chains. Firms are beginning to work together within and across sectors to remove technological, market, information, and economic barriers to safer products. This chapter presents some of the key drivers of business leadership in advancing safer chemicals and products and discusses challenges to innovation in safer chemistry.

From Safer Processes to Safer Products

Until the 1990s, the focus of chemical regulation in the United States was on a small number of individual chemicals used primarily in industrial production processes and known to be bad actors. Reducing and removing these problematic chemicals resulted in significant benefits to the environment and to workers previously exposed to dangerous chemicals. Little attention, however, was paid to chemicals incorporated into everyday products or to those chemicals that contaminated such products.

We are learning that small but constant chemical exposures from a wide range of everyday products may also adversely affect human health and the environment. These exposures are dispersed, generated from nonpoint sources, and therefore difficult to control. Phthalate additives to soften polyvinyl chloride (PVC) in children's toys and other products, polybrominated diphenyl ethers used as flame retardants in electronics, and bisphenol-A (BPA) lining food cans are all examples of chemicals used in everyday products that can now be found in wildlife and human tissues.[1] Additionally, a wide range of such substances as disinfectants, detergents, cosmetics, and pharmaceuticals are showing up in waterways, in part because they are not destroyed in traditional wastewater treatment facilities. The impacts of such chemical mixtures are nearly impossible to assess either individually or in total. However, research increasingly indicates that exposures to these substances, even at low levels, during critical windows of development may be problematic to human health (Colborn, Dumanoski, and Myers 1997; Canadian Environmental Law Association and Lowell Center for Sustainable Production 2009). Further, there is increasing scientific evidence that a variety of chronic illnesses may have links to chemical exposures, ranging from cancers to learning and behavioral disabilities and reproductive problems.[2] In such cases, redesigning products to eliminate hazardous chemicals from the start may be the most effective way to address chemical risks.

Starting in the late 1990s, significant attention began to be paid to assessing and controlling chemicals of concern in products and, more importantly, to transitioning from these chemicals to safer alternatives, thereby optimizing health, environmental, and innovation goals. In addition to new scientific understandings about exposures to chemicals and their potential health effects, a number of drivers have stimulated this transition, including new regulations, consumer pressure and campaigns against products of concern, demands from market leaders, and new tools for alternatives assessment and green chemistry. All of the drivers together are shifting markets for safer products.

Regulation and Compliance as Drivers of Safer Chemistry

Participating in a global economy requires compliance with countless chemicals regulations, many with evolving requirements and demands on companies and their supply chains. For example, companies have had to comply for more than 20 years with California's Safe Drinking Water and Toxics Enforcement Act of 1986. Known informally as Prop 65, the law requires the state to annually publish a list of chemicals known by the state to cause cancer or birth defects, or to pose reproductive hazards. Under the law, products sold in California containing chemicals on this list must be labeled as such.[3]

Increasingly, however, chemical policies from outside the United States are driving firms to revisit the types and amounts of chemicals used in their products. One example is the European Union's chemical policy overhaul known as Registration, Evaluation, and Authorization of Chemicals, or REACH. When REACH came into force in 2007, it significantly shifted the regulatory climate of chemicals used all over the world toward producer liability. REACH has required chemical manufacturers based in the EU member states and those importing into the EU to understand the toxicity of their chemicals and uses, exposures, and risks through the supply chain, and it has forced chemical-using companies to understand what chemicals are in their products and in what amounts. Further, given that REACH prioritizes chemicals of high concern for substitution (those that are carcinogens, reproductive toxicants, or persist in the environment or build up in our bodies), firms are being forced to examine what chemicals may be unavailable within their supply chains due to the costs of testing or restrictions. REACH challenges firms to understand their supply chains and prepare necessary information on chemical risks; yet it has sparked important cultural changes within supply chains, including (1) shifting the responsibilities to understand chemical toxicity, exposures, and uses, and to communicate that information onto the manufacturer of the chemical; (2) forcing collaboration within supply chains to share information and learn about chemical uses and alternatives; and (3) requiring that firms seek permission before their continued use of chemicals of concern (Fasey 2008). The first chemical registrations were submitted under REACH in the fall of 2010. The quality and thoroughness of the information received and its impacts in increasing chemical information and safer chemistry across supply chains has yet to be seen.

REACH arrived on the coattails of another European regulation that caused major changes in the electronics sector: the European Directive on Restriction of Hazardous Substances (RoHS), which prohibits the sale in the EU of electronic products containing specific heavy metals and flame retardant chemicals (European Parliament and the Council 2003). Like

REACH, RoHS requires that companies work with their supply chains to understand what hazardous substances are present in a final product as well as at what point in the supply chain the hazardous substances are introduced. RoHS has had significant impacts in states where electronics manufacturers produce significant exports to Europe. In these states, failure to comply with RoHS could have major impacts beyond the individual firms, and could affect the larger state economy (Lowell Center 2010).

Underscoring the importance of regulation in driving safer chemistry, one expert in the electronics field noted the implications of RoHS for innovation:

> Many of us practicing in the Cleaner Technology field have been working to develop lead-free soldering for electronics since the early 1990s. After more than a decade, we seemed little closer than when we started. Then the European Union RoHS Directive was passed and in less than three years, we have lead-free electronics. While our preceding efforts allowed us to meet the RoHS Directive's deadlines successfully, it's hard to discount the role that the regulatory requirement played in finally bringing lead-free products to market. (Lowell Center 2007)

While European and increasingly Asian regulatory requirements have played a large role in shifting markets toward safer chemicals, there has been only a slow shift at the federal level in the United States.[4] Almost a decade after the debates and final regulations on REACH and RoHS in Europe, the U.S. Congress and federal government have recognized the limits of the nation's toxic chemicals law, the Toxic Substances Control Act (TSCA). For a variety of reasons, TSCA has been a limited vehicle to advance application of safer chemicals and products (Lowell Center 2008). While revisions to TSCA have been introduced in Congress, they will likely not be instituted for several years.

In the absence of federal leadership, a range of states have introduced new safer products laws. U.S. states have traditionally been the innovators in environmental policies, and chemicals are no exception. Some U.S. state chemical policy directions include

- Single chemical restrictions: mercury, lead, phthalates, BPA;

- Chemical prioritization;

- Ingredient disclosure and labeling;

- Preferable purchasing requirements;

- Green chemistry, technical support, and clean technology economic development programs; and

- Alternatives assessment requirements.

While several states have introduced laws to restrict single chemicals of concern in products, such as mercury, lead, phthalates, polybrominated diphenyl ethers, and BPA, others have introduced broader comprehensive chemicals policies designed to address multiple chemicals and product types. States such as Washington and Maine have instituted laws that require prioritization of chemicals of concern, establishment of databases of chemicals of concern in children's products, and, when necessary, labeling requirements or restrictions. Many of the state policies have focused on advancing safer alternatives to problem chemicals through assessments of alternatives, mandatory substitution requirements, or technical assistance programs. Still other states are using the market forces of procurement to advance safer chemistry, particularly in the area of institutional cleaning chemicals used in public buildings and by regulating large governmental markets. Finally, California is using its global market strength (as evidenced by its Prop 65 requirements) through its Green Chemistry Program. Legislation introduced in 2009 requires the establishment of rules that would force product manufacturers to disclose product ingredients and undertake assessments of alternatives for substances prioritized as ones of concern. Companies could be required to substitute such substances if feasible safer alternatives exist.

Individually and collectively, these state regulations have played an important role in shifting markets for certain products, such as cleaning chemicals, flame retardants in electronics, mercury- and lead-containing products, and drinking bottles containing BPA. They have provided signals to manufacturers of high concern chemicals and products. Finally, the proposed California safer products regulations are likely to globally shift the way retailers and distributors of products assess chemical information and alternatives materials.

Consumers as Drivers of Safer Chemicals and Products

A large factor influencing corporate interest in the development of safer products through safer chemistry is consumer demand for those products. As concerns regarding chemicals have shifted from factories to products, so too have the affected constituencies—from workers and local community advocates to concerned parents and survivors of diseases with suspected environmental links. Consumer demand for greener products is most often the result of advocacy campaigns and pressure, which can lead to media attention and increased public awareness about the health impacts of specific chemicals or products. Advocacy groups, such as the Breast Cancer Fund, Greenpeace, and Moms Rising, have shown the potential to mobilize new constituencies to affect the marketplace. Such advocacy pressure occurs often as the result of highly publicized company mishaps and problems, new science indicating concerns regarding a particular chemical, regulations in another part of the world on the chemical, or evidence of a market leader instituting alternatives. For example, widespread publicity regarding lead in toys in 2007 lead to a re-evaluation on the part of many children's products companies to gain stronger control over their supply chains. Data indicating a buildup of polybrominated diphenyl ether flame retardants in people led many firms in the furniture and electronics industries to reevaluate their uses of such chemicals. While chemical concerns may or may not be scientifically valid, the "social risk" associated with public concern is just as important a factor in the sustainability decision making of many firms as the real or perceived health or ecosystem risks.

In many cases, consumer pressure has pushed markets to leapfrog regulation in advancing implementation of safer alternatives. One such example is the recent trend in plastic water bottles made with plastics not containing the controversial chemical BPA. A building block of polycarbonate plastic, BPA has been the center of debate in recent years over evidence that it may disrupt the body's hormone systems, potentially affecting pregnant women and children (Vanderberg et al. 2007).[5] While experts in the scientific community have continued to discuss the particular concerns posed by exposure to BPA, and regulatory agencies have varied in their assessments of how much risk this chemical poses, consumers have largely decided that BPA is enough of a concern that they have begun to purchase products without it. Within a matter of three years, advocates were able to bring so much media and public attention to concerns regarding BPA that the reusable bottle business, despite initial reluctance to change, rapidly shifted materials. For example, responding to customer demand, outdoor equipment company REI opted to voluntarily remove BPA from any of its products intended to come into contact with food or beverages.

REI did so despite publicly stating that based on the evidence it had reviewed at the time, the company remained unconvinced that BPA was a problem (Torrie 2009, 24). Whether the scientific community was in agreement about BPA's toxicity or not, market forces effectively surpassed this debate and provided consumers with options for water bottles made without BPA. In fact, concerns about BPA provided an opportunity for manufacturers of alternative materials, such as Eastman Chemical, which captured the market with its Tritan copolyester.[6]

While the BPA experience shows the power of market forces to bring about rapid changes in commerce, significant impact can also be seen through long-term engagement with industry. A coalition of health care workers, hospitals, environmental advocates, and other organizations interested in greening the health care sector known as Health Care without Harm (HCWH) has worked with group purchasers for health care supplies for more than a decade. When the U.S. Environmental Protection Agency found that hospital waste incinerators were the leading source of dioxin, a highly toxic byproduct of chlorine combustion, advocates saw an opportunity to transition an entire industry through market pressure. Believing that health care facilities had an ethical duty not to create health hazards in the service of treating disease, HCWH sought a phase-out of medical devices made with PVC and diethylhexyl phthalate (DEHP) because these substances pose serious threats to human health during their manufacture, use, and disposal (Tickner et al. 2001).[7] By partnering with the small number of group purchasing organizations that supply most of the nation's hospitals, HCWH has been able to successfully shift portions of the medical device market to ensure that life-saving equipment not containing PVC and DEHP is available to hospitals.[8] The organization has had similar successes with mercury-containing medical devices, latex, and, more recently, flame retardants. To stimulate the market for innovation in safer materials, HCWH organized CleanMed, an annual trade show for less toxic medical products.[9]

Kaiser Permanente, the largest managed health care organization in the United States and long-time HCWH partner, has gone beyond participating in these efforts and become a leader in the sector in its own right. In 2008, Kaiser Permanente announced its creation of a global health and safety initiative aimed at "[driving] markets for cleaner energy, safer products, and innovative green technologies" in the health care sector (Sissell 2008). In this way, market-based initiatives can have far-reaching impacts that build and grow along supply chains until significant and long-lasting changes are seen.

Similarly, the advocacy coalition behind the Campaign for Safe Cosmetics has successfully begun to shift markets toward safer cosmetics in the absence of federal regulation. Begun in 2004, the Campaign for Safe Cosmetics now includes more than 100 organizations concerned about the use of often untested and potentially toxic chemical ingredients in many cosmetics and personal care products used by the public every day. With the support of these organizations, the campaign has effectively used stricter regulation in Europe to leverage consumer demand for less-toxic cosmetics, resulting in some 1,300 cosmetics companies that have publicly pledged to remove from their products within three years ingredients known to cause cancer, reproductive toxicity, mutations, or birth defects, and to publicly report their progress toward this goal.[10] Greater consumer awareness of the potential dangers of many cosmetic ingredients has had a tremendous impact on the beauty industry, including product reformulations to decrease or eliminate the amount of high-profile ingredients, participation by more mainstream cosmetics companies, and an increase in sales for environmentally friendly, less-toxic products in the United States, making it the fastest growing sector of the market for personal care products.[11]

The growing availability of information about chemical ingredients in products is educating consumers and thereby pushing chemical substitution in the consumer product and retail sectors. Many manufacturers are beginning to place product ingredient information on their websites for consumers in response to consumer demand. Several searchable databases exist to allow consumers to know more about the products they purchase every day. For example, the Environmental Working Group maintains a database for safer cosmetics known as Skin Deep.[12] Such resources are valuable to consumers who wish to make informed product choices before shopping. Recently, this database concept has advanced to a new level of convenience in the era of smartphones. Good Guide, an organization established to provide consumers with the information they need to make informed purchases, features some 70,000 products used every day, each given a sustainability score to allow easy decision making. With the release of the Good Guide application for the iPhone, customers are now given the opportunity to make real-time assessments of products they purchase: while at a store, consumers can pick up an item they would like to know more about, scan the barcode, and Good Guide will return the product's score on the spot.[13]

Products themselves are often a source of valuable information. To date, more than 300 different labels exist for use in an array of different kinds of products. Some of these labels are verified by an independent third party, some are self-declared statements by the maker of the product, and other labels go beyond a logo to communicate more detailed information to consumers who can then decide which attribute of the product is more important to them and choose accordingly (Torrie 2009, 9).

Increasing Influence of Leading-edge Firms and Retailers in Moving Markets to Safer Chemicals and Products

Consumers are not alone in their power to affect markets. Increasingly, large consumer product manufacturers and retailers are also pulling their suppliers directly into the search for safer chemistry. Consumer product companies rise and fall on the value of their brand name and understand that when concerns about particular chemicals in a product are raised, it is the brand name held accountable by consumers, not the often-unknown chemical manufacturer. Additionally, many manufacturers have noted that with increasing consumer pressure there is growth in the "green products" market. There is a profit motive for makers of green products. A recent survey found that consumers are willing to pay as much as 8 percent more for a product if it is made in an environmentally sustainable way (Sissell 2008, 31). For companies that proactively seek improved formulations and manufacturing practices involving chemicals to create their products, a very real payoff exists with loyal consumers willing to pay a price premium for products they can feel confident are safer for themselves and their families. The growth of organic foods as the fastest-growing segment of the food industry demonstrates the potential opportunities for profit with greener products. Similar shifts are occurring in area of household cleaners and health and beauty aids.

Product manufacturers are being driven toward safer chemicals by a number of factors that vary by sector and firm. As a result of concerns about particular chemicals, treatment of workers overseas, and regulatory requirements, many companies in the footwear and apparel sector have moved rapidly in the past several years to undertake programs to shift toward safer chemicals and products through the establishment of lists of chemicals of concern and programs that reduce the overall impact of products. For example, Nike established its Considered

Chemistry program to develop safer materials that reduce toxicity, water use, and generation of greenhouse gasses. SC Johnson, a family-owned company with a long history of environmental consciousness, developed its Green List process to screen chemicals in its products and shift toward increasingly safer chemicals. The company has also committed to public disclosure of product ingredients. Hewlett Packard and Apple, in response to growing regulatory pressures on the electronics industry, have instituted programs to substitute chemicals of concern. Apple has established broad design principles that prohibit broad classes of chemicals in their products. Some firms, such as Dell, have published broad chemical policies that indicate the goals and directions the firms are taking in advancing safer products.

However, the retail sector has become a critical market force in the past five years in advancing safer chemicals through supply chains (Sissel 2008). Retail giant Walmart awakened much of the business community in 2006 with an announcement that it would ban three chemicals from products sold in its stores as a first step in a larger chemical restriction program, the goal of which was to "identify and replace potentially hazardous substances" from the products on its shelves (ibid., 26–27). Similarly, Target has announced its own initiative to strengthen the standards by which products manufactured for the company are measured. Additionally, Toys R Us has initiatives to restrict the presence of lead, a family of plastic softeners known as phthalates, and other priority substances. The company has gone so far as to mandate that suppliers of products made only for Toys R Us should immediately eliminate nickel-cadmium batteries (ibid., 27). Boots, a corner pharmacy in the United Kingdom, has found sustainable chemistry to be a key differentiator for them in the marketplace. Boots not only retails but also manufactures its own products, giving the company significant control over its supply chain. In this way, companies manufacturing products to be sold at these and other retailers, as well as their suppliers, are suddenly forced to better understand the chemicals and materials used to make those products, and to find alternatives to substances targeted by retailers quickly and completely or risk those products being rejected for sale. If these firms were not already working to better understand their supply chains in an attempt to make safer products, these and other similar initiatives by retailers ensure that they will in the future.

New Opportunities for Safer Materials through Green Chemistry and Design for Environment

While there has been increasing attention toward understanding product chemical contents and toxicity and eliminating materials of concern, the 1990s brought in new thinking in science and engineering to eliminate hazards at the design stage of chemicals and products. Despite quiet beginnings, the new attention to chemicals of concern combined with new demand for consumer products safe from chemical hazards has resulted in the blossoming of this thinking in designing new, safer alternatives. In 1998, chemists Paul Anastas and John Warner published *Green Chemistry*, a book documenting an emerging philosophy of chemistry dedicated to the creation of substances that are environmentally benign from production to use and disposal through the use of twelve principles of design. Green chemistry is an approach to chemistry that ensures that chemical feedstocks, reactions, byproducts, waste products, and the final desired product are as benign to human health and the environment as possible. Green chemistry encompasses the toxicity, waste, energy, and physical hazards of chemicals through their life cycles (Anastas and Warner 1998). If one thinks about the build-up of chemicals in the environment and their potential impacts as failures in design, then green chemistry can be viewed as a solution to chemical hazards where life-cycle toxicity becomes a design factor equal in importance to cost and performance.

Since the publication of Anastas and Warner's book, there has been a flurry of academic, government, and industrial activity around education, research and developmental, and application of green chemistry. The U.S. Environmental Protection Agency and the American Chemical Society host an annual Presidential Award in Green Chemistry, which rewards academic research and industrial innovation in advancing safer chemistry. The award applications demonstrate the economic value to firms in reducing waste, regulatory compliance costs, and liabilities. The annual international symposium on green chemistry brings together hundreds of experts from academia, government, and industry to explore research and application innovations.[14] The pharmaceutical sector has established the Pharmaceutical Green Chemistry Roundtable to support precompetitive research to develop innovations that overcome cross-sectoral challenges.[15] Several organizations, such as Beyond Benign, a nonprofit green chemistry education institute, are developing K–12 and university green chemistry curricula to train a new generation of chemists who will understand the implications of the materials they produce as well as how to make them safer.[16] Finally, the state of Michigan has linked green chemistry to economic development through its Green Chemistry Executive Directive, which established a state green chemistry program that combines sectoral collaboration with education and economic incentives to promote green chemistry.[17]

Whereas green chemistry focuses on the development of new molecules that are inherently benign, design for environment (DfE) is another approach gaining momentum to stimulate the application of existing or on-the-horizon chemicals that are safer. The DfE approach ensures that chemical selections are made with the intent of continually improving products. While the number of green chemical choices may be limited, DfE instructs companies to choose the best available alternative today and prepare for a better alternative tomorrow. Like green chemistry, DfE is not a fixed target but a tool to develop increasingly sustainable products. At the U.S. Environmental Protection Agency (EPA), a DfE program has been established to focus on screening alternatives to chemicals of concern to ensure they are the safest available option in their class—what might also be termed the functional use or service the chemical provides. Over the years, the DfE program has developed several well-respected voluntary partnerships with industry and other stakeholders in an effort to provide scientifically rigorous resources to industry seeking to voluntarily improve the health and safety profile of their products.[18]

A key component of DfE is alternatives assessment, a framework by which companies can evaluate chemicals or materials against common criteria and against each other. These criteria (e.g., explosivity, carcinogenicity) are chosen for each assessment and can be customized to the individual needs of the process, product, or company involved. In this way, alternatives assessment provides insight into the best alternative chemical or material for a specific substitution opportunity. Companies can make informed choices and be aware of any trade-offs that might be involved with choosing one option over another (Rossi, Tickner, and Geiser 2006). The EPA Formulator's Initiative shows how the DfE model can help stimulate the marketplace for safer alternatives. The initiative brings together cleaning product formulators to explore alternatives to chemicals of concern in such products as surfactants, solvents, and fragrances.[19] A partnership with the nonprofit Green Blue led to the development of a database called Clean Gredients, which provides a listing of alternative chemicals for specific functional uses. The EPA DfE program established the minimum toxicity criteria for calling a chemical a safer alternative, and manufacturers must obtain third-party certification that their products meet these criteria before the alternative can be listed as safer. Cleaning product formulators then can choose ingredients that represent the safest alternatives in a particular class. This model could easily be extended to other product types and functional uses of chemicals.

Barriers to Safer Chemistry

While there are significant drivers for safer chemistry throughout supply chains, there are also significant barriers faced by firms in moving their product lines toward safer chemicals and materials. Such barriers range from getting information on chemical formulations and toxicity through supply chains to lack of incentives for safer products. While the challenges vary by firm, they are similar across sectors. These can be divided into three types of barriers: technical, policy, and cultural.

Technical barriers to safer chemicals and products include

- Technical barriers that can compromise product performance;

- Alternatives that lack data, are difficult to implement, are too costly, or just do not exist;

- Lack of tools, data, and support to move toward safer materials (toxicity, use, materials tracking, design, etc.); and

- Lack of centralized data systems within firms to track chemical supply chain information and toxicity.

Policy barriers to safer chemicals and products include

- Limited programs to distinguish preferable materials;

- Lack of standards for "green";

- Disjointed regulatory authorities and requirements; and

- Lack of incentives for green chemistry.

Cultural or educational barriers to safer chemicals and products include

- Lack of communication up and down supply chains;

- Lack of leadership commitment and integration of environment, health, and safety into design (lack of a strong business case);

- Lack of education in greener synthesis/toxicology among chemists; and

- Consumers, purchasers, and manufacturers who are often not informed about safer options.

Technical and Policy Barriers

Understanding what problematic chemicals are present in a product, how they got there, their function in a product, and their toxicity is the first step in finding safer alternatives. Obtaining this chemical information is a primary barrier to safer chemistry among many firms in the United States, particularly smaller firms without large purchasing power. This requires an ability to map and communicate effectively along supply chains. Yet supply chains leading to finished products are often extremely complex with multiple, unconnected suppliers located across the globe. The supply chain picture becomes even more complex when talking about complex products, such as a jet engine that may have hundreds of parts from multiple suppliers. However, even a single raw chemical used in a product may have multiple suppliers depending on prices and supply at a specific point in time. While most product manufacturers can identify and obtain some information from tier 1 suppliers (direct suppliers), it becomes increasingly difficult to obtain good information from tier 2 suppliers and beyond. Even chemical manufacturers face a significant problem in understanding how their chemicals are used by downstream purchasers. Despite these limits, firms responsible for brand-name products have an incentive—due to legal obligations or brand image—to discover and understand when, in what quantity, and for what purpose chemicals, particularly those of concern, are being introduced into any material that will appear in a finished product. Without tracing a supply chain back to its origin, a company cannot say with any confidence that its products are really "nontoxic," "safe," or otherwise labeled as free of a specific substance of concern.

Even when companies can get information on product formulation, basic information on chemical hazards to the environment and to human health is largely unavailable. The most information on toxicity that a firm might obtain is a Material Safety Data Sheet, which provides only very limited toxicity information, inadequate to make informed decisions about materials. This makes it difficult for firms to identify chemicals of concern, prioritize substances for action, or identify safer alternatives.

These gaps in information can be traced to several factors, including lack of testing requirements for most existing chemicals in commerce, the ability of firms to claim significant amounts of data as confidential business information to protect market share, and the possibility that disclosing such information could lead to future liability (Lowell Center for Sustainable Production 2008, 72). Whatever the factors responsible for making this data unavailable, without it companies are unable to fully understand the extent to which problematic chemicals are used in their products, and neither are they able to assess what alternatives might offer similar performance with an improved health and safety profile.

Through the use of nondisclosure agreements, third parties, and other data-sharing initiatives, companies can begin to fill in chemical data gaps over time. Once armed with this information, however, some companies may find they lack the technical capacity to implement a chemical management system sophisticated enough to go beyond focusing on single "bad" chemicals to begin gathering information on "good" chemicals (Tickner and Geiser 2004). If technical capacity is removed as a barrier, companies may also find that the menu of suitable chemical alternatives is limited. In some instances, these alternatives do not yet exist, and in other cases, the use of the alternative might require capital investments in new equipment. Small and medium-sized firms especially may lack the resources for such an investment (Coffin 2009). A final barrier to removing problematic chemicals in favor of safer substitutes is uncertainty of future regulation. Once substantial time and resources have been invested in addressing a hazardous chemical, finding an alternative, and investing in any new equipment necessary to process the alternative, companies want some assurance that the chemical or material at the center of these investments will not be the subject of future regulation. Without confidence that this is the case, a company may choose to stay with "the devil they know" rather than make changes to their product or processes and risk future toxicity or regulatory surprises (ibid.). One of the challenges in this regard is that toxic chemicals are regulated in different ways by myriad federal and state agencies with often conflicting requirements. No single agency focuses on safer chemistries and products. In the case of BPA, for example, while the U.S. EPA has developed an action plan for finding alternatives to high concern uses of the chemical, the agency cannot look at alternatives in food contact materials because these are under the Food and Drug Administration's jurisdiction. Chemicals and materials tend to be treated as legal and jurisdictional entities, not as design problems.

Once safer alternatives are in use resulting in a safer product, firms may then be faced with a reduced return on their investment when competing with other "nongreen" products. While most companies want to ensure that their products are known first as "high performing, cost-effective" products and not "green" products (which can often bring the connotation of lower performing), they do want to be distinguished in the marketplace and ensure that competitors cannot make unsubstantiated green claims. In response to growing customer demand, many products sold today are marketed with any number of claims of positive environmental traits, few of which have been validated (Torrie 2009). Terms such as "all natural" or "biodegradable" can have more than one definition frequently used in marketing, and, as is the case with some product labels, these terms often lack the verification of any third-party oversight and are simply proclaimed by the maker of the product.[20] Unlike organic foods, which must be grown in accordance with a standard enforced by the U.S. Department of Agriculture, many of the terms on product packaging today are simply advertising gimmicks used to sell conventional products.[21] While the Federal Trade Commission is authorized to prosecute misleading marketing, this rarely happens (ibid., 29–30). Such marketing practices are known as "greenwashing," and while a testament to the power of the market for green products, companies that are truly making environmentally superior products have difficulty differentiating these products in the marketplace from their greenwashed competition.

Despite its potential benefits, there are few incentives for green chemistry research, development, and application. Incentives such as research credits, tax breaks, low-income loans, and venture capital support do not exist for green chemistry. A federal Green Chemistry Research and Development Act was introduced in Congress in 2004; despite its passage in the House of Representatives, the bill has never passed the Senate. The bill would provide for a small amount ($35 million) of research and development funds through the National Science Foundation and establish an interagency committee on green chemistry. Few states have instituted green chemistry research and development programs. And the federal government financial commitment to green chemistry and design for environment research, support, and networking is currently less than what a single chemical cancer study in animals might cost. While a significant call to action and financial backing for clean energy has occurred at the federal and state levels, such a call has not occurred for chemicals. Only a fraction of funding for chemical safety is dedicated to designing safer, more sustainable chemicals and processes. The vast majority is dedicated to in-depth scientific assessments of risks. For example, despite evidence indicating that BPA use in food can linings can present an exposure and health risk, the U.S. National Institute of Environmental Health Science dedicated $30 million in research funding to explore how the chemical might disrupt hormonal systems. Not a single dollar was dedicated to research on alternatives to the chemical that would lead to innovation and potential health benefits (Spivey 2009).

Cultural and Educational Barriers

Newer, greener products can become a secondary consideration, particularly during difficult economic times, when profit margins are low. Green chemistry and sustainability considerations are particularly challenging when dealing with low-profit-margin products. Within many firms, environment and health and safety departments are viewed as "enforcers" whose job it is to put barriers to production. In essence, environment and health and safety have been separated from design. Design has focused on two main factors—cost and performance—while environmental and health considerations have been considered an additional cost, not a criteria for design. While some firms have overcome this division through leadership commitment to sustainability, in other firms where government or customer specifications are strong, product lines change rapidly, or are heavily dependent on consumer confidence, it may be difficult for the environment to be considered on par with other factors in design choices.

Furthermore, chemists and designers have lacked education on toxicity, health and safety, and life-cycle risks. Most chemists are trained to design molecules without consideration of their impacts on society. Only a handful of green chemistry courses exist in U.S. academic institutions, and only one doctorate program currently exists in the field. While design schools are increasingly focusing on energy and material use, material toxicity has generally been neglected. Finally, business schools do not generally train the next generation of business leaders in the value of health and environment for the bottom line.

Summary and Conclusions

There are an increasing number of drivers that are motivating supply chains to move toward safer chemicals and products. While much of the discussion about supply chain sustainability to date has focused on issues of climate, resources, and human rights, chemical safety is becoming an importantly greater aspect of sustainability efforts in firms. Drivers such as new regulations in Europe and the states, market pressures from large retailers and product manufacturers, and consumer demand are creating greater willingness among firms to undertake efforts to understand product chemistry and find safer alternatives to ingredients of concern. These drivers are likely to increase in the coming years. New scientific tools, such as green chemistry and design for environment, are creating new opportunities for firms to innovate in safer products. While there are significant challenges to the design and application of safer products, forward-looking firms that respond to the drivers toward safer products and identify ways to overcome challenges will be at a competitive and market advantage in the future.

Websites

Beyond Benign: www.beyondbenign.org
Environmental Working Group: www.ewg.org
EPA Design for Environment Program: www.epa.gov/dfe
European Chemicals Agency: www.echa.europa.eu
Health Care without Harm: www.noharm.org
Investor Environmental Health Network: www.iehn.org
Lowell Center for Sustainable Production, Chemicals Policy and Science
   Initiative: www.chemicalspolocy.org

References

Anastas, P., and J. Warner. 1998. *Green Chemistry: Theory and Practice.* Oxford: Oxford University Press.

Canadian Environmental Law Association and Lowell Center for Sustainable Production. 2009. "The Challenge of Substances of Emerging Concern in the Great Lakes Basin: A Review of Chemicals Policies and Programs in Canada and the United States." Report prepared for the International Joint Commission Multi-Board Work Group on Chemicals of Emerging Concern in the Great Lakes Basin, Lowell, Mass., and Toronto, Ontario.

Coffin, Melissa. 2009. "The Impact of Trichloroethylene Alternatives in Metal Cleaning Applications on the Worker Experience." MA thesis. Lowell: University of Massachusetts.

Colborn, T., D. Dumanoski, and J. Petersen Myers. 1997. *Our Stolen Future*. New York: Plume.

European Parliament and the Council. 2003. Directive 2002/95/EC, "Restriction on Hazardous Substances." *Official Journal of the European Union*, January 27. http://eur-lex.europa.eu/LexUriServ/LexUriServ.do?uri=OJ:L:2003:037:0019:0023:en:PDF.

Fasey, Andrew. 2008. "REACH Is Here, the Politics Are over, Now the Hard Work Starts." *Chemicals Policy and Science Initiative*, April. http://www.chemicalspolicy.org/downloads/REACHisHere4-2008.pdf.

Lowell Center for Sustainable Production. 2007. "Clean Tech: An Agenda for a Healthy Economy." *Lowell Center for Sustainable Production*, December. http://www.sustainableproduction.org/downloads/UMLCleanTechDec2007.pdf.

Lowell Center for Sustainable Production. 2008. "Options for State Chemicals Policy Reform." *Lowell Center for Sustainable Production*, February. http://www.chemicalspolicy.org/downloads/OptionsforState ChemicalsPolicyReform.pdf.

Lowell Center for Sustainable Production. 2010. "Clean Tech: An Agenda for a Healthy Economy." *Lowell Center for Sustainable Production*, January. http://sustainableproduction.org/downloads/CleanTechLong-Final2-10_001.pdf.

Rossi, Mark, Joel Tickner, and Ken Geiser. 2006. *Alternatives Assessment Framework*. Lowell, Mass.: Lowell Center for Sustainable Production.

Sissell, Kara. 2008. "The New Regulators." *Chemical Week*, April 14–21, 26–31.

Spivey, A. 2009. "NIEHS Funds Human BPA Research." *Environmental Health Perspectives* 117 (December 1): A541. doi: 10.1289/ehp.117-a541.

Tickner, Joel, and Ken Geiser. 2004. "The Precautionary Principle: Stimulus for Solutions and Alternatives-Based Environmental Policy." *Environmental Impact Assessment Reviews* 24:801–24.

Tickner, Joel, T. Schettler, M. McCally, T. Guidotti, and M. Rossi. 2001. "Patient Health Risks Posed by the Use of Di-2-Ethylhexyl Phthalate (DEHP) in PVC Medical Devices: A Review of the Literature." *American Journal of Industrial Medicine* 39:100–11.

Torrie, Yve. 2009. *Best Practices in Product Chemicals Management in the Retail Industry*. Lowell, Mass.: Lowell Center for Sustainable Production.

Vanderberg, Laura, Russ Hauser, Michele Marcus, Nicolas Olea, and Wade V. Welshons. 2007. "Human Exposure to Bisphenol A." *Reproductive Toxicology* 24:139–77.

Notes

1 U.S. Centers for Disease Control, National Center for Environmental Health, "Fourth National Report on Human Exposure to Environmental Chemicals," Atlanta, Ga., 2009. http://www.cdc.gov/exposurereport/; and Environmental Working Goup, "Body Burden—The Pollution in Newborns," July 14, 2005, http://www.ewg .org/reports/bodyburden2/execsumm.php

2 CHE Toxicant and Disease Database, http://www.healthandenvironment .org/tddb

3 "Proposition 65," *California Office of Health Hazard Assessment*, http:// oehha.ca.gov/prop65.html

4 China and South Korea have instituted requirements similar to those in Europe.

5 See also "Bisphenol-A," *Environmental Working Group*. http://www.ewg .org/chemindex/chemicals/bisphenolA

6 "Eastman Tritan," Eastman Chemical, Innovation Lab, http://www .innovationlab.eastman.com/InnovationLab/Tritan/index.html

7 See also "The Issue," *Health Care without Harm*, http://www.hcwh.org/ us_canada/issues/toxins/pvc_phthalates

8 "Alternatives to PVC and DEHP," *Health Care without Harm*, http://www .hcwh.org/us_canada/issues/toxins/pvc_phthalates/alternatives.php

9 http://www.cleanmed.org/

10 "About Us," *Campaign for Safe Cosmetics*, http://www.safecosmetics .org/article.php?list=type&type=34; and "The Compact for Safe Cosmetics," *Campaign for Safe Cosmetics*, http://www.safecosmetics.org/section.php?id=51

11 "About Us."

12 Skin Deep Cosmetic Safety Database, *Environmental Working Group*, http://www.cosmeticsdatabase.com

13 "Good Guide Delivered to Your Phone," *Good Guide,* http://www .goodguide.com/about/mobile

14 "Green Chemistry." *U.S. Environmental Protection Agency*, http://www .epa.gov/gcc/

15 "ACI/GCI Pharmaceutical Green Chemistry Roundtable," *American Chemical Society*, http://portal.acs.org/portal/acs/corg/content?_nfpb=true&_ pageLabel=PP_TRANSITIONMAIN&node_id=1422&use_sec=false&sec_url_ var=region1&__uuid=6e43e562-2fce-4389-ae3e-0f7c03d629b9

16 "Our Mission," *Beyond Benign*, http://www.beyondbenign.org/about/ about.html

17 "Green Chemistry," *Michigan Department of Natural Resources and Environment.* http://www.michigan.gov/deq/0,1607,7-135-3585_49005---,00.html

18 "Green Chemistry & DfE," *Green Chemistry and Commerce Council,* http://www.greenchemistryandcommerce.org/greenchemistry.php

19 "Design for Environment," *U.S. Environmental Protection Agency*, http:// www.epa.gov/dfe/

20 "Compilation of Terms Marketing Green Products: A 'Green'Glossary," *Green Chemistry and Commerce Council*, http://www.greenchemistryandcom merce.org/downloads/MarketingTerms110110.pdf

21 "The Sins of Greenwashing Home and Family Edition," *TerraChoice*, http://sinsofgreenwashing.org

PART II

Managing Responsible
Global Supply Networks

CHAPTER 8

Designing Socially Responsible Supply Networks

Creating an Environmental Management System Design

Dan L. Shunk

Companies do not compete with companies any more—supply networks compete with supply networks. This recognition has led us to begin to conceive the design of a global environmental management system (EMS) that meets the needs and requirements for global supply network transparency as well as certification through the International Standards Organization's ISO 14000 series. This chapter covers a number of key issues surrounding the design of socially responsible supply networks, including competition among supply networks; the global business implications of ISO 14000; the requirements for socially responsible supply networks, for an Environmental Self-Assessment Tool (ESAT), and for an EMS; and a conceptual design for an EMS.

Introduction and Context

As we evolve to a much more sustainable business environment, we are finding that sustainability is really in the eye of the beholder. In this chapter, I define sustainability as the point at which we can claim to be living within our biophysical parameters. But I will emphasize in this chapter the notion of how we get to sustainable development in the complete life cycle of a product. To that end, sustainable development in this chapter will be the process or journey to get to sustainability. The third generation of most of our manufacturing enterprises is evolving. In generation one, we really focused on the internal operations of the industry. And we concentrated on simple, basic concepts such as design and manufacturing, and on how to get a product or service into production. The second generation began to look at how to streamline that activity within the four walls of a single enterprise. During this generation, the extension to the internal enterprise functions was achieved. Concepts such as "lean" and "six sigma" have become predominant in the thinking of manufacturing strategy around the world. But now we enter a new era, and the new era is the extension of the extended enterprise. This means really focusing on what Porter (1990) calls the competitive differentiation that can be achieved through sustainability, but we must also recognize that it is not simply the four-walls factory or four-walls business development organization that will participate in this. The paradigm is shifting from companies competing with companies to supply networks competing with supply networks. This paradigm of competing supply networks is supported by research done by Rice and Hoppe (2001) and others at MIT.

Rice and Hoppe (2001) propose that the fundamental building block for competition tomorrow is going to be supply networks competing with supply networks. In this chapter, I will call that distributive collaborative sustainable commerce. It is "distributed" in that I must understand how all the elements within my supply network participate in the ultimate creation and delivery of a product or service. It is "collaborative" in that stand-alone organizations cannot simply build walls around their activities. They must integrate and ultimately synchronize what they are doing with their compatriots upstream and downstream. Finally, we have the concept of "sustainable." We have learned that a second- or third-tier supplier using lead-based paint can truly detract from the aura of a toy manufacturer halfway around the world. This horror story was played out a few years ago and evolved to an awareness that first-, second-, and third-tier suppliers have as much impact on the sustainability of the end product or service as the original equipment manufacturer (OEM). As we look at the world of sustainability, we must take this into consideration. We must understand how these organizations will compete. We are fundamentally changing the game to look at business from a distributive collaborative sustainable commerce viewpoint focusing on value chains that are global compared to point solutions that are local. The mantra of this is that we will build by making new investments that promise return, and we will operate more effectively to increase the cash earnings without increasing the capital employed. To do this, we must harvest the operations that are not earning their cost of capital and do not have a decent prospect of doing so. But the intriguing change has come from what the trends are as they relate to trends in supply networks. Supply networks today compete not on a narrow focus but on a much wider focus, as was highlighted in the lean aircraft initiative by MIT about a decade ago and as now embodied in the lean sustainment initiative.[1]

Today, companies are much more sensitive to their overall new product development concepts by bringing in supplier knowledge and bringing in their willingness to participate in the design process. Moreover, the concept of sustainability now ripples through the entire distributed and collaborative design network in an evolving way. But we face dilemmas. We face financial dilemmas based upon the triple bottom line, such as "why do I wish to collaborate with my supply base and share the profits with them and share the risks from a sustainability standpoint?" We face dilemmas from an environmental standpoint, such as "why do I need to share this risk when it is my supply networks' partners' responsibility to deliver something that is sustainable?" And finally we share the social risks, such as "why would I help my supply network partners improve their positions in their neighborhoods while simply supporting my neighborhood?" These concepts of financial, environmental, and social dilemmas are driving this sustainable triple bottom line extension into the world of supply networks.

ISO 14000 and the Business Implications

To build on the notion of distributed, collaborative, sustainable commerce as the foundation for sustainable supply networks, we have found that there are international standards evolving to support this concept. ISO 14000 is one that we will discuss in detail in this chapter.[2] ISO 14000 is a family of international standards created and maintained by the International Standards Organization (ISO). ISO 14001, dated 2004, is a standard for environmental management system requirements, which we will discuss in detail later in this chapter. ISO 14004, published in 2004, is a standard for environmental management system principles, systems, and support that are required. ISO 14000.42 is the standard that deals with environmental management. ISO 14047 demonstrates some examples of applications of these standards, and ISO 14000.40 begins to highlight some life-cycle views that we need to include in our systems thinking. These standards, along with ISO 15288, which deals with life-cycle management and other standards that are fostered at the international level, serve as the backdrop for distributed collaborative sustainable commerce.[3] The ISO 14001 compliance requirement is based upon their philosophy that this is an assistance standard. It tells audiences that have an interest in sustainable supply networks what needs to be addressed and it addresses directly some of the fundamental issues in implementing these. The following list highlights some of these issues.

- Top management must understand that sustainability at the supply network level is of critical importance.

- We must understand how these standards can support the creation of an environmental policy at local, national, and international levels.

- We must talk about the scope and scale of environmental management systems and how they will play out in the 21st century.

Key considerations must include the coordination of the standard with other policies, the requirements by interested parties, the guiding principles needed to make this happen, the specific local and regional conditions to which we must address specific applications of these standards, the commitment to achieve sustainability, and the commitment to comply with legal requirements.

In parallel with the ISO 14000 series has been the development of international standards such as RoHS/WEEE, where we begin to ask our complete supply network to validate the content of bad materials in our electronic products. RoHS stands for Restriction of Hazardous Substances. The Waste Electric and Electronic Equipment (WEEE) directive in essence says that we are delivering electronics, at least in Europe, with huge amounts of strategic materials that have negative environmental implications. The RoHS/WEEE directive of August 18, 2005, specifies that we must avoid the use of heavy metals if at all possible, and that the proposed maximum concentrations are 0.1 percent by weight for materials such as lead, mercury, hexivalent chromium, polybrominated biphenyls, and polybrominated diphenyl ethers (RoHS/WEEE 2005). It also limits cadmium to less than .01 percent by weight. The penalties for this include removal of the product from the delivery mechanism within the supply network and penalties for the individuals of up to six months in jail or a

$500,000 fine. But more importantly, this says that we are now beginning to quantify what the complete supply network can provide as it relates to sustainability and the direction that we wish to have for sustainable development. If a second- or third-tier supplier is using lead-based solder, for example, as they assemble the printed circuit board that goes into the motherboard, that goes into the electronics assembly, that goes into the final electronic product, I have got a second- or third-tier supplier that must document that lead content. By definition, that entire supply network is now responsible for the sustainable development of the end product as compared to the OEM, although the OEM still maintains the responsibility to document what this means.

Adding to the Intermediation–Disintermediation Criteria

In a paper written by the author a few years ago (Shunk et al. 2007), the concept of intermediation (I) and disintermediation (D) was highlighted. Intermediation arises when a supplier is accepted by the supply network and "interjects" its products or services into the network. Disintermediation is just the opposite. When a supplier is "disintermediated," they are removed from the supply network. From a supply network perspective, this view of I–D is very important—you, as a supplier, either have a role to play or you do not. Literature review and interviews with key supply network executives has found that several drivers already exist for the I–D decision making. We have determined that there are currently eight candidate drivers to the I–D cycle:

- Economic: Transaction costs must be less for intermediaries to continue to be desired.[4]

- Information/knowledge sharing: It is just not "provide me the parts" anymore. "What really matters is making the transaction seamless and making sure the customer has access to the product" (Pinto 2000).

- Core competencies: The notion of strategic make or buy comes to play in outsourcing the entire logistics, parts identification, parts acquisition, and parts delivery functions.

- Industry structure: New forms of "communities" are being formed to streamline operations, establish standards, and achieve leverage.

- Time or availability: Clearly, a major metric is order-to-order fulfillment time

- Technology: Is the Internet changing the global distribution game plan? Can de facto, national, or international standards be established that allow distribution functions to address their portion of intellectual property?

- Logistics: "Deliver" is still a major part of the supply network functions of "plan, source, make, and deliver."

- Culture: Collaboration requires sharing, and sharing requires a cultural migration to at least "coordinated control," and probably requires "centralized control" to truly succeed.

Industry is now telling us and ISO is now mandating that a ninth driver exists that will foster either an intermediated role for a supplier or a disintermediated role for a supplier. That new driver is

- Environmental: Can the supplier document what they are providing from an environmentally benign view? Can the supply network look into the operations of the supplier and verify that they are performing to global environmental standards?

This environmental transparency is driving the creation of socially responsible supply networks.

A survey conducted by Business for Social Responsibility found that "85% of participating companies believe that internal alignment and supplier ownership are the most important elements of creating sustainable supply chains" (BSR 2007). BSR's big push is to streamline the internal operations of the firm and to change the way supply chains are addressed—migrating from "policing supply chains to developing holistic solutions."

The business impact of this is summarized by Accenture in their white paper titled "The Sustainable Supply Chain."[5] Accenture found that "the best-performing organizations on cost and service are typically also ahead of the curve on implementing sustainability across all parts of their end-to-end supply chain."

To be a successful provider of products to the global market:

- Clearly, the internal processes of the firm must be flexible, efficient, and effective.

- But with intermediation rampant on a global scale, internal focus is not enough.

- The supply chain must be deemed "value producing," and one of the most recent additions to the criteria for this is the concept of "sustainable supply networks."

- Finally, there is a positive correlation between how a company performs and its commitment to sustainability. More studies addressing the business view are needed as we address the economic aspects of the triple bottom line. Here many documented case studies are required to reinforce the notion of the sustainable supply network.

Requirements for Designing Socially Responsible Supply Networks

Socially responsible supply networks cannot just be fixed, they must be designed. And the call for collaborative sustainable design was emphasized at the round table on science and technology for sustainability at the annual meeting held June 15, 2004 (National Academies 2004). This task force of learned individuals headed by William Clark, cochair of the Kennedy School of Government at Harvard, and James Mahoney, cochair from the National Oceanic and Atmospheric Administration, identified seven topical areas that needed to be addressed as we begin to think about the design for socially responsible supply networks:

- A gap exists between knowledge and action.

- There is a great but untapped potential for learning from experience. There is substantial world experience, but lessons learned are rarely developed as input into contemporary systems.

- There is a need to foster mandatory user–producer interactions with suppliers and customers in a collaborative sense, and the collaborative dialogue of knowledge coproduction must continue throughout the enterprise.

- End-to-end systems are an important link to knowledge. We must have, as they point out, visibility. Successful programs involve end-to-end integrated systems that connect basic scientific predictions or observations with several steps to outputs that are directly relevant to the decision making.

- The value and vulnerability of bridging these boundary-spanning organizations is difficult. User–producer dialogues can be strained along the supply network for a variety of reasons. Dialogues may fester because of pressures being placed upon suppliers by customers or on customers by stakeholders of the need for more and more sustainability designed into the product.

- Recognize that there must be innovative risk-taking involved, and there must be some safe spaces defined for contributors to test various ideas. Efforts to link knowledge to action in sustainable development often involve radical institutional innovations. To shoot the messenger would be an unwise thing to do. And safe spaces are required to allow aggressive innovation to take place.

- There is a need for appropriate targets and metrics. Successfully linking knowledge to actions for sustainability generally requires a clear and readily understood statement of the beneficial outcomes that successful completion of the project would deliver. That knowledge base of the financial achievements of supply network integration is missing from the current thought patterns and environmental management systems of today. We are developing case studies, but the economics of sustainability is still the weak link in the triple bottom line.

Designing Socially Responsible Supply Networks: An EMS Viewpoint

The ISO 14000 series of international standards requires that an environmental management system be developed to provide organizations with complete visibility and accountability for their contribution to the sustainable development of their products or services. ISO 14000 uses a classic "plan-do-check-act" philosophy. But we have found in our research that developing stand-alone methodological approaches for every one of our corporate initiatives results in conflicts in these organizations. We have also found that there is a philosophical approach that can be developed as an umbrella design concept. For quality improvement, for streamlining the business, and for environmental improvement, this is called DMAIC:

define, measure, analyze, improve, and control. Mikel Harry (1999), in his classic six sigma text, introduced this concept of DMAIC with a statistical flavor to it to improve the quality of the product being produced. We have taken this concept of DMAIC, and we now use this as the umbrella concept for all continuous improvement processes. By doing so, we are now forming a critical mass of talent that understands the methodology and that can begin to cross-fertilize intellectually with their peers. DMAIC is based upon the following concepts:

- Define: What problem needs to be solved?

- Measure: What is the current capability of the process? What are the key metrics of the process? And what are the targets of opportunity for this process improvement?

- Analyze: When and where do opportunities exist and how do we go about capturing those improvement opportunities in a structured manner?

- Improve: What are the improvement tools and strategies needed to actually accomplish a sustainable development?

- Control: What controls or metrics can be put in place to sustain the gain once the gain is achieved?

Let's walk through DMAIC as it relates to ISO 14000 and the design of an environmental management system.

Define

ISO 14000.1 does not establish absolute requirements for what the EMS system must do. Our EMS design, which we will discuss in a moment, is developed so the company must define its own environmental policy. It must identify what aspects it wishes to control, what aspects it can influence, and what legal aspects must be present. This is truly in the spirit of $y = f(x)$, and there are huge supply network and sustainable supply network implications here. Because, as we understand, supply networks compete with supply networks, and the OEM has the responsibility but may not have the total authority over its partners in the field to participate in an upright fashion. So the definition of an environmental management system must take into consideration all of these aspects.

Measure

ISO 14000.1 says that we must align the environmental management system with the policies and the laws. We must also understand the technical options for various scenarios.

Analyze

ISO 14000.1 says that the management must address what resources are required, who is accountable, what the roles are within the organization of these individuals, what education and training will be needed to make this change happen, what communication plan will be in place, and how we will inform our members of our supply networks of these implications.

Improve

ISO 14000.1 asks how we conceive new approaches to the system needs. How do we improve the system? How do we then document the accomplishments? How do we document the policies, objectives, targets, and so on, and how do we control the resulting system design?

Control

How do we wish to maintain the gains that we have achieved?

As you will see in the following examples, control is based upon two fundamental building blocks that are needed. The first dictates what we call the environmental self-assessment tool, ESAT. The second dictates what is required from an environmental management system, EMS, to make this happen.

The ESAT is needed to allow the supply network to assess the current overall qualitative and quantitative status as compared to the desired status of the sustainable network. In today's parlance, this is called the prioritized value chain development and definition. It established the "D" in DMAIC, but it addresses it from a complete supply network perspective. The EMS makes this vision, this definition, if you will, come to life. It addresses the framework for capturing, storing, and providing access to the status, policy, best practices, education and training required to support this development, and documents needed to be created.

Let's think about the ESAT. As you view this chapter, you need to understand that we are building this ESAT on a building block that we created in the lean movement many years ago called the lean enterprise self assessment tool, LESAT.[6] This is a public domain tool for looking at lean that looks at 21 categories of policy, leadership, processes, and infrastructure. The ESAT must do similar activities. This ESAT will have several expected outcomes, including the recognition by the supply network that environmental sustainability is mandated for the complete supply network, the definition of what categories of sustainability need to be qualitatively and quantitatively addressed, and the formulation of a plan. Last, but certainly not least, is the buy-in by all supply network participants that the prioritized categorization of EMS categories must be understood and embraced by the entire supply network for this to be successful.

The second element of the ISO 14000 systems perspective is the creation of the EMS itself. Here, from a systems perspective, we propose the process shown in figure 1.

The flow of the environmental management system is to define, measure, analyze, improve, and then control. In addition, various controls drive the definition and analysis portions of the flow. We have environmental policy in every country in the world; every community in the world is

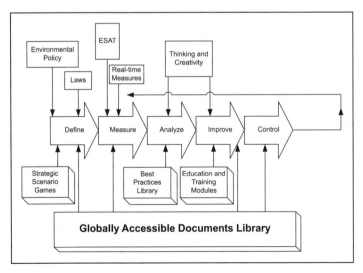

Figure 1   A Structured environmental management systems view.

creating environmental policy. We have laws, and we must understand the policies and the laws of the local region and fold that into our definition phase. We also have the results of the ESAT, which prioritizes where we as the supply network believe we must focus our attention. We have feedback coming through the system of actual accomplishments. All of that activity is called above-the-line activity, and they are all the controls from the outside. There are also three major databases that are pictured in this diagram (figure 1) that cannot be overlooked. The first are called strategic scenario games. This highlights that distributed collaborative sustainable commerce is a strategic development that must be embraced by leaderships within the organization. Various strategic scenarios can be captured in this data structure to begin to populate that strategic plan. The second major database in the environmental management system is the best practices library. This is hard to come by these days but is mandatory for organizations to understand what others are doing and what benefits can accrue by embracing the notion of sustainability.

The last is the education and training modules. By creating a series of interactive online modules, we believe that the workforce, the collaboration, and the buy-in by all parties can be successfully nurtured by having a learned, knowledgeable worker environment evolve. Finally, underpinning all aspects of the environmental management system is a globally accessible documents library containing virtual documents that would be well-defined and captured and populated by every participant in the supply network for each product or service that they perform. For example, that second- or third-tier supplier who populates a printed circuit board would document in the globally accessible documents library the content of lead that went into the overall soldering process. This relatively complex EMS does not exist yet. But as we evolve to this global availability and global awareness that sustainable networks are absolutely critical to create, we must then understand how to create this EMS of the future.

Closure: Making Change Happen

This chapter addresses the fundamental shift taking place in the world of sustainability, from a focus on individual processes to a world of supply networks competing with supply networks. For supply networks to successfully meet their sustainability requirements, visibility in a collaborative sense must be achieved. To achieve this visibility, individual organizations must be willing to document and participate in sessions that would define the key metrics and key targets of opportunities to achieve a sustainable environment. Then the network of organizations must come together in a virtual collaborative sense that will allow them to achieve complete visibility up and down the entire supply network through their EMS. By doing so, by offering that there is an ESAT to allow these organizations to come together and an EMS facilitating the documentation of the results throughout the supply network, we stand a much better chance of achieving sustainable supply network processes in the long term.

References

BSR. 2007. "Beyond Monitoring: A New Vision for Sustainable Supply Chains." Business for Social Responsibility, July 5. http://www.bsr.org/reports/BSR_Beyond-Monitoring-Report.pdf.

Harry, Mikel J. 1999. *Six Sigma: The Management Strategy Revolutionizing the World's Top Corporations.* New York: Doubleday, Random House.

National Academies. 2004. "Roundtable on Science and Technology for Sustainability." June 15. http://sites.nationalacademies.org/PGA/sustainability/PGA_050406.

Pinto, J. 2000. "Disintermediation Stirs up Industrial Automation." Controls Intelligence & Plant Systems Report, March. Available at http://www.jimpinto.com/writings/disintermediation.html.

Porter, Michael E. 1990. *The Competitive Advantage of Nations.* New York: Free Press.

Rice, James B., Jr., and Richard M. Hoppe. 2001. "Supply Chain vs. Supply Chain: The Hype vs. the Reality." *Supply Chain Management Review*, September–October, 46–54.

RoHS/WEEE. 2005. "Restriction of Hazardous Substances." Directive 2002/95/EC/Waste from Electrical and Electronic Equipment, 2002/96/EC. Directive of August 18. http://eur-lex.europa.eu/LexUriServ/LexUriServ.do?uri=CELEX:32005D0618:EN:HTML.

Shunk, Dan, Joseph Carter, John Hovis, and Aditya Talwar. 2007. "Electronics Industry Drivers of Intermediation and Disintermediation." *International Journal of Physical Distribution and Logistics Management* 37, no. 3: 248–61.

Notes

1 "Lean Sustainment Initiative," MIT Center for Technology, Policy, and Industrial Development, http://web.mit.edu/ctpid/www/lsi.html

2 ISO 14000 family of standards, "Environmental Management," http://www .iso.org/iso/iso_catalogue/catalogue_tc/catalogue_tc_browse.htm?commid=5480 8&published=on&includesc=true

3 ISO 15288 Standard, "Life Cycle," http://www.iso.org/iso/search.htm?qt=I SO+15288&searchSubmit=Search&sort=rel&type=simple&published=on

4 Jerry Ashton, "Disintermediation Defined," *CFO Advisors*, http://www .cfoadvisors.com/Default.asp?PAGE_ID=8

5 Accenture White Paper, "The Sustainable Supply Chain," 2008. Available at www.accenture.com

6 Lean Enterprise Self-Assessment Tool (LESAT), http://lean.mit.edu/ products/lean-enterprise-self-assessment-tool-lesat

CHAPTER 9

Green Purchasing Policy Development and Implementation by Higher Education

Brian K. Yeoman

Green purchasing policies are a critical foundational component of sustainable business practices. Urged by stakeholders to take definitive action to increase spending on green products and services, colleges and universities began in the late 1990s to formulate responses. The National Association of Educational Procurement fashioned a plan to harvest the knowledge and expertise of its members to create a definition of green purchasing and a green purchasing policy implementation roadmap with the objective of speeding sustainable business practice acceptance in higher education. Collaboration of multiple higher education organizations (American College and University Presidents' Climate Commitment, Association for the Advancement of Sustainability in Higher Education, and Higher Education Associations Sustainability Consortium) was certainly a key aspect to the end products. The history of green purchasing in higher education and the processes and the tools created and deployed are captured herein as well as citations of best practice institutions in the creation and deployment of green purchasing policies.

Introduction

Beginning in the late 1990s, colleges and universities were being pushed by their stakeholders—students, alumni, vendors, staff, faculty, and parents—to take definitive and positive action in increasing their spending on the purchase of green products and services as a critical component of the broader international sustainability movement. As is the case in all large-scale change movements, there were pioneers who were eagerly blazing a path to a place that most institutions had not seriously considered. As strange as it may seem now, one of the first and most important barriers to overcome was defining what exactly a green product was, and, therefore, what green purchasing was.

The Green Purchasing Definition and Current Practice

In March of 2007, the National Association of Educational Procurement (NAEP) formally published its green purchasing definition:

- Green Purchasing is the method wherein environmental and social considerations are taken with equal weight to the price, availability, and performance criteria that colleges and universities use to make purchasing decisions.

  - Green Purchasing is a serious consideration of supply chain management.

  - Green Purchasing is also known as "environmentally preferred purchasing (EPP), green procurement, affirmative procurement, eco-procurement, and environmentally responsible purchasing," particularly within the U.S. Federal government agencies.

  - Green Purchasing minimizes negative environmental and social effects through the use of environmentally friendly products.

  - Green Purchasing attempts to identify and reduce environmental impact and to maximize resource efficiency.[1]

While NAEP's members can take advantage of this definition, there is nothing that binds them to it. It provides a substantive definition that removes from the institution the responsibility of defining what is "green." The launch of the definition became a success that was soon followed by the often-difficult task of implementation. Fortunately this had been anticipated in the long-term planning process. NAEP took the steps necessary to address this critical issue. It did so by strategically engaging its membership in a highly creative process, which will be detailed further later.

NAEP successfully partnered with SciQuest, a Cary, North Carolina, software firm focused on the higher education sector to conduct the first-ever green purchasing survey (Yeoman and Zoetmulder 2010). The survey was conducted in January of 2009. There were 126 responses representing 101 institutions received from more than 4,166 individuals at 1,246 institutions. There were fewer than 30 questions in the survey. The plan was to conduct this survey on an annual basis to track the penetration of green purchasing in higher education and, when appropriate, to make topical additions on germane issues to inform the membership and the broader community at large regarding issues surrounding green purchasing. The results of the survey were analyzed by NAEP and SciQuest. Presentations were made at the executive and professional level at the NAEP national convention, press releases were made, webinars were conducted, and several abstracts were submitted to leading higher education sector organizations including the National Association of College and University Business Officers (NACUBO) for further dissemination of information. The media picked up on the press releases by the parties, and a large number of follow-up articles and interviews followed, thus reaching many more professionals in more than the purchasing trade press.

The green purchasing survey was repeated in early 2010 with great success, with 230 respondents of more than 4,000 individuals participating in the second year of the survey. As in the first year, the central question was, do you have a formal green purchasing policy? Five unique questions were added to the survey to identify any implications of the severe economic recession that was in place during all of 2009, and to identify green purchasing training experiences. Thus, the objective to track the trends of green purchasing policy in higher education had its first comparative data opportunity. Webinars were aired, press releases were again made, and presentations at national conventions were conducted.

Higher education owes the federal government a great deal of gratitude for any sustainable business practices in place in the academe. The fact that the federal government has been willing to lead in the arena of sustainable business practices stems from the President's Council on Sustainable Development (PCSD) created by President Bill Clinton in June 1993 by Executive Order 12852.[2] Because the federal government was willing to take the first steps in greening its procurement policies, it has made it acceptable for the higher education sector to follow. The federal government took its boldest green procurement steps in 1998. Interestingly, even with the ice being broken by the federal government more than ten years earlier, the vast majority of higher education institutions, 76 percent, did not have a green procurement policy in place in the 2009 survey, and 68 percent did not in 2010.

Higher education is an 800-year-old institution steeped in tradition and thus incredibly conservative. Even so, an uptake of only 32 percent after more than 10 years is indicative of the task that lies ahead for the sector. The good news is there are always leaders in every sector, and higher education has its leaders. Some of the leaders represented in the 32 percent of respondents with a green purchasing policy in February 2010 are

- Arizona State University
- Duke University
- Oberlin University
- University of California System represented by UCLA
- Rutgers University
- University of Washington
- Georgia Institute of Technology
- Villanova University
- Berea College
- University of Colorado
- Syracuse University
- University of Florida

One can create a green purchasing policy at this point by simply drawing from some of the more detailed examples provided by schools such as Arizona State University, Oberlin College, Rutgers University, and University of Florida.[3]

The green purchasing policy used at Rutgers is a great example policy. Rutgers's policy contains the following statement:

> It is the objective of Rutgers to support the 3 R's of waste management, namely Reduce, Reuse, and Recycle, and conserve energy and water when purchasing supplies, equipment, and services. In so doing Rutgers intends to minimize the harmful effects of their use and final disposition upon the environment. Rutgers is committed to actions designed to conserve and protect the environment, and will continue to

implement those actions whenever possible and economically feasible. It is the responsibility of Rutgers' Purchasing Office in conjunction with all Rutgers departments to promote the development and use of environmentally friendly products and services.[4]

Please note that the purchasing office has the responsibility for the university. The activities are many and varied and include issues such as the need to identify new and environmentally friendly products and services to meet needs, purchase from suppliers that are environmentally sensitive in their daily operations, encourage reevaluation of packaging and packing materials, specify attributes that products are expected to possess, evaluate purchases of chemicals, and evaluate supplier environmental record. As one can see by reading just a few issues addressed in the Rutgers's policy, green purchasing is a very complex issue requiring a major and concerted commitment. Securing that commitment in higher education has been a long and continuing journey.

Historical Beginnings

In the early 1990s, as social factors began to articulate more socially and environmentally responsible questions on campus operations, some higher education leadership began to feel the need to take action. Top leadership became more directly involved in green/sustainability actions with the space created by the formation of the President's Council on Sustainable Development (PCSD) led by then vice president Al Gore and co-chaired by Kenneth Lay, the chief executive officer of Enron, and by Ray C. Anderson, founder and chief executive officer of Interface.

The space created by the PCSD was enlarged substantially by the United States federal government and can be traced to the issuance of Executive Order 13101 by President Clinton on September 14, 1998.[5] The order was titled "Greening the Government through Waste Prevention, Recycling, and Federal Acquisition." Executive Order 13101 directed federal agencies to consider the following in acquisition planning:

- Elimination of virgin materials requirements

- Use of recycled content, biobased, and environmentally preferable products

- Human health and environmental attributes, including product reuse or recyclability, life-cycle costs (e.g., operations and maintenance costs), toxic and hazardous constituents, and ultimate disposal

- Revision of existing specifications, descriptions, and standards to enhance the procurement of environmentally preferable products and services

- Use of EPA guidance "to the maximum extent practicable" in identifying and purchasing environmentally preferable products and services

- Required government contractors to follow EPA's green purchasing guidance.

This was the genesis of green purchasing policy in the United States.

The NAEP Journey

Because there were pioneer institutions in the higher education sector, NAEP leadership cultivated relationships with those institutions that had responded to stakeholder demand on their campuses. Leadership sought to harvest their lessons learned by featuring them and began the process of trying to educate its membership in green purchasing practices. NAEP leadership struggled mightily with the big questions, such as what is a definition of a green product and service, and what would a green purchasing policy look like in higher education? Leadership clearly understood the broadest question, which was why green purchasing? And why higher education?

Leadership also understood that the higher education sector was responsible for the transformation of myriad natural resources into billions of pounds of products and millions of tons of packaging material, the expenditure of trillions of gallons of fossil fuel and billions of tons of greenhouse gas emissions, and the expenditure of untold hours of labor. Finally, higher education's primary stakeholder—the students—were actively applying pressure to improve environmental performance on campus. The timing appeared right for the NAEP to step to the forefront. NAEP recognized the consequences of this procurement activity as impacting all living systems and that further decline could be avoided if it began to act.

NAEP leadership knew that as higher education struggled to define and chart a path away from this destructive behavior, the purchasing department would represent the single-most tangible evidence that higher education was responding. Campus senior leadership would need a strong strategic partner. Why should it not be the purchasing department? Purchasing clearly was the most logical strategic departmental partner by choice on campus.

Why is purchasing a logical choice? Simply put, it is because 15–18 percent of the institutional budget passes through the typical procurement process on an annual basis, second only to salaries and wages in payroll. What better way to influence behavior than through a process that can be shaped to define the sustainability and green procurement objectives of the institution through the use of specifications and concentrated term contracts in the supply chain. And for good measure, those members of the academe who might choose to be resistant would not have much to stand on because of all the federal government was doing. This cleared a huge hurdle, that green purchasing was not a violation of federal grant and contract guidelines. Lastly, the procurement process contains most if not all of the low-hanging fruit or, for that matter, the fruit on the ground. This demonstrates that the institutions are in fact "walking the walk" instead of "talking the talk" to those stakeholders who have been increasingly louder in their clamoring for increased green purchases of goods and services.

Many of the goods that higher education purchases serve a limited function for a short time and then are discarded as waste. Higher education uses massive amounts of material, in addition to that used for personal use by its employees. There is that sticky problem of the "town and gown" syndrome to be contended with, and in many instances the early pioneers were coming from that environment. Thus, NAEP leadership thought that procurement officials could play the critical role of turning around and shrinking the environmental footprint of the campus and positively affecting the personnel in the organization. The challenges became how to educate the senior institutional leadership and how to move the NAEP members toward a more holistic and enlightened view.

The Green Purchasing Policy Roadmap

NAEP staff had decided to conduct an intensive Sustainability Institute in 2007. The staff also concluded that this could be the perfect venue to attempt the creation of a green purchasing policy roadmap for higher education. The October 2006 Association for the Advancement of Sustainability in Higher Education (AASHE) meeting on the Arizona State University campus had been such a tremendous success that it was abundantly obvious that Tempe was a prime site for the first Sustainability Institute. It also was the case that Arizona State had some technology that could be adaptively applied for the purpose of creating the roadmap. So it was with great fanfare that NAEP began the process of marketing its world-class faculty for the 2007 Sustainability Institute with the full plan including the process of creating the roadmap. The institute was to be conducted the first week of May 2007. Many of the authors of chapters in this reference set were institute faculty that May. They contributed significantly to the growth of green purchasing in higher education. Fifty-four participants from higher education were enrolled.

The catalyzing vision statement posed to roadmap construction participants was "Visualize that the President of your institution has given you the responsibility to implement a 'green purchasing program' including a 'green power' purchasing authorization under a broad institution-wide sustainable development initiative." NAEP staff had previously identified seven detailed questions designed to assist the participants in the discovery process for formulating a plan to implement a green purchasing program:

- Who are your technical and policy resources? (i.e., peers, professional organizations, consultants, web searches, other public resources)

- What information and data do you need to begin this task? (i.e., commodities, dollars, transactions, policies, procedures, state laws, federal laws, state and federal regulations, cooperatives)

- When is it likely that the green purchasing program can be implemented? (i.e., in months 1, 6, 12, 18, 24)

- Where and how will you include your noncampus stakeholders in the formulation of your program? (i.e., regents, system administration, vendors, regulators, neighbors, political subdivisions)

- How will you approach the implementation with your institution's students? faculty? staff? (i.e., tactics, techniques, policies, procedures)

- What financial and human resources will you need to implement a program?

- What are the critical success indicators for your institution with regard to a green purchasing program? (i.e., metrics, outcomes, costs, feasibility).

The Process

The seven questions were asked by ASU's professional facilitators, and the responses provided by the 54 institute participants in each of the six groups of NAEP Sustainability Institute participants were captured. Each group of six or more participants engaged in dialog addressing the questions as posed, and each group was facilitated by a trained Arizona State University Decision Theater professional facilitator.[6] The facilitator captured the responses in a live interactive session, and the responses were coalesced into a document that was subsequently published on the NAEP website for the entire membership to review.

Ninety days later NAEP staff asked for volunteers from the original participant group to serve as a steering committee. Thirteen volunteers stepped forward. The volunteers were asked to consider the data provided and to force rank the participant responses using their best professional opinion. The results were tabulated in an Excel spreadsheet.

Throughout the fall and winter of 2007, NAEP worked with a smaller team of institute participants to generate the roadmap. The goal of the group was to share their work and assist with other institutions that were getting ready to embark upon their journey to create a green purchasing policy for their institution. NAEP felt that the roadmap could be used with little modification and would not require the re-creation of the hard work undertaken in Tempe. The roadmap was formally released in monograph form by NAEP in February of 2008 and is available at naepnet.org. NAEP staff used the annual convention in April of 2008 to offer multiple presentations of the roadmap to the membership. The roadmap was released to all Higher Education Associations Sustainability Consortium (HEASC) members following the formal launch to the membership.[7]

NAEP submitted conference abstract proposals to AASHE and to NACUBO for the Green Purchasing Policy Roadmap, and both were accepted. The AASHE presentation was given in November of 2008 and was the highest-rated session of the conference. The NACUBO presentation was made in March of 2009 and was also favorably received.

Sustainability Leadership Lessons from the History of Higher Education Purchasing

The higher education sector in this country has many professional organizations that provide leadership to their professional members and lend overall knowledge to the sector. One of the leading organizations is NACUBO. This is probably the largest and most influential higher education professional organization because they represent the chief business officers. The Society of College and University Planners represents the planning and the budgeting professionals on campus. The American Association of Higher Education Facilities Professionals, the source of the single-largest nonpayroll expenditures on campus, exists to work with and inform physical plant professionals. The procurement professional in the sector looks to NAEP for their sector-wide leadership on omnibus issues involving procurement.

So where was the NAEP from 1998 until today? In a few words, largely transparent but quietly plotting to lead. Membership-based professional organizations typically suffer from a lack of funding and from a lack of influence and vision. If the members do not recognize the need for action, these organizations rarely jump out and charge forward on any given issue. In this case however, NAEP tried quite unsuccessfully to influence its members early and often. In early 2000, the leadership proposed a partnership with a certain nonprofit to examine this issue and was firmly but politely told by its members, "We don't want any of that green stuff; we don't believe in it." And further, "Why is that nonprofit anymore knowledgeable than we are?" Working somewhat covertly, the leadership invited and encouraged "green" presentations and the broader notion of sustainability at its annual meetings. NAEP also encouraged and began to produce quarterly columns in its official publication, *The Journal*, believing that the membership needed to know what was taking place outside the world of higher education on the topic of sustainable development and green procurement.

In the fall of 2003, NAEP hired a sustainability/green procurement staff person/topic expert and immediately began the process of upgrading its professional development offerings and upgrading its technical resources on the website. One of the first offerings was a compendium of the existing green purchasing policies in place in the higher education sector. It also began the process of planning a sustainability track at its annual meeting. Leadership recognized that the sustainability movement had developed a robust body of theory and that sustainability was beginning to move beyond theoretical development to the level of pilot implementations in higher education. Meanwhile green procurement remained an emergent field, particularly so in higher education. While leadership saw business applications encompassing industrial and service sectors, the application of sustainability principles to the purchasing practices of higher education had received virtually no attention. Thus, leadership sharpened its focus on understanding the issue of sustainable development in higher education and began to postulate the strategic nature of green procurement therein.

The Plan

NAEP concluded a lengthy planning exercise in 2005 focused on a five-year planning schedule, which found the following major points:

- Build interest and competence in sustainability issues in the membership.

- Increase the purchasing professionals' influence on campus.

- Define green purchasing.

- Develop deployment strategies.

- Promote green purchasing through articles and presentations.

- Promote NAEP and green purchasing at other higher education organizations.

- Create a roadmap for implementation of green purchasing in higher education.

- Promote the roadmap in multiple higher education professional organizations.

- Test the green purchasing policy roadmap.

- Survey higher education to assess effectiveness.

- Revise the required elements of the definition and the roadmap based upon the data analysis.

Doreen Murner, the chief executive officer of NAEP, was instrumental in identifying the demand for an intense training session on green procurement and sustainable development. She set out to address this need through the creation of the Sustainability Institute to be conducted with a world-class group of instructors. This institute was to focus on the implementation of sustainable business activities of the higher education enterprise; therefore, it would be totally unique due to the nature of the research activity, the decentralized nature of the college and university power structure, and the relatively conservative social climate. Leadership felt that the implementation of sustainability principles had moved barely incrementally with a reliance on education, individual initiative, and changed minds to achieve what little change that had occurred. NAEP realized that this had to change in order to succeed. The objective was to alter the very slow movement that had been buttressed by programmatic changes across several academic and business practices to create a dynamic flexible yet effective change process.

Leadership also felt that, with numerous instances of recent dramatic increases in energy costs, institutions would be willing to invest more in energy-efficient products and construction materials that could pay off more quickly in energy savings, thus providing institutions another value to consider to get them to "go green," while saving "green." The notion in those days was that equating energy efficiency with green procurement was a virtual no-brainer and could be buttressed by the EPA's Energy Star program and the requirements coming from the federal government for federal agencies. Thus, this rising interest in green products that could save money would lead to a pathway to demand for other green/sustainable products and services.

NAEP went about recruiting a world-class faculty, hotel, site selection, and creating the hype to sell the four-and-a-half-day institute in the spring of 2005. After an intense marketing campaign of more than four months, there was insufficient registration to conduct the institute. NAEP had to deal with the reality of procurement's standing in the higher education sector. The institute would have been a financial failure. Leadership considered putting on the institute anyway, but sound business management overrode the rationale that there was a vertical marketplace to be had. The harsh reality was that procurement officials in the pecking order of higher education simply did not have enough power and influence to be able to routinely seize upon a strategic initiative and act independently of their bosses—typically the chief business officer. The chief business officers had not yet "seen the light" on the procurement end of the sustainability issue even though they were heavily involved in the investment and socially responsible portfolio conversations on campus.

This was a bitter pill for NAEP and a very low time in the green procurement effort to move forward in the higher education sector. NAEP learned from this early failure and got a little good luck. As fate would have it, a wonderful, brand-new organization, the Higher Education Associations Sustainability Consortium (HEASC), was formed in December 2005 by leaders of several higher education associations to support and enhance the capacity of higher education to fulfill its critical role in producing an educated, engaged citizenry with the knowledge needed for a thriving and civil society. The founding organizations recognized that fulfilling their mission in the 21st century was going to require a much more holistic, systemic, collaborative approach to their work and that of the stakeholders they serve. NAEP was a founding member.

According to the HEASC.org website, "the goal for HEASC members is to learn from each other, work together on joint projects, get access to the best expertise and information on sustainability, and to keep a collective, ongoing focus on advancing education for a sustainable future over time." This was the perfect opportunity to leverage in green procurement by providing expertise in exchange for access to many other segment of the higher education sector. A partial listing of member organizations taken from the website follows:

- American Council on Education (ACE)

- National Association of College & University Business Officers (NACUBO)

- National Association of Educational Procurement (NAEP)

- Association of Higher Education Facilities Officers (APPA)

- Society for College & University Planning (SCUP)

- American Association of Community Colleges (AACC)

- American Association of State Colleges & Universities (AASCU)

- Association for the Advancement of Sustainability in Higher Education (AASHE)

- Association of Collegiate Conference & Events Directors-International (ACCED-I)

- ACPA-College Student Educators International (ACPA)

- Association of College & University Housing Officers-International (ACUHO-I)

- Association of Governing Boards of Universities & Colleges (AGB)

- National Association of Independent Colleges & Universities (NAICU)

HEASC membership elevated NAEP's efforts because the organization was so very skilled at supporting its members' work in advancing sustainability by

- Promoting and enhancing each others' sustainability efforts;

- Providing a forum for sharing and exchanging information, knowledge, and experiences;

- Building the capacity of higher education associations to make sustainability a goal of their programming and practices;

- Enhancing professional development, including training in sustainability for higher education association staff and their constituents;

- Reorienting professional development programs to address sustainability; and

- Connecting higher education associations to the best expertise, resources, and information in sustainability for higher education.

This experience revealed that planning, building, and purchasing by colleges and universities was becoming more heavily influenced by green and sustainable considerations than could be seen from the lens of one profession. Nonetheless, the experience reinforced NAEP's long-term plan to increasingly focus the green buying power of the 2,000+ members toward making green and socially responsible product and service information available to members. Thus, the education of the members became the top priority with the planning to conduct a world-class sustainability institute reignited. Thus, renewed by the experiences of early 2006 with the other higher education associations, NAEP submitted multiple abstracts to other HEASC member's annual meetings in hopes of introducing the notion of green purchasing to those organizations and particularly to the bosses, and it sharpened its commitment to establishing a singular definition of green purchasing for all of higher education by the close of that calendar year. NAEP was fortunate to have its suggested session titled "Why Green Purchasing" selected for presentation at the inaugural meeting of AASHE in Tempe, Arizona, in October of 2006. The meeting was attended by more than 700 individuals, and the session was warmly received.

Bolstered by this reception, NAEP redoubled its commitment to education and to providing the higher education sector as well as its membership with a definition of green purchasing that is holistic, flexible, and understandable for everyone on every campus in America. In the process, NAEP understood that the definition had to address all three legs of the sustainability platform: economy, equity, and environment. NAEP devised a process to engage in the necessary dialog with the members to harvest their previous work, ideas, and concerns. All of the requisite expertise to do this existed with the membership. Drawing from the experience of the Natural Step and its consensus-building process, a draft of a green purchasing definition was iterated seven times to members of NAEP, each time narrowing the focus and tightening the definition.[8] When NAEP arrived at a consensus, the definition was vetted with the HEASC member organizations and distributed widely throughout higher education. This returns us to the opening of this chapter because the NAEP vision is a whole-systems approach where there is no finish line but more likely a model more on the order of biological systems that are cyclical in nature, as opposed the linear models that are dominant throughout the business processes of the world. NAEP feels as if it has made a material contribution to the broader acceptance of sustainable business practices in the higher education sector. The data from the second green purchasing survey confirms the trend of broader adoption, deeper deployment, and wider acceptance coupled with an increasing number of institutions positioning themselves to take definitive action in the next year.

Consistent with the early history of the green purchasing movement, the federal government has continued to hone its activities and broaden its lead as a role model for higher education. Two notable green purchasing executive orders have been issued since 2007. They are Executive Order 13423, "Strengthening Federal Environmental, Energy, and Transportation Management," dated January 24, 2007, issued by President George W. Bush; and Executive Order 13514, "Federal Leadership in Environmental, Energy, and Economic Performance," dated October 5, 2009, issued by President Barak Obama.[9]

These executive orders strongly set green purchasing policy with goals and objectives for federal agencies' acquisition of goods and services through the use of sustainable environmental practices, including acquisition of biobased, environmentally preferable, energy-efficient, water-efficient, and recycled-content products. These executive orders established a very high standard and cleared the way for more aggressive adoption and implementation by higher education.

The NAEP website includes links to these important seminal bodies of policy. The green purchasing definition is consistent with these latest federal initiatives, and the Green Purchasing Policy Roadmap recognizes the important sources as potential models and examples of what is possible in the public sector purchasing space. In a continuing effort to assist member institutions, NAEP encourages feedback and comments about this critically important topic of green purchasing. NAEP stands ready to make adjustments based upon the consensus approach described earlier in the chapter. There can be no doubt that further definition and procedural adaptation will need to be made over the evolution of the implementation of green purchasing policies in higher education.

The Near-Term Future

There are perhaps two major topics that most likely will shape green purchasing in the immediate future. The first is that for a very long time it has been the case that procurement professionals have been chasing the pot of gold at the end of the rainbow when it comes to "green" or "eco" labels, and the results have been mixed at best. The reasons for this are many, but chief among them have been the degree to which independence could be demonstrated by the owner of the certification system, the costs of certification, the criteria used to confirm a product as green, and the robustness of the testing methodology. All of those are important characterizations of where purchasing has been and, to some extent, where purchasing is now. A single, ubiquitous, valid product certification simply cannot usefully exist for professional procurement personnel. That is not to say that the magazine *Good Housekeeping*, now in the business of putting its label on green products, and Walmart, who is talking about doing something similar for retail consumer products, will fall short of the mark, but it is to say that for professional purchasers those efforts simply will not be good enough.

The second issue likely to be shaping green purchasing in the future is the ability to clearly and concisely capture data about the "spend" in the vast enterprise resource systems employed by higher education. In these difficult financial times, the amount of pressure that procurement professionals are feeling about green purchasing activity is significant. And quite frankly, the pressure to stand back and wait for something better to happen is a crutch that some will opt to take. The fact is, the need for a solid data capture system could never be better made than right now. Thus, when purchasing departments most need the data to support the green purchasing decisions they are making, the tools they need to do so are sorely lacking.

Vision for 2015

There can be little doubt that the two primary drivers that will clarify any ambiguity in the higher education sector regarding the breadth and depth of sustainable business practices as evidenced by the role green purchasing policy plays in higher education are the ACUPCC's voluntary efforts to achieve climate neutrality and the tremendous influence created by leadership and application by the federal government in greening the supply chain. Since June of 2007, 675 college and university presidents have signed the American College and University Presidents' Climate Commitment.[10] The range of institutions engaged in this exciting, publically reported and recorded effort is a mirror of higher education, including some of the smallest most technically oriented institutions to the largest public universities. This bodes well for the higher education purchasing profession.

According to the ACUPCC website, "the American College & University Presidents' Climate Commitment (ACUPCC) is a high-visibility effort to address global climate disruption undertaken by a network of colleges and universities that have made institutional commitments to eliminate net greenhouse gas emissions from specified campus operations, and to promote the research and educational efforts of higher education to equip society to re-stabilize the earth's climate. Its mission is to accelerate progress towards climate neutrality and sustainability by empowering the higher education sector to educate students, create solutions, and provide leadership-by-example for the rest of society."

These institutions have got to clearly understand that for success to be in the offing, they must make fundamental change in that 800-year-old culture. The three major undertakings for higher education are, first, realizing and accepting the fact that society is demanding change in the sector. Second, in responding to society, higher education has to accept the accountability that if it is going to accept compensation for creating change agents in the form of undergraduate and graduate students, there is a fundamental expectation that the institution must lead by example. And finally, there is a clear public expectation that higher education will create and implement activities, policies, programs, and projects that are scalable, reproducible, and financially viable.

If they are to succeed, these institutions must develop green procurement practices as part of the transformational change they face and to meet their ACUPCC commitment. This means that a fully integrated, holistic approach to green procurement has to be developed and deployed for the year 2015. This will be a major undertaking for higher education and for the purchasing professionals therein. It can and must be done. The critical components of an integrated holistic green purchasing program are as follows:

- Increased organizational visibility

- Shared mission, vision, and strategy

- A seat for purchasing at the leadership level

- Increased skills in professionals

- Robust data systems

- Relationship management focus

Increased organizational visibility is necessary for institutional success. Climate neutrality can only be achieved through the supply chain and the 16 to 18 percent of institutional spending that flows through the process. The public processes required of those institutions that are ACUPCC signatories superimpose a higher and greater level of institutional commitment and accountability. Presidents and chancellors once visibly linked to the success of a green purchasing program will provide all of the necessary support to allow the program and related project to succeed. In essence, when the chief executive becomes the champion, there is every reason to believe that significant results are achievable.

Following on the heels of the actions that will be taken by the chief executive is the critical step of achieving consensus around a shared mission, vision, and strategy for the elimination of greenhouse gas emissions. The early results clearly demonstrate that this is an essential step. When sufficient dialog has taken place, the academic culture can get behind the process. These are intelligent individuals who know that the second-largest slice of an institution's budget is the supply chain, which provides maintenance, operations, and capital funding. They also know that they can directly affect the procurement cycle in both a positive and negative manner. When shared mission, vision, and strategy exist, it is possible that the synergy that is achieved truly is greater than the sum of the parts. Faculty and staff know that purchasing departments can deliver the results that senior level leadership has committed itself to by signing the ACUPCC document.

The quest to maintain a shared mission, vision, and strategy is not an easy course to follow. The long-term success of the green purchasing program will not have a chance of succeeding while the purchasing department is functioning as a third- or fourth-tier functional department in the institution. To advocate such a thought would be folly. It is the case that purchasing departments, particularly at large public sector institutions, must be elevated to the leadership level of the institutions. It is illogical to think that the second-largest element of the budget and the place where the "rubber meets the road" on greenhouse gas emissions would not be elevated to the leadership level to benefit from direct interaction with the champion and to serve the champion in his or her quest to meet their publically avowed goals and objectives under the mission and vision. It is the primary building block in the strategy, and it mirrors what is taking place in the private sector.

Clearly, if the purchasing department is going to be performing this critical role, the skill sets held by departmental personnel need to be updated. It can no longer be assumed that buying is buying, or contracting is contracting. Understanding the intricacies of an integrated holistic approach to operating the supply chain where equal consideration is given to environment and equity after a career of only valuing economy is a dramatic shift in behavior. There is no reason to believe that this cannot be accomplished, but to reach that state will require investing in personnel, reinvesting in them, and monitoring their performance against the goals. This will also mean that personnel will have to have tools that will make it more likely that they will be successful. As an example, if the enterprise resource platform that the institution employs is multiple generations behind the current state of data collection and ease of use and, most importantly, its reporting capabilities are weak, a disaster may be in the making.

Robust data systems are a critical component of the 2015 view. It has been a slow evolutionary process in higher education to get more controls in place for the second-biggest slice of the budget (the purchase of goods and services), but the time has arrived when this issue is addressed. Leadership will have to be willing to invest in the tools to enable the success of the purchasing department because it cannot reach its higher objectives without equipping the supply chain with the requisite knowledge and systems to make the chief executive's objectives reality. Driven in part by the ACUPCC's public reporting requirement, which is hosted on the AASHE website, chief executive officers cannot afford to fail in meeting their commitment before their peers, boards, students, faculty, and staff. Better data systems are in the offing.

Along the way, green purchasing policy will make major contributions to the fundamental shift in the process to understanding the principles of the total cost of ownership. This is very critical for institutions because they are here for the long term, and their spending patterns are here for the long term. Thus, it is a logical extension that the evolution of life-cycle analysis, which is a very legitimate academic pursuit, would become codified in software solutions to support the mission, vision, and strategy of the higher education sector.

Thus, purchasing policy once properly situated organizationally; adequately staffed; and sufficiently trained, tooled, and committed to a consensual shared mission, vision, and strategy can make a huge shift in the higher education sector to relationship management. The 2015 environment is one in which the total cost of ownership is celebrated by all sustainable business partners. Long gone is the attitude that the supply chain process for higher education is an adversarial one. This shift will fundamentally boost the entire higher education purchasing profession into high gear. That is to say, that when energy is expended in supply chain management, it can be totally focused upon achieving results that are commonly held, agreed to by all, typified by a long-term relationship, and focused upon delivering value consistent with the mission and vision, not the lowest possible price. When the parties within the institution recognize the power of this approach, we will truly be able to say that we have transformed the supply chain and that we are doing great things for the institution and the planet and all other living things.

And because we will have excellent data systems, we will be able to record and report. Thus, being able to measure what is taking place in the supply chain, higher education will have an opportunity to definitively know the answer to the questions of how we are doing and how we compare. We will be able to do this because AASHE, after multiple years and multiple pilots, has successfully launched a sustainability index created by higher education specifically for higher education. Its name is STARS, the Sustainability Tracking Assessment and Rating System, and by 2015 it should easily be the norm that every college and university will be collecting data and reporting publically on the AASHE website. There are six identified categories in which specific performance targets must be met to secure points toward the overall college or university rating. Green purchasing is weaved into many sections of the tabulations in a very significant manner, including a unique purchasing section. Thus, the importance of green purchasing is reinforced by the scoring charts for the overall ranking, which is used by a wide range of people to make decisions about colleges and universities ranging from where to attend, to where to work, to where to donate.

The second major driver that defines what 2015 looks like is the federal government. Beginning with President Clinton and Executive Order 13101 and spurred on by President Bush with Executive Order 13423, the federal government has been blazing the trail in green purchasing. In October 2009, President Obama signed Executive Order 13541, which is titled "Federal Leadership in Environment, Energy, and Economic Performance." This is the most significant enhancement to the green purchasing movement in more than 10 years. It creates tremendous goals and objectives for all federal agencies. It also creates numerous flow-down regulations for federal grants and contracts awarded to higher education. Some of the significant elements of the executive order follow:

- EO 13514 mandates numerous specific actions including a requirement that 95 percent of new contract actions, including task and delivery orders, for products and services meet a requirement for use of sustainable environmental practices, including the purchase of products that are non-ozone depleting or are non-toxic or less toxic alternatives where such products and services meet agency performance requirements. The executive order also requires that agencies buy paper of at least 30 percent post-consumer content, and it stipulates that uncoated printing and writing paper be used. In the arena of electronic equipment, it specifically requires that there be procurement preference for EPEAT-registered electronic products and that for electronic equipment, Energy Star– and FEMP-designated electronic equipment be procured.

These purchasing policies will cause higher education to move comfortably and with harmony toward a broader acceptance of green purchasing policy. The marketplace will follow quickly, having been given the signal from the federal government that they are moving in this direction. The marketplace will respond with more favorable terms and conditions such that the perception of a barrier to green purchasing policy adoption by some in higher education will have been mitigated.

It is ironic that the genesis of green purchasing has its roots in federal executive orders and that another major push on the higher education sector for the future will come again from the ratcheting up of the performance by federal example. It will be very interesting to see how these two major forces—higher education's voluntary actions through ACUPCC and AASHE and the exemplary model being created and executed and flowing down by the federal government—will influence higher education.

References

Yeoman, Brian, and Eric Zoetmulder. 2010. "Green Procurement Trends within Higher Education: 2010 NAEP Green Procurement Survey Results—Complete Results." PowerPoint presentation, available at http://www.naepnet.info/documents/sustainability/2010_naep_green_ procurement_survey_results.ppt#259.

Notes

1 See the National Association of Educational Procurement (NAEP) website, http://www.naepnet.org

2 Exec. Order No. 12852, 58 Fed. Reg. 126 (July 2, 1993), http://www .archives.gov/federal-register/executive-orders/pdf/12852.pdf

3 Arizona State University, *PUR 210: Green Purchasing*, http://www.asu .edu/aad/manuals/pur/pur210.html; Oberlin College, *Green Purchasing Policy*, http://www.oberlin.edu/sustainability/portfolio/docs/OC_green_purchasing_ policy.pdf; Rutgers University, *Rutgers Green Purchasing Policy and Guidelines,* http://purchasing.rutgers.edu/green/Images/Rutgers_Green_Purchasing_

Policy.pdf; and University of Florida, *Sustainable Purchasing*, http://fa.ufl.edu/uco/handbook/handbook.asp?doc=1.4.12.16

4 *Rutgers Green Purchasing Policy and Guidelines*, http://purchasing.rutgers.edu/green/Images/Rutgers_Green_Purchasing_Policy.pdf, 2

5 Exec. Order No. 13101, 63 Fed. Reg. 179 (Sept. 16, 1998), http://www.epa.gov/epp/pubs/13101.pdf

6 Arizona State University Decision Theater, http://dt.asu.edu/about/team

7 Higher Education Associations Sustainability Consortium, http://www2.aashe.org/heasc/about.php

8 The Natural Step, http://www.naturalstep.org/

9 Exec. Order No. 13423, 72 Fed. Reg. 17 (Jan. 26, 2007), http://edocket.access.gpo.gov/2007/pdf/07-374.pdf; and Exec. Order 13514, 74 Fed. Reg. 194 (Oct. 8, 2009), http://edocket.access.gpo.gov/2009/pdf/E9-24518.pdf

10 American College and University President's Climate Commitment, http://www.presidentsclimatecommitment.org/

CHAPTER 10

The Role of the Chief Purchasing/ Supply Office in Sustainable Business Practice

Phillip L. Carter and James C. Hershauer

Chief purchasing officers (CPO) are positioned to turn corporate statements about sustainability into corporate practice on sustainability both within the organization and with their supply networks. Is this happening? Because organizations spend up to 80 percent of their cost of goods sold with suppliers, many of their sustainability initiatives, if they are to have a significant impact, must be directed at the supply base and the internal customers for the goods and services purchased from the supply base.

Through a series of studies from 2006 through 2009, CAPS Research has led the way in understanding what is happening and how it is being accomplished. Based on these interviews, surveys, and case studies, this chapter will discuss how CPOs have and can approach the important responsibilities and opportunities that they have naturally devolved to them. The opportunities are immense.

The structure of this discussion is based on *Process Guide for Supply Management Environmental Sustainability* (Hershauer 2008). The guide was developed based on discussions with CPOs and their managers and an extensive review of company sustainability statements. Because supply management groups were in an early adoption phase of sustainability in 2008, five stages were identified as needed to achieve supply management environmental sustainability. Because efforts have matured since that study, this chapter adapts the stages to three key areas of decision making. The three areas are establishing the role of the CPO in executing corporate sustainability commitments, establishing goals for key metrics, and working with key suppliers and internal customers.

The Opportunity: The Pivotal Position of Supply Management

Chief purchasing officers (CPOs) are at the crossroads of both the top-down and bottom-up sustainability movement of sustainability initiatives. Because of the large amount of company spending they manage or advise on, they are in a position to greatly influence the impact of that spending on the "greenness" and "equity" of purchased goods and services. CPOs, because they must partner with internal customers on the spending, are also in a position to influence the thinking and orientation of the internal customer about the need for specifying green goods and services and qualifying acceptable equity suppliers. Gattiker, Tate, and Carter (2008) have claimed that different industries will have differing adoption rates for green strategies. Working to help establish industry standards and protocols common to all suppliers will simultaneously help to level and to raise the playing field; however, there will still be enormous opportunities for industry leaders and high risks for industry laggards when it comes to making tough choices to improve the sustainability of the spending.

The Role of the CPO in Executing Corporate Sustainability Commitments

Gattiker, Tate, and Carter (2008) found that unclear definitions concerning corporate sustainability and lack of mutual understanding of metrics to choose and goals to set were impeding progress by corporations in achieving success related to corporate sustainability commitments. The chief purchasing officer is uniquely positioned to create operational definitions for the conceptual definitions typical of corporate sustainability commitments.

Converting Corporate Statements to Operational Definitions

Corporate statements might define supply web environmental sustainability as a set of interorganizational processes for interacting with suppliers regarding monitoring and lessening environmental impact in supplier operations and in the related upstream products and services received by suppliers. The CPO must then work with internal customers to help them determine specifications for incoming products and services that are consistent with the internal need for product or service performance, the corporate environmental commitment, and current industry environmental standards. The CPO might also help establish ISO 14000 certification for all internal operations as a predecessor to supplier development programs that assist suppliers in achieving ISO 14000 certifications. Many early attempts to interpret corporate commitments have quickly moved to requiring suppliers to achieve a standard such as ISO 14000 certifications. In many cases, this external requirement transpired prior to having the firm's internal operations achieve the same certifications. Many survey responses in the set of CAPS Research studies found this type of recurring response from suppliers. Suppliers are naturally very dissatisfied with buyers that arbitrarily require them to meet a standard that the buying company has not achieved and often does not understand.

Regarding equity, corporate strategy might define supply web equity sustainability as having no child labor used anyplace upstream in the supply web, protecting the health and safety of all workers upstream in the process, and protecting the rights of workers in all upstream operations. Many firms have attempted to accomplish this by establishing a corporate code of conduct and adopting the same code as the supplier code of conduct. This leaves the CPO in the position of interpreting a code that was not developed for the wide myriad of cultures in the supply base firms. The code may sometimes violate the norms and customs that exist in many different global locations of supplying organizations. Successfully qualifying suppliers can be quite difficult in this setting and may require creating unique operational definitions that are acceptable to the supplier and the internal customer for each country of origin. Construction engineering and management firms are keenly aware of these differences. Requirements for a certain percentage of local suppliers can exacerbate these decisions.

Creating Industry Standards

It is important to try to anticipate future industry standards so that product and service design decisions are not obsolete prior to delivery of first units. Car manufacturers in the United States can certainly attest to the pain of not recognizing the rapidly changing expectations from all stakeholders. Most car manufacturers are now heavily engaged in several industry partnerships and consortia to level the playing field and to advance the entire industry. A key to advancing the entire industry is creating supply chains for many new forms of lightweight materials and many new forms of power systems. Advancing the automotive industry even requires that entirely new networks of sources of alternate power must be created.

Multiple and Varied Roles

Gattiker, Tate, and Carter (2008) identified numerous sustainability roles for the CPO and supply management team. These include managing existing relationships subject to new constraints, protecting the organization from liability, identifying and learning from suppliers that are leaders in sustainability action, handling sustainability communications, gathering information and data, monitoring for compliance, recognizing exceptional supplier sustainability performance, searching for innovative supplier solutions, qualifying new environmentally preferable suppliers, and coordinating sustainability efforts of all internal organizational functions through dissemination of practices and facilitation of negotiations.

During the early stages of organizational efforts on sustainability, it is critical that existing supplier relationships must be maintained and managed. Operationally, a corporate conception of a sustainability definition that eliminates all existing supplier relationships by fiat is doomed to failure. Existing supplier relationships are often based on years of interaction to build a certain level of trust with and reliable performance of the supplier base. From an operational perspective, it is imperative that the supply management team determine operational practices that allow them to develop existing supplier relationships to meet sustainability objectives. This often requires mutual problem solving and early supplier involvement in establishing operational definitions. It is also possible that a key supplier may provide the leadership necessary for the entire industry to move forward on a sustainability agenda. Power in some organizational supply chains may be with a key supplier rather than with the original equipment manufacturer (OEM) or large retailer. Each supply chain may require a different set of operational definitions. The CPO is in the pivotal position to allow sustainability efforts to flourish while maintaining the necessary existing supply base.

In any case, the supply management group ultimately handles both strategic and tactical communication, gathers information and collects data, and then monitors key metrics for compliance and recognition. Recognizing and rewarding a high-performing supplier for sustainability excellence may create more supplier peer pressure on other suppliers rather than trying to enforce some strict decree about meeting a minimum threshold of sustainability performance. Minimum thresholds often inhibit real gains for a metric by also becoming the implied maximum level of performance and discouraging truly innovative alternative solutions.

Supply management needs to understand the regulations and risks of suppliers from both supplier facility and upstream material perspectives. The CPO is again uniquely positioned to protect the buying organization from risks imbedded in its product/service bundle through supplier action or inaction. The risk of a supplier stoppage due to environmental noncompliance or worker equity violations may be even more important in some industries and for particular materials and services.

Action Plan

The steps required to create an action plan were developed by Hershauer in a prior study.

> To understand corporate environmental sustainability in the context of supply chain environmental sustainability, supply management leadership should take 4 basic steps in conjunction with corporate leaders. These steps include: (1) deciding when to roll out CEO statements to suppliers, (2) establishing rules of engagement for commodity manager interactions with suppliers, (3) determining if a policy is needed for environmental sustainability as a part of supplier accreditation, (4) deciding if, when and how to roll out a supplier code of conduct and/or environmentally preferable (green) purchasing. (Hershauer 2008, 3)

Establishing Goals for Key Metrics

First, one must understand and define what is meant by sustainability success. Both environmental and equity metrics must then be developed.

Supply Management Sustainability Success

Supply management sustainability success can be defined as establishing mutual expectations for sustainability among a buying organization's internal customers and its supply base. "This requires that the buying organization conduct a self-assessment before embarking on supplier assessments. This will allow the buying organization to define sustainability and success in the context of their industry and organizational setting"

(Hershauer 2008, 2). Sustainability success of internal operations and the related supplier base will thus be somewhat unique to the context of materials, services, and products of the industry that the buying organization operates in. In addition, each industry that suppliers reside in may require a somewhat unique set of metrics and goals.

Environmental Metrics

On the environmental side, "the family of metrics should generally include (but may not be limited to): (1) GHG [greenhouse gas] emissions, (2) hazardous substance usage and waste, (3) net water consumption and waste, (4) total supplier waste to landfills and (5) total supplier energy consumption" (Hershauer 2008, 4). Esty and Winston (2006) have identified 10 areas for measurements; however, not all will apply to most supplier bases. The five listed above are essential for most third-party reporting schemes that currently exist.

Equity Metrics

On the equity side, the electronics industry, through its Electronic Industry Citizenship Coalition (EICC), has provided the best guide to areas for metrics in its industry code. Based on the EICC Code of Conduct, it is recommended that the family of metrics for all upstream global suppliers also include (but not be limited to) (1) child labor avoidance; (2) occupational injury and illness; (3) sanitation, food, and housing; (4) fair business, advertising, and competition; and (5) nondiscrimination.[1] The EICC provides links to the many international efforts in these and related areas. These references include groups such as the United Nations, the International Labor Organization, the International Standards Organization, and the Ethical Trading Initiative. "At current levels of supply management sustainability, the key focus with these metrics is to learn the current industry status and to focus on improvements year over year from a baseline" (Hershauer 2008, 4).

Defining Success

Gattiker, Tate, and Carter (2008) found several key areas for defining the success of supplier sustainability efforts. They include (1) environmental benefit; (2) environmental compliance (which may be measured as reduced likelihood of regulatory noncompliance); (3) operating cost savings; (4)

operating revenue increase; (5) conventional investment analyses; (6) total cost of ownership; (7) life-cycle analysis; (8) reputation enhancement; (9) regulation avoidance; and (10) reduced likelihood of an environmental accident (oil companies should particularly note this one). They found that success did not require standard investment justification if there was a clearly defined offsetting benefit, which needs to be quantifiable. They also found that participants believed that the metrics need to be enduring and consistent over an extended time. One-time and one-off benefits generally cannot keep a sustainability program going.

Working with Key Suppliers and Internal Customers

Working with key suppliers and internal customers requires directly addressing several issues. Important issues include identifying barriers, overcoming resistance, and enlisting top management support.

Barriers

Gattiker, Tate, and Carter (2008) and Gattiker (2006) have found numerous barriers to starting and maintaining sustainability efforts at the CPO level. These two surveys identified such issues as (1) current corporate policies that contradict sustainability efforts; (2) lack of C-level commitment; (3) buy-in from employees who carry out the decisions; (4) acceptance of environmentally preferable materials by internal customers; (5) absence of third-party standards; (6) a focus and reward for getting low cost; (7) the size and complexity of the organization and supply base; (8) a high degree of corporate decentralization in supply decisions; (9) lack of prior leadership by the supply group on energy and water; (10) lack of system support and such analysis tools as life-cycle analysis; (11) current job descriptions and reward structures that do not include anything on sustainability; (12) lack of standard metrics for analyses; and (13) lack of scientific evidence about potential new materials and processes.

Overcoming Resistance

Ashenbaum (2008), Gattiker, Tate, and Carter (2008), and Gattiker (2006) have also discovered ideas and solutions for overcoming these barriers. Many of these are the standard organizational practices for overcoming resistance to change. They include such practices as (1) procuring top management leadership and endorsement; (2) adopting material and process changes that are cost neutral or better; (3) creating a funding pool specifically for sustainability investments; (4) releasing new policy statements; (5) participating in generation of acceptable third-party standards for the industry; (6) sponsoring needed research regarding new materials and processes; (7) determining measurement boundaries, if any, regarding how many upstream levels to be responsible for; and (8) creating a corporate weighting scheme for the multiple sustainability objectives so that tradeoffs can be made appropriately and consistently. In addition, Gattiker found that "a sales-oriented approach was found to be counterproductive. After all, causing a user to adopt a product that does not meet cost or performance requirements is a short-term victory at best. Instead, the program managers' advocacy role is mainly one of generating interest and providing information (such as cost, performance, environmental attributes and health effects), as well as materials for user trials" (Gattiker 2006, 3).

Two additional considerations in overcoming resistance to sustainability efforts are perceived practicality of the sustainability effort and perceived connection to recruiting and retention of top talent. "A hard reality is that some green initiatives do not have an appropriate cost-value tradeoff (or at least one that is capturable) and might need to be abandoned. Green strategies benefit the company in the area of talent retention. The perception is that younger talent makes a potential employer's stance on green issues a key factor in whether to accept a job offer" (Ashenbaum 2008, 6). Internal customers may find the sustainability effort to be more credible if green efforts that are proven to be detrimental to performance are actually abandoned by the organization rather than being forced upon internal customers when the evidence is overwhelming against the change.

Top-Down Execution

Hershauer has previously identified three necessary steps to ensure top management involvement and communication.

> To get started, a supply management group should take 3 basic steps. Step 1 is to create a corporate executive-level position or team for supply management environmental sustainability.

Step 2 is to include sustainability management tools in the strategic sourcing process to guide spend area managers on how they should interact with suppliers regarding environmental sustainability (depending on the criticality of the relationship). Training programs for commodity managers and suppliers will be essential to this step. Training should include concepts such as creating supplier code of conduct, creating a "green" purchasing policy, revising supplier scorecards to reflect environmental sustainability processes and goals and initiating audited environmental management systems (EMS) similar to those developed by ISO.[2]

Step 3 is to establish a plan for encouraging and introducing supply chain innovations such as joining or forming a leading industry-based eco-friendly association such as the Electronic Industry Citizenship Coalition,[3] establishing a GHG baseline and have suppliers work to reduce their annual emissions year over year, and exploring life-cycle, industry-level supply-chain solutions. (Hershauer 2008, 3–4)

These steps require top-down commitment and communication. Common approaches to the top-down execution found by Gattiker, Tate, and Carter (2008) were (1) establishing a leadership team of the CPO with other business function leaders; (2) using independent third-party auditors; (3) creating a holistic risk assessment of the supply base; and (4) creating top-level contingency plans for failures. Ashenbaum (2008) suggested that a top-down approach should include the creation of a cross-functional leadership team, the creation of policies and governance, and the creation of a common sustainability scorecard.

Take Specific Actions and Demonstrate Success

A common thread woven throughout the reports from CAPS Research is that specific actions must be initiated and success must be demonstrated in order to accomplish sustainability buy-in from both internal customers and the supply base. The key to this is a top-level openness to innovations and approval of trial-and-error changes in the area of sustainability. The CPO is in the pivotal position to encourage and monitor the success of such innovations. Gattiker (2006) provides an excellent example of what a successfully executed action plan might look like using two environmental purchasing program managers to scan the market for materials and technologies. These managers serve as advocates for changes in materials and technologies that are more environmentally friendly based on a corporate environmental purchasing policy created at the executive level. Although departments must consider the suggestions, adoption is totally voluntary based on a full evaluation of price, quality, performance of functions, and availability as well as environmental, health, and equity issues.

Although models for more complex analyses such as total cost of ownership and life-cycle analyses do exist, the point is that most organizational cultures are not open to starting with such models for sustainability innovations. Initial efforts must generally be more transparent to both internal customers and suppliers. Several recommended actions can be gleaned from the studies by Ashenbaum (2008), Gattiker (2006), Gattiker, Tate, and Carter (2008), and Hershauer (2008):

- Search for suppliers ranked near the top in independent sustainability ratings.

- Ask for percentage of recycled material in products received.

- Ask for a summary of green initiatives.

- Ask for proof of year-over-year improvements in sustainability metrics.

- Ask for self-reports of sustainability efforts through existing supplier information portals.

- Update supplier scorecards to include a sustainability factor in addition to the typical cost, quality, and delivery dimensions.

- Include sustainability factors in new requests for proposals.

- Start with a visible and successful project.

- Initially provide both green and nongreen alternatives for internal customers.

- Provide well-qualified credible trainers for use of new materials.

- Use suppliers with a recycling commitment.

- Take advantage of new green products and services that are being introduced into the marketplace daily.

- Use standards from independent third-party organizations rather than establish unique organizational ones.

While traditional process improvement approaches would suggest beginning with a single pilot study to demonstrate success, gaining sustainability buy-in from throughout an organization will require the inclusion of a cross-section of suppliers and products and services in initial programs to demonstrate the corporate commitment at all levels and to learn about challenges that may differ by industry, product, and service. Supplier maturity regarding sustainability will also continue to differ by the industry represented by the supplier. Example case studies have been reported by Flynn (2009) and Gattiker (2009). The experiences in these two organizations are consistent with the general guidance provided in this chapter. Their stories are useful in understanding the specific actions required and possible outcomes.

The Road Ahead

As the sustainability movement moves beyond the current early adoption phase to maturity, the role of the chief purchasing officer will continue to expand to include the entire global supply web that an organization draws from and influences. These connections will need to be through high-level executive commitments and various industry associations and third-party auditing groups. In addition, CPOs will need to be actively engaged in encouraging and understanding the setting of standards that influence the long-term viability of the firm. The cooperation between the supply side of an organization and the market side will also become increasingly important as society and regulators understanding the implications of life-cycle analyses and total cost of ownership models.

References

Ashenbaum, B. 2008. *"Green" Corporate Strategies: Issues and Implementation from the Supply Management Perspective*. Tempe, Ariz.: CAPS Research.

Esty, Daniel, and Andrew Winston. 2006. *Green to Gold*. New Haven, Conn.: Yale University Press.

Flynn, A. 2009. *The Greening of Expedited Packaging: A U.S. Postal Service and Supplier Collaboration*. Tempe, Ariz.: CAPS Research.

Gattiker, T. 2006. *Environmental Purchasing for Indirect Materials*. Tempe, Ariz.: CAPS Research.

Gattiker, T. 2009. *ISO 14000 at Veris Industries*. Tempe, Ariz.: CAPS Research.

Gattiker, T., W. Tate, and C. R. Carter. 2008. *Supply Management's Strategic Role in Environmental Practices*. Tempe, Ariz.: CAPS Research.

Hershauer, J. 2008. *Process Guide for Supply Management Environmental Sustainability*. Tempe, Ariz.: CAPS Research.

Notes

1 Electronic Industry Citizenship Coalition, "Electronic Industry Code of Conduct," version 3.0 2009, http://www.eicc.info/PDF/EICC%20Code%20 of%20Conduct%20English.pdf

2 http://www.iso.org

3 http://www.eicc.info

CHAPTER 11

Sustainable Marketing and Marketing Sustainability

Eric J. Arnould and Melea Press

This chapter provides a basic understanding of the nascent relationship between marketing and sustainability. In this chapter we introduce and clarify several terminological distinctions and marketing issues that pertain to sustainability. We provide examples from industry to illustrate the discussion. Specifically, we discuss sustainable marketing, marketing sustainability, the sustainable marketing organization, and sustainable consumer behavior.

Introduction

The aim of this chapter is to provide a baseline understanding of the relationship between marketing and sustainability. We are most concerned with sustainable marketing, or aligning organizational processes and goals with general principles of sustainable business practice; marketing sustainability, how an organization carefully goes about communicating their sustainability goals, successes, and challenges; the sustainable marketing organization, which is an organization that takes on a profound sustainability initiative and must adjust to new goals; and sustainable consumer behavior, which describes the ways that consumers engage with and think about sustainability.

What Is Sustainable Marketing?

Sustainable marketing is an approach to marketing that ideally aligns internal organizational processes and organizes resources that create value for stakeholders (e.g., owners, shareholders, employees, value chain partners) and through which the external natural and social environments are enriched by the activities of the firm. This approach is used most effectively by organizations that have clearly stated values and goals for their desired effect on their own economic viability as well as on the natural and social environments they operate within. A lack of clarity and integration of organizational, environmental, and community goals constrains successful sustainable marketing.

The term "sustainable marketing" applies when an organization takes the perspective that it operates within a finite resource system and thus has a responsibility to its current and future stakeholders to make strategic decisions for the long-term benefit of the entire system. There are several common frameworks that organizations use to develop sustainable strategies. Some sustainability frameworks place value on incorporating the costs of ecosystem services into operations; some try to mimic natural systems in new product development and operations; some try to minimize the firm's overall carbon footprint; and some try to change technologies they deploy in order to enhance rather than diminish natural resources. In addition, there are different ways to approach the concept of sustainability itself, for example, as a resource scarcity problem, an issue of integrity and morality, or as a normative guide to conduct (Thompson 2010).

Sustainable marketing is a process, not a state; marketing is undertaken in the service of sustainability goals. This process commits a firm to make continuous improvements toward the goal of increasing the resilience of the social environment and restoring the natural environment it operates within, in addition to thriving as an economic entity. Actions an organization might take toward greater sustainability include increasing operational efficiencies, for example, by deploying lean manufacturing principles. The process often includes a commitment to reducing use of virgin raw materials and increasing use of recycled, recaptured, and repurposed materials. Firms develop new profit centers by closing loops in their operations that reduce waste and capture these repurposed materials. Sustainable marketing commits a firm to reduce the discharge of wastes into the natural and social environment that are hazardous to health or compromise future environmental, community, or economic viability. Achieving zero negative net impacts is an ideal but not realistic goal under current conditions.

Sustainable marketing differs from conventional marketing in its holistic approach to decision making, monitoring, and evaluating organizational actions and consequences. That is, when an organization commits to sustainable marketing, overarching sustainability goals become the guiding force behind all operational decisions at all levels of the organization. Sustainable marketing also differs from conventional marketing in its commitment to rendering organizational processes transparent to stakeholders, enlisting multiple stakeholders in value creation, and in its concern with rendering product life cycles and value chains benign in their effects on natural and social environments. Sustainable marketing will often take on the triumvirate of the triple-bottom-line approach to business and to business reporting; that is, its stakeholder communications may include information about the environment, society, and the economic viability of the firm.

Belz and Peattie (2009) see sustainable marketing as a macromarketing concept insofar as macromarketing is concerned with the effects of marketing on whole systems, such as institutions, value chains, or industries rather than with dyads of exchange partners as in traditional marketing theory and practice. They also see sustainable marketing as involving major changes in outlook and activities on the part of both producers and consumers, taking on the triple-bottom-line approach. We concur that sustainable marketing requires adopting a new paradigm that embraces the whole system as a working unit.

For example, in contrast with the classic tactical marketing mix elements of price, place, product, and promotion, a sustainable marketing strategy might adopt four other tactical dimensions involving, first, customer solutions that go beyond product or service-based benefits to providing triple-bottom-line benefits that address consumers' societal or environmental concerns; second, a commitment to customer costs that incorporate the social and environmental costs of products throughout the product life cycle; third, customer communications, which entails ideas of firm transparency; and, finally, convenience, which means that firms go beyond conceptions of customer exchanges focused only on sales or even customer lifetime value to approaches that incorporate access, sharing, and alternative models of product use and disposition (Belz and Peattie 2009, 33).

Large organizations as well as small ones have embraced sustainable marketing. Walmart has embraced a multipoint program that incorporates more sustainably sourced and more environmentally benign products in its inventory. Walmart also has an entire section of their website dedicated to "Green Living," where they feature articles about living more sustainably and saving money through wasting less, and suggest products that are "earth friendly."[1] While Walmart has been both criticized and praised for their embrace of sustainability, it continues to develop expertise in sustainable marketing, recently experimenting with increased local sourcing of produce, for example, to reduce transport-related carbon emissions.

Nonprofits are an especially important feature of the sustainable marketing landscape, typically providing third-party certification and monitoring for private-sector firms' sustainable marketing efforts. For example, the Marine Stewardship Council (MSC) was created in 1996 by Unilever, one of the world's largest buyers of frozen fish, together with the World Wildlife Fund. It is now a fully independent, global charitable organization. The MSC has developed a labeling scheme for sustainable seafood products that provides incentives for fisheries to be managed sustainably. Once a fishery has been certified, strict guidelines govern use of the MSC logo. Use of the MSC logo on fishery products is only permitted where there has been independent verification that the product originated from an MSC-certified fishery. Through their certification and labeling programs, MSC helps organizations, including big retailers such as Walmart, with their sustainable marketing. The cost of certifying a fishery is $20,000 to $100,000 or more, depending on the size of the fishery. However, these costs may be offset by the opportunities that certification creates for firms. These opportunities include reduced exposure to critical activism, financial risk reduction, market share retention, or avoidance of future regulations. There are also opportunities for revenue enhancement through product differentiation from farmed fish, for which the environmental costs are increasingly publicized, and through increased market share, premium pricing, and the public relations benefits of MSC branding (CCIF 2002, 28–29). A good example of sustainable marketing is provided by Burgerville, USA, a regional fast-food chain headquartered in Tacoma, Washington, discussed briefly in a short case that follows.

Burgerville, USA

Burgerville, USA can be classified as a sustainable marketing organization, but more importantly, sustainability is a key element of their marketing strategy. Burgerville is a fast-food restaurant with a commitment to developing their employees' skills and goals, minimizing the negative environmental impacts of the business, and contributing to the communities in which they are located, as well as to corporate growth and profitability. Burgerville pays close attention to its entire value chain, working closely with producers to locally source as much of their inputs as possible. For example, they purchase locally sourced seasonal produce throughout the year; they are famous for seasonal berry milkshakes and Walla Walla onion rings. One of Burgerville's biggest marketing and sourcing victories came in working with Country Natural Beef to increase beef supplies. The initial problem was that the ranchers could not provide Burgerville with the quantity it needed. Instead of giving up on local sourcing, Burgerville worked with ranchers to help them get their operations to a scale that Burgerville could rely on. After eight years of efforts, Burgerville started buying the consortium's beef. The process took longer than expected, but customer response to this marketing/sourcing effort has been enthusiastic. Interestingly, Burgerville management was not sure what customer response to the local sourcing initiatives would be, but it is clear from favorable press and robust economic returns that customers have been enthusiastic (Leahy 2007).

Burgerville also works with partners to procure wind power and to recycle and compost their waste materials. A good example of Burgerville's commitment to operational sustainability is their waste diversion programs. The company worked with a small local start-up firm to develop a successful biodiesel production and marketing program to handle the massive amounts of waste cooking oil from the stores. In addition, 39 Burgerville locations with access to commercial services are composting, recycling, or both, and 21 locations offer customers the option to sort their waste in the dining rooms or employees will sort waste collected from tables. In 2008, Burgerville was already more than 50 percent of the way toward the ultimate 85 percent diversion goal (BioCycle 2010).

As part of their internal marketing program, Burgerville offers all employees affordable health care, and they have programs in place to increase employee leadership skills. The chain pays at least 90 percent of health care premiums for employees who work at least 20 hours a week. The company claims that this contribution to the community "leg" of the sustainability "stool" resulted in savings by cutting turnover, boosting sales, and improving productivity (Needleman 2009). Burgerville communicates ongoing sustainability efforts on their website, which has details about their environmental and social endeavors.[2] Burgerville leadership also speak about their sustainability efforts at sustainability and industry conferences.

What Is Marketing Sustainability?

Marketing sustainability is an ongoing demonstration that an organization has made commitments toward general sustainability goals. Ideally, sustainability goals would be understood and worked on by every employee in the organization, enunciated in every piece of internal and external communication the organization produces, and incorporated into every product the organization makes and the practices it instills.

Marketing sustainability is an approach to interacting with internal and external stakeholders in ways that deliver resources, provide benefits, and enrich immediate stakeholders, the natural environment, and the social environment in which such interactions occur. Products, services, ideas, and experiences may all be sustainably marketed, but just as a market orientation affects the entire firm, so does marketing sustainability. The organization must integrate these goals throughout the product life cycle from cradle to grave, or in more recent closed loop thinking, from cradle to cradle.

Marketing of sustainability differs from the conventional approach to defining and conveying market offerings by adopting a future orientation such that the consequences of marketing activities today do not adversely affect the ability of people in the future to meet their needs. Transparency measures, corporate social responsibility initiatives, and sustainability reports are one way to market sustainability. These have strengths and weaknesses. They can provide a clear structure for reporting certain agreed-upon metrics. However, reports are often voluntary and not independently verified. They also provide a venue for increased and sometimes ill-informed or biased stakeholder scrutiny.

An organization that is interested in marketing sustainability should be cautious not to make false or exaggerated claims about their efforts. Skepticism, cynicism, and a desire for transparency on the part of stakeholders can make some organizations fearful about marketing their sustainability efforts. However, positioning efforts in terms of an ongoing journey, clearly pointing to both successes and failures, and adopting transparency about the process will help with truthful marketing of sustainability and will favor the long-term success of this approach. Good examples of the mixed results that may accrue to organizations from marketing sustainability are included in our case study on Clorox's Green Works brands.

Marketing Sustainability: Clorox Green Works

Clorox, a traditional marketer of fast-moving consumer nondurable cleaning products, recently dedicated itself to improving its pro-environmental positioning. In January 2008, Clorox launched its first new brand in 20 years, a collection of natural cleaning products called Green Works. But the launch of Green Works does not necessarily mean that Clorox has become a sustainable marketing organization because this would require an internal commitment to sustainable process improvements in the use of raw materials and energy. In addition, Clorox still makes conventional products such as Formula 409 cleaner, which contains 2-butoxyethanol, a substance that is readily absorbed through the skin and is routinely screened out by institutions with environmentally preferable purchasing screens on cleaning products.

It does mean that Clorox has embraced the so-called green marketplace, and management has realized that certain market segments care about what is in their cleaners because of concerns about toxicity, allergies, or downstream environmental impacts of waste cleaning products. Clorox marketing executives had noticed that the 1 percent market share held by green niche brands such as Method and Seventh Generation seemed to belie survey results that have shown for many years that slim majorities of consumers are theoretically interested in buying more sustainable and healthier products. Management decided this was an underexploited market.[3] Clorox identified three reasons consumers were not following through on their pro-environmental attitudinal preferences: concerns about effectiveness, expense (most environmentally friendly cleaners cost twice as much as conventional ones), and inconvenience (in the past, niche products tended to be available only at local cooperative and natural food stores). Pricing and distribution (availability) considerations fall plainly within the traditional domain of marketing action.

In response to this market opportunity, Clorox developed products that were 99 percent petrochemical-free and matched or beat standard cleaners in consumer tests of effectiveness. Thanks to Clorox's volume production capabilities and leverage with suppliers, their new products could be priced at a 20 percent to 25 percent premium to conventional products.

Green Works is one of the most successful launches of a new cleaning brand in recent memory. In 2008, Green Works held more than a 40 percent share of the natural home cleaning market. The first-year success of their product single-handedly grew the natural cleaning product market by more than 80 percent by selling Green Works through their current distribution chain in more than 24,000 stores alongside their regular household cleaning products.

Is Green Works really green? Clorox claims that each one of the five cleaners is at least 99 percent "natural." However, the use of this term is unregulated; hence, its use may raise doubts in the minds of critical observers and increasingly savvy consumers. Nonetheless, most ingredients in the cleaners can be "naturally derived." According to the label, alkyl polyglucoside comes from coconut oil and ethanol and glycerin from corn oil. While this kind of sourcing is potentially more sustainable than using petroleum-derived alternatives, serious issues related to rainforest habitat destruction in Borneo as a result of harvesting coconut oil have been raised, and there are environmental and food policy concerns associated with corn-based ethanol. This highlights the complexity of issues associated with so-called green products. Consumers may harbor concerns about product toxicity to humans, pets, and the environment, but they are also concerned about social and environmental issues associated with the entire value chain for green products.

According to their website, Green Works sets stringent standards to ensure that its cleaners are at least 99 percent natural—that is, derived from renewable resources, biodegradable, and free of petrochemicals. Green Works attributes the remaining 1 percent to a preservative and green coloring and claims the company is working to find alternatives. Clorox has committed to transparency about the Green Works line by listing ingredients on the product and providing responses to questions at their blog and through their *Shades of Green* journal. Critics argue that because no industry standard definitions currently exist for natural cleaners, Green Works is simply deeming itself green against its own internal standards without external verification.

The Green Works case has implications for those interested in the increasing incidence of co-branding alliances of for-profit firms with nongovernmental organizations (NGOs). Green Works products qualified for the EPA's "Design for the Environment" label, certifying that they are free of the most toxic chemicals. But Clorox wanted to go further. The logo of the respected environmental NGO the Sierra Club also appears on all Green Works labels. In return for its endorsement, the Sierra Club receives an undisclosed fee based partly on Green Works sales. Within the Sierra Club, the reaction to this co-branding deal was contentious. It was not clear how Sierra Club leadership came to the conclusion that Green Works lived up to its pro-environmental claims. Charges were leveled against executive director Carl Pope's executive committee for selling out the good name of the Sierra Club. The decision generated a lot of reaction from members of the Sierra Club, some of whom asked for a national referendum on the Clorox decision. Chapter leaders in northern Michigan resigned over the deal.

The co-branding alliance of the Sierra Club with Clorox underlines both the potential upside for major brands enlisting endorsements from environmental organizations and the danger for nonprofit environmental groups of endorsing profit-making companies' products. For Clorox, the co-branding move may be all upside, but if independent tests undermine its product claims, it risks a cynical backlash. For the Sierra Club, co-branding puts at risk its independent reputation, but it appears to have been a harbinger of a new direction for environmental organizations formerly committed to a purely preservationist model of environmental defense.

On another note, despite their commitment to the natural product line, Green Works' critical stakeholders may question how much Clorox has done to internalize the sustainability commitment expressed in their marketing communications into their research and development, operations, and manufacturing. If this commitment had infiltrated the entire organization, there might never have been a controversy or issue with the Sierra Club endorsement. While Green Works may be "better" than a petroleum-based or chemical alternative in terms of toxicity and sourcing, it is far from perfect.[4]

What Is a Sustainable Marketing Organization?

A sustainable marketing organization (SMO) is committed to ongoing, measurable improvements in its relationships with its external natural and social environments, and to internal organizational processes consistent with general sustainability goals. Much like a market-oriented organization integrates the needs of the customer into every aspect of the organization, an SMO integrates sustainability goals and values into every aspect of the organization and uses this orientation as a tool to help with every decision the organization makes.

SMOs will adopt suitable goals and values that should be diffused into every aspect of the organization. Ideally, these values and goals are repeated often and known and understood by every stakeholder of the organization, including those throughout the value chain. Thus, an SMO will have the ability to address sustainability issues throughout its value chain with transparency and confidence.

A sustainable marketing organization is one in which sense-making capabilities for capturing and internal dissemination of knowledge are oriented to the detection of unmet needs in the immediate stakeholder community it can best serve. This is done while capturing information about the external natural and social environments as well, with the goal of mutual enrichment. The SMO is characterized by smarter, more efficient, less wasteful use of all resources that contribute to the delivery of market offerings.

In an ideal sense, there are a few key differences in orientation between a sustainable marketing organization and a conventional marketing organization. In the SMO, important economic profits are viewed as means to achieve sustainability goals rather than ends in themselves. Also, the SMO firm is driven by the overarching goal of achieving organizational resilience both in the short- and long-term time horizons.

A sustainable marketing organization stretches natural resource use by striving to increase the productivity of a given unit of virgin resource by a measurable, meaningful amount while at the same time seeking to identify and incorporate alternative recycled or renewable resources into its operations. This commitment addresses issues of overharvesting and resource depletion. It also commits to the use of closed-loop production systems so that waste is treated as a resource and reused. SMOs also seek to replace goods with services. They may lease the services provided by products, rather than selling products themselves. Thus, when a product becomes obsolete or outlives its useful life, the company has maintained ownership over the product and is prepared to take it back for recycle or remanufacture. In other words, the end of the product life cycle has been built into the business plan. SMOs invest in restoring, maintaining, and expanding ecosystems to sustain society's needs. Through these actions they also avoid regulation and customer cynicism and discontent (Willard 2009, 8).

Ten Steps for Transitioning to a Sustainable Marketing Organization

Transitioning to a sustainable marketing organization must proceed incrementally. But imagine these steps as pieces of a pie rather than sequential stages. In step 1, the firm develops a sustainability policy as a core goal.

In step 2, the firm builds a long-term commitment to a sustainability ethic at the top of the organization. In step 3, the firm identifies and supports sustainability champions within the firm and across functional areas. In step 4, concrete measures are taken to educate employees about the value of sustainability in driving down costs, increasing resilience, and adding value to product-service offerings. Some, like Walmart, may wish to make a personal sustainability commitment a part of every employee's formal performance review process. In step 5, the firm initiates and sustains a dialog with government and nongovernmental sustainability interest groups about industry best practices and government regulations. Regulatory compliance is a must and overperformance is a plus. In step 6, the firm develops an assertive sustainability action program integrated into the strategic planning process. In step 7, functional areas or departments are brought together by leadership to work together to respond flexibly to emerging sustainability challenges. Competing intrafirm interests such as engineering, marketing, and sales must work together to develop solutions to these challenges. Rewarding real engagement in the sustainability journey can induce employee enthusiasm and creative problem solving. In step 8, the commitment to sustainability is backed with money allocated to research and development, marketing communications, and sales to implement sustainable action programs. In step 9, marketing communications conveys to customers what the firm is doing. This is not simple in today's climate of suspicion toward corporate sustainability initiatives and may require enlisting third-party certifying organizations in the communications effort. In step 10, the customers' response to sustainability initiatives is monitored through an active market research program. The dynamic nature of the sustainability market space requires regular monitoring and flexible adaptation (McDaniel and Rylander 1993; see also Epstein 2008).

Marketing departments and officers may take the initiative in bringing the sustainability concerns of customers to the attention of management as well as serving as advocates for this transition. Marketers can attempt to heighten sustainability awareness among personnel while focusing on those issues most germane to the firm's product or service lines. It is essential to teach the lesson that sustainability is a cross-functional issue and is simultaneously an intra- and interfirm (value chain) issue. As integrator/implementer, marketing units and officers can bring cross-functional teams together to tackle product life cycle–related sustainability challenges. Marketers can also initiate changes in business practices such as instigating formal cradle to cradle, natural step, design for environment, or other procedures into product/service development, regularly including sustainability issues in consumer research, and incorporating sustainability attributes into marketing communications campaigns (Fuller 1999, 115–16).

As with any strategic orientation, there are unexpected outcomes for SMOs from taking on a sustainable marketing orientation. Some of these are positive, and some are dangers. First, the main unexpected positive outcome of taking on a sustainable marketing orientation is that employees often become deeply engaged with the organization in ways they had not been previously. This kind of employee engagement often leads to greater creativity and innovation in the organization. As the organizational commitment literature suggests, greater commitment to the workplace leads to positive word of mouth, fewer missed days of work, and greater employee productivity when at work.

Second, one must consider the potential pitfalls. One concern organizations have when adopting a sustainability initiative is that their journey will be scrutinized by customers and other constituents. While we are used to seeing organizations engaged in "greenwashing," we now see them engaging in "sustainability washing." That is, constituents perceive that they make minor efforts toward their stated sustainability initiative but do not really commit to the sustainability journey as does a truly sustainable marketing organization.

Contemporary customers are skeptical and often cynical. They are interested in transparency that goes beyond numbers and are often willing to spend time researching organizations. Because of the amount of information available online, thoughtful, careful, honest, and transparent organizations may set themselves up for controversy if they preach greater sustainability than they are actually engaging in. This is why we suggest that organizations take on sustainability initiatives cautiously, that they state their successes and set-backs as part of a journey toward greater sustainability, and that they take care not to overpromise and underdeliver. InterfaceFLOR provides an excellent example of a sustainable marketing organization.

A Sustainable Marketing Organization: InterfaceFLOR

InterfaceFLOR, is the world's largest manufacturer of modular carpet in the world and a leading example of a sustainable marketing organization. The founder, Ray Anderson, experienced an epiphany in 1994 after which he could no longer run his business as he had for the previous two decades. In videos available online, he has sometimes referred to himself as a "plunderer of the earth," and since his epiphany has worked toward the goal of eliminating "any negative impact Interface has on the environment by 2020."[5] The firm has also worked with organizations in their supply chain and around the world to help other corporate leaders with their own sustainability journeys.

As people at Interface began working toward becoming a more sustainable organization, they recognized the importance of the global ecosystem to the existence of their business and to the future of the world. The company's ultimate goal now is to become a "restorative enterprise," meaning that Interface will ultimately make a net positive contribution to the global ecosystem.[6]

InterfaceFLOR distinguishes its sustainability initiative from a green initiative. Sustainability highlights a systems perspective that affects operations and guides decision making at all levels of the organization, including relationships with suppliers and customers.[7] While Interface fields a team to drive and measure progress toward greater sustainability, the sustainability goals set for the organization are embraced, enacted, and pushed by all employees.

Interface lists 10 areas that the company focuses on to achieve their sustainability goals. These include reevaluating raw materials; using bio-mimicry; working toward carbon neutrality; combating climate change; engaging employees; reevaluating energy use; using life cycle assessments; eliminating waste; closing the loop by turning waste into valuable, reusable products; working with supply chain partners; and addressing greenhouse emissions associated with transportation. These areas seem to provide a basis for innovation, measurement, and action. Examples are discussed briefly below.

Innovation

A bio-based raw material involves the search for alternatives to oil-based materials, especially renewable resources. Interface is currently making commercial modular carpet out of polylactic acid fibers derived from maize and other starch containing agricultural plant materials and waste products. These fibers can be produced without using heavy metals and with less water than petrochemical polymers, and the waste products can be composted.[8]

Biomimicry uses nature as an inspiration for sustainable designs and processes. Interface has used this principle to help develop lines of carpet tiles that incorporate "organized chaos" into their design, and thus fit together in seemingly random and seamless patterns, a critical need for carpet tiles that are not all replaced simultaneously. Interface also used biomimicry to develop a carpet tile adhesive-free installation system that releases no volatile organic compounds and can be installed without damaging underlayment.[9]

Action

Interface engages employees and tries to improve their lives. One way they do this is by creating a healthier and safer work environment through actions already discussed. The company sees benefits for their organization from these efforts in the form of increased productivity, higher retention rates, and a culture of innovation. Employee engagement is measured and tracked with a yearly survey of all employees. Interface organized a program called Cool CO_2mmute, where employees calculate their own carbon emissions from commuting, and Interface splits the cost of the offsets with them. In addition, since 2002, Interface has calculated and offset the carbon emissions from company cars and, since 1997, from business air travel.[10]

Measurement

Life cycle assessment (LCA) involves detailed analysis and evaluation of raw material extraction and processing, manufacturing, transportation and distribution, use, reuse, maintenance, and recycling or final disposal with the aim of reducing raw materials use, cost, and waste and increasing recycling, reuse, and value-added production. LCA is applied to all of Interface's products.[11]

Interface developed Mission Zero, which commits them to eliminate any negative impact the company has on the environment by 2020. Part of this is taken care of by reducing their carbon emissions and purchasing carbon offsets for those they cannot reduce. Interface also started a program called Cool Carpet in 2003. This program measures the carbon footprint of the carpet using LCA, which looks at every part of the carpet's life cycle from raw materials to manufacture, shipping, and disposal. Interface then purchases carbon offsets to balance the footprint.[12]

In working toward its sustainability goal, Interface not only engages every employee in the organization, the company also provides information and opportunities for every partner in their value chain to engage in sustainability efforts. In addition, Interface is at the forefront of manufacturing and climate change policy issues, and continuously pushes for proactive management of all aspects of organizational operations.

What Is Sustainable Consumer Behavior?

Sustainable consumer behaviors (acquisition, use, and disposition processes) are those that mirror and complement the behaviors of sustainable businesses. Such behaviors seek to minimize the use of virgin natural resources; increase the use of recycled, reused, and repurposed resources; reward value chains organized around sustainable principles through ongoing exchange; and engage in cocreative processes of value production with sustainable marketing organizations.

From a managerial perspective, key differences between sustainable consumer behavior and a conventional understanding of consumer behavior are that sustainable consumer behaviors explore the benefits of market offerings that emphasize use value over display or status values and look for ways to transcend common property challenges. For example, consumers interested in more sustainable consumption take account of a wide range of criteria in their purchases of food, cleaning products, toiletries, furniture, and even building products. Common examples are preferences for fair trade and organic food and for environmentally friendly cleaning products, for example, Seventh Generation or Green Works products, and toiletries that are not tested on animals. Some consumers are experimenting with such novel resource-sharing schemes as car and bicycle sharing offered by either commercial or governmental entities. Some consumers also favor local, independent shops and producers, for example, Burgerville, USA. Studies in both North America and Europe find that consumers are increasingly willing to compromise on price, brand, convenience, and, in some cases, product performance in order to ensure that their purchases are in line with sustainability principles (McDonald et al. 2009, 140).

To contend with common property resource depletion problems, sustainable consumer behavior looks to various third-party verifiers (e.g., forestry products certified by the Forestry Stewardship Council and seafood certified by the Marine Stewardship Council) to support a sustainability journey. Rather than just focusing on the immediate benefits in making purchase decisions, consumers also take the product life-cycle costs and effects into account, including conditions of sourcing, lifetime energy requirements, and disposal facilities.

This being said, consumers most often do not apply sustainability principles consistently across product categories. In the end, they may sacrifice sustainability attributes for more conventional considerations (Bartiaux 2008). In short, sustainable consumption practices in some sectors and some countries are well developed and actively pursued. In other sectors, this is not the case (McDonald et al. 2009, 143).

While product/service offerings have increased dramatically, problems of product/service availability, choice, and information constrain more sustainable consumer behavior (Newholm and Shaw 2007), which suggests many opportunities for marketers to provide effective information and better product choices and improve the distribution of more sustainable product lines.

In terms of information, it seems that rather than desiring detailed analysis of all the possible sustainable purchasing criteria, consumers interested in sustainability want simple advice from trusted, independent sources, such as the British website which.com, the Fair Trade label, or perhaps, as in the Clorox example, the Sierra Club. These days, third-party certifications are often necessary to create a climate of trust around firm sustainability claims. In the absence of this sort of information, consumers may ignore green or ethical criteria altogether, or simplify the process into a "buy/do not buy" decision. Overall, the simpler the information supplied (providing it is from a trusted source), the more likely it is to be incorporated into sustainable consumer decision making (McDonald et al. 2009, 143). However, the proliferation of sustainability certification schemes and labels including private-label schemes, such as those being developed by Walmart (Gunther 2009) and Tesco, are currently complicating the information environment for consumers. That being said, the value of information should not be overemphasized. There is not, as some have assumed in the past, a linear relationship between information provision and more sustainable consumer behavior, and consumers make their own assumptions and assessments of risk (see Szasz 2007).

Many firms and consulting companies are still promulgating general segmentation schemes to try to profile the green or sustainable lifestyle consumer (Ginsberg and Bloom 2004).[13] While these schemes may have their uses, the effort to develop a general segmentation scheme is not the best approach to encourage more sustainable consumption. This is because marketing sustainable consumption is not like the marketing of other goods and services and cannot be approached in a traditional way. This is clearly seen by the longstanding and overall low levels of uptake of green and other sustainable products and services and the enduring gap between pro-environmental values and purchase and consumption behaviors.

There are two main reasons for this. One lies in the nature of consumer lifestyles. There are two aspects to the lifestyles issue. First is the finding that contemporary lifestyles rather than being coherent and unified are instead partitioned. Thus, a young mother may be highly motivated to ensure that her new baby consumes environmentally benign, locally sourced, chemical-free, organic foods for health reasons, but she may at the same time drive a large, gas-guzzling, polluting, and nonrecyclable SUV because of misplaced concerns for the safety of that same child.

Moreover, it is quite evident that consumers will rarely accept products and services that make their domestic routines more "rigid" in temporal or spatial scheduling, or that they feel are regressive in terms of everyday standards of comfort and convenience (Shove 2003). They will instead prefer those products and services that give them greater flexibility in performing domestic tasks. For example, promotion of resource pooling as an environmentally or socially beneficial alternative to divisible and privatized consumption is likely to face opposition because it makes life less flexible and constrains individuals' alternative uses of their time and other resources (Spaargaren and van Vliet 2000, 67).

The second, more challenging issue is that much consumer behavior is organized in terms of routines. More formally stated, much behavior falls into the domain of what social scientists sometimes call practical reason (Sahlins 1976), practical consciousness (Giddens 1991), or dispersed practice (Warde 2005). These are matters of habit and are not directly influenced by inputs of novel information. Thus, in affluent consumer cultures when we are cold we turn a thermostat; when in the dark, we flip a switch to light a room; when bored, we power up an electronic diversion; when dirty, we jump in a warm bath; and when short of bread, we hop in a transport conveyance powered by nonrenewable energies to run to the store, and so on. Most of us never give these actions a second thought; they are mindless; and we are disconnected from the shared but largely invisible social and environmental costs of the private benefits we derive from these acts of consumption.

The other main reason why marketing sustainable consumption cannot be approached through traditional segmentation and targeting strategies lies in the way in which many of the goods and services implicated in unsustainable consumption are provided to consumers. A good many products and services depend upon the presence of preexisting expert systems that constrain alternative choices or render them expensive. "Once the citizen-consumer has been 'connected' to the water works, the sewage system or the electricity grid, the consumer has become a 'captive' consumer. Captive consumers cannot just shift from one system to another without losing resources (money, knowledge, skills) that have been invested in the present networks" (Spaargaren and van Vliet 2000, 64). Furthermore, every time a consumer makes use of these expert systems in exchange for money, the systems are reinforced. And it is not just mundane resources such as water, sewer, or power that are implicated. Most products and services are still produced and marketed based on a linear production model that makes it difficult if not impossible to return or recycle obsolete or broken items back into the production process without incurring incremental costs. The loops are not closed; consider the example of used batteries. These expert systems, sunk costs, and incremental costs of change prevent consumers from moving freely between different systems of provisioning, even where other more sustainable options are available, which often enough there are not.

So even if people are striving for more sustainable lifestyles and patterns of domestic consumption, the possibilities offered or not by collective marketing or governmental systems of provisioning are of strategic importance. As Spaagaren and Van Vliet (2000) point out, when concern for more sustainable living encounters low levels of sustainable innovation in systems of provisioning, the result is a lack of sustainable consumer behavior. On the other hand, consumers will only accept more sustainable products and services under the condition that these innovations fit into the overall organization of their households and lifestyles, which, it will be recalled, are partitioned rather than unified (Bartiaux 2008; and Spaargaren and van Vliet 2000, 65). When modestly priced, convenient, and effective sustainable products are offered, such as Burgerville burgers, Interface carpet tiles, or Clorox Green Works, some people will adopt them.

Alternatively, when distributed practices are rendered into integrated practices or when practical consciousness is rendered into discursive consciousness through civic and commercial dialog or through the emergence of communities of practice like those associated with brand or consumption communities (Hobson 2001; Schau, Muniz, and Arnould 2009; Warde 2005), consumers also may be motivated to adopt more sustainable alternative lifestyle practices. Researchers have identified some such sustainable communities of practice within affluent consumer cultures. Thus, voluntary simplicity, downshifting, anticonsumption groups, and slow living each have specific and subtly different meanings and relate to slightly different ethically driven projects associated with more sustainable lifestyles. There is also a national inflection to some of these movements with anticonsumption flourishing in the United Kingdom and France, and slow living finding resonance in Italy. Voluntary simplicity and downshifting seem to have caught the attention of some in the United States (Newholm and Shaw 2007).[14]

As a result of the emergence of these communities of practice, an issue in sustainable consumer behavior concerns whether and to what extent sustainable consumption should be conceived of or promoted as a form of social action. Some argue that the movement of more sustainable products into the mass market risks reducing sustainability to a misguided belief that consumers can shop their way to a better world, a criticism also leveled at fair trade marketing schemes (Dolan 2005). Such thinkers argue that to retain a sense of social action, there needs to be more cocreation of value between producers, retailers, and consumers. This element of social action they see as important to helping to move toward an overall consumer culture in which consumers are willing to contemplate some reduction of overall personal consumption rates in defense of a more sustainable planet and future (Newholm and Shaw 2007, 263).

There have been and will continue to be many failures as well as successes in the sphere of sustainable consumption. Sustainable goods and services can be offered in ways that do not fit contemporary consumers' lifestyles because they adversely affect prevailing standards of comfort, convenience, and propriety. Products and services may also be turned down by consumers because their adoption, use, and maintenance do not fit with the organization of domestic time, space, and lifestyle. Sometimes sustainable products fail at the production line because they are designed and produced from a narrow engineering perspective, such as the early generation of electric cars. Or well-designed products fail because of their mode of provisioning, for example, when consumers are not acquainted with the channels used for car-sharing services, or when they have lost their trust in the electric utility provider (E7 Working Group 2000; and Spaargaren and van Vliet 2000, 72).

Summary

In this chapter, we discussed sustainable marketing, marketing sustainability, the sustainable marketing organization, and sustainable consumer behavior, and we provided explanations and examples for each term. First, we clarified that sustainable marketing must render organizational processes transparent to stakeholders, enlist stakeholders in value creation, and attempt to render product life cycles and value chains benign in their effects on natural and social environments. We suggested that sustainable marketing goes beyond the traditional product, price, place, and promotion to include providing triple-bottom-line benefits, incorporate the social and environmental costs of products throughout the product life cycle, engage in customer cocreation of value and transparency, and create new distribution approaches that incorporate access, sharing, and alternative models of product use and disposition.

Second, we discussed marketing sustainability, the ongoing demonstration that an organization has made commitments toward general sustainability goals. We cautioned organizations against making false or exaggerated claims about their efforts and highlighted the importance of clearly stating successes and failures and being as transparent as possible about the process to facilitate long-term success of this approach.

Next we discussed the sustainable marketing organization (SMO), highlighting its commitment to ongoing, measurable improvements in its relationships with its external natural and social environments as well as to its internal processes. A sustainable marketing organization develops sensemaking capabilities for capturing and internally disseminating sustainability knowledge. Ideally, SMOs adopt goals and values that diffuse into every aspect of the organization and that are known and understood by every stakeholder of the organization, including those throughout the value chain. We identified 10 steps for transitioning to a sustainable marketing organization.

Finally, we discussed sustainable consumer behaviors. These behaviors of acquisition, use, and disposition processes mirror and complement the behaviors of sustainable businesses. Sustainable consumer behaviors explore the benefits of market offerings that emphasize use value over display or status values and look for ways to transcend common property challenges. We highlighted strategies that consumers use to attempt sustainable behaviors, such as car sharing, purchasing locally made products, and buying products that have been third-party certified. We pointed out difficulties in changing consumer behaviors. For example, nonsustainability is built into the systems of provisioning for many consumables. Further, taken-for-granted norms of comfort, convenience, and value are resistant to retrenchment. Finally, there is a dearth of offerings that provide substantial improvements in sustainable qualities.

References

Bartiaux, Françoise. 2008. "Does Environmental Information Overcome Practice Compartmentalisation and Change Consumers' Behaviours?" *Journal of Cleaner Production* 16:1170–80.

Belz, Frank-Martin, and Ken Peattie. 2009. *Sustainability Marketing: A Global Perspective.* West Sussex, UK: John Wiley & Sons.

BioCycle. 2010. "Compostable Cup for Quick Service Chain." *BioCycle* 51, no. 3 (March): 6. http://www.jgpress.com/archives/_free/002036.html.

Conservation and Community Investment Forum (CCIF). 2002. *Analysis of the Status of Current Certification Schemes in Promoting Conservation.* San Francisco: CCIF.

Dolan, Catherine S. 2005. "Fields of Obligation." *Journal of Consumer Culture* 5 (November): 365–89.

Dunn, Collin. 2008. "Introducing Clorox's Green Works Cleaners." *Treehugger,* January 14. http://www.treehugger.com/files/2008/01/clorox-green-works.php.

E7 Working Group. 2000. "Social Trust and the Electricity Industry: An E7 Contribution." E7 Working Group Report, October. Montréal, Canada: E7 Network of Expertise for the Global Environment. http://www.e8.org/upload/File/ST_&_Electricity_Industry.pdf.

Epstein, Marc J. 2008. *Making Sustainability Work.* San Francisco: Berrett-Koehler.

Fuller, Donald A. 1999. *Sustainable Marketing.* Thousand Oaks, Calif.: Sage Publications.

Giddens, A. 1991. *Modernity and Self-Identity: Self and Society in the Late Modern Age*. Cambridge: Polity Press.

Ginsberg, Jill Meredith, and Paul Bloom. 2004. "Choosing the Right Green Marketing Strategy." *MIT Sloan Management Review*, October 15, 79–84.

Gunther, Marc. 2009. "Inside Wal-Mart's Sustainability Index." *GreenBiz*, July 14. http://www.greenbiz.com/blog/2009/07/14/inside-wal-marts-sustainability-index.

Hobson, Kersty. 2001. "Sustainable Lifestyles: Rethinking Barriers and Behaviour Change." In *Exploring Sustainable Consumption*, edited by Maurie J. Cohen and Joseph Murphy, 191–212. Oxford: Pergamon/Elsevier.

Kamenetz, Anya. 2008. "Clorox Goes Green." *Fast Company*, September 1. http://www.fastcompany.com/magazine/128/cleaning-solution.html.

Leahy, Kate. 2007. "Local News, 7/15/2007." *Restaurants & Institutions* 117, no. 11: 55–56.

Lee, Evelyn. 2009. "Is It Green? Clorox Green Works." *Inhabitat*, August 12. http://www.inhabitat.com/2009/08/12/is-it-green-clorox-green-works.

McDaniel, Stephen W., and David H. Rylander. 1993. "Strategic Green Marketing." *Journal of Consumer Marketing* 10, no. 3: 4–10.

McDonald, Seonaidh, Caroline Oates, Maree Thyne, Panayiota Alevizou, and Leigh-Ann McMorland. 2009. "Comparing Sustainable Consumption Patterns Across Product Sectors." *International Journal of Consumer Studies* 33:137–45.

Needleman, Sarah E. 2009. "Burger Chain's Health-Care Recipe." *Wall Street Journal*, August 31, B4. http://online.wsj.com/article/SB125149100886467705.html.

Newholm, Terry, and Deirdre Shaw. 2007. "Studying the Ethical Consumer: A Review of Research." *Journal of Consumer Behaviour* 6 (September–October): 253–70.

Sahlins, Marshall. 1976. *Culture and Practical Reason*. Chicago: University of Chicago Press.

Schau, Hope Jensen, Albert Muniz Jr., and Eric J. Arnould. 2009. "How Brand Communities Create Value." *Journal of Marketing* 73 (September): 30–51.

Shove, Elizabeth. 2003. "Users, Technologies and Expectations of Comfort, Cleanliness and Convenience." *Innovation: The European Journal of Social Sciences*. 16 (June): 193–206.

Siegelbaum, Heidi. 2008. "The Dubious Road to Clorox's New GreenWorks Product Line." The Greenwash Brigade, *American Public Media*, January 21. http://www.publicradio.org/columns/sustainability/greenwash/2008/01/the_dubious_road_to_cloroxs_ne.html.

Spaargaren, Gert, and Bas van Vliet. 2000. "Lifestyles, Consumption and the Environment: The Ecological Modernization of Domestic Consumption." *Environmental Politics* 9 (Spring): 50–76.

Szasz, Andrew. 2007. *Shopping Our Way to Safety: How We Changed from Protecting the Environment to Protecting Ourselves*. Minneapolis: University of Minnesota Press.

Thompson, Paul B. 2010. "What Sustainability Is (And What It Isn't)." In *Pragmatic Sustainability: Theoretical and Practical Tools*, edited by Steven A. Moore, 15–29. New York: Routledge.

Warde, Alan. 2005. "Consumption and Theories of Practice." *Journal of Consumer Culture* 5, no. 2: 131–53.

Willard, Bob. 2009. *The Sustainability Champion's Guidebook*. Gabriola Island, B.C.: New Society Publishers.

Notes

1 http://instoresnow.walmart.com/Sustainability.aspx

2 http://burgerville.com/sustainable-business/

3 See, for example, www.lohas.com

4 Sources for this discussion of Clorox Green Works are Dunn (2008), Kamenetz (2008), Lee (2009), and Siegelbaum (2008).

5 See video on YouTube, http://www.youtube.com/watch?v=1uoRe9vOzec. See also http://www.interfaceglobal.com/Company.aspx

6 http://www.interfaceglobal.com/Sustainability/Our-Journey.aspx

7 http://www.interfaceglobal.com/Sustainability/Sustainability-in-Action.aspx

8 http://www.interfaceglobal.com/Sustainability/Sustainability-in-Action/BioBased-Raw-Materials.aspx

9 http://www.interfaceglobal.com/Sustainability/Sustainability-in-Action/Biomimicry.aspx

10 http://www.interfaceglobal.com/Sustainability/Sustainability-in-Action/Supply-Chain.aspx; and http://www.interfaceglobal.com/Sustainability/Sustainability-in-Action/Employee-Engagement.aspx

11 http://www.interfaceglobal.com/Sustainability/Sustainability-in-Action/Life-Cycle-Assessment.aspx

12 http://www.interfaceglobal.com/Sustainability/Sustainability-in-Action/ Cool-Carpet.aspx

13 See also http://www.lohas.com/

14 See, for example, www.newamericandream.net

CHAPTER 12

Aligning Consumer Decisions and Sustainable Energy Objectives

Energy Efficiency in the Residential Retrofit Market

Charlie Wilson and Hadi Dowlatabadi

Making existing homes more energy efficient is an important challenge for sustainability, and particularly for greenhouse gas emission reduction. Home owners' decisions to retrofit their homes with efficient building envelope and energy system technologies play a crucial role in this challenge. The policy and business communities try to induce and influence these decisions through an "inform, incentivize, assure" approach. This approach has had only limited success in stimulating energy retrofits over the last 30 years despite the apparent cost-effectiveness of energy efficiency. This stands in stark contrast to the ever-growing popularity of amenity retrofits such as remodeled kitchens, loft or basement conversions, and landscaped gardens. Such retrofits received no inducements and often cost more than their energy retrofit counterparts. An investigation of home owners' retrofit decisions helps explains why: amenity retrofits are motivated by emotional, aesthetic, and social signaling characteristics that energy retrofits lack. This points to an unexploited potential for an alternative piggybacking approach to promoting energy efficiency in the home. Such an approach would reduce the effort, cost, and inconvenience of distinct energy retrofit decisions by packaging energy-efficiency measures into amenity retrofits. As well as allowing businesses in the amenities supply chain to differentiate their service offering, this piggybacking approach would also help align policymakers' objectives with home owners' retrofit decisions.

Energy Efficiency in the Home

The year 2010 was historic for energy efficiency in the home: it featured in the State of the Union Address alongside the financial crisis, health care reform, and nuclear disarmament. In President Barak Obama's words: "We should . . . give rebates to Americans who make their homes more energy-efficient" (Obama 2010). The Home Star Energy Retrofit Act submitted to Congress in April 2010 duly established some $6 billion of tax credits to be disbursed over a two-year period to home owners in lump sums of up to $3,000 for appliance and equipment upgrades, and up to $8,000 for whole home retrofits.

Why the interest in energy efficiency in the home? Reducing residential energy use has repeatedly been identified as an important low, or even negative, cost component of a climate change mitigation strategy, which also contributes toward a host of other policy objectives relating to local employment, energy security, air pollution, and health (Metz et al. 2007; Dietz et al. 2009). The residential sector in the United States uses 21 percent of the national energy supply, of which roughly three-quarters is electricity and the remainder natural gas and fuels used directly in the home for heating (EIA 2010). This contributes 21 percent of the United States' CO_2 emissions or 18 percent of total greenhouse gas emissions (EIA 2009).

The energy efficiency of the 1–2 million new homes built each year in the United States can be ratcheted up through regulation, codes, standards, zoning laws, and other policy levers operating mostly at the state or municipal level. However, around 130 million homes have already been built (JCHS 2009a). Houses are also very long-lived physical assets, so the challenge of improving residential energy efficiency primarily concerns retrofits to existing homes.

Around 44 percent of energy used in existing U.S. homes is for space conditioning (heating and cooling) and a further 12 percent for water heating (Gardner and Stern 2008). Efficiency measures, particularly upgrades to homes' building envelopes and energy systems, offer by far the largest potential reductions in household energy use (Gardner and Stern 1995). Weatherization, or sealing and insulating building envelopes, reduces the demand for space conditioning. Weatherization measures include weather-stripping; draft-proofing; cavity insulation; triple-glazed, low-emissivity windows; and energy-efficient doors. Efficient energy systems reduce the energy needed to meet that demand. Energy system measures include high-efficiency furnaces or boilers, programmable thermostats, and hot water tank and pipe insulation. All these technologies are proven, widely available, and cost-effective insofar as their upfront cost is ultimately repaid through energy savings.

The potential energy savings from these types of weatherization and energy system measures throughout the U.S. housing stock is in the ballpark of 30–35 percent of total energy use (Gardner and Stern 2008). This proportion may be considerably higher in older or less efficient homes. This chapter is concerned with how these energy savings can be achieved. Our central argument is that it is essential to align home owners' interests in improving the feel and function of their home with policymakers' interests in promoting energy efficiency, and the business supply chain's interests in offering an attractive value proposition to home owners. At the heart of this alignment challenge lie home owners' decisions to retrofit their homes.

Sustainable business strategists emphasize the importance of aligning the interests of a wide range of stakeholders. In addition to what Esty and Winston (2006) call the consumers and the rule makers, we emphasize the importance of business partners and competitors as a third category of stakeholder. The premise for our argument is that the prevailing policy approach to promoting energy efficiency in the home fails to recognize some important characteristics of home owners' retrofit decisions. This has indirectly reinforced competition and fragmentation rather than partnership between the energy and amenities supply chains. The result is a misalignment between the interests of home owners, policymakers, and businesses.

In developing our argument, we begin by looking at policymakers' assumptions about how best to promote energy efficiency in the home by influencing home owners' retrofit decisions. We argue that the prevailing inform, incentivize, assure approach is of limited success because it fails to account for how retrofit decisions are actually made. We present empirical evidence from our own research to support this argument, drawing out important differences between preretrofit and postretrofit decision characteristics, and between amenity and energy retrofit decisions. Based on our analysis, we develop a specific set of proposals for a piggybacking approach that uses the supply chain for amenity retrofits to promote energy efficiency in the home. Drawing on business strategy and supply chain management expertise, we set out a clear business case based on enhancing the value proposition for retrofitting home owners. Furthermore, we suggest how policymakers can support this value proposition. The result, we argue, is more effective policy for realizing energy savings and the potential to transform the functioning of the residential retrofit market based on an understanding of home owners' needs and decisions.

The key innovation of this chapter is to treat the improvement of residential energy efficiency not as an energy-efficiency challenge but as a retrofit challenge. This simple reframing of the issue allows new business models and service offerings to be explored that align different stakeholders' interests.

In dealing with any complex web of interrelationships in an industry supply chain, it is critical that clarity be used in the terminology. Following are key terms used throughout this chapter.

Retrofits are any activity to replace, upgrade, renew, or improve all or part of an existing home. As used here, "retrofits" encompasses various other terms including home improvements, renovations, and remodeling. We further distinguish energy retrofits and amenity retrofits. Energy retrofits are changes to the thermal performance of a home's building envelope (windows, doors, walls, etc.) or to a home's energy systems (heating, cooling, ventilation, hot water, etc.). Energy retrofits can potentially improve energy efficiency, though this is not always the case. Energy retrofits are targeted by energy efficiency policies. Amenity retrofits are changes to a home's living and functional spaces (kitchens, bathrooms, living rooms, garage, garden, etc.). Amenity retrofits do not generally improve energy efficiency, though this is not always the case. Amenity retrofits are not targeted by energy efficiency policies.

The supply chain is the network of firms or other entities involved in providing a product or service to a final user. We also use the term "supply chain actors" to denote all these firms and entities. The energy supply chain includes the supply chain actors who enable or carry out energy retrofits. The energy supply chain includes product manufacturers, home improvement retailers, home contractors, and utilities and government agencies. The amenities supply chain includes the supply chain actors who enable or carry out amenity retrofits.

Inform, Incentivize, and Assure: The Prevailing Approach for Promoting Energy Efficiency in the Home

To paraphrase the legal concept and proverb: a home is the home owner's castle, a private space largely outside the domain of direct regulatory influence. More than two-thirds of U.S. households own their homes (JCHS 2009b). Realizing energy savings across the majority of the U.S. housing stock therefore depends on the weatherization measures and energy system upgrades decided upon by home owners, both in their own homes and in their rental properties. Put simply, the key to delivering energy efficiency into the home is home owners' retrofit decisions. So the starting point for influencing home retrofit decisions toward sustainability is to understand how such decisions are made.

A wealth of behavioral research over the last 30 years has shed light on many aspects of household energy demand and energy-efficient technology adoption (for a review, see Wilson and Dowlatabadi 2007). We know that information that is nontechnical, personally relevant, from a trustworthy source, and delivered through social networks rather than mass media channels tends to be more effective at influencing behavior (Kempton, Darley, and Stern 1992; Rogers 2003). We also know that publicly made commitments and collective or group action further support behavior change (Staats, Harland, and Wilke 2004). We know that financial incentives that are immediate, simple to administer, and available at the point of sale tend to be more effective (Stern et al. 1986). We know that households' knowledge and recall of how much energy they use tends to be fairly simplified and incomplete, as does awareness of how much different behaviors and technologies contribute to overall energy use (Kempton and Montgomery 1982; Wilson 2008a). We know that generally held values relating to the environment, health, or wealth tend not to explain energy-related behavior (Gatersleben, Steg, and Vlek 2002). We also know that positive attitudes and intentions toward energy efficiency and conservation tend to be constrained by contextual factors such as costs, established norms, and regulations (Stern 2000). We know that energy-related behavior tends to be shaped by domestic routines and habits (Shove 2003). We also know that decisions often tend to be made using rules of thumb or heuristics over a limited time and based only on partial information (Kahneman 2003).

Note that these findings are all intentionally expressed as tendencies. There is considerable variability across a population of households in terms of energy demand as well as lifestyles, behavioral routines, and responsiveness to energy price changes. As a result, there is no one-size-fits-all approach to influencing energy-related decisions or behavior. There is, however, a prevailing approach to promoting energy-efficient retrofits that is informed by many of these research findings as well as the limited scope for regulatory intervention within home owners' castles. This prevailing approach can be characterized as "inform, incentivize, assure."

Information makes home owners aware of energy-efficient investment opportunities, technology options, beneficial outcomes (including financial savings), and supporting policies. Over the longer-term, information can play a role in more broadly educating and sensitizing home owners about energy efficiency. The information approach includes advertising and awareness campaigns, home energy audit schemes, real-time energy-use monitors, and energy performance product labels.

Incentives improve the financial attractiveness of energy-efficient investment opportunities (by reducing upfront costs) and can increase the salience of financial savings. The incentive approach includes grants, rebates, and low-interest loans.

Assurance improves home owners' confidence and certainty in the beneficial outcomes of energy efficiency, and in the ability of supply chain actors to deliver those outcomes. Ross (2008) describes assurance as the peace of mind that customers gain from a transaction. The assurance approach includes knowledge and skills development for retrofit contractors, training programs, and accreditation bodies to maintain and enforce standards.

A prime example of this inform, incentivize, assure approach is provided by the White House Council on Environmental Quality convened by Vice President Joe Biden in 2009, which recommended how billions of dollars of stimulus money earmarked for energy efficiency should be spent. The task force's October 2009 "Recovery through Retrofit" report identifies "a series of barriers [which] have prevented a self-sustaining retrofit market from forming" (CEQ 2009, 1). These barriers are identified as access to information, financing, and skilled workers, so the report recommends action in these three areas. On information, recommendations include developing a standardized home energy performance measure and label. On financing, recommendations include simplified ways for home owners to fund retrofits through low-cost loans rolled up into mortgages or property taxes. On skills or quality assurance, recommendations include developing national standards to qualify energy-efficiency and retrofit workers as well as industry training providers.

These recent stimulus-driven measures are the latest in a long continuum of efforts by governments and utilities targeting energy efficiency in the home as a potential means of reducing energy demand (Gillingham, Newell, and Palmer 2006; Linden, Carlsson-Kanyama, and Eriksson 2006). In the United States between 1989 and 1999, $23 billion was spent by utilities on programs that encouraged energy-efficient technology adoption and behavior (Loughran and Kulick 2004). In the residential sector, weatherization and energy system technologies were the most commonly promoted. That weatherization still occupies a headline role in policy efforts indicates the limited success of efforts thus far. Energy efficiency remains important to environmental, energy, and social policy objectives, but delivering on these objectives also remains difficult.

Assumptions and Misconceptions about Home Owners' Retrofit Decisions

The inform, incentivize, assure approach tries to encourage home owners to make energy-efficient retrofit decisions. Underpinning the approach is a basic conceptualization of these decisions as being broadly rational. Rationality here implies that home owners are motivated by outcomes, are informed about these outcomes and the options for achieving them, and make optimizing decisions based on this information (i.e., they select the option that best achieves the outcomes). An additional assumption of the inform, incentivize, assure approach is that home owners are financially oriented; hence, information on the cost-effectiveness of energy-efficient investments is assumed to influence decisions, as are incentives that further improve their financial attractiveness.

Our own work started from the premise that this was not the whole picture. Despite considerable expenditure and effort in the United States and elsewhere, home owners remain stubbornly resistant to retrofitted energy upgrades. We believed that the way in which home owners actually make decisions about energy retrofits did not fit the rational, financially oriented decision making implicitly assumed by the inform, incentivize, assure approach.

To characterize retrofit decisions realistically, Wilson (2008c) asked more than 800 home owners (in British Columbia, Canada) a battery of questions about why and how they made their decisions, and what they were deciding at different stages. Our survey sample was intentionally biased toward home owners who were actively deciding about home retrofits, both energy retrofits and amenity retrofits.

Retrofit Decisions: Before the Fact versus After the Fact

Our research revealed two important findings that supported our suspicion that the inform, incentivize, assure approach was missing something in its assumptions about home owners' retrofit decisions. First, by comparing the responses of home owners at different stages of the retrofit decision process, we found evidence that decisions are not a discrete event but an often long, drawn-out process. This is intuitively obvious; what is important, however, is that key decision characteristics change over this process. In particular, the motivations and decision rules reported by home owners in the run up to, during, and after their retrofits differ systematically. Figure 1 summarizes some of these differences by contrasting survey responses from home owners before and after carrying out retrofits.

Our second key finding, drawing on these data, was that the decision characteristics reported by home owners after completing retrofits correspond well with the model of rational, financially oriented decision making assumed by the inform, incentivize, assure policy approach. After the fact, home owners tend to report being motivated by financial and general comfort-related outcomes (see figure 1 next to "stronger postretrofit"). They also tend to report that they fully considered all the different options (optimizing decision rules in figure 1) or followed expert or other advice to inform their retrofit decisions (advice and guidance decision rules). Because much of the work done to investigate retrofit decisions asks home owners after the fact (and this applies to both academic studies and contractors' customer feedback and evaluation studies), it is not surprising that home owners' motivations and decision rules are thought to be broadly rational.

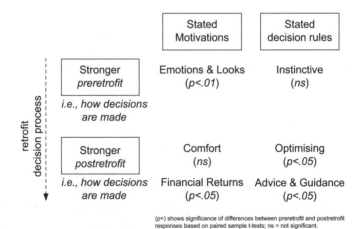

Figure 1   Characteristics of retrofit decisions, before and after the fact.

However, as figure 1 shows, how home owners report their decisions after the fact does not necessarily mean this is how they actually make their decisions before the fact. Decision characteristics reported by home owners before carrying out retrofits tend to emphasize emotional and aesthetic motivations. Preretrofit, home owners also tended to report choosing between options by using gut instincts or an innate sense of what was right (instinctive decision rules in figure 1). Additional work, not shown in figure 1, found that social norms also play a role in energy retrofit decisions (Wilson 2008b). This is further supported by a growing body of evidence on the influence of social norms on different types of energy-related behavior (Schultz et al. 2007). This composite impression of emotional, aesthetic, normative, and instinctive retrofit decisions is very different from the broadly rational, financially oriented model reported by home owners after the fact. It also helps explain why information, incentives, and quality-assurance-type inducements offered by policymakers to home owners are only of limited success. These inducements fail to target the before-the-fact characteristics of the decision process that they are trying to influence.

Retrofit Decisions: Amenity versus Energy

A third finding of our research into the retrofit decision process points to a novel means of tackling this mismatch between policy inducements and energy retrofit decisions. The potential solution lies with amenity retrofits. The Joint Centre for Housing Studies (JCHS 2009a) has compiled the amounts spent by home owners in the United States on energy-related, amenity-related, and other types of retrofits including structural features (roofing, siding), nonenergy systems (plumbing, wiring), and disaster repair. For every dollar spent on energy retrofits, approximately five dollars are spent on amenity retrofits.

Retrofits of all types are also very frequent. In 2007, 58 percent of home owners reported undertaking at least one retrofit project at some point in the previous two years (JCHS 2009a). Amenity retrofits are reported by home owners more than twice as frequently as energy retrofits, although these may be undertaken concurrently. Amenity retrofits are roughly as common as all other types of retrofit combined.

That more is spent on amenity retrofits, and more frequently too, tells us that the before-the-fact characteristics of amenity retrofit decisions are more motivating for home owners. And of course, this is without any information, incentives, or other inducements from policymakers. So how are these amenity retrofit decisions made?

Our survey sample included a substantial proportion of home owners undertaking either pure amenity retrofits or mixed amenity–energy retrofits. Compared to pure energy retrofit decisions, these decisions with an amenities component tended to be even more motivated by emotions, looks, and social norms, all bound up in instinctive choices. So the preretrofit and postretrofit differences in decision making shown in figure 1 were even more emphatic. Again, this is intuitively obvious. Compared to amenity retrofits, energy retrofits lack any emotional, aesthetic, or even visible appeal. Energy retrofits are often born of the necessity to replace poorly functioning equipment or renew worn out parts of the home. In contrast, home owners' decisions to spend substantial sums of money on a remodeled kitchen or bathroom, a garage or basement conversion, or simply new flooring and decoration are motivated by aspirations, feelings, desires, looks, and other considerations to do with the home. These considerations are in turn influenced by a morass of personal and social factors relating to status, taste, identity, lifestyle, and meaning (Aune 2007). Table 1 generalizes these differences between amenity and energy retrofit decisions.

The inform, incentivize, assure approach treats building envelope and energy system upgrades as the outcome of a distinct, energy-related retrofit decision. Information and services are aimed at motivating home

TABLE I

Contrasting Characteristics of Amenity and Energy Retrofit Decisions

Decision Features	Amenity Retrofit Decisions	Energy Retrofit Decisions
Prevalence	Common	Less common
Main parts of the home	Kitchens, bathrooms, conversions, outdoor areas	Windows, doors, heating & ventilation systems
Motivations	Emotions, aesthetics (social norms)	Thermal comfort, financial returns
Strength of motivations (for initiating decisions)	Strong	Less strong
Decision rules	Instinctive	Instrumental (optimize outcomes)
Social role	Status, identity (symbolic) comfort, modernity (practical)	Comfort (practical)

owners to decide on energy retrofits that they would not otherwise have done, or to improve the efficiency of energy retrofits to which they are already committed. But home owners are already making decisions to spend substantial sums on amenity retrofits, and—compared to energy retrofits—more frequently to boot. Why not piggyback on this existing pattern of behavior?

Compared to the inform, incentivize, assure approach, this piggybacking approach reduces the incremental effort, inconvenience, time, and expense of improving home energy efficiency. These are important characteristics of supply chain actors' value proposition to home owners. Packaging energy measures into amenity retrofits also ties energy efficiency explicitly to the social signaling role of home amenities. Interestingly, it also allows the amenities to motivate home owners to undertake retrofits in the first place, but the energy retrofits provide financial and comfort benefits as well as a ready-made, after-the-fact rationalization for all the effort and money expended.

Using the Amenities Supply Chain to Promote Energy Efficiency in the Home

The challenge is to find ways of packaging energy-efficiency measures into amenity retrofits. This must involve both policy inducements and business supply chains, which is a major departure for both. A goal shift is required away from inducing new and additional energy retrofit decisions toward inducing incremental, energy-related modifications to existing amenity retrofit decisions. This goal shift allows the alignment of home owners' decisions with both policymakers' objectives and supply chain actors' commercial interests.

The Business Case for Packaging Energy Measures into Amenity Retrofits

The inform, incentivize, assure approach relies either directly on home owners or indirectly on actors in the energy supply chain. Not only does this approach fail to constructively use the differences between energy and amenity retrofits shown in table 1, it also drives a wedge between the energy supply chain and the amenities supply chain. The contractors, expert advisors, and other service providers who form the energy supply chain are specialized or focused on building envelopes or energy systems with little connection to amenities. Like policymakers, they treat energy retrofits as the result of a distinct type of retrofit decision.

The piggybacking approach proposed here offers new business opportunities for these energy supply chain actors as well as the broader supply chain for amenity retrofits. Crucially, this begins with an understanding of home owners' decisions and creative thinking about home owners' overall experience as a basis for enhancing the value proposition offered by supply chain actors (MacMillan and McGrath 1997). Ross (2008) calls this an emphasis on customer intimacy through which companies seek to enrich their relations with customers by delivering information, service, innovative products, and interactions that add value.

Womack and Jones (2005) summarize what customers really want from their suppliers as being complete solutions, attained and implemented with as little cost, time, and effort on the part of the customer as possible, and without the customer having to search for other providers to complete the solution or merge disconnected sources. Bundling the product or service so that this can be achieved with minimal decisions and effort ensures that "ease of sourcing and completeness of the solution and not the product or service that constitutes the key value of the customer" (Ross 2008, 21).

This is central to the value proposition of the piggybacking approach because it centers on "making the search process less complicated, more convenient, less expensive, and more habitual" (MacMillan and McGrath 1997, 135). Similarly important is improving the convenience and comfort of the decision-making process so home owners can use the sort of instinctive decision rules explained earlier in the context of figure 1.

These sources of customer intimacy arise by treating home owners' decisions as being about retrofits and not about energy efficiency, based on an understanding of the underlying decision process. Offering energy measures as part of an amenity retrofit creates a source of competitive differentiation that arises from making consumers "aware of a need in a way that is unique and subtle" (MacMillan and McGrath 1997, 134). Home retrofits are the need or want for which the supply chain should provide.

Despite the potential business opportunities of the piggybacking approach, packaging energy measures into amenity retrofits is a major challenge for business. A simplified supply chain for energy-efficient windows includes: (1) material/component suppliers; (2) manufacturers; (3) distributors (sometimes bypassed); (4) retailers (sometimes bypassed);

(5) contractors (sometimes bypassed); and (6) final users. Data on the numbers of firms represented at each stage has been reported by Thorne (2003) and Will and Baker (2007). From only 5 glass manufacturers, there are then 4,000 window products manufacturers. There are about 200,000 contractor businesses (not including 330,000 self-employed contractors) to work with the 130,000,000 homes. The supply chain for retrofits, particularly at the contractor level, is highly fragmented, with disintegration not just between amenities and energy contractors but also between different types of energy contractors (ibid.).

Using the amenities supply chain to promote energy efficiency to home owners would rely on new alliances between accredited energy contractors (doing the work) and amenity contractors (doing the selling). Knowledge and skills transfer as well as training and business development programs would be needed as alternatives to subcontracting or joint venture arrangements. Mechanisms to manage risks and reputations would be needed, although it is likely that existing government quality assurance schemes could play a central role. More broadly, particularly given concerns over some irresponsible contractors, due attention must be given to ensuring quality and enduring workmanship. This suggests trialing the proposed incentive through established brand name contractors with more internal resources as well as higher reputational risk. Ultimately, the success of the piggybacking approach depends on the expanded, diversified value proposition being attractive to home owners.

The Policy Case for Packaging Energy Measures into Amenity Retrofits

Policy can and should support businesses in overcoming these challenges. Targeting energy-efficiency policy at supply chains rather than individuals or households is well-trodden ground. It falls under the rubric of market transformation and includes training and accreditation, new product development, standards, and innovations in the delivery of products and services. Various reports review and evaluate these initiatives by utilities, state agencies, and others (e.g., Nadel et al. 2003). Examples of best practice are widely known, as are initiatives for their dissemination (e.g., CEE 2005). And they can be readily extended to the supply chain for amenity retrofits as a means of promoting energy efficiency in the home in the piggybacking approach.

Take financial incentives as an example. Currently, financial incentives are a key mechanism for supporting supply chain activities. Table 2 compares the prevailing type of home owner–targeted incentive with a proposed amenities supply chain–targeted incentive. The home owner–targeted incentive takes the form of a rebate for energy-efficiency measures purchased or installed as part of an energy retrofit. The amenities supply chain–targeted incentive takes the form of a grant for energy-efficiency measures sold as part of an amenity retrofit. Both incentives have the same objective: inducing the adoption of energy-efficiency measures by home owners. Both incentives work in the same way: reducing the net cost of energy-efficiency measures to home owners. Both incentives could have

TABLE 2
Redesigning Energy-Efficiency Incentives

	Existing: *Home Owner–targeted incentive*	**Proposed:** *Amenities supply chain–targeted incentive*	*Rationale of Proposed Incentive*
Incentive marketed and paid to	Home owners	Amenities contractors (or home product stores) but passed on to energy contractors and/or home owners	Reduce bureaucracy and decision burden for home owners Leverage influence of supply chain actors on home owners and expand service offerings of amenity contractors Encourage new business alliances and knowledge/skills transfers between energy and amenity contractors
Type of home owner benefiting	Home owners deciding on energy retrofits, e.g., to replace worn-out equipment	Home owners deciding on amenity retrofits, e.g., to improve look and feel of home	Target much larger segment of home owners undertaking amenity retrofits Use emotional, aesthetic and normative motivations for retrofit

(Continued)

Benefit to home owner	Delayed cash flow benefit (postinstallation rebate), subject to paperwork	Immediate cash flow benefit (point-of-sale grant) with no paperwork	Incentives passed on by supply chain actors to home owners through lower net cost contract (assuming competitive markets)
Cost of managing incentive program	High: individual applications from, and program marketing to, many dispersed home owners	Low: aggregated applications from, and program marketing to, fewer supply chain actors	Applications for incentives managed and aggregated by supply chain actors Fewer, more clearly identifiable number of actors for targeted (and so more effective) marketing

the same monetary value: for example, set equal to the social benefit of the energy-efficiency measures. However, the incentives differ in terms of their target, their delivery, and their administration. The central feature of the amenities supply chain–targeted incentive is that it turns energy efficiency from a stand-alone investment into an incremental add-on.

Table 2 reinforces the point that in addition to potentially inducing the uptake of more energy-efficiency measures, redirecting incentives from home owners to amenities contractors may have more transformative effects on the supply chain for delivering energy efficiency into people's homes. The existing home owner–targeted incentive acts through the energy supply chain indirectly by inducing demand for efficiency measures. The proposed amenities supply chain–targeted incentive acts through the amenity and energy supply chains directly by inducing contractors and stores to market an expanded service offering based on new business relationships and skills. Such changes are more likely to persist if and when the incentives are phased out.

Criteria for Promoting Energy Efficiency in the Home

This chapter has argued for both policy and business communities to look to the supply chain for amenity retrofits as a means of promoting energy efficiency in people's homes. This argument rests on two straightforward observations. First, home owners' decisions to undertake retrofits require time, effort, resources, and a cognitive burden that information, incentives, and assurance cannot easily surmount. Business models, supported by policy, can circumvent these characteristics of energy retrofit decisions and so enable strategic differentiation (MacMillan and McGrath 1997). Our proposed approach is to package energy measures into the amenity retrofits already being decided upon and carried out by home owners.

This piggybacking approach is supported by the second observation. Far more is spent by home owners on amenity rather than energy retrofits, and more regularly too. Treating energy efficiency as a retrofit challenge rather than an energy-efficiency challenge demonstrates that the supply chain for amenity retrofits is well placed to influence this common type of decision of home owners.

This piggybacking approach can be summarized in three criteria for businesses seeking to promote energy efficiency in the home: circumvent, contact points, cross-sell.

- Circumvent: Reduce decision effort for home owner; piggyback on existing decisions rather than trying to induce new ones.

- Contact points: Leverage existing points of contact between home owners and the supply chain rather than trying to create new ones.

- Cross-sell: Through these contact points, package energy-efficiency measures into broader retrofit services and business models.

Examples of these criteria acting in concert include

- Walk-through energy audit as part of pre-contract home visit;

- In-home servicing of energy system equipment and training on maintenance and system tune-ups as part of amenity retrofits; and

- Complementary energy products with free installation as part of amenity product sales from home product stores over a certain amount.

In all cases, the same challenges around supply chain fragmentation arise, requiring new business models, alliances, joint ventures, and skills and knowledge transfer between energy and amenity contractors. We do not consider these insurmountable if these changes allow supply chain actors to enhance and differentiate their value proposition to home owners.

This would mean energy-efficiency policies, incentives, and marketing and business models could become more effective. Whereas the prevailing inform, incentivize, assure approach that targets home owners can help sensitize and stimulate demand for energy retrofits, the piggybacking approach that targets the amenities supply chain can ensure that this demand is easily and conveniently supplied. This broader approach to transforming the market aligns policymakers and the business supply chain with how home owners actually make retrofit decisions. The resulting approach to promoting energy efficiency in the home has the hallmarks of a sustainability strategy: comprehensive, integrated, and aligned.

References

Aune, M. 2007. "Energy Comes Home." *Energy Policy* 35, no. 11: 5457–65.

Consortium for Energy Efficiency (CEE). 2005. *Residential Home-Performance Programs: National Summary*. Boston: CEE.

Council on Environmental Quality (CEQ). 2009. "Recovery through Retrofit." Report of the Middle Class Task Force of the White House Council on Environmental Quality convened by the Vice President of the United States. October 2009. www.whitehouse.gov/administration/eop/ceq/initiatives/retrofit.

Dietz, T., G. T. Gardner, J. Gilligan, P. C. Stern, and M. P. Vandenbergh. 2009. "Household Actions Can Provide a Behavioral Wedge to Rapidly Reduce U.S. Carbon Emissions." *Proceedings of the National Academy of Sciences* 106, no. 44: 18452–56.

Esty, D. C., and A. S. Winston. 2006. *Green to Gold*. New Haven, Conn.: Yale University Press.

Gardner, G. T., and P. Stern. 1995. *Environmental Problems and Human Behavior*. Boston: Allyn & Bacon.

Gardner, G. T., and P. Stern. 2008. "The Short List: The Most Effective Actions U.S. Households Can Take to Curb Climate Change." *Environment* 50, no. 5: 12–24.

Gatersleben, B., L. Steg, and C. Vlek. 2002. "Measurement and Determinants of Environmentally Significant Consumer Behavior." *Environment and Behavior* 34, no. 3: 335–62.

Gillingham, K., R. Newell, and K. Palmer. 2006. "Energy Efficiency Policies: A Retrospective Examination." *Annual Review of Environment & Resources* 31:161–92.

Joint Centre for Housing Studies (JCHS). 2009a. *The Remodeling Market in Transition.* Cambridge, Mass.: Joint Centre for Housing Studies of Harvard University.

Joint Centre for Housing Studies (JCHS). 2009b. *The State of the Nation's Housing: 2009.* Cambridge, Mass.: Joint Centre for Housing Studies of Harvard University.

Kahneman, D. 2003. "Maps of Bounded Rationality: Psychology for Behavioral Economics." *American Economic Review* 93, no. 5: 1449–75.

Kempton, W., J. M. Darley, and P. C. Stern. 1992. "Psychological Research for the New Energy Problems: Strategies and Opportunities." *American Psychologist* 47, no. 10: 1213–23.

Kempton, W., and L. Montgomery. 1982. "Folk Quantification of Energy." *Energy* 7, no. 10: 817–27.

Linden, A.-L., A. Carlsson-Kanyama, and B. Eriksson. 2006. "Efficient and Inefficient Aspects of Residential Energy Behaviour: What Are the Policy Instruments for Change?" *Energy Policy* 34, no. 14: 1918–27.

Loughran, D. S., and J. Kulick. 2004. "Demand-Side Management and Energy Efficiency in the United States." *The Energy Journal* 25, no. 1: 19–43.

MacMillan, I. C., and R. G. McGrath. 1997. "Discovering New Points of Differentiation." *Harvard Business Review* 75, no. 4: 133–45.

Metz, B., O. R. Davidson, P. R. Bosch, R. Dave, and L. A. Meyer. 2007. *Climate Change 2007: Mitigation of Climate Change.* Contribution of Working Group III to the Fourth Assessment Report of the Intergovernmental Panel on Climate Change, 2007. Cambridge: Cambridge University Press.

Nadel, S., J. Thorne, H. Sachs, B. Prindle, and H. S. Elliott. 2003. *Market Transformation: Substantial Progress from a Decade of Work.* Washington, D.C.: American Council for an Energy Efficient Economy.

Obama, Barak. 2010. "Remarks by the President in the State of the Union." *WhiteHouse.gov,* January 27. www.whitehouse.gov/the-press-office/ remarks-president-state-union-address.

Rogers, E. M. 2003. *Diffusion of Innovations.* New York: Free Press.

Ross, D. F. 2008. *The Intimate Supply Chain.* Boca Raton, Fla.: Taylor & Francis.

Schultz, P. W., J. M. Nolan, R. B. Cialdini, N. J. Goldstein, and V. Griskevicius. 2007. "The Constructive, Destructive, and Reconstructive Power of Social Norms." *Psychological Science* 18, no. 5: 429–34.

Shove, E. 2003. *Comfort, Cleanliness, and Convenience: The Social Organisation of Normality*. Oxford: Berg.

Staats, H., P. Harland, and H. Wilke. 2004. "Effecting Durable Change: A Team Approach to Improve Environmental Behavior in the Household." *Environment and Behavior* 36, no. 3: 341–67.

Stern, P. C. 2000. "Towards a Coherent Theory of Environmentally Significant Behavior." *Journal of Social Issues* 56, no. 3: 523–30.

Stern, P. C., E. Aronson, J. M. Darley, D. H. Hill, E. Hirst, W. Kempton, and T. J. Wilbanks. 1986. "The Effectiveness of Incentives for Residential Energy Conservation." *Evaluation Review* 10, no. 2: 147–76.

Thorne, J. 2003. *Residential Retrofits: Directions in Market Transformation*. Washington, D.C.: American Council for an Energy Efficient Economy.

U.S. Energy Information Administration (EIA). 2009. *Emissions of Greenhouse Gases in the United States 2008*. Washington, D.C.: EIA.

U.S. Energy Information Administration (EIA). 2010. *Annual Energy Outlook*. Washington, D.C.: EIA.

Will, A., and K. Baker. 2007. *The Performance of Remodeling Contractors in an Era of Industry Growth and Specialization*. Cambridge, Mass.: Joint Centre for Housing Studies of Harvard University.

Wilson, C. 2008a. "Energy Efficient Home Renovations Are Not Financial Investments." International Association for Energy Economics (IAEE) Conference, June 18–20, Istanbul, Turkey.

Wilson, C. 2008b. "Social Norms and Policies to Promote Energy Efficiency in the Home." *Environmental Law Reporter* 38:10882–88.

Wilson, C. 2008c. "Understanding and Influencing Energy Efficient Renovation Decisions." Institute for Resources, Environment & Sustainability. Ph.D. diss., University of British Columbia, Vancouver, B.C.

Wilson, C., and H. Dowlatabadi. 2007. "Models of Decision Making and Residential Energy Use." *Annual Review of Environment and Resources* 32:169–203.

Womack, J. P., and D. T. Jones. 2005. *Lean Solutions: How Companies and Customers Can Create Value and Wealth Together*. New York: Free Press.

Note

The research described in this chapter was made possible through support from the Climate Decision Making Center (CDMC) located in the Department of Engineering and Public Policy at Carnegie Mellon University, created through a cooperative agreement with the National Science Foundation (SES-0345798).

CHAPTER 13

Making It Happen

A Practical Guide to Achieving Energy Sustainability and Self-Sufficiency

Thomas E. Kiser

America's path to energy sustainability and self-sufficiency is much easier to tread than most people realize. It lies straight through buildings. The energy-consumption goliath that buildings represent is a growing problem. We must start thinking of buildings as part of the supply chain that both gulps energy and is a major contributor to the threat of global warming. New buildings are designed primarily to meet maximum energy load demands—not generally to optimize energy performance. Existing buildings have not been retrofitted to employ even the most basic and affordable energy-efficiency strategies.

Buildings in the Energy Supply Chain

While much public attention has been focused on the transportation sector as the primary culprit in creating the carbon emissions crisis we face today, the truth is that vehicles are not the major guilty party. Transportation emissions actually account for just a little more than one-fourth of our total greenhouse gas emissions.[1]

Buildings are the real problem. They account for nearly 40 percent of carbon dioxide emissions in the United States, use more than 40 percent of our country's energy, and consume about 70 percent of the electricity. Buildings are a part of all supply chains. Much of the energy consumed by buildings is wasted through inefficient technology and outmoded systems for heating and cooling. Modern electronics and appliances that are essential to today's workplace and home lifestyles are continuously adding to "plug load." Most home owners understand little about how energy is consumed in their homes and workplaces and have only rudimentary knowledge about how to reduce energy costs. Landlords have little incentive to upgrade properties with more efficient energy systems because they generally shift the burden of energy costs to tenants either through higher rents or by directing responsibility for utility bills to the individual renter through lease agreements. Adding to the impact of buildings on the environment is the fact that about half of the electricity used by buildings is produced by coal-burning power plants—one of the largest sources of greenhouse gas emissions.[2]

It is way past time that people are educated that this is a different world; our energy needs can no longer be met through an out-of-date, extremely wasteful supply system that continues to rely on high-polluting, carbon-based materials as its primary source of fuel. We have to learn to view energy as a valuable commodity, one that must be used wisely and well if we are going to leave a sustainable economic legacy for generations to come. We must start thinking of buildings in particular as part of the supply chain that gulps energy and is a major contributor to the threat of global warming.

Growing Demand

The power demands of a 21st-century, information-driven society that is heavily dependent upon sophisticated electronic mechanisms to carry out a mammoth number of daily life tasks cannot continue to be met by an energy system first put in place in the 19th century. Problems exist both upstream and downstream in the energy supply web. Our energy production methods are hugely inefficient, wasting tons of natural resources daily that are then buried in the ground or vented into our skies and bodies of water as residual products that are extraordinarily harmful to our environment. Our national grid for transmission and distribution of energy is greatly overtaxed and vulnerable to collapse. The centralized structure of our national energy system—a negative result of deregulation of the power industry—makes it extremely vulnerable to disruption from weather conditions, natural disasters, and terrorist threats. The inefficient way we use energy in our workplaces, institutions, and homes drives up the cost of energy tremendously and further pollutes our environment with the way most waste heat is vented.

The United States is already the largest consumer of energy in the world, gulping a whopping 21 percent of the world's supply of energy while accounting for less than 5 percent of the world's population.[3] Energy consumption by the average American is five times the world average.[4]

Our power demands are anticipated to grow by leaps and bounds in the coming years. Projections are that total electricity demand will increase 30 percent by 2035 from 2008 levels. The largest growth—42 percent—is expected to come in the commercial sector as dependence on electronic devices to carry out work-related tasks continues to escalate. Residential demand for electricity is projected to climb 24 percent while demand growth in the industrial sector is predicted to be a relatively miniscule 3 percent as new, less-energy-intensive industries replace old manufacturing plants.[5]

Some of the growth in electricity use will come from the ever-increasing share of electricity drawn to meet total energy needs. The share of electricity that households use to meet total power needs is expected to increase from 41 percent in 2008 to 48 percent by 2035. The amount of electricity consumed for commercial use to meet total energy needs will jump 5 percent from 54 percent in 2008 to 59 percent in 2035.[6]

Solutions Are Out There

The good news is that solutions exist today to meet the twin challenges of an ever-growing demand for energy and the urgent need to halt global warming. Numerous ideas are being explored for modernizing and significantly improving the efficiency of the first two components of our energy system—generation and distribution—in ways that will reduce our dependence upon fossil fuels and shrink greenhouse gas emissions.

Most promising in terms of having a rapid impact on reduction of energy consumption and shrinkage of carbon footprints are the solutions for improving energy efficiency at the load, the end point of our energy system. It really is not that hard to make all types of buildings much more energy efficient and environmentally sustainable. The job can be done by applying simple engineering principles and innovative thinking to the use of readily available technology that has been around for many years.

This is the focus of my company—PSI. We have been doing it for 30 years and saving energy consumers a lot of money in the process. In simple terms, what we do at PSI is holistically analyze a building's energy needs and consumption patterns and then design an individualized energy system that creates an immediate revenue stream through reduced operating costs. The techniques that we employ generally result in 20 to 60 percent savings on energy bills and a reduction of carbon footprints by 30 to 90 percent. And we are achieving those levels of savings for buildings of all kinds—single-family homes, multifamily dwellings, commercial buildings, institutional facilities, and manufacturing plants. PSI has won several awards for creating novel, individualized energy systems that both cut energy bills and shrink carbon footprints for almost all of these types of structures.

The concepts and tools we use to do this are relatively simple. They are methods that anyone can learn to use and, applied on a global scale, can contribute immensely to solving both our energy consumption and climate change crises. Specifically, what we do at PSI is

- Abandon the use of steam;

- Render ductwork obsolete by pressurizing all confined spaces;

- Integrate a facility's structure, function, and purpose into the energy system to recapture waste heat and recycle it to produce more energy;

- Incorporate renewable energy in the most efficient way to provide direct current to meet small load demands and serve as a supplemental energy source for peak load times; and

- Design systems and create maintenance protocols with an eye toward long-term sustainability, including increasing the life cycle of the equipment.

In a nutshell, we maximize energy efficiency at the load while reducing costs and shrinking carbon footprints. PSI is all about saving money and increasing the life cycle of energy systems. It is that simple.

Start with Building Design

The starting point is the inversion of the way the vast majority of energy systems for buildings are designed today. Most system designers rely on concepts and components for power production and delivery that date from the 19th century. Certainly, these outmoded methods are not capable of producing and delivering energy at optimum efficiency to meet the complex demands of a 21st-century society.

Additionally, designers create plans aimed at meeting the maximum energy needs of a structure, providing enough power to compensate for extreme conditions and demand loads at all times. As an example, building energy systems in the United States to produce enough power 24 hours a day, 7 days a week to heat a structure when the external temperature is 0 degrees Fahrenheit in winter, and to cool it when the temperature is above 100 degrees in the summer—even if temperatures in a region only reach those extremes a few times a year. The systems also generate enough power at all times to meet demands when all building operations requiring energy are running at full capacity and the maximum number of people occupying the facility are in place. These practices result in tremendous energy waste.

We must turn that approach to energy system design upside down and begin creating systems that aim for optimum efficiency instead of peak load, maximum demand. Customized systems that integrate the purpose and function of a facility into the energy system design must be crafted to meet the advanced, complex energy requirements of today, not the Industrial Revolution.

At PSI, we learned a long time ago that most consumers purchase a great deal more energy than they actually use. For example, residential consumers generally use just 1 unit of energy for every 10 purchased. Commercial and institutional consumers use 1 of every 5 units purchased. Industrial consumers use 1 of a minimum of every 3 bought. All of the leftover energy—all the energy consumers are buying but then not using—is vented into the atmosphere as waste heat. This is the primary reason why buildings are the major source of greenhouse gas emissions, making a junkyard of our sky.

To counter this waste and simultaneously shrink both energy costs and carbon footprints for any building, the design process at PSI is founded on the application of what we call the "Kiser Quotient." This formula stipulates that "energy needed should be equal to or greater than energy purchased." Our goal at PSI is to reverse the current consumption ratios and make sure that consumers are purchasing—at a minimum—just one-third of the energy they actually need. This is our starting point. In some cases, where energy-intensive processes are a major component of a building's function, such as in manufacturing facilities, our energy system designs actually can reduce this ratio to just 1 unit of purchased energy for every 10 units needed. This tremendous energy cost savings is achieved primarily through the capture and recycling of rejection heat.

PSI designs energy systems that incorporate demand management as a fundamental component. The systems we create provide optimum energy efficiency at partial load, ramping up for the power necessary to counterbalance extreme conditions only when those conditions actually occur. To reverse the analogy used above, a PSI-designed energy system produces enough heat to offset zero degree external temperatures only when the temperature actually drops to that level in winter, and it generates enough cooling power to countervail summer temperature readings of 100 degrees or more just when the thermometer hits that high point. Our systems automatically adjust power output down when people are not occupying a space and equipment is idle. Designing for demand management to gain optimum efficiency swiftly reduces energy costs by cutting back on the amount of energy that must be purchased to match system requirements and power needs. In turn, achieving optimum energy efficiency reduces carbon footprints by simply reducing the amount of energy that must be purchased, and reducing the amount of waste heat that is vented into the atmosphere as greenhouse gas emissions.

Good energy system design also includes factoring in the purpose for which the structure is or will be used since 75 percent of the energy consumed by a building is needed to meet occupancy and use requirements. Incorporating building functions into the energy system design is a tremendous way to reduce energy costs, but it calls for a more innovative approach to design than typically is brought to bear today.

Designers must look inspirationally at the purpose of a building, identifying opportunities to maximize efficiency through recapturing and recycling waste heat. Every person, machine, and electronic device at work in a building produces rejection heat that can be used to offset energy requirements. The goal for any energy system design should be to achieve zero waste.

At PSI, we have developed several different methods that contribute to reaching that goal. One is a sustainable strategy, what we call our "liquid chimney," for capturing carbon dioxide in the exhaust streams of natural gas appliances and mixing it with treated water to produce hot water that is recycled to produce more energy. It is an efficient and safe alternative for steam in many applications.

Approximately 98 percent of the rejection heat produced by the natural gas appliances is captured through the liquid chimney strategy. With the recycling of this thermal energy, PSI has developed a cool, nonpressure vessel liquid chimney strategy that sequesters carbon dioxide into calcium carbonate that is harmless to the environment. The liquid chimney operates at approximately 80 percent efficiency in capturing and transforming the carbon dioxide, meaning that just 20 percent of the usual amount of this particular greenhouse gas is vented into the atmosphere.

On behalf of a snack food producer, PSI recently designed an energy system for a new manufacturing facility that included installation of heat recovery units over the ovens used to cook snack food chips. These liquid chimneys capture the waste heat expelled during the cooking process. This design feature contributed to a 30 percent reduction in the amount of energy consumed per pound of snack food produced at the plant.

Shut Down Steam

PSI begins designing for optimum efficiency by abandoning the use of steam. America is addicted to steam, much like the world is. And the world is way overdue for breaking this addiction. Steam as a mode of meeting 21st-century power needs is way past its expiration date. It is an expensive and wasteful means of producing energy that is dependent upon an aging infrastructure requiring vast amounts of money to maintain its operation and safety.

The technology to replace steam—getting rid of chimneys—has been around for 25 years. But there is an ingrained resistance to retiring it. First, proposals to shut down steam often are met by that age-old, knee-jerk human reaction of "This is the way we've always done it. This works. Why do we need to change?" That argument is bolstered by the fact that most building facilities staff are hired and trained to maintain steam systems. They frequently are reluctant to endorse proposals that would require learning new ways of operating more efficient systems and more sophisticated technology.

The truth is that steam is very inefficient, operating at a 20 to 50 percent efficiency rate. And all the rejection heat emanating from steam is vented into the atmosphere, both wasting energy and adding to a facility's carbon footprint. Steam's inefficiency starts with its production. Large amounts of water—a very precious resource in many parts of the United States—are necessary to create steam. Additionally, changing water into steam is a very energy-intensive process—one that does not vary regardless of the load, the amount of power required by the consumer at any point in time.

A total of 960 British thermal units (Btu)—the measurement of the amount of energy required to heat one pound of water by one degree Fahrenheit— must be generated to convert one pound of water into steam.[7]

Most of the heat wasted in a steam boiler—as much as 10 to 41 percent—is lost through the distribution system, including load heat extraction, leaks, condensation, and radiated heat from the boiler skin. The second-largest amount of heat loss is through combustion exhaust, with losses ranging from 17 to 35 percent. All of this rejection heat generally is released into the atmosphere, adding substantially to a building's carbon footprint.

Another drawback to a steam-powered energy system is that the very nature of the system degrades the equipment. Steam produces perfect water as it condenses. Perfect water attracts impurities in the pipes through which steam is distributed; therefore, perfect water is very corrosive, constantly eating away at the pipes through which it flows. Additionally, the solid matter collected by the perfect water eventually settles to the bottom of the steam boiler through which the water is recycled to make more steam. The solid matter builds up as sludge in the bottom of the boiler, corroding the metal boiler skin and inhibiting equipment efficiency.

With the technology available today, the use of steam should be kept to an absolute minimum in energy system design. PSI restricts the use of steam to circumstances in which it is essential, such as to meet sanitation requirements or to create humidity to preserve precious objects like those in a museum.

PSI was one of the first energy system design firms to recognize the value of getting rid of steam. We have been employing alternatives since the 1980s, using low-heat sources whenever possible to power decentralized hot water systems that deliver heat at a much higher efficiency. In contrast to the 50 percent efficiency of a steam boiler system, a hot water system operates at an average efficiency of 90 percent with an efficiency range of 79 to 97 percent. Heat losses through combustion exhaust are reduced to 2 percent to 20 percent in a hot water system. Losses through most of the distribution system, including load heat extraction, leaks, and condensation, are eliminated.

Often a PSI energy system design relies upon natural gas as its power source. The United States has a plentiful supply of natural gas. In addition, natural gas is relatively clean burning because, unlike other fossil fuels, it does not need to be transformed to create energy.

Natural gas becomes a cost-effective fuel source in a PSI energy system design because it can be modulated to meet load demand. Steam cannot be. Additionally, natural gas is a tremendous source of thermal energy that can be recaptured hydronically through PSI's liquid chimney strategy. As much as 90 pounds of water can be produced and captured by a liquid chimney strategy for every 1,000 cubic feet of gas burned, thus reducing the need to purchase and draw in freshwater as well as energy provided by a utility.

One of the very first major alternative energy systems we installed— back in 1986—at a Ford Motor Company plant in Sandusky, Ohio, delivered almost $1.7 million in annual savings right off the bat with a two-year payback on the initial investment. And that was after PSI replaced coal at $1.88 per million Btus with natural gas at $5.20 per million Btus. Another system we designed in 1987 saved a glass manufacturing factory about $3.9 million a year in energy costs and paid for itself in just over one year.

A side benefit of PSI's liquid chimney is that it eradicates the need for pressure vessels. And pressure vessels, as we all know, can be quite dangerous. Without consistent maintenance and constant monitoring, pressure vessels can malfunction with sometimes disastrous consequences. In worst-case scenarios, pressure vessels can blow up, endangering the lives of any nearby workers.

Redefining Ductwork through Pressurization

After we abandon steam, PSI also abandons ductwork—another very inefficient component of most heating and cooling systems. A ductless energy system, such as PSI employs, consumes just one-eighth of the energy needed to push air through ductwork. Therefore, consumers who install a ductless system see an immediate drop in their energy bills because much less energy is required to make such a system work. They also experience an immediate reduction in their carbon footprint because less fossil fuel is burned to create power and more waste heat is captured for recycling, thus fewer greenhouse gas emissions are vented into the atmosphere.

One reason that a ductless system needs much less energy to function is that air does not like being forced through artificial tunnels, particularly if those tunnels are square. Air also retards the movement of energy, acting as an insulator rather than a conductor. Therefore, the energy required to power the equipment needed to push air through ductwork actually is about seven times greater than the power needed to fulfill a facility's total air needs. One-tenth of an inch of pressure is essential to pressurize ductwork in a home. A full inch is necessary to pressurize duct work in an industrial setting. In a ductless system, just one one-hundredth of an inch of pressure is required to pressurize a room or a whole factory.

PSI has patented a concept for moving air by pressurizing confined spaces. Our process blows in enough air to create an indoor pressure level that, in effect, seals the space. The indoor air pressure acts as a counterforce to keep out external hot or cold air that attempts to infiltrate while allowing a slight outward escape of indoor air that otherwise is kept circulating in natural patterns. The natural properties of air circulating within this pressure vessel then become an additional energy-efficiency tool because air is an insulator, not a conductor, of energy. PSI's patented air-handling unit, called Bigfoot, blows cool air into the upper levels of a confined area. As it is compelled to by nature, the weightier cold air tries to fall to the lower levels, only to meet the counterforce of lighter weight hot air, created by the waste heat generated by the people and equipment operating at floor level, that is trying to rise to the upper levels.

Air does not mix. It tends to stratify; in other words, cold and hot air stay separated. PSI's pressurization process destratifies air, trapping in between the continuous flow of cooler air across the upper levels and rising waste heat from the lower levels the air that already has attempted to fall or rise and is now blending and circulating in a comfortable mix. Through stringent computer control, the temperature at floor level can be controlled at plus or minus two degrees of desired conditions constantly by adjusting the air pressurization balance inside the structure.

A bonus benefit is that positive building pressurization helps exhaust fans operate more efficiently in clearing indoor air of particulates. PSI has had measurements demonstrating that air quality can jump as high as 300 percent in an industrial setting when a building is pressurized. The greater operational efficiency of the exhaust fans also extends the life cycle of the equipment, another cost-savings benefit.

Give the System a Brain

Essential to using building air pressurization as an optimal efficiency heating and cooling system is giving the energy system a brain. We call the brains we give the energy systems we design our "Global Control." Basically, Global Control functions as an autopilot that flies building pressurization. Its sophisticated central nervous system feeds a continuous stream of data into the custom-written software that functions as the brain, making Global Control capable of automatic, rapid response to changing conditions inside and outside a facility to maintain consistent air balance throughout a building.

Global Control's central nervous system is composed of many strategic meters and submeters. Every piece of equipment that is a component of any energy system designed by PSI is routinely monitored. Energy production, transmission, and consumption are tracked and metered in real time. If a piece of equipment uses gas, electricity, or water—and PSI is responsible for the Btus it consumes—it is metered. Changes in external conditions—temperature fluctuations, wind direction, humidity levels, etc.—also are measured constantly. Airborne contaminants that are irritants or pose possible dangers, such as carbon dioxide, smoke, haze, and explosive vapors, also are measured as to degree and concentration.

An added benefit to Global Control is that this extensive submetering becomes an energy-efficiency strategy as well. Submetering and close monitoring of equipment energy consumption can, by themselves, cut energy costs by 5 to 10 percent.

Another advantage to submetering is that it allows for different algorithms to be applied to different applications, such as swimming pool heating versus office space heating. Additionally, individual meters can be isolated for equipment shutdown, adjustments, and repairs without disrupting the data collection or operation of the rest of the energy system. Individual system components also can be isolated through submetering, again allowing specific component overrides without disrupting the entire system.

Using the data fed in by the metered central nervous system, Global Control takes a comprehensive snapshot of system performance every 60 minutes. Every hour around the clock, seven days a week, Global Control tallies the energy ballot for all system components and impact factors, adjusts the system automatically to compensate rapidly for changing conditions, and ensures that energy-efficiency goals are being achieved. Global Control also enhances energy demand management capability by enabling easy system adjustments such as scheduling facility heating, ventilating, and exhaust fan functions to coincide with production schedules.

This enhancement of demand management capability further ensures the optimum energy efficiency of the system.

Surprising as it is to many people, that is not the way most energy systems are managed today. Instead, as stated before, most systems operate continuously at levels designed to meet peak load demands and extreme conditions. The result is tremendous built-in waste in our energy systems. The vast majority of the energy produced at any one time really is not needed and has no place to go except into the junkyard we have made of the sky, adding to the debris collecting there.

Another major benefit of Global Control is that it helps increase the life cycle of the equipment by providing an hourly pulse on how the system is functioning. Individual system components that are not operating at optimum efficiency are identified quickly and system operators are alerted so that needed adjustments and repairs can be made expeditiously. Such close monitoring and control guarantees the long-term sustainability of the entire energy system.

Incorporate Renewable Energy

More of the two-thirds ratio of the Kiser Quotient that calls for use of energy derived from sources other than paid utility companies can be fulfilled through the incorporation of renewable energy into system designs. All types of renewable energy—solar, wind, geothermal, thermal, biofuel, anything and everything that can be used to make energy in a clean and efficient way—can make a valuable contribution to reducing energy costs and slashing carbon footprints for buildings if incorporated wisely and well into a total energy system concept.

The problem with renewable energy today is that these resources generally are not being used in the most efficient way. We need to get a whole lot smarter in the way we think about and employ renewable energy to gain maximum value from it.

Many green energy proponents dream of a world in which all energy is derived from renewable sources. Unfortunately, this is not a realistic concept. Replacing fossil fuels with renewable energy is not a practical solution for satisfying the enormous global appetite for energy—no matter how appealing this solution appears to be on the surface. The facts are that most types of renewable energy—again, whether we are talking wind, solar, geothermal, thermal, or biofuels—cannot be produced or transmitted at the quantities and voltage necessary to be the reliable, consistent sources of energy needed to meet daily demand on a national scale.

For example, wind turbines only produce medium-pressure voltage that must be passed through a transformer to increase the voltage substantially in order to match electrical grid standards. In addition, there are limitations on where wind turbines can be placed because they must be strategically located in areas with at least a seven-mile-per-hour wind stream. Solar energy creates very low pressure voltage so it must be produced extremely close to the end user to be cost effective and efficient. Even with continuing advances in the technology of deriving energy from renewable sources, it is unlikely that this means of producing energy will be capable of serving as a total replacement for fossil fuels anytime in the relatively near future.

However, renewable energy incorporated into the design of a total energy system for any size facility and produced onsite or very nearby can make a substantial contribution to improving energy efficiency, reducing costs, and scaling back greenhouse gas emissions. In particular, renewable energy, stored in batteries and coupled with natural gas, provides a terrific answer to meeting peak load demands as needed. Using renewable energy in this manner increases its efficiency and cost effectiveness twentyfold. It also eliminates the tremendous amount of waste heat that results from the consistent flow of enough energy to meet peak load demands at all times, as most energy systems are designed to do today.

Solar energy is especially effective when used as a supplemental power source and fed directly as direct current to a nearby end user to meet low-voltage power needs, such as lighting and personal computers. Incorporating photovoltaic solar energy to produce direct current to power direct current loads increases the efficiency of solar energy by 25 percent. Thermal solar also is a very cost effective method of supplementing a hydronic energy system and increasing its efficiency.

Other examples of ways to incorporate renewable energy efficiently into an energy system design include the following. All are techniques PSI has employed in various green energy system designs.

- Ground source heat recovery can be used to heat or cool a hydronic loop.

- A pond more than 12 feet deep can function as a cooling tower in summer, providing cool water for a hydronic loop, and a warm water source in winter when temperature inversion occurs after ice forms on the top of the pond and warm water is forced to the bottom.

• Energy produced close to the end user by wind turbines also can be stored in batteries and used as direct power to power direct current loads to significantly reduce peak load costs and brownout vulnerability.

The true key to incorporating renewable energy effectively and efficiently into an energy system design is to think innovatively. Every designer should consistently be asking himself or herself, "What can I do with renewable energy in this particular project to achieve maximum energy efficiency for this structure?" When that question can be answered successfully for every energy system created, America will be well on its way to achieving the goal of the Kiser Quotient—purchasing just a single unit of energy for every three that are needed.

Conclusion

The energy-efficiency model at the load that is detailed in this chapter is one of proven effectiveness. Systems such as these are making huge differences in the energy savings earned daily by manufacturers, commercial enterprises, institutions, and individual building owners all over the United States. They also are helping to substantially shrink the amount of greenhouse gases these structures release daily into the atmosphere. And finally, they are dispelling the myth that green technology is more expensive. Systems designed according to the model outlined here generally cost 10 to 15 percent less to construct than traditional energy systems and are much more efficient to operate, cutting energy costs by as much as 60 percent for some structures.

Notes

1 Environmental and Energy Study Institute, "Transportation and Energy Program," available at http://www.eesi.org

2 Environmental and Energy Study Institute, "High Performance Green Buildings," available at http://eesi.org

3 Center for Sustainable Solutions, University of Michigan, "U.S. Energy System," available at http://css.snre.umich.edu/facts

4 World Watch Institute, "Making Better Energy Choices," available at http://www.worldwatch.org

5 U.S. Energy Information Administration, *Annual Energy Outlook 2010*, p. 65, available at http://www.eia.doe.gov/oiaf/aeo/

6 Ibid., 57, 59

7 Aware Services, from the Organization Resources Counselors, Inc., "Cost of Energy Required for Evaporation," http://www.aware-services.com/orc/costs/htm

CHAPTER 14

Sustainable, Clean, Carbon-Neutral Bioenergy while Cleaning Air and Water

Mark Edwards

In the name of energy security, U.S. policymakers have chosen to heavily subsidize corn ethanol production to the exclusion of other feedstocks. The unintended consequences of ethanol include massive subsidies; severe air, soil, and water pollution; and social inequity from subsidies and the health problems caused by agricultural chemical pollution. Algal biomass provides a sustainable and clean feedstock for liquid transportation fuel that does not compete with food crops for fossil resources. Algal biofuel production can include remediation of wastewater, recovery and recycle of waste nutrients, and carbon dioxide (CO_2) capture and sequestration from smoke plumes and other waste sources. Algal biofuels hold promise to provide economically sustainable, socially positive, and environmentally friendly production of liquid transportation fuels.

Carbon-Neutral Bioenergy

Energy security plays havoc with environmental policies, economics, and society. Politicians talk a good game but too often do the opposite. Political leaders in the United States enacted comprehensive antipollution policies and then promptly exempted the worst polluters, including the oil companies, agriculture, biofuel producers, and refiners (Hogue 2007).

The world demand for liquid transportation fuels continues to escalate at about 3 percent annually, which increases demand but diminishes supply, escalating fuel prices. Developing countries such as China, India, and Indonesia are increasing their fuel consumption by more than 12 percent annually, which pushes prices even higher. Speculators are betting that future supplies will be tight and their future options will be profitable. Adding risk to accelerating consumption is the fact that single production, refinery or distribution failure, or storm or terrorist damage could double or triple the cost of a barrel of oil almost overnight.

Unless the United States is able to find domestic solutions for liquid transportation fuels, the annual bill for oil imports will exceed $1 trillion annually within 10 years, devastating the economy. The rising cost of transportation fuels creates severe social inequity by pushing up the cost of transportation, food, clothing, and other consumer goods. Those with the least means must pay more for necessities, which acts like a regressive tax.

Fossil fuels and the many products derived from them, including plastics, fertilizers, pesticides, and herbicides, leave an appalling environmental legacy in air, soil, and water pollution. Transportation fuels pollute with heavy loads of CO_2, nitric oxide, and black soot particulates that magnify global warming, deplete the ozone layer, and lead to severe respiratory illnesses as well as heart disease and cancers.

The United States has 600 coal-fired power plants that supply 64 percent of the country's electricity. Burning coal is the leading cause of smog, acid rain, global warming, and air toxins. Each year, each 500-megawatt coal plant generates millions of tons of pollution, including 3.7 million tons of CO_2, 10,000 tons of sulfur, 500 tons of black soot particulates, 10,200 tons of nitric oxides, and more than 200 tons each of hydrocarbons, arsenic, and mercury (Freese and Clemmer 2006). Each power plant also consumes more than 2 billion gallons of freshwater for cooling.

A coal plume downwind of a coal-fired power plant's supply chain includes the coal mine, rail transportation, coal storage at the site, and the power plant exhaust plume. Poor coal miners and power plant operators are trapped in the coal plume with their families. The coal plume causes social injustice for those disadvantaged people who suffer from significantly higher occurrences of kidney, lung, heart disease, and cancers as well as diminished property values.[1]

The reciprocal of our consumptive, environmentally and socially destructive fossil energy economy would be a sustainable, clean, carbon-neutral energy system that cleans air and water. A sustainable and clean energy system should be reliable for at least seven generations and should not pollute air, soils, or water. "Carbon neutral" means the process adds no additional carbon to the atmosphere. Ecofriendly energy production would be ideal if it also cleaned air, water, and other waste streams. The nanotechnology solution that can supply these benefits relies on the oldest yet simplest energy system on Earth—photosynthetic algae (Edwards 2008, 82).

Renewable clean energy sources such as wind, waves, solar, and geothermal will have a substantial impact on the energy grid and may eventually displace coal. However, these energy sources will not provide liquid transportation fuels that will be needed for decades to power legacy consumer vehicles as well as tractors, trucks, trains, ships, and planes. More than 96 percent of our oil imports are liquid transportation fuels and, with the exception of electric vehicles, only biofuels offer an opportunity to displace oil imports. Currently, electric vehicles powered with current generated by a coal-fired power plant have twice the carbon footprint as a gas-powered vehicle.

The U.S. energy program that pushes corn ethanol makes sense to politicians because it provides farmers with much-needed income in the form of subsidies and higher prices. However, the science and unintended consequences of massive corn production for nonfood purposes makes no sense. If government experts and politicians were looking for a sustainable and clean biofuel feedstock, they made the worst possible choice (Edwards 2007, 82).

Ethanol Biofuel

Global warming combined with rising prices and scarcity of fossil fuels have pushed several countries to pass legislation to meet the growing demand for liquid transportation fuel with biofuels (Jacobson 2009). Corn- and sugarcane-based bioethanol constitute 90 percent of the commercial-level biofuel that exists in the market today (REN 21 2009).

Sugarcane ethanol provides a biofuel solution for Brazil with its extensive flat, rain-fed land. Brazilian ethanol creates severe environmental impacts that may be fatal to the industry including clear-cutting forests and pushing small farmers off prime lands and into the rain forests as well as soil erosion and air and water pollution. Brazil depends on a large fishery around the mouth of the Amazon, and the nitrogen and phosphorus runoff will create a dead zone like the one in the United States at the mouth of the Mississippi River that will be catastrophic for the country. The United States lacks proper soils and climate for several potential biofuel feedstocks including sugarcane, cocoa, rapeseed, coconut oil, and jatropha, a succulent indigenous to South America.

Although ethanol and biodiesel production continue to increase, assessments of production potential, environmental impact of biomass production, and carbon sequestration show that biofuels based on these feedstocks fail to comply with sustainability criteria (Hoekman 2009). Increased corn acreage for biofuel production has raised concerns regarding disruption of global food supply, soil erosion, fertilizer and pesticide pollution, greenhouse gas (GHG) emissions, reduced crop biodiversity, and biocontrol ecosystem service losses (Donner and Kucharik 2005).

Corn ethanol production in 2009 produced roughly 9 billion gallons of ethanol—less than 2 percent of U.S. oil imports for 2009—while consuming more than

- 44 million acres of prime cropland to grow the feedstock

- 2 trillion gallons of freshwater to irrigate

- 5 billion gallons of diesel fuel to farm and transport the feedstock

- 20 million tons of agricultural chemicals

Ethanol production causes severe environmental pollution of air, soils, and water. Each acre of corn production used for ethanol adds about 2.25 tons of CO_2 to the air (Dias de Oliveira, Vaughan, and Rykiel 2005). Nitrogen fertilizer and soil bacteria combine to create nitrous oxide (N_2O), which adds to GHG. Nitrous oxide has an atmospheric lifetime of 120 years and a global warming index of 260 compared to CO_2's global warming index potential of 1 (Shindell et al. 2005).

Fertilizers used for corn can lead to an accumulation of arsenic, cadmium, uranium, and other heavy metals that are absorbed by food plants. Phosphorus and potassium come from mines in only a few countries; reserves are extremely limited, and prices are rising. Corn farmers also apply an average of 82 pounds of potash per acre to corn fields, 80 percent of which is imported (Huang 2004).

Conversion of ecologically vulnerable wetlands, rainforests, peatlands, savannas, and grasslands into new croplands creates enormous biofuel carbon debts by releasing several magnitudes more CO_2 than the annual GHG reduction that these biofuel would provide by displacing fossil fuel (Sawyer 2008). Biofuel production using corn grain, soybean, and wood biomass require more fossil energy than the energy content of the biofuel (Pimentel and Patzek 2007). Even if all U.S. corn and soybean land were converted to fuel, only 12 percent of gasoline and 6 percent of the diesel demand could be met (Tilman et al. 2009).

Food crop feedstocks drive up the cost of food and all the inputs to food production. When the cost of food rises, people on food stamps who have a dollar a meal to spend on food either have less food to eat, or they buy cheaper food with more fat and less nutrition. A viable global biofuel industry will not emerge unless these critical environmental, economic, and social equity concerns are addressed (Henry and Devereaux 2009).

Advanced Feedstock

The many biofuel mandates already in place illustrate the need for development of advanced feedstock biofuel (Harte 2010, 1). Advanced biofuels yield a net life-cycle reduction of at least 50 percent in GHG emissions compared with fossil fuels and offer additional advantages for the environment as well as for local economies. Potential biodiesel feedstocks include algae, enzyme hydrolysis of forest waste and switch grasses, thermal depolymerization of organic waste to form biocrude, and direct biological synthesis of more complex biofuels.[2] Algae-based biofuel stands out as the most promising for fast development.[3]

Enzyme hydrolysis and cellulosic ethanol appear to be at least a decade away. Al Darzins, group manager at the National Bioenergy Center and the National Renewable Energy Laboratory, works on the problem of breaking down corn's cellulosic biomass. He describes the structure of corn stalks as similar to cement with rebar (iron rods) running through it (Darzins 2007).

Cellulosic feedstock sources such as corn, grasses, and forest wastes are severely handicapped because their short-chain hydrocarbons can be converted only to weak alcohols such as ethanol. Many algal species offer longer carbon chains that can be converted into gasoline or other fuels that contain even more energy such as biodiesel, aviation gas, and jet fuel, JP-8.

Algae use the sun's energy to convert water and CO_2 into chemical energy in plant bonds. Each molecule of CO_2 sequestered yields a molecule of glucose, plant sugar, and gives off six molecules of pure O_2 to the atmosphere. Each day algae produce 70 percent of the oxygen in the atmosphere, more than all the forests and fields combined. Each pound of algae sequesters two pounds of CO_2. Algae synthesize roughly 0.8×10^{11} tons of organic matter daily, constituting about 40 percent of the total organic matter grown on the planet (Goyal 2002).

In the oceans and on land, algae captures CO_2 and sequesters it in green plant bonds that fall to the bottom of the water column and integrate with soil matrix or algal eaters whose biomass eventually decomposes in water or soils. Algae cultured for biofuels can produce fuels made with no fossil fuel. Algae recycle carbon that would otherwise have been released to the atmosphere. Carbon neutral applies because no new fossil carbon is added to the atmosphere. Each gallon of algal biofuels displaces one gallon of fossil fuel, except for ethanol. Ethanol, which is 200-proof corn whiskey, yields only 64 percent of the energy of gasoline. Algae diesel has 30 percent more energy than gasoline. Therefore, algae diesel provides roughly twice the energy per gallon as ethanol.

Algal biofuels are clean because the only thing released to the environment during production is pure oxygen. Burning algal fuels produces no black soot particulates or heavy metals. Algal biofuels create no black soot particulates because the fuel is essentially vegetable oil and has not been fossilized.

Extensive research in the 1970s and 1980s examined the use of microalgae as an advanced energy feedstock with applications being developed for biodiesel, bioethanol, and biohydrogen gas production (Huntley and Redalje 2007). Algae have far higher photon conversion efficiency than land-based feedstocks and can synthesize and accumulate large quantities of neutral lipids (biodiesel) and carbohydrates (bioethanol) along with such other valuable coproducts as vitamins, minerals, micronutrients, astaxanthin, and omega-3 fatty acids.

Why Algae?

Current biofuel feedstocks not only consume precious cropland, trillions of gallons of water, and billions of gallons of diesel fuel but they also provide a dismally low yield. Commercial algal farms have the photosynthetic potential to produce 5,000 gallons of oil per acre annually while corn typically produces 18 gallons an acre (Hu et al. 2008).

Algal biomass grows in ponds, tanks, or tubes called biofactories, or in cultivated algal production systems. Algae use affordable and plentiful inputs that will not run out: wastewater, CO_2, and natural or artificial light. Algae prefer diffused light that is not too bright, so some systems use

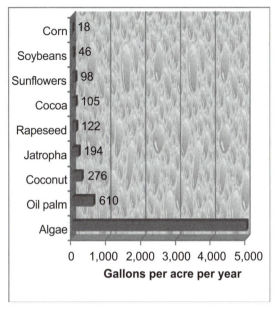

Figure 1   Oil production potential.

shading that both limits light and diffuses light. Various species produce best at different temperatures, so some systems use recycled water on the outside of the biofactory to maintain optimum temperature.

Algae consume considerable CO_2, and the cost can be minimized by siting the biofactory near a power or manufacturing plant the produces CO_2. Nutrients may be provided from wastewater, brine water, leeched compost, or other fertilizer source. Harvest often occurs daily or continuously, and the remaining culture contains considerable residual nutrients that may be recycled and reused. Closed systems maximize culture control and minimize water loss to evaporation. Algaculture systems that use high-saline water such as agricultural waste streams or brine water (or municipal wastewater) offer the advantage of cleaning water as well as producing algal biomass.

Algae double their biomass daily, so harvest may occur continuously by filtering, centrifuge, flocculation, or laser. The cells suspended in the broth are separated from the water, and algal oil is extracted from the recovered biomass and converted to biodiesel or other biofuel. Biomass composition varies by variety but may be 40:25, oil to protein, with about 25 percent carbohydrates and 10 percent ash or waste (Sommerfeld 2010). After the oil component is used for biofuel, the remaining high-protein biomass may be demoistured and stored in a convenient form such as a cake, which does not require refrigeration and has about a two-year shelf life. The algal cake may be made into anything made with soy, corn, or wheat flour or into food ingredients, fodder, fertilizer, fine medicines, or other components.

Part of the spent biomass may undergo anaerobic digestion to produce biogas that generates electricity that powers the biomass mixing and water transport (Lantz et al. 2007). Effluents from anaerobic digestion may be used as a nutrient-rich fertilizer for more algae production or as nutrient-rich irrigation water. Some of the power generated from the biogas is consumed in biomass production, and excess energy may be sold to a grid.

Algal biodiesel production is carbon neutral because the power needed for producing and processing the algae can come from the methane produced by anaerobic digestion of the biomass residue remaining after oil extraction. The modest additional energy requirements to mix, harvest, and separate the coproduct may also come from other noncarbon sources such as wind or solar.

Algal biomass components, lipids (oils), starches, and proteins are processed into a variety of products, including any fuel that can be made from crude oil. Crude oil is made of algae fossilized from ancient oceans. Algal biofuels simply skip the 400 million years nature required to fossilize the fuels.

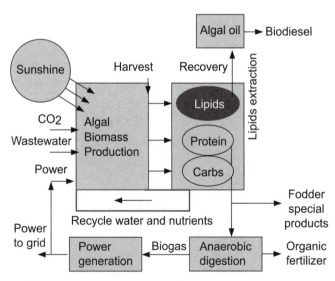

Figure 2   Algaculture carbon-neutral bioenergy production system.

The potential product mix offers almost infinite variations, depending on algae strain and production parameters. The desired product outcomes drive strain selection, growth parameters, and processing. Enhanced algal strains selected through screening natural varieties, hybridization, and bioengineering will enable producers to optimize biofuel production. The chemical structure of the algal species determines how much energy will be released when the chemical plant bonds are burned.

Natural Resource Consumption

Algal feedstock can be grown using no or minimal natural resources needed by food crops—fertile soil, freshwater, fossil fuels, or fossil agricultural chemicals. Algae can be grown on noncrop lands such as abandoned land, saline/coastal areas, or arid and desert lands for which there are no competing demands (Edwards 2010, 9).

Agriculture in the United States uses 80 percent of the available freshwater, and several regions face impending water shortages (DOE 2006). Therefore, any feedstock should consume minimal freshwater for growth and refining. Half the water stored in the Earth's crust, brine water, contains too much salt for land plants or human use, but algae thrive in brine and even saltier ocean water. Substantial saline groundwater resources, roughly 15 billion acre-feet of brine water, are contained within several huge aquifers in the U.S. Southwest (Huff 2004). The arid climatic conditions coupled with plentiful desert land, sunlight, and saline water in the region can support a diversified and strong algal biofuel industry.

Algae can recover and reuse growth nutrients such as nitrogen and phosphorous from a variety of waste streams such as agricultural run-off, animal feed operations, and industrial and municipal wastewater. Algae provide sustainable bioremediation of these wastes while producing clean water for economic and social benefits (Shilton et al. 2008).

Algae can also couple carbon-neutral fuel production with CO_2 sequestration from other power industries, which can generate carbon credits (Dismukes et al. 2008). Arizona Public Service received a $70.6 million grant to feed algae CO_2 from two sources: captured from a coal-fired smokestack and directly from the smoke by flueing the smokestack gas into an algae culture (St. John 2009). Algae consume two pounds of CO_2 in each pound of algal biomass and release only one gas to the atmosphere—pure oxygen.

A defined set of technology breakthroughs will be required for the optimum use of algal biomass for commercial biofuel production (Edwards 2008, 188). The major advancement will be stable, scaled production. Arizona State University Polytechnic has demonstrated the first stable algal biofuel production in a field setting, but the project footprint was less than an acre. The next vital step will be scaling production to 40 or 100 acres and cultivating algae year-round.

Earthrise Nutraceuticals in Southern California produces 500 tons of human food-grade algae annually on a small farm. The 30 one-acre ponds are 18 inches deep, and Earthrise grows only during the seven warm months of the year. Algae-based human food, nutraceuticals, and animal feed offer algae farmers several times the price associated with commodities such as fuel. Most algal business models plan to harvest the oil and sell the other coproducts for their highest value.

Year-round algal biomass production represents an important challenge. In colder months, closed or semiclosed growing systems need modest heat to sustain high productivity. Greenhouses with solar panels to harvest solar energy or that operate with the heat from geothermal would substantially contribute to continuous production. Indoor production capability reduces water loss due to evaporation and enables continuous water and nutrient recycling while mitigating environmental pollution.

Considerable investment is flowing into algal fuels. Exxon Mobil recently invested $600 million into a joint venture with Craig Venter's Synthetic Genomics for research into next-gen algal fuels. Large oil and gas companies, many utilities, and the airlines are all investing in algae for both carbon capture and oil production. Sapphire Energy announced it will produce 1 billion gallons of algal fuel per year by 2018 (Bruemmer 2010).

Corn versus Algal Feedstock

The reasons algae will displace corn ethanol as the biofuel feedstock of choice are summarized in table 1. Corn is not sustainable as a biofuel feedstock because it takes far too much cropland, water, fertilizers, pesticides, and herbicides. Corn ethanol costs too much to produce in terms of total energy, economics, and environmental pollution.

Corn ethanol farmers receive direct and indirect subsidies for nearly every production input, including water and the power to pump water as well as payments for growing corn. Subsidies encourage overconsumption of fossil resources, pollution, and waste. The United States would be well

TABLE I
Corn Ethanol and Algal Biofuel Comparison

Parameter	Corn	Algae
Renewable and sustainable	No, massive consumption of inputs is nonsustainable	Yes, positive ecological footprint
Gasoline equivalent energy	36 percent less energy than gasoline	Equal to or 30 percent more energy than gasoline
Consumes millions of acres of cropland	Yes, about 44 million acres in 2010 for corn ethanol	No cropland
Consumes trillions of gallons of clean water	Yes, about 2 trillion gallons in 2008	No, algae clean wastewater; use brine water
Pollutes air and soils	Yes, CO_2, nitric oxides, fertilizers, chemicals	No, algae give off only pure oxygen
Creates dead zones in wetlands, rivers, lakes, estuaries, and oceans	Yes, agricultural run-off	No, water recycled, reused, and often remediated
Causes massive ecological destruction	Yes, extracts nonrenewable fossil water, erodes soils, and pollutes wells	No ecological destruction
Systemic water pollution	Millions of tons of fertilizers, herbicides, pesticides, and fungicides	No or minimal water pollution in closed or semiclosed systems
Erodes soils	Yes, about 6 tons per acre per year	No erosion, no land cultivation or irrigation
"Eflation," ethanol-induced food price increases	Yes, burning food for fuel decreases supply and increases food prices	No, produces proteins, starches, and lipids and adds to the food supply
Decreases exports due to eflation	Yes, due to price spikes in grains and animal feed	No, produces fodder, animal feed, and nutrients
Requires $20 billion in subsidies to sustain the industry	Yes, ethanol is nonsustainable without massive subsidies	Yes, but far lower subsidies than ethanol
Consumes massive fossil fuels in feedstock production	Yes, tractors, trucks, harvesters, fertilizers, chemicals, refining	No, light tractors, trucks, and fertilizers
Vulnerable to a single weather event or disease vector	Yes, a drought or severe storm can destroy a crop	No, when the sun shines, algae grows; it goes dormant in bad weather
Need for special engine designs due to alcohol	Yes, alcohol degrades the engine	No need for special engines
Cannot be distributed by pipeline because it mixes	Yes, absorbs condensation and dilutes fuel	No, can be distributed by pipeline
Positive energy value, yields more energy than it takes to produce	No, yields less energy than it consumes in production	Yes, energy positive

served to create a farm and energy policy that shifts subsidies from corn ethanol to biofuel production that is sustainable and nonpolluting.

America's path forward for bioenergy needs a quick course correction because the current model is not sustainable in economic, environmental, or social terms. Algal biofuels offer considerable benefits including a bioenergy future that is sustainable, clean, and carbon neutral. Algal biofuel production reverses the pollutive path and cleans water and air pollution while providing coproducts such as food, food nutrients, feed, fertilizers, and fine medicines that provide substantial benefits to human societies.

References

Bruemmer, Rene. 2010. "10 Major Innovations to Look for in the Coming Decade." *The [Montreal] Gazette*, January 2. http://www.montrealgazette. com/technology/.

Darzins, Al. 2007. "Cellulosic Ethanol." Presentation at the Arizona State University Conference on Sustainable Energy, Tempe, Arizona, May 30.

Department of Energy (DOE). 2006. *Report to Congress on the Interdependence of Energy and Water*. United States Department of Energy, December.

Dias de Oliveira, Marcelo E., Burton E. Vaughan, and Edward J. Rykiel Jr. 2005. "Ethanol as Fuel: Energy, Carbon Dioxide Balances, and Ecological Footprint." *BioScience* 55, no. 7: 593–602.

Dismukes, G. C., D. Carrieri, N. Bennette, G. M. Ananyev, and M. C. Posewitz. 2008. "Aquatic Phototrophs: Efficient Alternatives to Land-Based Crops for Biofuels." *Current Opinions in Biotechnology* 19:235–40.

Donner, S. D., and C. J. Kucharik. 2005. "Corn-Based Ethanol Production Compromises Goal of Reducing Nitrogen Export by the Mississippi River." *Proceedings of the National Academy of Sciences* 105:4513–18.

Edwards, Mark. 2007. *BioWar I: Why Battles over Food and Fuel Lead to World Hunger*. Tempe, Ariz.: LuLu Press.

Edwards, Mark. 2008. *Green Algae Strategy: End Oil Imports and Engineer Sustainable Food and Fuel*. Tempe, Ariz.: CreateSpace.

Edwards, Mark. 2010. *Abundance: A Green Algae Strategy for Sustainable Food*. Tempe, Ariz.: CreateSpace.

Freese, Barbara, and Steve Clemmer. 2006. "Gambling with Coal: How Future Climate Laws Will Make New Coal Power Plants More Expensive." *Union of Concerned Scientists*, September. Available at http://www.windpoweringamerica.gov/pdfs/workshops/2007_summit/clemmer.pdf.

Goyal, S. K. 2002. "A Profile of Algal Biofertilizer." In *Micro Fertilizers*, edited by S. Kannaiyan, 250–58. Delhi: Narosa Publishing House.

Harte, Julia. 2010. "EPA's Biofuel Mandates Based on Shaky Assumptions, Scientists Say." *Solve Climate News*, April 20.

Henry, L., and C. Devereaux. 2009. "Sustainable Biofuels." Discussion Paper 2009-07, Environment and Natural Resources Program, Belfer Center for Science and International Affairs and Sustainability Science Program, Harvard University.

Hoekman, S. K. 2009. "Biofuels in the U.S.: Challenges and Opportunities." *Renewable Energy* 34:14–22.

Hogue, Cheryl. 2007. "EPA's Program to Reward Environmental Excellence Gets a Bad Review," *Chemical and Engineering News* 85, no. 17 (April 23): 36–37. doi: 10.1021/cen-v085n017.p036.

Hu, Q., M. Sommerfeld, E. Jarvis, M. Ghirardi, M. Posewitz, M. Seibert, and A. Darzins. 2008. "Microalgal Triacylglycerols as Feedstocks for Biofuel Production: Perspectives and Advances." *Plant Journal* 54:621–39.

Huang, Wen. 2004. "U.S. Increasingly Imports Nitrogen and Potash Fertilizer." *Amber Waves*, February. http://www.ers.usda.gov/amberwaves/February04/Findings/USIncreasinglyImports.htm.

Huff, G. F. 2004. "An Overview of the Hydrogeology of Saline Ground Water in New Mexico." *Water Desalination and Reuse Strategies for New Mexico*. New Mexico Water Resources Research Institute, September.

Huntley, M., and D. G. Redalje. 2007. "CO_2 Mitigation and Renewable Oil from Photosynthetic Microbes: A New Appraisal." *Mitigation and Adaptation Strategies for Global Change* 12:573–608.

Jacobson, M. Z. 2009. "Review of Solutions to Global Warming, Air Pollution, and Energy Security." *Energy and Environment Science* 2:148–73.

Lantz, M., M. Svensson, L. Björsson, and P. Björsson. 2007. "The Prospects for an Expansion of Biogas Systems in Sweden." *Energy Policy* 35:1830–43.

Pimentel, D., and T. W. Patzek. 2007. "Ethanol Production: Energy, Economics, and Environmental Losses." *Reviews in Environmental Contamination and Toxicology* 189:25–41.

REN 21. 2009. "Renewable Energy Policy Network for 21st Century." *Global Status Report*. Available at http://www.ren21.net/.

Sawyer, D. 2008. "Climate Change, Biofuels and Eco-Social Impacts in the Brazilian Amazon and Cerrado." *Philosophical Transactions of the Royal Society B: Biological Sciences* 363:1747–52.

Shilton, A. N., N. Powell, D. D. Mara, and R. Craggs. 2008. "Solar-Powered Aeration and Disinfection, Anaerobic Co-Digestion, Biological CO_2 Scrubbing and Biofuel Production: The Energy and Carbon Management Opportunities of Waste Stabilization Ponds." *Water Science and Technology* 58:253–58.

Shindell, Drew T., Greg Faluvegi, Nadine Bell, and Gavin A. Schmidt. 2005. "An Emissions-Based View of Climate Forcing by Methane and Tropospheric Ozone." *Geophysical Research Letters* 32. doi: 10.1029/2004GL021900.

Sommerfeld, Milton. 2010. "Algal Biofuels." Presentation at the Algal Biomass Summit, Phoenix, Arizona, October.

St. John, Jeff. 2009. "APS Gets $70.5M to Feed Captured Carbon to Algae." *Greentechmedia*, August 16. http://www.greentechmedia.com/articles/read/aps-gets-70.5m-to-feed-captured-carbon-to-algae/.

Tilman, D., R. Socolow, J. A. Foley, J. Hill, E. Larson, L. Lynd, S. Pacala, J. Reilly, T. Searchinger, C. Somerville, and R. Williams. 2009. "Beneficial Biofuels: The Food, Energy, and Environment Trilemma." *Science* 325:270–71.

Notes

1 "Chronic Illness Linked to Coal Mining," *Science Daily*, March 27, 2008, http://www.sciencedaily.com/releases/2008/03/080326201751.htm

2 Biomass Research and Development Board (BR&DB), *Increasing Feedstock Production for Biofuels,* http://www.usbiomassboard.gov/pdfs/8_Increasing_Biofuels_Feedstock_Production.pdf

3 United States Department of Energy, *National Algal Biofuel Technology Roadmap,* https://e-center.doe.gov/iips/faopor.nsf/UNID/79E3ABCACC9AC14A852575CA00799D99/$file/AlgalBiofuels_Roadmap_7.pdf

PART III

Metrics and Supply Chain
Transparency

CHAPTER 15

Making Greenhouse Gas Management Practical for Business

Christopher L. Weber, Andreas Vogel, and H. Scott Matthews

Business interest in supply chain risk management, sustainability reporting, and ecolabeling is driven by several factors, including increased public environmental awareness and historically high energy prices. If a company wishes to retain a good environmental image to consumers, investors, and high-quality potential employees, it will need to continue learning about energy and environmental issues and methods. Thus, managing greenhouse gas emissions throughout supply chains is an increasingly important skill for businesses to learn. We outline the current state of greenhouse gas management (GHGM) tools, particularly life cycle assessment (LCA), and discuss their potential to help businesses become more environmentally sustainable. In its current state, such tools take considerable effort in upfront learning and data gathering, and we focus on how these tools can increasingly be made more practical for business. We argue that by combining the best aspects of the current tools, businesses can minimize the time and money needed to gather data and perform environmental assessments. Critically, we argue that the level of precision and effort should be dictated by the specific use the business has for the results. We illustrate these thoughts with a case study in managing supply chain greenhouse gases in the soft drink industry. A focus on practical GHGM will in turn lead to more time for interpretation and management, helping businesses to decrease their supply chain costs and risks, maintain good relationships with their suppliers and retailers, build brand value, and attract young talent.

Introduction: Greenhouse Gas Management, Life Cycle Assessment, and Business

Since the early 1970s, the passage of laws restricting environmental emissions, regulation, and consumer/investor awareness have made businesses more aware of their environmental impacts. The recent global focus on energy and environmental issues, particularly climate change, has the international business community seeking tools to further understand, quantify, and publicize both their environmental impacts and their efforts to reduce these impacts. Further, drivers such as increasing energy costs, changing consumer preferences, and climate change policies (Weber, Matthews, and Vogel 2008) are compelling businesses to broaden their viewpoints to include not just impacts taking place at their facilities but also impacts embedded in their supply chain and in the use and disposal of their products. Several overlapping methods and tools exist for greenhouse gas management (GHGM), most related to the growing field of life cycle assessment (LCA), aka "carbon footprinting" of products or entities (Matthews, Hendrickson, and Weber 2008; Suh et al. 2004).

LCA is a scientific method designed for comprehensive "cradle-to-grave" assessments of the energy use and environmental impacts of products and services (Hendrickson, Lave, and Matthews 2005; Vigon et al. 1993). The method has roots in economics, environmental engineering, and supply chain optimization. LCA was originated to answer relatively simple comparative questions such as the better environmental choice for grocery shopping bags (paper versus plastic). Despite these modest beginnings, the method has now developed into its own discipline, bringing together engineers, scientists, and social scientists from several traditional disciplines. A quickly growing number of environmental consultancies specifically focus on performing LCAs, and several software and database tools are available.

Business interest in LCA originally stemmed mostly from an understanding of supply chain vulnerabilities and complexities, and this remains an important driver for LCA in business. However, with growing public awareness and concern over environmental issues, LCA has grown in importance to many businesses for several other reasons, such as making comparative environmental claims on a company's products and avoiding scrutiny and potential embarrassment from the campaigns of environmental nongovernmental organizations (NGOs). Specifically, increasing business interest in LCA is being driven by three broad classes of concerns, both internal and external to the business:

- Supply chain risk management (internal usage)

- Insight and decision support for product or process design (internal usage)

- Retailer or investor requirements such as carbon labeling, sustainability reporting (external usage)

LCA allows businesses to understand supply chain vulnerabilities, such as the risks of higher energy costs or increased regulation of an environmental contaminant such as greenhouse gases. It can also allow businesses to benchmark their energy usage or environmental progress against industry standards and support environmentally preferable purchasing decisions. In a slightly broader context, LCA can support decision-making about the design of products, including not just supply chain vulnerabilities but also the use and disposal of the products, both of which are important for how consumers judge a product or brand's sustainability.

More recently, the use of LCA has become more important from an external perspective. Announcements from several major retailers that energy or environmental data, or both, will be required from suppliers in the near future has led to perhaps the most important reason for interest—a requirement for businesses to report in order to secure future shelf-space in leading retail stores. Additional external uses of such data, such as for sustainability reporting and climate disclosure to mandatory or voluntary greenhouse gas registries, are also playing a leading role.

These different internal and external uses of greenhouse gas information require firms to gather different types of data and ensure different levels of precision. For example, simply determining "hot spots" for design planning requires much less precision than presenting that life-cycle greenhouse gas emission data in a label on the product, where it may be subject to legal or consumer challenge. Moreover, different types of products may have different specific needs as well. For example, some products have energy use and emissions associated with their use (e.g., appliances, autos, and electronics) while others do not (household furnishings, food and beverages, plastics). Services clearly constitute different challenges than physical products, and product-service systems, for example, leasing of products, are different still. Food products require detail of non-energy-related greenhouse gas emissions, such as nitrous oxide and methane, which may not be as important for other products.

Despite the substantial learning that it can offer, detailed GHGM in the business world has been held back by concerns over the substantial time and resources that typical LCAs require. Because such studies are comprehensive in scope, they require massive amounts of data from the business's own facilities and from its suppliers, in turn requiring large amounts of staff time and consultants' fees. Standards describing the methods of LCA, such as the International Standards Organization 14040 series or the PAS 2050 standard from the British Standards Institute and Carbon Trust (BSI 2008), specify when more general data types can be used;[1] however, these standards remain inscrutable and difficult to navigate for many nonexperts. This has led to efforts to simplify or streamline the process of LCA through alternate methods, different data sources, and various simplifications (Hendrickson, Lave, and Matthews 2005; Graedel 1998).

This review will focus on the current state of the LCA field and how greenhouse gas management could be made more practical for businesses. A background section will discuss the concepts of LCA, especially related to how life cycles vary between different business and product types. We then briefly discuss the currently available methods and their practical limitations. Finally, we discuss how various business goals relate to the different methods and data sources available, followed by an illustrative case study.

Understanding Product and Service Life Cycles

Before discussing detailed methods and data for LCA, we first introduce the concept of product life cycles and the general differences in product classes. We use the term "product" to denote a physical good, service, or product–service system. There are several phases defining the life cycle of a good or service, and different products will have different shares of impacts in these various phases. Figure 1 shows a typical definition of a product life cycle that consists of five stages: raw material extraction, material processing, manufacturing, usage, and end of life (waste management). The stages proceed linearly but have several potential feedback loops, for example, recycling (where waste returns to material processing), remanufacturing (to manufacturing), or reusing (to use). We add in another dimension that is not typically included in the scope of LCA, product and process design. Product design informs which materials end up in

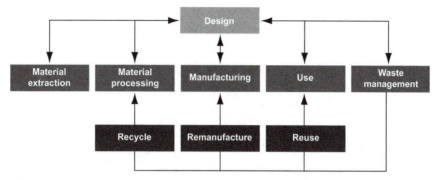

Figure 1   Phases of a product life cycle and linkages between phases.

the product, how the product is used, and its potential for reuse/recycling while process design informs the way the product is made and thus the emissions associated with the production phase.

We focus this review on greenhouse gas emissions, although all the concepts are generalizable to other environmental impacts. In terms of greenhouse gas emissions, products can have impacts in different stages of their life cycles. Figure 2 shows a schematic of different industry types and where their direct impacts on climate change tend to occur. The figure orders sectors roughly from bottom to top from primary sectors (those

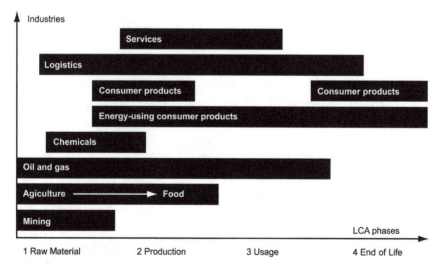

Figure 2   Schematic of life-cycle stages and industry groups' impact profiles over the stages.

involved near the beginning of supply chains) to secondary sectors (manufacturing) and service sectors. In general, secondary and service sectors require output from the more GHG-intensive primary sectors at some point in their supply chains, and thus all the sectors are linked through supply chain interactions (also known as "indirect" emissions of manufacturers or service providers).

As is evident in figure 2, all primary sectors such as mining have impacts in the raw material phase, although for oil and gas, another raw material, impacts tend to be dominated in the production phase (refining) and the use phase (the combustion of gasoline, diesel, etc.). Agriculture can be considered a raw material, and some agricultural products are used directly (i.e., fruits, vegetables, nuts) while other products (e.g., corn and soy) tend to be further processed into other food products (processed food, meat, and dairy products) such that their impacts occur more in production phases. Most consumer products have their direct impacts in the production and end-of-life phases, although a special case is energy-using products such as appliances, transportation equipment, and electronics, which have substantial use phase impacts. Logistics occur throughout all the life-cycle phases and have impacts that are usually allocated to the product that is being moved or stored. Service sectors produce an intangible product and have little to no end-of-life impacts but can emit greenhouse gases in the production and usage phases.

It is important to remember that the different industry groups do not exist in isolation. Consumer products, for instance, require minerals and chemicals from the mining and chemicals sectors (metals, plastics, etc.) to make components and final goods. Services, although they tend to be thought of as relatively low-impact compared to the "dirty," energy-intensive industries such as chemicals, raw materials, and so on, require products such as computers and equipment, which in turn require chemicals and raw materials in their supply chains. Thus, as these relatively energy-intensive sectors are the most exposed to potential cost increases from climate change policy, no supply chain is free from risk due to the ubiquitous usage of energy-intensive materials to make products and services.

LCA and "Footprinting": Considering the Whole Life Cycle

Delineating these supply chain interactions between businesses that produce final goods and those producing intermediate goods is at the core of life cycle assessment. These interactions are what make LCA different from other tools such as some entity-level tools and initiatives, for example, the Greenhouse Gas Protocol, the most widely used standard for calculating a company's greenhouse gas emissions, and the Carbon Disclosure Project, an investor-led initiative requesting emissions data from large companies. These initiatives separate emissions into three tiers or scopes but only require reporting of the first two tiers, direct emissions and emissions from purchased energy. The third scope, including emissions from the company's value chain, use and disposal of its products, and all other emissions associated with an entity, is where LCA is used.

By requiring businesses to report only emissions in the first two scopes, such tools miss a large portion of the greenhouse gas emissions in the production of a good, estimated previously at around 74 percent for an average sector of the U.S. economy (Matthews, Hendrickson, and Weber 2008). While analyses of direct emissions alone can be helpful for some of the goals businesses might have for environmental analysis, such as compliance with mandatory emissions reporting, they are far from ideal for such uses as supply chain risk management and labeling. The reasons why can perhaps best be explained through examples.

Figures 3 and 4 show some example numbers for "cradle-to-gate" (i.e., raw material extraction through production but excluding use and end-of-life) emissions of $1 million worth of products from various industries in the 2002 U.S. economy in two different formats.[2] The method used to obtain these average results is discussed below. Figure 3 shows

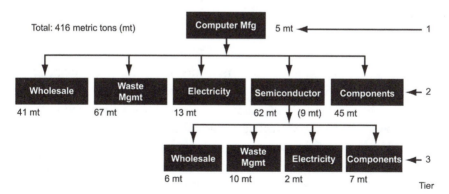

Figure 3 Example industry LCA results (adapted from the EIO-LCA web model, http://www.eiolca.net/) for the production of $1 million of computers in 2002.

a breakdown of emissions from the manufacture of a computer, which emits 416 metric tons (mt) CO_2e GHG emissions to make the $1 million of computers. Emissions are represented at each level of the supply chain, with the top of the tree (tier 1) representing final assembly, the second tier representing the assembly facility's suppliers, and the third tier representing the suppliers to these suppliers. Of course, the schematic only shows a fraction of the inputs to make a computer, and thus the nodes do not add up to the total.

The "direct" emissions from making the computer, occurring directly at the assembly facility, represent only 5 of the 416 total tons. Adding in the emissions from the electricity used at the assembly facility yields only 18 tons (5 tons direct + 13 tons electricity) of the 416 tons CO_2e in the supply chain. Thus, the scope 1 and 2 "footprint" of the computer assembler yields a very small fraction of the total cradle-to-gate life-cycle emissions. Perhaps more surprisingly, the total emissions associated with the top 5 contributors to computers' supply chain emissions (wholesale trade, waste management, electricity, semiconductor manufacturing, and other components) amount to only around half (230 tons) of the 420 mt CO_2e of GHG emissions associated with making computers, which shows how a complex supply chain such as computer production can have large shares of emissions occurring in many small contributing supply chain components.

Figure 4 shows an alternate view, giving the fraction of life-cycle emissions for five different product types (computers, coal, iron and steel, legal services, and apparel) occurring at various supply chain tiers, this time including all suppliers at that tier. The differences between coal mining, where around 80 percent of the total cradle-to-gate emissions occur in the first tier of the supply chain (directly at the coal mine) and more advanced products such as apparel, legal services, and computers are striking. For example, the first tier percentage of total emissions varies from around 1 percent for computers to around 20 percent for apparel, 40 percent for iron and steel, and 80 percent for coal mining. As a product gets more advanced and has longer supply chains, the supply chain depth necessary to capture a large fraction (say 90 percent) of life-cycle emissions increases: it takes only two tiers to capture 90 percent of coal mining's GHG emissions, three tiers for iron and steel, four for apparel, five for legal services, and six for computers.

These examples show the importance of examining the entire supply chain in the calculation of cradle-to-gate GHG emissions for products or industries. Even an industry very close to raw material extraction, coal

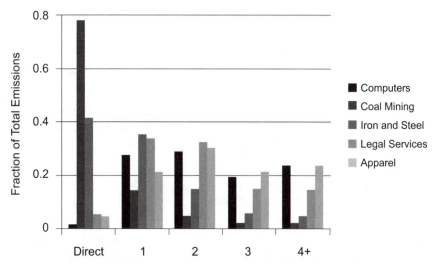

Figure 4 Percentage of cumulative life-cycle GHG emissions at the direct and first 3 supply chain tiers (and remainder of 4th and above tiers). Note: For each set of five columns in the figure, the order from left to right is computers, coal mining, iron and steel, legal services, and apparel.

mining, has more than 20 percent of its emissions outside of the scope 1 and 2 boundary required for reporting. This is true for almost any product or industry; a company trying to measure its exposure to price increases due to climate legislation thus needs LCA methods to truly understand its risks.

Usage and End of Life: The Downstream Phases

The results shown in figure 4 are general and intuitive; more complicated products have more complicated supply chains and thus more complicated life-cycle emissions profiles. However, until now we have only quantitatively discussed the upstream phases of production and materials. A full view of GHGM also needs to capture the downstream use and disposal phases, which may or may not be important to businesses conducting LCA, depending on their goals and the type of product they make.

As compared to raw material acquisition and production, which are generally historic and will yield increased precision by increased scrutiny of supply chains, usage and end of life are predictive of the future use and disposal of a company's products. In other words, emissions occurring downstream from a company are much harder to calculate than those occurring upstream from a company. This detail makes generating precise numbers for the total life-cycle emissions associated with a product difficult; however, with consistent metrics, comparison between products in the use phase can still be worthwhile. Examples include the Energy Star program, EPA fuel economy ratings for automobiles, and many other rating schemes. Due to this standardization, comparisons of use-phase emissions may be easier to perform than calculations for supply chain production emissions.

The end-of-life phase is complicated in both absolute and comparative metrics, however. Like the usage phase, end-of-life emissions depend on an assumption of how a product will be disposed of, recycled, remanufactured, or reused. In some cases, especially for remanufacturing, businesses may have good data on recovery rates for products. However, recycling becomes more difficult—should a company get credit for making a product recyclable but without any recycled content? Vice versa? Or only if the product contains recycled material that can be traced directly back to the company's own first generation products? These issues require some level of practitioner judgment, which has led to some criticism of LCA tools as being inexact. In general, however, the inclusion of use and end-of-life phases, even if inexact, will better help businesses to fully understand the life-cycle impacts of their products and how improvements may be made.

Methods for Life Cycle Assessment: Process versus Economic Input–Output

After a brief discussion of different impacts that could be considered, we now move to discuss some common methods for LCA and GHGM. The main methods for conducting LCA are process-based methods and economic input output methods.

Process (Engineering) LCA

A number of institutions worldwide have been developing LCA approaches and databases since the early 1990s. In the United States, the Society for Environmental Toxicology and Chemistry and the Environmental Protection Agency (EPA) have spearheaded the development efforts (Vigon et al. 1993). The International Standards Organization has produced and subsequently modified standards internationally. Other groups, including the British

Standards Institute, in conjunction with the Carbon Trust, the World Resources Institute, and the World Business Council for Sustainable Development, have published or are working on greenhouse gas–specific standards for businesses and products. These LCA standards are based on process engineering models that identify and quantify resource inputs and environmental outputs at each life-cycle stage. This approach requires collection of detailed data directly from companies or studies published in literature.

Input–Output (Economic) LCA

A complementary approach to process LCA uses economic input–output models to capture the upstream supply chain of results, though use and disposal phases are not included. Economic input–output LCA (EIO-LCA, aka environmental input-output analysis, EIOA) uses publicly available economic and environmental data to arrive at comprehensive, industry-wide environmental impacts (Hendrickson, Lave, and Matthews 2005). The economic models behind this method, called input–output models, are developed by most countries' statistical agencies every few years (two to five years is typical). The input–output model is combined with energy and environmental data for different economic sectors to describe the entire supply chain to make a good or service in economic and environmental terms. The method can only determine impacts from raw materials up to the manufacturing stage; thus, the use and disposal phases must be treated separately. A key parameter for the method is the level of detail available in a country's input–output table because many countries use rather aggregated sectors (such as having only one sector for the chemical industry), producing potentially large errors when modeling specific commodities (such as a specific chemical within the sector).

Strengths and Weaknesses of the Basic Methods

Many authors have described the strengths and weaknesses of the two main approaches to LCA (see, e.g., Minx et al. 2008). Generally, process LCA is seen to be the most appropriate method for product-level analysis due to its high level of product specificity; data can be gathered, allocated, and summed to fully describe a specific production system of a specific product (measured either in mass or number of units). This stands in contrast to EIO-LCA, where specificity is low in general due to aggregation of unlike products within economic sectors and a reliance on economic prices (which vary) to measure production.

Given its specificity, process LCA has been the focus of most international standards for LCA and "footprinting" of products. However, process LCA suffers from two major weaknesses that EIO-LCA can help overcome. The first is aforementioned high levels of time and money necessary to fully complete an LCA for even a single product. Perhaps worse, there are relatively few opportunities for economies of scale because data collection and allocation for one product may or may not help in an LCA of a second product. With EIO-LCA, once a model has been completed (public data gathered for energy and greenhouse gas emissions by sector), performing a scoping LCA takes a matter of seconds, as the online implementation of several countries' models at the well-used website eiolca.net shows.[3]

Process LCA also suffers from "cut-off" issues related to unavailable data or processes considered too insignificant to gather data for. Because each additional process considered within the scope of the study requires additional data, at some point process LCAs cut off processes deemed to be outside of the "system boundary." The choice of system boundary is somewhat arbitrary, and several studies have estimated the errors involved with cutting off at a system boundary to be significant (> 50 percent of total impacts for some products [Lenzen 2001]). EIO-LCA has the theoretical advantage of being a fully complete model in that the supply chain extends upstream to comprise all impacts from all inputs to a product, including services and capital investments (with additional data on capital flows within an economy), which are usually ignored in process LCA.

Hybrid Methods: Leveraging the Strengths of Both Methods

Given the relative strengths and weaknesses of both methods, a combination of the best attributes of both would achieve the theoretically best LCA results, in terms of producing the most accurate results at least cost. Many practitioners of LCA have thus proposed various methods for "hybrid LCA" using both methods to differing degrees (Suh et al. 2004; Minx et al. 2008). The sophistication of hybrid methods varies considerably but can be as simple as either method in isolation (Hendrickson, Lave, and Matthews 2005; Minx et al. 2008).

Meeting Business Needs: A Practical Approach to GHGM

With this brief background in mind, we discuss how LCA can be moved from an academic and research method to a useful, informative, and practical tool for business planning. We begin the discussion with the various goals businesses may have in conducting LCAs. We then discuss data needs and data availability to meet these different goals, since data drives both the quality and the cost of LCA studies. Finally, we discuss the potential role of business software in helping businesses overcome the financial and knowledge hurdles that LCA can present.

Different Goals for LCA Studies and Their Data Requirements

As discussed earlier, businesses conduct LCAs with different purposes in mind:

- Supply chain risk management (internal usage)

- Insight and decision support for product/process design (internal usage)

- Retailer/investor requirements, for example, carbon labeling, sustainability reporting (external usage)

Again, a key difference between these goals is whether data will be gathered internally or approximated with external data. This distinction has ramifications for data quality and specificity. Managing greenhouse gases throughout supply chains is rather data-intensive, and several different types of data are often used. There is an inherent tradeoff between the specificity of results and the time and effort needed to achieve that specificity.

Table 1 reviews the potential data types a business may use in conducting an LCA, describing the level of specificity (the term "facility" represents any single geographic location whether a factory, store, or farm), the units in which the data is available, and whether the data is allocated from facility to product.

Greenhouse gas emissions data can either be measured directly or estimated through the use of energy or activity data and emissions factors

TABLE I
Data Types for Compilation of LCAs

Name	Level of Analysis	Units	Product or Facility
Primary facility-level data	Facility	CO_2e/yr	Facility level or product level
Secondary LCA data	Process or product	CO_2e/kg (usually)	Product level (usually)
Registry-type data	Facility or group of facilities	CO_2e/yr	Facility level
EIO-LCA (top-down)	Group of industries	CO_2e/\$/yr	Supply chain of facilities

for energy types or activities. For example, a facility will take data on yearly energy usage (natural gas, electricity, etc.) and multiply by CO_2 emissions factors for natural gas boilers and for the local electricity mix (WBCSD/WRI 2007). Of course, this calculation only yields emissions per facility per year, not per product. Converting between facility-level and product-level data is simple when a facility performs only one task or produces one product; however, when multiple products are produced, the emissions must be allocated to the various products, coproducts, and by-products. For example, dairy farms produce dairy products as well as meat and leather, and the impacts associated with the facility must be allocated between these products. This point remains a contentious one in GHGM (WBCSD/WRI 2007; Ekvall and Weidema 2004; Kim and Dale 2005).

Primary data, or data gathered directly from the facility or supplier of interest, is clearly preferred where it is available because only this data type is truly representative of the product or supply chain being studied (given a certain spatial and temporal context for the study). Supply chains vary over time and space, and picking this context is an important step in defining the goal and scope of a study. However, there should be a limit to the amount of primary data gathered for any given study, since each additional primary data point, particularly deep in a product's supply chain, increases the cost and effort involved with a study. Thus, other data (secondary data) can and should be used where appropriate to limit the effort associated with a study. The key is to meet the specificity and precision required for the business goal while minimizing cost.

Three main data types are available. The first data type is previous LCAs. Several databases exist worldwide for prior LCAs, some free and others proprietary. Theoretically, secondary LCA databases represent a clear second-best solution to gathering additional primary data. However, any LCA's usefulness to another study is limited by its representativeness to the supply chain under question because production practices, energy efficiencies of processes, and many other parameters vary over time and in different locations. How representative a prior study is to current practice depends on its age and location as well as how quickly technology and production practices change for the product or supply chain in question.

Greenhouse gas registries, such as the Climate Registry in North America and various government-sponsored mandatory registries worldwide, provide facility-level data for facilities, usually in the form of direct emissions and emissions from purchased electricity.[4] The main drawback with this data type is that making use of registry data requires allocation because the registries will list only emissions data per facility, not per product or component.

The final data type is from input–output LCA databases. Some of the existing secondary LCA databases include input–output data while other educational tools exist online using national input–output tables.[5] This data is highly available and allows comparison between different countries of production; however, it exists only for aggregated sectors as opposed to specific products, and it uses variable production costs as the unit of measurement for products, somewhat undesirable given variations of prices of time and between similar products within a category (e.g., organic versus conventional apples).

Matching Needs with Methods: A Least-Cost Approach

Given the different needs and goals companies have and the different data and methods available to meet these goals, we suggest a least-cost approach to achieving satisfactory results for greenhouse gas management activities. In theory, the method and data used to perform the study should use the minimum time and money for data gathering and calculation in order to achieve the needed level of precision. In other words, we argue that general data should be used wherever possible to avoid costly primary data collection, and further, that scoping analysis is critical to reveal which data are important enough to warrant the extra costs of primary data collection.

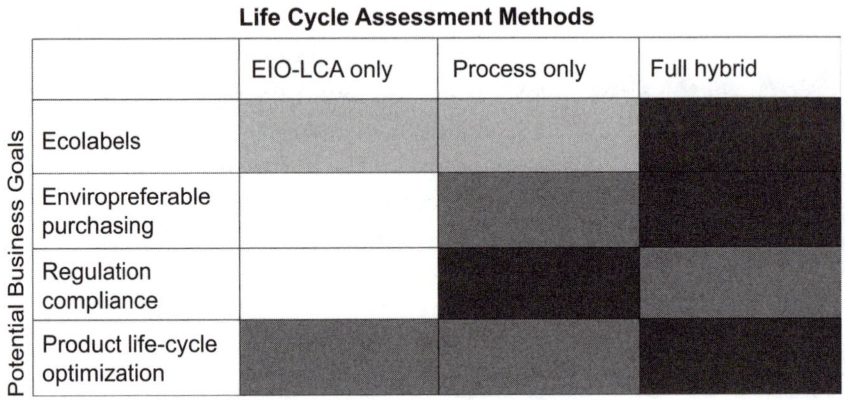

Life Cycle Assessment Methods

	EIO-LCA only	Process only	Full hybrid
Ecolabels			
Enviropreferable purchasing			
Regulation compliance			
Product life-cycle optimization			

Potential Business Goals

Figure 5   Life cycle assessment methods.

The needed level of precision varies for different LCA purposes and, as stated earlier, depends on whether the results of the LCA are intended for internal or external eyes. We summarize how the different methods and data types might be matched with goals in figure 5. Generally EIO-LCA, the most general and thus least-cost approach, will only be marginally applicable to most business applications without further refinement. However, for general insight into the life cycles of products or supply chains, EIO-LCA can provide a good deal of information for a relatively small investment.

In contrast, a pure process analysis, the most detailed and thus most costly approach, will be needed for some purposes, notably compliance with regulation, where general data is of little use. Process analysis can also yield valuable insights into product life-cycle optimization and environmentally preferable purchasing when primary data is available from suppliers. However, its issues (such as cut-off error) make it less than completely satisfactory for external uses such as making product claims via ecolabels—a complete and consistent method is needed to compare across products within a class, and a complete analysis can only be achieved at reasonable cost using hybrid analysis.

In general, we suggest that hybrid analysis of some type is the most useful method for most purposes a business will have for LCA. Even when it is unnecessary to use primary data due to concern over liability and product claims, such as in internal product insight, hybrid analysis will yield the most consistent and accurate results at a reasonable cost. Further, as hybrid analysis can yield both industry-level and product-specific results, it is the most reliable method for comparing between products such as in carbon labeling or environmentally preferable purchasing decisions.

The more difficult question is how to combine the data types in each particular case. It seems reasonable to suggest, as many authors and standards have, that primary data should be used for important subprocesses in a supply chain while average or secondary data, possibly from input–output sources, should be used to complete the system for smaller, less important subprocesses (Minx et al. 2008). We suggest the following routine as the most practical approach to modeling a company's supply chain and approaching a full LCA:

1. Perform a scoping analysis using EIO-LCA and simple assumptions for distribution, use, and disposal phases to get a general idea of where in the life cycle the biggest impacts exist. Because several models already exist, this step should represent a relatively small investment for relatively large reward in insight.

2. Gather primary data from one's own facilities and providers of purchased energy. This data will always be important regardless of project goal because the emissions occurring directly at a company's facilities can represent some of the easiest potential improvements in supply chain emissions.

3. Determine where additional primary data is necessary to achieve the goal of the study. Often this can be determined by using a rule such as a certain amount of contribution to overall supply chain emissions, for example, representing above 1 percent of total emissions.

4. After collecting primary data, recalculate supply chain emissions and assess whether the study's goals have been met.

A generic product's life-cycle emissions profile will include major contributions and more minor contributions. The first step of the approach uses a structural EIO-LCA approach for scoping in which flows represent major and minor contributions. Simple first-order calculations for use and disposal phases will yield an approximate size for these flows. The goal of the study (internal or external usage) will determine where the cutoff between major and minor contributions will be. Primary data should be gathered for all major contributions from the business's own facilities and key suppliers, with the best available secondary process data when primary data is unavailable. For minor contributions, as well as the contributions of less-studied inputs such as services, EIO-LCA data is adequate and sometimes the best available.

Case Study

We complete this review with a case study illustrating how a company would use this practical method to explore the carbon footprint of its products or supply chain. We use a relatively simple product, soft drinks, for illustrative purposes while acknowledging that more complicated products will by necessity be more complicated. A preliminary scoping assessment is performed using input–output LCA for the production phase combined with process data and assumptions for distribution, use, and disposal. The scoping exercise then informs which data need to be gathered in more detail using direct measurement or calculation at the facility, secondary data sets, suppliers, or GHG registries.

Upstream Supply Chain

We begin with a scoping assessment of the production phase of soft drink manufacturing. This first-tier assessment using the 2002 EIO-LCA model

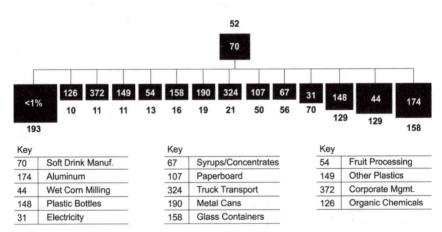

Key	
70	Soft Drink Manuf.
174	Aluminum
44	Wet Corn Milling
148	Plastic Bottles
31	Electricity

Key	
67	Syrups/Concentrates
107	Paperboard
324	Truck Transport
190	Metal Cans
158	Glass Containers

Key	
54	Fruit Processing
149	Other Plastics
372	Corporate Mgmt.
126	Organic Chemicals

Results represent the production of US $1 million (in 2002 dollars) of soft drinks produced in the United States in 2002. All numbers are in metric tons of CO$_2$e with the number below representing the total supply chain beneath the node and the number above representing the direct emissions at the facility represented by the node. Supply chain nodes are numbered by sector of the economy and are shown in the key. The size of the node is roughly proportional to the sector's total supply chain emissions.

Figure 6   Scoping LCA using EIO-LCA for soft drink manufacturing.

is shown in figure 6 for some of the major impact categories for soft drink manufacturing.[6]

In total, to produce $1 million worth of soft drinks, around 880 metrictons of greenhouse gases are produced according to the input–output model. Figure 6 shows the first-tier suppliers that represent greater than 1 percent of total supply chain emissions, with the remainder represented at bottom (node "< 1%," representing 193 of the 885 tons CO_2e). The supply chain GHG emissions to produce soft drinks come from a wide variety of sources, from direct energy use and emissions at the facility (50 tons of the total 880 tons CO_2e), purchased electricity by the soft drink manufacturer (80 tons), and a wide variety of supply chain purchases, from syrups and sugars of corn and fruit to aluminum, plastics, glass, and paperboard for packaging. Of course, logistics throughout the supply chain, such as truck transportation and wholesaling of the purchased supplies contribute, as well as a long list of minor contributions such as organic chemicals, corporate management (i.e., energy use in office

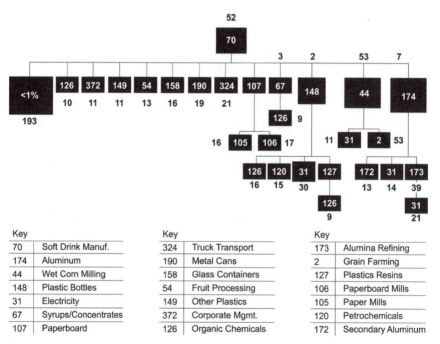

Figure 7 Detailed scoping analysis including all supply chain subtiers representing more than 1 percent of total supply chain emissions to produce $1M of soft drinks.

buildings), and several other contributions less than 1 percent, including air travel, services and consultants, and various other supplies.

However, the scoping analysis should not be limited to first-tier suppliers, since suppliers further up the supply chain (e.g., suppliers of suppliers) may also represent a significant amount of emissions. Figure 7 shows a more detailed scoping analysis where all significant suppliers are identified (defined here as > 1% of supply chain emissions, but the cutoff is arbitrary, as seen in the following). Now it is clear that it is not so simple as to gather data from aluminum can, corn syrup, and plastic bottle suppliers but rather that the supply chains of each of the soft drink producer's suppliers matters as well.

A total of 28 supply chain nodes lie above the 1 percent cutoff, representing 14 first-tier suppliers and their upstream suppliers. If the soft drink maker were able to gather data for the supply chains of each of these 14 first-tier suppliers, it would then have primary data representing around 78 percent of its supply chain emissions. However, if it were only to gather first-tier data (as opposed to data representing the entire supply chain upstream of the facility) for even all of the 28 supply chain facilities that lie above the 1 percent threshold, it would achieve only 48 percent of its supply chain emissions, which shows the importance of both setting the cutoff threshold low enough and including what has been called the "long tail" of supply chains, whereby the sum of small contributions leads to a large share of total emissions.

This brings up the question of effort versus completeness—how low should the cutoff be set? Already 28 upstream facilities would require a good deal of time and money for data gathering if all primary data was sought. To show how quickly this number can expand if a lower cutoff threshold were used, the calculation was repeated at 0.1 percent. Now 180 facilities are included, with still only 64 percent of supply chain emissions represented by direct emissions at these 180 facilities. This would represent substantial time and money for not a large improvement in study quality. One option would thus be to consult secondary data sets for well-studied suppliers, such as aluminum production, plastic bottles, and corn syrup. The advantage of consulting secondary LCAs for such products is that the entire upstream supply chain will be included if a past study is available; thus, improved estimates of large chunks of upstream emissions could be obtained at smaller cost than primary data gathering.

The scoping analysis shows several areas of concern for the producer's upstream supply chain. Direct energy use and electricity are clear contributors, as is the main ingredient in soft drink manufacture, syrups and sugars from corn and fruit. The various methods of packaging the product, from aluminum cans, plastic bottles, and paperboard cases, are also of clear importance. After this, the contributions get somewhat smaller in scale, though transport and logistics should clearly be of concern. Each of these major contributions—aluminum, plastics, glass, paperboard, flavoring syrups, and energy/electricity, deserve more detailed data gathering while the remainder of the supply chain could be modeled as industry average using the input–output data.

Usage and Disposal Phases

So far, only upstream emissions have been considered. Because beverages do not use energy after being produced, use-phase emissions are minor compared to the emissions to produce the soft drink. For the distribution phase, the producer would need to gather data on average delivery distances to the point of sale, and potentially on energy use during display or retailing (such as in display cases in retail stores, in soda machines, etc.). Shipping that uses both company-owned and third-party trucks should be included; at least for the company fleet, a good estimate of fuel usage is probably already available and could easily be converted to emissions using online tools for direct emissions (such as WBCSD/WRI 2007).

Of particular importance to this case study would also be the disposal/recycling phase because one of the biggest environmental impacts associated with soft drinks is the solid waste associated with their packaging. Data on recycling rates for the various modes of packaging would be needed, as well as data on recycled content used in the containers the producer purchases.

Case Study Conclusion

The scoping assessment for a soft drink producer showed several important subprocesses in the production of soft drinks—direct energy usage, purchased electricity, syrups and sugars, aluminum, plastics, glass, and paperboard. Of course, if product-level assessment (e.g., for a carbon label) was the goal of the study, this industry average would need to be split into the various delivery mechanisms for the soft drink—cans, bottles, and boxes—and the variations in production practices between different kinds of soft drinks would need to be identified. Because soft drinks have high weight-to-value ratios, the distribution phase is likely to be important as well, although it depends on the average distance traveled in distribution and the energy efficiency of the fleet moving the drinks. Finally, because a large proportion of the upstream supply chain was in the production of packaging materials (around 42 percent of the total), the recycling stage will clearly be important for the company, although this stage is somewhat harder to quantify in LCA.

Conclusions

As we have shown, business interest in supply chain risk management, sustainability reporting, and ecolabeling is being driven by several internal and external factors. If a company wishes to retain a good environmental image to consumers, investors, and high-quality potential employees, it will need to continue learning about its impacts on the environment, particularly on climate change, while constantly striving for continuous improvement. Life cycle assessment provides an important tool for businesses to understand and manage their greenhouse gas emissions.

That said, LCA currently takes considerable effort from business. Time and effort spent on performing LCAs, gathering supplier data, and reporting to retailers, NGOs, and government is time not spent performing other vital business tasks. Thus, LCA must adapt to business just as business is adapting and learning to perform LCA. We have presented a summary of some of the main methods and issues in supply chain and life cycle assessment for greenhouse gas management with a focus on making LCA as practical as possible for business. In its current state, LCA takes considerable amounts of time and money. Methods vary in their specificity and involved effort, and much of the current literature discusses using the best of both main methods of LCA in hybrid analyses.

With the combination of the best of these current methods, it is possible for business to begin gathering data and performing assessments without the large investments of time and money that LCAs have typically taken. More importantly, however, by combining input–output LCA scoping with primary and secondary data for important processes, businesses can begin reducing the greenhouse gas impacts of their products through better process and product design at minimal cost, a true win-win for business and society.

References

BSI. 2008. *PAS 2050:2008 Specification for the Assessment of the Life Cycle Greenhouse Gas Emissions of Goods and Services*. London: British Standards Institute.

Ekvall, T., and B. P. Weidema. 2004. "System Boundaries and Input Data in Consequential Life Cycle Inventory Analysis." *International Journal of Life Cycle Assessment* 9, no. 3: 161–71.

Graedel, T. E. 1998. *Streamlined Life-Cycle Assessment*. Upper Saddle River, N.J.: Prentice Hall.

Hendrickson, C. T., L. B. Lave, and H. S. Matthews. 2005. *Environmental Life Cycle Assessment of Goods and Services: An Input-Output Approach*, 1st ed. Washington, D.C.: RFF Press.

Kim, S., B. E. Dale. 2005. "Environmental Aspects of Ethanol Derived from No-Tilled Corn Grain: Nonrenewable Energy Consumption and Greenhouse Gas Emissions." *Biomass & Bioenergy* 28, no. 5: 475–89.

Lenzen, M. 2001. "Errors in Conventional and Input–Output Based Life-Cycle Inventories." *Journal of Industrial Ecology* 4, no. 4: 127–48.

Matthews, H. S., C. T. Hendrickson, and C. L. Weber. 2008. "The Importance of Carbon Footprint Estimation Boundaries." *Environmental Science and Technology* 42:5839–42.

Minx, J., T. Wiedmann, J. Barrett, and S. Suh. 2008. *Methods Review to Support the PAS Process for the Calculation of the Greenhouse Gas Emissions Embodied in Goods and Services*. London: DEFRA.

Suh, S., M. Lenzen, G. J. Treloar, H. Hondo, A. Horvath, G. Huppes, O. Jolliet, U. Klann, W. Krewitt, Y. Moriguchi, J. Munksgaard, and G. Norris. 2004. "System Boundary Selection in Life-Cycle Inventories Using Hybrid Approaches." *Environmental Science & Technology* 38, no. 3: 657–64.

Vigon, B. W., D. A. Tolle, B. W. Cornaby, H. C. Latham, C. L. Harrison, T. L. Boguski, R. G. Hunt, and J. D. Sellers. 1993. *Life Cycle Assessment: Inventory Guidelines and Principles*. EPA 600/R-92/245. Washington, D.C.: U.S. Environmental Protection Agency.

WBCSD/WRI. 2007. *The Greenhouse Gas Protocol*. Geneva: World Business Council for Sustainable Development and World Resources Institute.

Weber, C. L., H. S. Matthews, and A. Vogel. 2008. "SAP White Paper: Climate Change: Challenges and Opportunities for Business." Palo Alto, Calif.: SAP White Papers, 1–16.

Notes

1 "ISO 14040: 2006. Environmental Management: Life Cycle Assessment Principles and Framework," International Standards Organization, http://www.iso.org/iso/catalogue_detail?csnumber=37456

2 Green Design Institute, "Economic Input-Output Life Cycle Assessment (EIO-LCA) model," http://www.eiolca.net/

3 Information at http://www.eiolca.net/ is compiled and implemented by the Green Design Institute at Carnegie Mellon University.

4 See the Climate Registry, http://www.theclimateregistry.org/

5 Green Design Institute, "Economic Input-Output Life Cycle Assessment (EIO-LCA) model," http://www.eiolca.net/

6 Ibid.

CHAPTER 16

Wind Power, Energy Technology, and Environmental Impact Assessment

Hannes M. Hapke, Zhaohui Wu, Karl R. Haapala, and Ted K.A. Brekken

Wind power provides a mature electricity-generating technology that has the potential to substitute a share of the traditional thermal electricity generation. The chapter introduces wind power generation, its development over the past years, and current technology trends. The discussion focuses on environmental assessment of energy sources, particularly wind power. For this purpose, the concept of environmental life cycle assessment (LCA) is introduced, and a case study of an Oregon wind power plant is presented. The results of the case study show a short energy payback time from the wind power plant. This results in a rapid offset of greenhouse gas emissions from the manufacturing process during the operational phase of the power plant, and the further operation of the wind power plant supports the reduction of greenhouse gases from electricity production.

Introduction

Power generation for the existing electrical grid is largely based on the combustion of fossil fuels. Global concerns have been raised regarding the environmental sustainability of the system due to life-cycle impacts, including land losses from fuel extraction and impacts of combustion emissions. The urgency to reduce carbon emission of fossil fuel–based energy motivates governments and businesses to find viable alternative energy sources. In the first decade of the new millennium, we have seen concerted efforts to develop such alternative energy generated by wind, solar, biomass, and so on. This chapter focuses on wind energy and has three objectives. First, we will offer an overview of the major alternative energy sources and their environmental impact. Second, we focus on wind energy, its history, and key technology issues with wind power energy. Lastly, we examine the environmental impact of wind farm. To do so, we introduce the life cycle assessment (LCA) method to quantify the environmental impact of a wind turbines. The empirical analysis uses commercially available data as well as information from an existing wind power plant. The LCA study suggests that environmental benefits of avoiding typical electricity production greatly outweigh the impacts due to wind turbine construction and maintenance.

Major Electricity Generation Sources and Their Environmental Impact

In this section, we will first discuss various alternative energy sources and their environmental impact. Then we will focus on wind energy and introduce the LCA method to evaluate the environmental impact of wind farms.

As illustrated by table 1, sources of electrical energy vary by region. The three major sources are conventional thermal, hydroelectric, and nuclear energy. Conventional thermal electricity generation, which is based on the combustion of fossil fuels, continues to dominate. Fossil fuels commonly used for energy generation are coal, oil, and natural gas. These fuels are a nonrenewable resources extracted from the earth using a variety of

TABLE 1
World and Regional Electricity Use by Source

	Conventional Thermal (%)	Hydroelectric (%)	Nuclear (%)	Others Renewable (%)
North America	66.2	13.4	18.0	2.4
Central/South America	28.1	67.5	1.8	2.7
Europe	52.6	15.5	27.4	4.6
Euroasia	63.6	18.4	17.7	0.2
Middle East	96.5	3.5	–	–
Africa	80.5	16.7	2.3	0.4
Asia and Oceana	76.2	13.1	9.6	1.1
World Total	66.0	16.7	15.2	2.1

Source: U.S. Energy Information Administration, "Electricity," http://www.eia.doe.gov/fuelelectric.html.

methods that can disturb sensitive ecosystems. Combustion can release radioactive substances, mercury, carbon dioxide, and other gaseous emissions that can be harmful to humans and the environment. Nitrogen oxides and sulphur oxides form acid rain, which can damage structures and kill plants and organisms.

Hydropower takes advantage of the kinetic energy of flowing water. Environmental concerns of hydroelectric energy generation include changes to rivers and surrounding ecosystems and impacts resulting from the large amounts of materials that are required for construction. Nuclear energy, which is derived from uranium, is a nonrenewable energy resource. Uranium must be mined and refined prior to use. Nuclear energy production uses large volumes of water and results in radioactive solid waste, which are cause for environmental concern.

Wind energy is able to reduce environmental impacts of electrical energy generation systems and complement these existing energy generation technologies. Once a wind park is constructed, additional impacts are small and mainly due to maintenance and repair activities. As shown in figure 1, the impact of electricity production from wind is much lower than for other sources, due mainly to maintenance activities. Environmental concerns have been raised regarding wind farms, however, and include potential impacts on birds, such as death from colliding with turbine blades and interference in migratory corridors and loss of arable land. Residents in close proximity to wind turbines worry about reduced property values due to aesthetic impacts and noise pollution. Such impacts are difficult to quantify in conducting environmental analysis, and decisions on wind often rely on policy-based decision making. Later in this chapter, we will apply LCA method to evaluate the environmental impact of wind energy.

Wind Power

A brief illustration of the history of wind power will help to understand the evolution of wind power technology.

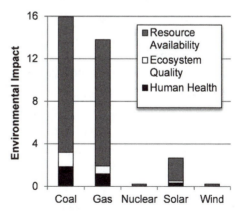

Figure 1   Environmental impact (MPt) of 104 TJ of electricity by source.

For thousands of years, wind power has been an energy source used by society for many purposes. The use of windmills has been recorded in ancient Persia, Tibet, and China for water pumps and grinding mills. Wind energy has also been captured and converted to other forms of energy for centuries. The first wind turbine for electricity production was built in 1891 by Danish engineer Poul la Cour. However, until the mid-20th century, the use of wind power for electricity mainly focused on supplying remote systems and charging small batteries.

The first major developments toward wind turbines for megawatt-scale electricity production were made in the 1940s. At that time, Palmer Putnam designed a 1,250 kW wind turbine for the S. Morgan Smith Company. The blades swept an arc with a 53 m diameter, which created the largest swept area until the 1980s. The sophisticated design also included state-of-the-art, pitch-regulated control of the turbine blades, in which the turbine blades changed their angle toward the wind to have a constant rotational speed. This design became standard for designs in the years to come. Putnam's wind turbine failed and was dismantled in 1945. Shortly thereafter, a 200 kW Danish wind turbine prototype was installed on the Danish island Funen in Gedser. It produced 2.2 million kWh between 1956 and 1967 (Ackermann 2005). Its three-blade design with an upwind rotor became an industry standard in the years to come.

The oil crisis during the 1970s boosted wind turbine technology development and generated commercial interest and investment. Governments worldwide funded research projects for larger turbines and new blades technologies. However, commercial turbines reaching the megawatt levels for power production were not produced in large numbers until the 1990s. Wind energy is a growing source of electricity and a promising complement to current energy generation technologies. In 2009, wind provided 2 percent of global energy needs (340 TWh), yet installed capacity continued to exhibit doubling every three years.[1] At this rate, wind power capacity would top 1.9 million megawatts by 2020. The United States, China, and Germany hold more than half of the world's installed capacity for wind energy. As shown in figure 2, U.S. wind energy generation is predicted to experience rapid growth and then remain level at about 200 million megawatt hours annually through 2020 (EIA 2010).

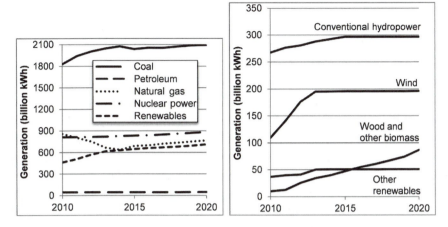

Figure 2   Projected growth of electricity generation: a) major sources and b) renewable sources (EIA, 2010).

Modern Wind Turbine Technology

Wind turbine technology has seen considerable developments over the last half century to make it a viable and competitive energy generation alternative. In this section we discuss some of the key technological issues associated with modern wind turbine design and challenges in wind energy development.

Power and Energy Capability

Turbine output power is strongly dependent on the wind speed. For very low wind speeds, usually around 4 meters per second (m/s) or less, there is insufficient power available to run the turbine. When the wind increases above this cut-out speed, the turbine begins to turn and produces power. The electrical power produced is approximately proportional to the cube of the wind speed, up to the rated, or nameplate, electrical power of the wind turbine. Once the turbine reaches rated power output, any increase in wind speed requires the blades to be turned into the wind, or feathered, to effectively "spill" the excess power, so the capabilities of the mechanical and electrical system are not exceeded. The turbine will produce its rated power output as the wind speed increases until the wind speed reaches an unsafe level. The turbine is shut down at unsafe wind speeds.

Advances in blade and tower manufacturing and construction have enabled very large turbine sizes, with most modern wind turbines having tower heights of 80 meters or more and blade lengths of 50 meters or more. The blade length of some of the newest large turbines is equal to or longer than the wing length of the largest commercial passenger airplanes. Longer blades give the turbine a larger swept area, which increases energy capture, and higher towers give the turbine access to stronger and steadier winds at higher elevations.

For modern, large wind turbines, the rated output is typically around 2 MW to 3 MW, and the yearly average power output is typically around 30 percent of the rated power. The ratio between rated (i.e., nameplate) power rating and yearly average power output is called the "capacity factor." It varies depending on the wind characteristics for a specific site. This means that a 2 MW wind turbine operating with a capacity factor of 30 would generate 600 kW on average. Several major manufactures have demonstrated turbines at 5 MW and larger, but there are presently construction and transportation limitations to the widespread deployment of these very large turbines.

Variable Speed Operation

Early modern wind turbines, such as those first installed in the 1980s in California, were typically equipped with fixed-speed generators. These have the advantage of robustness due to their simplicity but can suffer from suboptimal performance. Optimal aerodynamic performance requires that the rotational speed of the blades vary with wind speed, when possible. Presently, the large wind turbines from all major manufacturers feature variable speed control, which is commonly achieved in one of two ways. The first is using a doubly fed induction generator. This is an induction generator with a grid-connected stator and polyphase windings on the rotor, permitting the injection of current by an external power converter (through slip rings) to control the rotor frequency and hence the rotational speed. The advantage of this design is that variable speed operation is achieved, but the power converter only handles the power in the rotor, which is generally around 30 percent of the total machine power, thus reducing the cost of the converter compared to the total machine rating.

The second major method to achieve variable speed control is using a synchronous generator connected to the grid through a power converter that provides the buffer between the fixed grid voltage and frequency and the variable frequency and voltage of the synchronous generator. The advantage of this design is that the converter has complete control over the active and reactive power as well as harmonics and power quality issues. The disadvantage is that all the power goes through the converter, requiring a converter that must at least match the wind turbine rating. This results in a larger, more expensive converter.

Direct Drive

The majority of large, modern wind turbines incorporate a multistage gearbox to couple the low rotational speed of the blades to the high speed required by the electrical generator. A typical large wind turbine may have a blade rotational speed of approximately 15 rpm and a generator rotational speed of approximately 1,200 rpm. This requires a very large gear ratio and a tremendous amount of torque on the blade-shaft side of the gearbox. The gearbox is a critical stress point in the system, and gearbox failures and maintenance issues have plagued some designs. Performance issues associated with the wind turbine gearboxes have lead to a large academic and commercial interest in so-called direct drive designs that do not require a gearbox. In these designs, a very large electrical generator is directly connected to the blade side of the main shaft, bypassing the need for a gearbox. There is a trade-off in this approach in terms of generator construction difficulty and cost.

Challenges of Wind Energy Development: Location and Power Grid

In countries like the United States, developments for onshore wind power plants are driven by two constraints: area constrains and megawatt constrains.

Recent wind farm development has led to an almost saturation of the wind turbine locale in countries like Germany or Denmark. Favorable areas for wind power plants with high wind speeds and large distances to residential areas have been used; therefore, the wind industry is focusing on two possibilities: repowering and using turbines for lower wind speeds. Repowering means that existing wind turbines that have reached their lifetime of 20 years are dismantled and replaced by state-of-the-art turbines, which provide a much higher power generation on the same area. In the past, wind sites with an average wind speed of 8.5 m/s were favored, whereas a reduction to 7.5 m/s as an average wind speed can increase the market multiple times over. Turbines for lower wind speeds are designed to extend the possible areas for wind power plants.

Megawatt constraints mean that wind power plants are limited by the electric grid connection. The connection is simply not strong enough to handle more wind power. The only solution to this constraint is an upgrade or overhaul of the electric grid system to integrate more wind power into the electric grid. With ambitious renewable energy targets, the electric grid has to be upgraded from a centralized production network to a decentralized electric grid to accommodate different sources of renewable power generation.

A large market exists for offshore wind energy. The offshore wind market has become attractive for many wind turbines suppliers, such as Siemens and Vestas. The smoothness of the ocean surface allows higher wind speeds with less turbulence compared to land. Increased isolation from people eases restrictions on turbine noise and placement. However, offshore wind power presents many technical challenges. Most current offshore turbines are mounted on monopiles driven into shallow-water reefs. Placing a turbine in deep water requires innovative floating designs and difficult mooring schemes. Wave action and salt water vapor add to the mechanical stress on the system. Because of the large installation and maintenance costs for offshore turbines, turbine manufacturers are attempting to increase the power production of the individual turbines to a level of 6 or 8 MW. To increase the number of possible offshore locations, turbine manufacturers are specifically developing offshore turbines that can be placed into deep-water areas.

Life Cycle Assessment of Wind Energy: A Case Study

Earlier in this chapter, we pointed out that wind energy has the least environmental impact relative to other energy sources. In this section, we introduce LCA, a method to evaluate the environmental impacts of a product or service. LCA is widely accepted and standardized internationally through ISO 14040.[2] In LCA, impacts of all product stages—material extraction/material processing, manufacturing, use, and end of life—are considered. Results may be interpreted on the basis of a single score such as the ecoindicator points, as described later. It allows business managers and policymakers to consider the environmental implication associated with product design, production process, and product usage and disposal.

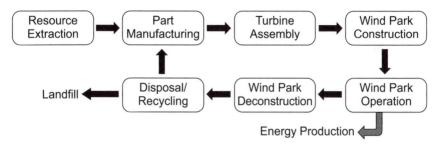

Figure 3   Life cycle of a modern wind power plant.

An LCA of a wind mill or a wind park can also inform business deci-sions on the basis of emissions trading and environmental offsets (Hapke et al. 2010).

An environmental impact comparison for several electricity sources has been undertaken using LCA. These studies employed life-cycle inven-tory data within the ecoinvent database, and the ReCiPe 2008 World H/A impact assessment method.[3] We carried out an LCA to assess the effects of the stages of the life cycle of a wind power plant depicted in figure 3. We focus on the life cycle of wind turbine production and wind farm opera-tions. The production of individual wind turbines, wind park operation, and disposal were considered.

Manufacturing material and energy information in the LCA software have been used to model turbine component production. Our analysis is based on power data and information for a wind park, or wind power plant, in northern Oregon consisting of 100 Vestas V82 (1.65 MW) turbines. We use wind speed and power data research provided by a power company to determine capacity factors for an actual wind park. Capacity factor refers to the ratio of energy output of a wind generator compared to the maximum possible energy output over a period of time. Due to the lack of detailed information, the impacts from the transport, final assembly, and construction were neglected. Earlier studies suggested that transportation-related impacts are insignificant compared to man-ufacturing stage impacts. A lifetime of 20 years was selected as a functional unit for the LCA, which is typical for the industry. The key components are listed in table 2.

The Eco-indicator 99 H/A method evaluates effects of inputs and outputs according to eleven impact categories including carcinogens (C), respiratory organics (RO), respiratory inorganics (RI), climate change (CC),

TABLE 2
Masses of the Main Components of a Modern Wind Park and Related
CO_2 **Emissions**

Component	Weight (t)	CO_2 (t)
Foundation	832.00	87.6
Tower	135.20	281.0
Nacelle Shell	24.20	58.6
Blades (3)	22.20	36.8
Hub/Spinner	20.00	60.2
Gearbox	15.25	51.6
Generator	9.09	32.6
WTG Transformer	3.091	6.6
Internal Cables	0.822	2.5
Transformer Station	174.3	310.8

Source: Weight information is taken from Vestas Wind Systems A/S (2006).

radiation (R), ozone layer (OL), ecotoxicity (E), acidification/eutrophication (AE), land use (LU), minerals (M), and fossil fuels (FF). The three damage types include Human Health, consisting of C, RO, and RI; Ecosystem Quality, consisting of CC, R, OL, E, and AE; and Resources, consisting of LU, M, and FF.

Our analysis illustrates the relative environmental impacts of the components for 100 wind turbines, as well as one transformer station. As shown in figure 4, the wind turbine tower production, foundation

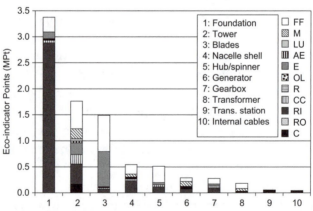

Figure 4   Impact of wind park components.

construction, and blade manufacture are the key contributors to the environmental impact of a wind park.

The inventory network for an entire wind park using a capacity factor of 35 percent is shown in figure 5. Only processes contributing to greater than 0.22 percent of environmental impacts are displayed using the Eco-indicator 99 H/A method. Numbers in each box indicate positive and negative impact in terms of Eco-indicator Points (Pt), where a point represents one-thousandth of the annual environmental load of a European. Thus, negative impact represents avoided impact, or a benefit to the environment.

We found that over a 20-year life, the wind park will avoid about 10,000 GWh of energy generation, resulting in a benefit of about 280 MPt of environmental impacts. This demonstrates that wind turbines belong to a small group of products that can offset their other impacts across their

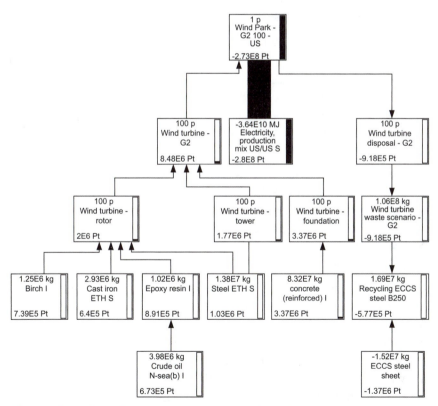

Figure 5   Life-cycle inventory network of wind power plant.

life cycle by displacing other technologies and their impacts. Thus, they have the potential to create a negative emissions balance.

The study suggests that deploying wind turbines in a wind park setting can take advantage of economies of scale. In effect, environmental impacts due to construction and manufacture of system-level components (e.g., substation) are allocated to a larger number of turbines. The energy payback time for a wind power plant is shorter than for a single turbine. Overall, for wind turbines and for wind power plants, the large amount of emission-free generated energy significantly outweighs the amount of energy consumed over their life. This has implications as energy companies face new carbon policies that allow trading of carbon credits. An advantage may be gained by exploiting economies of scale to further increase the margin of avoided carbon emissions over conventional, fossil fuel–based energy generation technologies.

Summary

In this chapter, we started with an overview of the major alternative energy sources and their environmental impacts. Then we discussed the wind energy technology and current challenges associated with wind energy development. In the end, we introduced the life cycle assessment method to evaluate the environmental impact of a wind farm. The LCA results suggest that a wind farm is able to offset the carbon emission associated with the production, operation, and disposal of wind turbines.

Wind power is one of the fastest-growing alternative energy sources—a low-carbon, renewable source of electricity that can deliver millions of watts of relatively low-cost power. The U.S. Energy Department projected that wind could meet 20 percent of total electricity demand by 2030—displacing half of natural gas–powered and 18 percent of coal-fired generation. While wind energy promises environmental benefit, the development of wind energy face various challenges as well. There is always the chicken-and-egg issue associated with commercialization of alternative energy. On the one hand, business organizations have to commit to a high initial investment of developing large-scale wind farms. On the other hand, the existing power grid is unable to handle all the wind energy electricity generated as the electricity storage technology is still under development. Furthermore, new transmission lines to carry electricity from parts of the country with lots of wind to places where demand is highest could cost $93 billion according to a National Renewable Energy Laboratory study. As a consequence, in the United States, government subsidy and incentive programs still play an important role in the growth of wind energy projects.

References

Ackermann, T. 2005. *Wind Power in Power Systems*. New York: Wiley.

Hapke, H., K. R. Haapala, Z. Wu, and T. K. A. Brekken. 2010. "Life Cycle Assessment of Modern Wind Power Plants." In *Proceedings of the Fifteenth Design for Manufacturing and the Lifecycle Conference* (ASME IDETC/CIE), Montreal, Canada, August 15–18.

U.S. Energy Information Administration (EIA). 2010. "Annual Energy Outlook 2010: With Projections to 2035." DOE/EIA-0383(2010). http://www.eia.doe.gov/oiaf/aeo/pdf/0383%282010%29.pdf.

Vestas Wind Systems A/S. 2006. "Life Cycle Assessment of Electricity Produced from Onshore Sited Wind Power Plants Based on Vestas V82-1.65 MW Turbines." Available at www.vestas.com.

Notes

1 World Wind Energy Association, "World Wind Energy Report," March 2010, http://www.wwindea.org/home/images/stories/worldwindenergyreport2009_s.pdf

2 "ISO 14040: 2006. Environmental Management: Life Cycle Assessment Principles and Framework," http://www.iso.org/iso/catalogue_detail?csnumber=37456

3 "SimaPro 7 LCA Software," http://www.pira-international.com/SimaPro-7-LCA-Software.aspx

CHAPTER 17

Metrics-Driven Sustainability

James Niemann

How sustainable is your corporation? Sustainability is a paradigm shift of significant proportion that could determine if your company will succeed or fail in the future. Creating a flexible business and system architecture to support your sustainability vision will allow the corporation to make swift decisions to take advantage of unforeseen opportunities in the future. Making the right investments in implementing software and metrics will be the difference between winners and losers in the future marketplace.

The challenge is making the metrics program broad enough to make a significant impact and achieve the goals while not trying to "boil the ocean." Improving sustainability is about fundamentally changing how products and services are produced and delivered to the customer. "Metrics-driven sustainability" recommends using and tracking business value as the key component to the vision. Ultimately, keeping internal and external stakeholders informed of the benefits of sustainability will make the program legitimate and enable a dramatic culture change.

The Need for Metrics

At some point each corporation will need to join the movement toward sustainability. The pain of no action will become greater than the sting of organizational change required to join the green culture that is upon our world. This pain will come in many forms including: lost revenue, government regulation, and loss of key employees. Once on the path to sustainability, the next question becomes "how sustainable is our corporation?"

How can a CEO measure if they have done everything possible to

- Have a public persona as a sustainable company;

- Protect the corporation from government penalties and fines;

- Change the culture to make being a sustainable company a priority;

- Build end-to-end supply chains with an appropriate environmental impact; and

- Protect the employees from long-term effects of the work they do?

Many corporate and public leaders are at this point of asking these questions; they are reading all the detailed literature about carbon footprint and wondering how to get their corporations working in this direction. Measuring success will be a major cornerstone of the drive toward sustainability.

Along with the movement toward sustainability, there is a massive increase in tracking technology that is generating an unprecedented amount of data. Smart devices are now tracking everything happening in the world, from driving information from your car to the energy consumption at the meter level on your home. With each of the devices being an addressable device on the Internet, the ability to process this data into information and make significant real-time decisions has reached a new level. With wireless technology and radio frequency tags, transmitting data about people and product movement to a new level of analysis is a reality.

As we have seen in the past with supply chain management systems, it is not the accumulation of the data that is important; it is what information is gleaned from the data and how that information is used to change the way we run our businesses, governments, and personal lives that will decide the winners in the market. As an example, product labeling has changed how products are made and what products we purchase. Before we had the detailed information on product labels, it was difficult to make the smart choices about the food we were eating. As companies start to gain institutional knowledge about sustainability, they will want to improve their practices; for this reason it is important to realize that flexible system architectures are necessary to allow movement from tracking one data element or process to another with relative ease. This agility will allow the corporation to make swift decisions to take advantage of unforeseen opportunities in the future.

With the need to jump into sustainability quickly, it is important to understand why you are taking this leap. This answer will provide a vision and give a picture of what sustainability will look like in your company in three to five years. With the vision in place, a roadmap of how to achieve these objectives will become the most important plan a company will build in this new world. Making the right investments in implementing software and metrics will be the difference between winners and losers in the future marketplace. Without a clear path to the future, companies will make investments in multiple areas that will not allow overall tracking and reporting of the success. This leads to the discussion about what metrics and systems are needed to make the sustainability vision a reality. Companies that create a proper vision, develop the roadmap, measure success, and govern the program will have the greatest chance at success.

Sustainability Vision

With so many pressures moving companies toward sustainability, understanding the overall vision is an important first step. The human tendency is to just get going and leave the strategy work behind. Without a vision, measuring success will be difficult. With an eye toward the end, focusing on business value is the best place to start to develop the vision.

Defining the Vision of Sustainability

Complete business transformation toward sustainability is at the highest level of the vision. This is not about changing one department or division. Sustainability needs to be across the company so that it becomes ingrained in the culture of every employee, group, product, and process across the enterprise.

Imagine corporate visions for sustainability five years into the future. What would have to be in place for customers, employees, governments, competitors, media, investors, and others to consider your corporation a leader in the movement toward sustainability? These visions can take many forms:

- End-to-end product sustainability program

- Green information technology

- Green facility certification

- Waste reduction

- Water-use reduction

- Energy-use reduction

An example of an encompassing vision is tracking the entire supply web for a product, from how the raw materials are developed to the retirement and waste created at the end of life. This perspective requires looking outside of the four walls of the enterprise and changes the relationship with suppliers and customers. This broad definition of vision has a significant impact on both the metrics and systems required to measure progress. For example, tracking the carbon footprint within one entity is difficult, but the enormity and complexity of the effort required to track all the data for all of the direct suppliers and customers for your products is a much bigger task. One data element might include all of the transportation costs for every use of one product after it leaves the factory, which could be an impossible task without adequate systems and metrics.

Another example is water-use reduction. Measurement could be defined as water required for building the product, but an enhanced measure is how much water the product will require to operate for the customer. These examples epitomize the need for proper planning and visioning. These are the kind of information issues that companies with maturing sustainability programs are trying to get their heads around.

The challenge is making the program broad enough to make a significant impact and achieve the goals while not trying to "boil the ocean." This is where looking to business value becomes the cornerstone of building the vision. To gain further information about business areas that can be part of your vision, SAP has created a sustainability map that shows the focus areas that are being adopted by their customers.[1] Focus areas (with one example topic in parentheses for each) include (1) executive management (financial risk and performance); (2) environmental health and safety (risk assessment and reduction); (3) operations (production energy management); (4) supply chain (green logistics); (5) product (sustainable design); (6) consumers (personal footprint); (7) human resources (labor compliance and human rights); and (8) information technology (green IT).

Business Value Is the Key to Measuring Success

Some companies might develop sustainability programs because it is the right thing to do, but most companies will only implement projects and programs because there is a true return on the investment (ROI). At a minimum, a sustainability or green project should at least pay for itself. In a more likely scenario, the program will provide many opportunities to drive value to the bottom line and will provide opportunities for new products and services into the future. Chief financial officers are now beginning to see that measuring sustainability will actually impact the other normal measures of a successful company.

Business value has both short- and long-term implications. If the CEO looks at just one project, they can find ROI, but one project is not going to solve the earlier questions about changing the culture and public perception. This value needs to be seen as a long-term strategic direction that will drive how investments will be prioritized to drive long-term sustainability.

With such broad performance improvement results, recognition from Wall Street, industry groups, and the government will become an output of the sustainability program. Taking benchmarks, measuring results, and reporting on progress are the keys to attaining this type of recognition. As an example, the Dow Jones Sustainability Index tracks the largest 600 North American companies and finds the top 20 percent in terms of sustainability.[2] This type of benchmarking also needs to be part of the vision to ensure that the process metrics and reporting are all addressed to make this type of recognition possible.

Transition from Vision to a Sustainability Roadmap

Integrating sustainability into the current business model and business system architecture will determine the success of attaining the vision. As stated earlier, sustainability needs to be integrated into every process across the enterprise. As each process is being redesigned and sustainability is taken into account, the architecture of business will be impacted. Software solutions supporting the business processes will change. This will ultimately impact the overall system architecture and solution design. Taking into account all of the required process changes and the related solution design becomes the first step to figuring out how to implement the vision and is the basis of building a roadmap of projects to deliver the three- to five-year sustainability program.

Software Solutions Supporting Sustainability

Because sustainability is relatively new to the business culture and the ultimate opportunities from sustainability are not completely understood, deciding on the software solutions to support sustainability will be critical. Flexible architectures will be required to support data collection, process change, and reporting. As with many software decisions, it is important to think about integration into the overall processes of the company. As an example, smart metering will be the foundation of the data-collection process for energy companies going forward. Integration into billing and power-generation systems will determine the success of the program.

This once again reiterates the importance of the overall vision. Significant investments might be required in software to support the process changes. Making each of the system-solution decisions independently could have a catastrophic effect and ultimately require a significant amount of rework to achieve an efficient enterprise architecture that is easy to maintain and flexible for future growth and opportunities. The lack of integration and planning will manifest itself most prominently in the ability to report progress and success toward the overall vision.

Integrated solutions are now available from enterprise software companies that support sustainability programs. As an example, SAP has integrated solutions, including:

- Sustainability strategy management

- Sustainability performance management

- Energy data management, smart metering

- Employee health and safety management

- Environmental performance, emissions management

- Carbon impact

- Product safety and stewardship

- Risk management

- Manufacturing integration and intelligence

- Recycling administration

- Recall management

- Product life-cycle management

- Supplier relationship management

As the entire solution architecture comes into view, building a roadmap to implement the architecture is the next level of planning.

Building a Roadmap to Support the Vision

Many business leaders select a first sustainability project and believe it is the cornerstone of the sustainability program. As an example, measuring the carbon footprint can be a first project; however, it is important to understand how that project will impact the overall multiyear program and the attainment of a complete sustainability vision.

Listing all of the initiatives that can be thought of to reach the vision or the "how" is the next logical step. This does not need to be a huge task with weeks of analysis. This is a rough map of all ideas that can be generated to accomplish the vision. It is important to collect rough order of magnitude estimates of effort, duration, and projected benefits during this stage. With this information, an analysis methodology can be employed to ensure projects are sequenced in the proper order to gain the maximum value. Criteria for analysis should include strategic alignment, time to benefit, process readiness, risk level, ease of adoption, and execution readiness.

Each initiative should provide a positive ROI. Finding the economic value is the key to this calculation and program success. First is to determine what detailed process change is being considered in each initiative. It is at the process-change level that the benefit can be calculated by a change in a key performance indicator (KPI). In the research and sustainability work done to date, there are many specific examples that have shown significant impact and have proven to have a nice ROI. Examples of benefits for a business case might include productivity increases, reduced direct material or energy costs, and reduced labor costs.

With business value as the driver to the vision of sustainability, the overall program becomes very compelling. Each project on the roadmap should have clear attainable value defined in a business case. It is important to realize that clear business cases are necessary for the projects that are executed in the early years of the roadmap. To complete the roadmap, less detail is needed initially for projects later in the roadmap. It is still important to calculate the rough benefits to make sure the specific projects should be included in the roadmap. As time passes, the business cases of the projects in the later years will need to be created and confirmed.

If the business case does not ultimately yield the expected benefit, a significant consideration to canceling the project should be given. This seems very obvious, but many times companies have pet projects that have been considered for years and it seems unbelievable that the project would be canceled. Taking on projects with little or no ROI has been the root of many program failures. This does not mean that every project with no ROI has to be canceled, for many times a project is foundational to a new direction a company is taking and the true ROI cannot be calculated. This is where the executives of the company are required to exercise leadership to make and execute these tough decisions.

Measuring Success with Metrics

After developing the roadmap to success in sustainability, the tracking of success is imperative to a long-term strategy and culture change. It is important to break the perception that sustainability projects are "philanthropic" and are only done because it is the right thing to do. Building a course of action to track success that includes measuring KPIs and periodically assessing the advancement and reporting progress will ensure that the vision of sustainability is delivered. Measuring performance using KPIs begins with measuring a specific process (operational KPIs) to validate how efficient or effective a process is performing. These operational measures will impact the financial KPIs, which measure the performance of running the company. Measuring sustainability in terms that are required by government and industry groups is very important and should be also be key part of your strategy, but measuring business value and ROI will allow a sustainability program to grow and contribute to the bottom line.

Process Measurement Is the Key to Gaining Business Value

Improving sustainability is fundamentally about changing how products are produced and delivered to the customer. Detailed process change provides the most likely method of achieving value realization. Changing the direct materials, manufacturing process, and transportation method are all examples of process change that could be implemented. It is important to understand the fundamental process changes that are being suggested by the vision to determine what to measure. During the design of the process change, the definition of the metrics should also be clearly established. These metrics will lay the foundation of success for the new process. Example process change metrics are

- Water consumption

- Process waste reduction

- Raw material consumption

- Transportation method usage or distance required

- Greenhouse gas emissions

- New energy sources consumption

- Packaging reduction

- Procurement sustainability enforcement

Once the process KPI is defined, it is important to do the value mapping to understand how a change in the KPI will be used to calculate the value or benefit gained from the process change. As an example, a reduction in packaging will have a unit cost savings that can be multiplied by the number of packages to determine the benefit generated. This cost savings would roll into a process KPI called "cost per unit." To complete the value mapping, the specific process would need to be evaluated against all other process changes that could impact that KPI. An agreement is needed with the steering committee to determine the final calculation of how much the process change impacted each unit movement in the KPI to ultimately determine the benefit achieved. This benefit can then be rolled up to the overall sustainability reporting on a periodic basis (monthly, quarterly, or annual).

Once the value mapping is complete, the results should be the cornerstone of the software design supporting redesign of processes. It is important to design-in the value that is expected from the process change. Many times the business case is not shared with the developers, and the intent of the process change is lost. Before making any software modifications or reconfiguring the enterprise resources planning (ERP) system, a complete understanding of the expected value should be reviewed and designed into the modifications.

Key to system design should be a flexible architecture. Because sustainability tracking and processes are relatively new, it should be anticipated that processes will require more modifications as more information is gathered and more institutional knowledge is acquired. Being able to reconfigure systems with short development cycles will be a key to success.

One thing to determine in the process design is how the change will be measured. Reporting has to be considered, not just an afterthought. How will the data be accumulated? What specific detailed fields will be needed to create the reports? What summary information is required to drive management reporting? Will the data be accumulated in the ERP system or the business intelligence environment? These reporting design requirements will have a significant impact on the solution design.

Financial Measurement Brings Together the Benefits

Just as important as measuring each individual process, it is important to roll the process change benefits into dashboard terms that make sense to the chief financial officer in terms of financial metrics. Improvements in operation processes typically lead to improvements in financial KPIs such as cost of goods sold, days of inventory on hand, total revenue, or outstanding receivables. As a general rule, it is advisable to show an impact to a financial KPI that is already tracked by the corporation. This way the sustainability project will show a real impact to the enterprise. If a new financial KPI is proposed and used, it is important that the KPI is recognized by the leadership team as a key addition to the performance dashboard for running the company.

With both the operational and financial KPIs set, it is important to relate these benefits back to the specific business case that was prepared to support the process changes. With business case benefits and improvement in financial metrics, a corporation has the ability to show that true bottom-line value of the sustainability program is achievable.

Program Metrics Keep the Focus on the Vision

As discussed earlier, many sustainability programs will focus on benchmarks or certifications that are outside the company. Many times these kinds of objectives within the vision will require program-specific KPIs. These are metrics that will be tracked for the length of the program but will typically not become part of the long-term metric framework for the corporation. Examples include product design requirements (durability, content, etc.); certification attainment through programs such as LEED certification, Green Globes, and Energy Star[3]; education and communication initiatives; supplier certification; knowledge management repositories; process documentation; government regulation adherence; and green IT. It is important that all of the program metrics are addressed in the system design. Their inclusion needs to be completely understood. If the measurement is going to be done as a manual process, this needs to be agreed to by the business unit supporting the project and the IT organization. This is where problems for implementation are created. It is not usually the core components but the side requirements that cause cost overruns and missed project deadlines. These project metrics are the key to reporting the project success and getting approval for the next sustainability project.

Measuring the Transformation Requires Baselines

Investing in sustainability will be difficult at best because most corporations do not exist just to become sustainable or green. Most companies are in business to sell a product or a service and create profit for the shareholders. Sustainability is something you do along the way. For a long-term program such as sustainability to gain momentum and ultimately become part of the culture, the leadership has to believe that making these investments is truly the most economical and cost-effective way to run the corporation. Therefore, it is important to find baselines by which to measure the progress toward the vision. These baselines for the process, financial, and program metrics will be the yardstick used to measure success. They will also allow benchmarking against peer groups to find opportunities for future progress.

Governance Drives Success

Just because a vision is in place does not ensure that a sustainability program will be executed flawlessly. A governance body needs to be leveraged to continually monitor the sustainability program including the process, financial, and program KPIs using a balanced scorecard approach. Making adjustments in the vision and strategy of the sustainability program is imperative as corporate sustainability knowledge grows. The governance group will also decide what reporting will be done about the sustainability program both internally and externally.

Monitoring and Reporting Sustainability Progress

Once the vision is in place and the project roadmap is accepted, the first project with a strong business case is selected, metrics are chosen, and baselines are taken, then it becomes time to start reporting on progress. Reporting can prove to be the most important component of the entire process. Many companies put reporting in place to just provide the basic data on a regular basis; however, leading companies build an analytic framework that allows modeling and decision support based on flexible business intelligence architecture. By moving beyond essential reporting activities, companies can turn strategy and data into actionable information that makes sustainability viable and profitable for the organization. Ultimately, corporations need to decide what is going to be reported and who is going to be accountable before they can develop the system infrastructure to support the vision.

Accountability Is Critical

Corporations spend millions each year developing reporting and analytic solutions. Leaders believe if they invest in the infrastructure, the users and accountability will come somewhat like a field of dreams. There is nothing further from the truth. From the inception of the initiative to creating an analytic framework, accountability for the solution and alignment to vision is critical. Some very basic components will help to ensure success in managing not only the reporting but the entire sustainability program. Basic components are outlined below.

Meaningful Content

This seems obvious, but many programs get so caught up in detail that they start reporting everything that is possible. Working to only report what is real information, not data, about the program is a key success factor. A significant amount of consideration is required to determine what will be reported. Remember the old adage—less is more.

Baselines and Targets

Setting KPIs is critical to the success of the program. Baselines have to be established to have a point to measure from. Agreed-upon targets will determine progress toward a successful outcome. Short-term targets (e.g., quarter end, annual) can confirm that the program is moving in the right direction and identify if adjustments are needed. Program-level targets provide the long-term vision and a point at which the program will be considered successful.

Data Transparency

The ability to understand the information being reported is critical to success. For example, the calculations that are performed to summarize the data need to be easily understood. If the information in the report is not easy to confirm, the accuracy and intent of the report will become the focus and not the information that is being presented about the sustainability program.

Cadence of Reporting

The performance management process needs to drive the reporting. A report hitting every managers' e-mail box once a month will probably not drive the sustainability program forward. This is a culture change that requires accountability. Regularly scheduled meetings to review the program will keep it on track. Reviewing the reporting has to be a key part of this meeting. Reporting not being used is a key indicator to one of two significant issues. First is that the reporting is not useful and needs to be modified. In this case, a review of the targets, baselines, and data will most likely reveal the issue. Second is that people are not comfortable holding others accountable, which is a critical component of program success. In this case a review of the governance and targets could uncover the underlying change management issue.

Reporting Content

Each program will have a different vision and definition of success that will drive reporting. Having a broad enough concept of the possibilities of reporting and analytics is going to be very difficult as the architecture is being considered. Below is a list of example areas that could be considered when building the framework. Example reporting and analytics contents include the following:

- Carbon management

- Product footprint

- Economic impact

- Green IT adherence

- Energy management

- Financial performance

- Safety standards

- Risk reduction

- Supply chain

- Recycling/reuse

- Stakeholder impact

- Strategy performance

- Sociological impact

- Environmental compliance

- Labor compliance

- Waste reduction algorithm

Another factor in the content of the reporting is the ability to accumulate the data needed to properly report to the external indices. If the vision of the corporation is to gain status or a reputation based on external sources, it is critical to understand these external reporting requirements from the inception. Example external indices include:

- Dow Jones Sustainability Index

- Financial Times Stock Exchange FTSE4Good Index[4]

- Global Reporting Index (GRI) reporting framework[5]

- UN Global Compact[6]

- Industry specific indices

Reporting Solution Considerations

We have discussed "what" is going to be reported in the section on reporting content. We also discussed the "who" and the "when" of the reporting in the section on accountability. Now we need to discuss the "how" to develop the reporting solution.

As you can imagine, putting this analytic framework together can be a difficult task. Many software companies are providing point solutions to solve individual parts of the sustainability puzzle. This is where having a vision and a roadmap is critical. If you purchase or build software to solve just one opportunity, for example carbon footprint, you run the risk of not providing an infrastructure for sustainability projects over the years to come. Companies, such as SAP, have developed complete solutions to support sustainability across the enterprise covering many of the functionality requirements and addressing integration, data collection, and performance analytics. Recommended software considerations are

- Integration: As the vision for sustainability grows, many different areas of the corporation will be impacted and data will be accumulated to track the individual programs. Integrated solutions provide many benefits for integrating the total solution to track the overall program and provide a common analytics framework. Without this integration, a company could wake up four or five years down the road with many individual solutions but not able to have the corporation picture in a single coordinated fashion toward the goal of sustainability. As we discussed earlier, the ability to track the process changes and roll that information into the financial KPIs will be a key success factor for the entire program.

- Data collection: The ability to collect data in an automated fashion is critical. Workflow, automated data requests, data validation, and approval processes should all be driven with some level of automation.

- Adjustments to data: Many times data needs to be normalized to deal with missing or anomalous data. The better software solutions allow for automated interfaces that can adjust the data based on rules. In addition, an audit trail is important to maintain a searchable record of every action taken to provide transparency and enforce high-integrity reporting.

- Automated KPI tracking: Focus on the metrics that will have the greatest impacts for your stakeholders. Leveraging a central KPI library that includes standard metrics is recommended. The KPI library functionality enables business users to create and update their own sustainability KPIs that may be composed of other standards, multiple tiers of subindicators, and calculations. All these KPIs should be stored in a searchable and filterable central library that allows users to share and reuse their work.

- Performance analytics: Powerful analytic functionality enables you to aggregate results and examine performance across multiple dimensions. Planning workbooks enable users to set targets or benchmarks for different organizations and sustainability indicators.

- Dashboards and scorecards: Sustainability practices and processes must work in concert with core business goals and strategies and must improve enterprise profitability. Therefore, it is necessary to create reporting and goal setting at relevant levels of the organization where the information is actionable, while making reporting more efficient and cost-effective.

Reporting has to enable the vision of the stakeholders. Perhaps most important, you need to have a management framework for guiding improvement through strategic planning, performance initiatives, and risk management. This is done by defining the content, setting the accountability, and introducing a flexible software framework to monitor and drive the attainment of the vision.

Sustainability Program Addresses Challenges for Future Generations

Sustainability is a paradigm shift of significant proportion that could determine if your company will succeed or fail in the future. Creating a business and system architecture to support your sustainability vision requires components such as a roadmap, governance structure, and reporting infrastructure to ensure success. Within these components are detailed objectives supported by process changes and financial goals that need to be supported by metrics to determine the success of the program. Finally, keeping internal and external stakeholders informed of the progress makes the program legitimate and a force for change to meet the needs of future generations.

Notes

1 SAP Global, "SAP Sustainability Map," http://www.sap.com/solutions/executiveview/sustainability/sustainability-map/index.epx

2 Dow Jones Index SAM, http://www.sustainability-index.com/

3 Bluestone Energy Services LTD, "Leadership in Energy and Environmental Design (LEED)," http://www.bluestoneenergy.com/leed_certification.html; Green Globes, "The Practical Building Rating System," http://www.greenglobes.com/; and U.S. Environmental Protection Agency and the U.S. Department of Energy, "Energy Star," http://www.energystar.gov/

4 Financial Times Stock Index for Good, "FTSE4Good_Index," http://www.ftse.com/Indices/FTSE4Good_Index_Series/index.jsp

5 Global Reporting Index, "GRI," http://www.globalreporting.org/Home

6 UN Global Compact, http://www.unglobalcompact.org/

CHAPTER 18

Regulatory Compliance, Sustainability, and Transparency in the Supply Chain

Robert Johnson

Industry-leading businesses are incorporating sustainability processes into their daily operations, signaling a paradigm shift in manufacturing that transcends traditional methods of doing business. Part of this shift can be attributed to significant changes in corporate supply chain management, data collection, reporting, and analysis practices.

Supply chain management is a critical component of an organization's sustainability program. The supply chain is the sequence of steps, often done in different firms or locations, that results in the production of a final good from primary factors. In fact, it is the driving force behind global manufacturing strategies.

Businesses must closely monitor and manage their manufacturing processes and those of their suppliers and partners to ensure compliance with regulatory compliance requirements and voluntary sustainability commitments. New operating models may be required as companies respond to a regulatory landscape that poses increased risk and complexity in manufacturing and product design.

Information management is the key to address today's supply chain management challenges. The demand for information is growing, and companies must efficiently manage huge volumes of data to meet their reporting obligations. At the same time, information management processes are becoming more complex. Today, organizations must understand and track in minute detail the chemicals, materials, designs, processes, and operations used to build and deliver their products, and to manage inputs from external partners, suppliers, and customers. Information is no longer a tactical necessity. It is a strategic requirement for organizations that expect to be at the leading edge of the global business environment.

Introduction

Supply chain management is changing. Increased public awareness and activism regarding key environmental issues—including global climate change, materials management, and product life cycle—are generating significant shifts in public policy that impact the way that companies design and manufacture their products. Industry-leading businesses are incorporating sustainability processes into their daily operations, signaling a paradigm shift in manufacturing that transcends traditional methods of doing business. Their ability to maximize the benefits by meeting tighter regulatory requirements and achieving new efficiencies that reduce operational risks and costs can be attributed to significant changes in corporate supply chain management, data collection, reporting, and analysis practices.

Companies that do business on a global scale must be prepared to address a new generation of strict regulations governing greenhouse gas (GHG) emissions management, product life-cycle management, and materials management including

- The European Union Emission Trading Scheme (EU ETS), Australia's National Greenhouse and Energy Reporting Act, and, in the U.S., the Environmental Protection Agency Mandatory Reporting Rule (MRR), Regional Greenhouse Gas Initiative (RGGI) and California Assembly Bill 32—laws that require the reporting of GHG emissions. EU ETS goes even further by requiring purchase of credits or "allowances" when companies exceed approved GHG emission limits;

- EU Restriction of Hazardous Substances Directive (RoHS) and Waste Electrical and Electronic Equipment Directive, Canada's Material Management Plan, and China's Measures on Environmental Management of New Material Substances—laws that mandate safe recycling and disposal of certain electronic products; and

- Registration, Evaluation, and Authorization of Chemicals (REACH)— the EU regulation with worldwide impact that governs the use of hazardous materials in product design and manufacturing processes.

Previously, companies regarded environmental regulations primarily as a compliance issue to be addressed at the facility level. Sanctions, usually consisting of agency-issued fines, were not typically seen as a significant impediment to operations or a threat to a company's standing in the market. Today, however, the stakes are higher than ever for corporate compliance and sustainability performance. Regulatory compliance and sustainability performance are now widely regarded as key business differentiators that are closely watched by investors, customers, and other external stakeholders. Because these issues have visibility from the production floor to corporate boardrooms, accountability for sustainability programs has moved up the chain of command from facility-level managers to senior executives, including the chief executive officer, chief operating officer, or corporate responsibility officer.

Failure to address these important issues can expose organizations to severe operational, financial, and asset risks that have a bottom-line impact. In extreme cases—for example, when an industrial accident results in a regional environmental disaster—they may even threaten a company's industry standing or its corporate brand. Typically, however, the business challenge of managing for compliance and sustainability is one that must be met on a more routine daily basis. Companies must now continually collect, process, and report on an unprecedented volume and variety of information in order to document the fact that they are meeting new regulatory requirements and achieving operational efficiencies that can lead to cost savings, productivity gains, or competitive advantages. REACH, in particular, places a significantly greater burden on businesses to disclose the materials they use in products or their manufacturing processes so consumers can understand what substances are used to produce goods they consume. Manufacturers and importers are responsible for managing the potential risks from materials, and they are required to submit detailed information regarding properties of their material substances to the European Chemicals Agency.

Investors also are closely monitoring companies' environmental performance. Influential nongovernmental organizations—such as the Carbon Disclosure Project (CDP), World Resource Institute, and Global Reporting Initiative—operate registries where companies voluntarily submit emissions data. Dow Jones's sustainability indexes and FTSE4Good evaluate compliance and sustainability performance from an investor's perspective. Institutional stockholders now regard environmental management as a key risk management indicator and a differentiator for investment decision making.

Additionally, market perceptions of compliance and sustainability can drive changes in consumer loyalty. Studies such as the "Consumer Greendex"—a scientific index of consumer behavior and material lifestyles based on a study, sponsored by the National Geographic Society and GlobeScan, of 17,000 individuals in 17 countries—shows "that environmentally friendly consumer behavior . . . has now increased from 2008 . . . [including] people's transportation patterns, household energy and resource use, consumption of food and everyday consumer goods."[1] Growing numbers of consumers now consider environmental sustainability and product safety among their key criteria for purchasing decisions.

A New Focus on Environmental Compliance and Sustainability

Initiatives aligning environmental and product life-cycle management with supply chain management are at a nascent stage of development in most organizations. Industry-leading businesses are incorporating carbon management, materials management, and product life-cycle programs into their daily operations, signaling a shift in manufacturing that transcends their traditional methods of doing business. A major part of this paradigm shift can be attributed to significant changes in data collection, reporting, and analysis practices for corporate supply chain management.

Market leaders are being rewarded for early adoption of best practices in compliance and sustainability for supply chain management. A survey conducted by analyst firm Accenture found that "there continues to be a business case for greening the supply chain, resulting in lower costs as well as environmentally responsible processes. Organizations that have achieved top performance in both cost effectiveness and customer service are more than twice as likely [as laggards] to actively model their supply chain carbon footprints and implement successful sustainability initiatives."[2]

No business is exempt from the need to address environmental issues affecting their supply chain relationships. Supply chains for even "simple" products, such as T-shirts or stuffed animals, include business partners across diverse geographic locations, according to a report from Business for Social Responsibility, an organization with more than 250 industry leaders as members worldwide. "Outsourced supply chain models are more attractive to businesses that are looking for financial and operational gain in countries where production costs and wages are substantially lower. As manufacturing becomes further removed from a company's headquarters, so does the control and transparency of business processes related to supply chain information management."[3]

At the same time, the impact of product life-cycle and material management mandates such as REACH and RoHS have also become more pronounced. So many of today's businesses depend upon a global supply chain and distribution model that even regulations adopted only in selected jurisdictions can drive companies to change their product design, material content, or operating processes, no matter where goods are manufactured.

To optimize environmental compliance management across their supply chains, companies must be able to communicate regulatory requirements to internal operational teams and suppliers and monitor compliance from raw material acquisition to product delivery and even disposal. Meeting material management requirements can be particularly tricky because regulations vary widely across jurisdictions. For instance, a material that is considered safe in one nation could be regarded as toxic in a neighboring country.

Despite growing momentum in support of environmental statutes, some corporate decision makers still regard regulatory requirements merely as burdens that add cost, not value, to business operations. They lag behind market leaders because their programs are focused solely on short-term cost avoidance rather than ensuring compliance and minimizing risk, maintaining employee health, and protecting the environment.[4] By contrast, industry leaders are now proactively embracing opportunities to produce and promote products that not only meet government rules but also strengthen the company's operational efficiency and its reputation for corporate responsibility.

Transition to Environmentally Friendly Supply Chain Strategies

GHG emissions reduction and sustainability initiatives require companies to demonstrate that they are taking steps to ensure compliance with applicable statues and emerging best practices. Treating these programs as strictly internal or one-off activities without taking into account their ongoing impact on suppliers' operations exposes companies to a variety of business risks—recurring costs, business interruptions, late-term material changes, manufacturing process delays, slow market launches, and reduced market options as countries change requirements. CDP suggests that there is currently a gap between companies and their suppliers based on measurements of strategic risk awareness, carbon reduction ambition, existing reporting capabilities, and implementation practices. "The challenge for suppliers now lies in bridging this gap. They must catch up to member companies in order to fulfill the goals to reduce emissions."[5]

Market-leading businesses are responding to this challenge by implementing enterprise-level programs designed to improve asset management and maintenance in order to lower GHG emissions and improve energy management. Programs addressing scope 1 (direct) and scope 2 (indirect) emissions are already deeply rooted, with stakeholder pressures driving most companies to monitor, collect, and aggregate carbon emissions from direct or indirect sources and benchmark their progress against mandatory or voluntary standards. Additionally, many companies—especially those that produce electronics products—are now going further by adopting programs that integrate a host of other environmentally friendly processes into their product design, material acquisition, manufacturing, packaging, product delivery to consumers, and end-of-life management. Experts regard these best practices as benchmarks of a sustainable supply chain (Yug 2008, 2).

Some suppliers have been slow to recognize the need to institute emission reduction targets, but with more companies discovering that scope 3 emissions, sources outside of a company's direct control, represent a substantial portion of their total GHG footprint, pressure is building. Original equipment manufacturers, especially those in the consumer products sector, are taking a more aggressive approach to collaboration with vendors. Most are working cooperatively with suppliers to identify potential emissions reduction strategies, but others are coercing their vendors by using carbon emissions management performance as criteria for procurement decisions.

Companies that want to extend progress toward their materials management goals are also looking to the supply chain to address those concerns. Businesses across every industry sector have adopted sophisticated outsourcing strategies because of their proven ability to lower product manufacturing costs. However, regulatory requirements and global manufacturing strategies are prone to risks associated with operating in jurisdictions that have different requirements for governing similar activities.

The goal of a sustainable supply chain strategy is not only to fulfill the individual customer's needs but also to meet the public's expectation for a given manufacturer by enhancing its perceived role in addressing social responsibility and environmental concerns. In exchange, the company will gain a competitive advantage in the industry.

Supply chain sustainability is the merging of product stewardship and product compliance. The first focal point is direct materials—because those are the elements that go into products—but indirect materials (those that support operations) also need to be sustainable.

In order to successfully transition to sustainable supply chain practices, organizations first need to align those best-practice work processes with their own operations, and build effective communication links to all stakeholders in order to communicate standards and expectations. This goes far beyond collecting raw data for reporting purposes.

Companies must first identify relevant stakeholders, including regulators, and identify how associated demands align with business processes. This may appear to be simple, but in many ways it is not. A company's operations team and its network of suppliers are primarily focused on their core mission of acquiring raw materials, maintaining efficient operations, and ensuring product delivery in a timely manner.

Although businesses have plenty of incentive to align their work processes with compliance and sustainability objectives, some companies, and even more of their suppliers, have found it difficult to make progress toward those goals. Many decision makers understand the benefits of incorporating environmentally friendly practices into their operations and are feeling increased pressure to do something about it, but they lack the metrics and the visibility into their supply chain to make it happen.[6]

Transparency of material-related information across all stakeholder interests enables organizations to proactively respond to a variety of potential issues that can arise between operations and suppliers. Without the ability to provide appropriate levels of visibility to each other, companies and their stakeholders risk significant production challenges. For instance, REACH requires operations personnel to ensure that neither internal manufacturing facilities nor suppliers are using substances that are prohibited under REACH. Company officials must find alternative materials, which require modifications in product design, and must identify materials that meet manufacturing requirements and procure those materials without incurring unacceptable costs or delays that might prevent them from reaching their production goals.

In order to enable these kinds of environmental compliance and sustainability decisions, companies must review their manufacturing process from raw material acquisition to packaging, including those of their suppliers, to determine if they are compliant with emerging material standards.

Collecting relevant materials compliance information is a complex process that can involve production activities dispersed across hundreds, or perhaps thousands, of facilities and discrete businesses. Automating that information management process at the enterprise level has become a best-practice strategy for minimizing both the risk of noncompliance and operational costs.

The Role of Integrated Information Technology Solutions

Information is the key. The converging demands of tighter regulatory requirements and an intensely competitive global marketplace are driving businesses to monitor and manage unprecedented quantities of environmental information in minute detail. Data on raw materials, chemicals, materials, designs, processes, and operations are needed to manage a product's life cycle while a rising tide of carbon emissions data must be collected and reported from both a company's own operations and its suppliers. At the same time, global economic pressures are putting companies under unprecedented pressure to keep costs down and revenues up. Managers are being told to do more with less and find smarter ways to operate their businesses in order to drive both sustainability and profitability.

Organizations that seek to drive growth by introducing new products and expanding into new geographical markets, or to become more competitive by turning to offshore suppliers, are finding that manual methods of managing environmental compliance and performance data can become exponentially more complex and time consuming (Gupta 2008). Even some companies that have automated systems are prone to keeping their information in silos within business units, departments, or programs, which sometimes leads them to miss out on opportunities to save time and money while improving performance.

To meet these challenges, companies need to implement enterprise-level information systems to collect, track, and deliver critical emissions and material information from a myriad of sources across their operations and their supply network. Forward-thinking companies are already implementing integrated software platforms that can help manage materials and GHG emissions information as well as many other sustainability-related challenges across a global enterprise. They are also adapting work processes and undergoing extensive training within their organizations and with their suppliers to ensure the success of these implementations.

For instance, a company that implements a RoHS compliance strategy will recognize that it must manage materials information that starts with product design and continues through the entire product life cycle. Not only does a large volume of data need to be gathered, it needs to be verified, updated, and disseminated to truly demonstrate compliance.

This requires an integrated information management solution—one that can provide up-to-date information regarding parts and components, whether those items are within the scope of regulations where the product will be delivered or not. This information needs to be seamlessly transferred to enterprise systems such as enterprise resource planning (ERP) systems or product life-cycle management systems so it can be used by engineers, product designers, procurement officers, and operational managers.

Materials management programs should be designed and implemented to enable users to collect and process large volumes of information from both internal and external sources and account for every applicable materials statute. Companies also need immediate access to voluminous lists of standards, technical specifications, recommended guidelines, and voluntary data reporting. This adds an additional level of complexity to companies' already elaborate information management requirements. Like parts inventory information, it must be up to date and able to be delivered directly to enterprise systems already in use for easy access by users who need it. A firm may need to use thousands of these standards to design and manufacture their products, ensure quality and worker safety, and minimize their impact on the environment. The standards must be readily available to the employees that need them, and because standards change frequently, companies must ensure that all employees are referring to the same version of each standard.

Practical Steps to Addressing Sustainability in the Supply Chain

Many companies are looking to reduce their carbon footprint by driving down emission reductions by suppliers. However, most have inadequate visibility across all tiers and levels of their supply and value chain. Few use a single hosted platform to improve such visibility. And a vast majority lacks the metrics to monitor or enforce sustainability throughout their extended supply chain. In short, they are "ill-prepared to drive the necessary changes that are required in today's carbon-constrained and price-sensitive market."[7]

Automating and digitizing materials management and carbon emissions information is an emerging best practice that companies are using to enhance their efficiency and enable their product design and manufacturing personnel to concentrate on their primary functions. To achieve their goals, companies must first facilitate visibility into suppliers' operational processes in order for manufacturers to drive downstream reductions in greenhouse gas. Best practices to support emission reduction programs begin with collecting and aggregating GHG data at the asset level, traceable back to the equipment level, in order to meet rising standards for transparency and verifiability. Improved communication with suppliers is also needed in order to facilitate a clear understanding of material regulations.

While most GHG management programs are focused on scope 1 and scope 2 emissions, companies now recognize that there are significant opportunities to lower their enterprise footprint by addressing scope 3 emissions. Recently, some companies have indeed achieved major GHG emission reductions by engaging their suppliers and partners and asking (or requiring) them to work together toward mutual benchmarks.

In order to ensure full compliance, managers need information management tools that provide visibility to ensure that all phases of product development are in accordance with all applicable regulations. Effective materials management programs distinguish themselves from others based on their ability to collect information from a myriad of potential sources, internal and external, and to streamline manufacturing processes to reduce regulatory costs and risks.

Companies that operate across multiple jurisdictions must be able to monitor and ensure compliance under requirements that involve widely varying information management processes. Also, because legislative trends continue to evolve, the tools that companies use should be agile enough to enable compliance with changing requirements for collecting and managing compliance data.

When companies use manual processes to collect and aggregate data from hundreds of spreadsheets, it can be difficult, if not impossible, to trace specific emissions back to the source. Detailed tracking at the asset level ensures traceability and accountability by reducing the risk of material reporting errors and enabling the company to take corrective measures, if needed.

Many organizations initially attempt to manage GHG emissions data—both their own and that of their suppliers—in the same way that they traditionally dealt with other types of environmental, health, and safety (EHS) data. Air, water, waste, refrigerants, and now GHG data—as well as material or material data, worker safety information, and more—are all being collected, processed, and delivered via manual processes and spreadsheets. These labor-intensive processes add unnecessary risks, costs, and complexity to business operations.

Industry leaders are taking a more strategic approach. They are implementing GHG emissions and materials information management solutions that are part of integrated enterprise-level software platforms for compliance and sustainability in order to achieve broader efficiencies and business benefits and manage risk.

Integrated enterprise software platforms, for example, help manage GHG data from emissions inventories to the trading floor while also fulfilling a host of other EHS compliance and sustainability needs. Operational complexity, risks, and costs shrink as duplicate systems and redundant work processes are eliminated. In addition, the systems generate valuable EHS business intelligence that executives can use to make informed technical and economic decisions on projects and investments to reduce their environmental footprint and drive growth. By gathering and merging information from across the enterprise, companies can project their GHG emissions levels and develop scenarios based on current or future costs of carbon allowances in order to develop an optimal carbon asset portfolio and trading strategies under market-based legislation like EU ETS and RGGI.

Looking to the Future

Sustainable business operations are an established megatrend that is changing how companies operate. As this trend continues to accelerate, it is shifting environmental performance expectations. Public concerns about product materials, water quality, air emissions, and other environmental sustainability continue to grow. Failure to act on those concerns will put products at risk of obsolescence, diminish the company's competitive position in the industry, and possibly threaten the future health and viability of the business itself.

CDP states that a growing number of suppliers are now engaged in initiatives to close the environmental compliance and sustainability performance gap with their corporate customers. Competitive and regulatory pressures are expected to reinforce that trend as more and more firms race to catch up to market leaders. Even laggard suppliers do not appear opposed to reducing the environmental impact of their operations and products; they simply view compliance as a drag on productivity and innovation.

A typical supply chain consists of a complex network of organizations that demonstrate widely varying acceptance of sustainable manufacturing processes. Differences in acceptance of sustainability best practices may result in increased volatility and risk among manufacturers, suppliers, and customers. Businesses will need to closely monitor and manage their supply chain's progress toward compliance and sustainability in order to reduce risks and achieve their performance goals.

In this new business era, reflecting societal concerns about materials management and climate change as well as other environmental issues is critical. Winning organizations will be those that thrive by making their supply chains engines of both sustainability and profitability.

References

Gupta, Anil. 2008. "Ten Best Practices in SAP Supply Chain Management." *TechTarget*. http://searchsap.techtarget.com/feature/Ten-best-practices-in-SAP-supply-chain-management.

Yug, Darin. 2008. "The Case for a 'Green' Supply Chain: Turning Mandate into Opportunity." White paper. Chicago: Diamond Management and Technology Consultants. http://www.diamondconsultants.com/PublicSite/ideas/perspectives/downloads/Green%20Supply%20Chain_Diamond.pdf.

Notes

Alvin Hayes contributed to this chapter.

1 "Greendex," *National Geographic*, http://environment.nationalgeographic.com/environment/greendex/

2 "Only One in 10 Companies Actively Manage Their Supply Chain Carbon Footprints, Accenture Study Finds," *Accenture*, February 25, 2009, http://newsroom.accenture.com/article_display.cfm?article_id=4801

3 "Perspectives on Information Management in Sustainable Supply Chains," Business for Social Responsibility, August 2007, http://www.bsr.org/reports/BSR_Info-Management-Supply-Chains.pdf, 21

4 Taylor Wilkerson, "Following Products Through the Green Supply Chain," *Awareness into Action,* http://www.awarenessintoaction.com/whitepapers/green-supply-chain-sustainable-programs.html

5 "Carbon Disclosure Project: Supply Chain Report," Carbon Disclosure Project, London, https://www.cdproject.net/CDPResults/CDP-Supply-Chain-Report_2010.pdf, 24

6 "Acceleration of EcoOperation: Achieving Success and Sustainability in the Supply Chain," BPM Forum, Palo Alto, CA, 2009, http://www.bpinetwork.org/reports.php

7 Ibid.

About the Editors and Contributors

Volume II

The Editors

GEORGE BASILE, PhD, is professor in the School of Sustainability and a senior sustainability scientist at the Global Institute of Sustainability at Arizona State University. He is an internationally recognized creative thinker in the field of sustainability. He has served as the executive director of the Decision Theater at ASU exploring decision making, resource intelligence, and sustainability; has served as chief scientist of the Natural Step, an international NGO focused on strategic planning for sustainability; and has led his own sustainability consultancy. He has led strategic sustainability efforts with numerous Fortune 500 companies and served on the boards of sustainability start-ups and NGOs. He has published and presented widely in the field of sustainability, including more than 30 articles and reports, and is coauthor of *Strategic Leadership toward Sustainability* (Blekinge Institute of Technology: Psilanders Grafiska, 2005).

JAMES C. HERSHAUER, DBA, is Emeritus Professor of management and affiliate faculty of the School of Sustainability at Arizona State University. Hershauer has received the award of Fellow in the Decision Sciences Institute and was editor of the *Decision Sciences Journal*. He has coauthored eight volumes about business practices on such topics as productivity, quality, and supply chains. He has published more than 50 articles in a wide variety of journals—his most recent paper, coauthored with Dan O'Neill and Jay Golden, was "The Cultural Context of Sustainability Entrepreneurship" (*Greener Management International*, no. 55, 2009).

SCOTT G. MCNALL, PhD, is professor of sociology and senior advisor to the president for sustainability at California State University, Chico, a university recognized for its sustainability efforts. McNall founded and directed the Institute for Sustainable Development and served as its executive director from 2007–2010. He also served as the university's provost for 13 years and as interim president for about 1 year. He is the author and editor of more than 60 books, chapters, and articles on such diverse topics as the Kansas Populists, Greek villagers, the military, Plains families, and sustainability. His most recent book is *Rapid Climate Change: Causes, Consequences, and Solutions* (Taylor and Francis, 2011), and his current research focuses on behavior change and residential energy use.

The Contributors

BRAD ALLENBY, JD, PhD, is Lincoln Professor of Engineering and Ethics and a professor of civil, environmental, and sustainable engineering at Arizona State University. He is also the director of the Center for Earth Systems Engineering and Management, and chair of the Consortium on Emerging Technologies, Military Operations, and National Security. He has spent more than 20 years in industry, ending his career as vice president for environment, health, and safety at AT&T. He is the author of *Reconstructing Earth: Technology and Environment in the Age of Humans* (Island Press, 2005) and *Industrial Ecology* (Prentice Hall, 1998).

ERIC J. ARNOULD, PhD, is the Distinguished Professor of Marketing and Sustainable Business Practices at the University of Wyoming. He has a background in cultural anthropology and, before his university career, worked as a consultant on economic development problems in many West African countries. He has served as a consultant for CVS, Transfair USA, H. J. Heinz, Vertical Communications, Colorado River Outfitters Association, JC Penney, Rainbird, USAID, United Nations Environmental Program, CARE, and a number of independent consulting firms. His research on consumer culture theory, economic development, services marketing, and marketing channels in developing countries appears in many social science and managerial periodicals and books.

TED K. A. BREKKEN, PhD, is an assistant professor in energy systems at Oregon State University. He studied electric vehicle motor design in 1999 in South Korea. He also studied wind turbine control at the Norwegian University of Science and Technology in Trondheim, Norway, in 2004–2005 on a Fulbright scholarship. His research interests include control, power electronics, and electric drives—specifically, digital-control techniques applied to renewable energy systems. He is codirector of the Wallace Energy Systems and Renewables Facility and a recipient of the NSF CAREER award.

PHILLIP L. CARTER, DBA, is the executive director of CAPS Research, a center jointly sponsored by the Institute for Supply Management and Arizona State University (ASU) and funded primarily by multinational corporations. Carter holds the Harold E. Fearon Eminent Scholar Chair of Purchasing Management in the W. P. Carey School of Business at ASU, is professor of supply chain management in the Carey School, and is Professor Emeritus at Michigan State University.

MELISSA COFFIN, MA, is a research associate for the Chemicals Policy and Science Initiative at the Lowell Center for Sustainable Production, where she focuses on the use of the precautionary principle in public policy. She coordinates the Green Chemistry and Commerce Council (GC3), a group of proactive industry, academic, and government organizations that work collaboratively to find green chemistry solutions within their supply chains and in finished products. She also staffs the Toward Tomorrow initiative, a joint venture of the Lowell Center program areas, designed to inspire a new generation of environmental and health leaders to create a more sustainable future.

HADI DOWLATABADI, PhD, is a professor at the University of British Columbia in the Institute for Resources, Environment, and Sustainability and with the Liu Institute for Global Issues at the university. He also worked at Carnegie Mellon University, Resources for the Future, and the Rockefeller Foundation. At the university, he came to understand uncertainty in the performance and economics of unproven technology and the impact of these on choices and public policy, subsequently trying to apply systematic thinking to energy technology evaluation and policy. He learned that technical performance and economics need to be augmented with environmental and social impacts of technologies. His work can be characterized as explorations into understanding how these issues interact dynamically and into what we do not (or cannot) know about them before we have to make decisions.

MARK EDWARDS, MBA, PhD, is a graduate of the U.S. Naval Academy, where Jacques Cousteau motivated and mentored his interest in the oceans and global stewardship. He has taught marketing, leadership, entrepreneurship, and sustainability in the Morrison School of Management and Agribusiness at Arizona State University for most of his career. He also served as CEO of TEAMS Intl., a software and assessment firm. He was a director of a Fortune 500 food company and has done extensive research and development on new food sources and consumer behavior and has served as a consultant for Monsanto, Pioneer Seeds, DuPont, Nabisco, Quaker Oats, General Mills, Borden, and other food and transportation companies.

KARL R. HAAPALA, PhD, is an assistant professor in the School of Mechanical, Industrial, and Manufacturing Engineering at Oregon State University. As a trainee in the Sustainable Futures NSF IGERT project from 2004–2008, he studied public policy at Southern University–Baton Rouge, Louisiana, and conducted research within the Laboratory of Process Metallurgy at the University of Oulu, Finland, and in collaboration with the Advanced Materials Technology Group at Caterpillar Inc. in Peoria, Illinois. His research addresses sustainable design and manufacturing challenges related to emerging technologies, including alternative energy and nano-manufacturing, life-cycle engineering, and manufacturing processes.

PHIL HAMLETT, MFA, is director of the MFA program in graphic design at the Academy of Art University in San Francisco and a regionally and nationally recognized design consultant. Prior to his current position, he served as the communications director for Turner & Associates, where he identified fundamental climate objectives, facilitated the development of core messages, and explored how best to communicate those messages. He has worked for such clients as Yahoo!, Adaptec, Macromedia, Ariba, PeopleSoft, IBM, AT&T, and Coca-Cola.

HANNES M. HAPKE, MS, is a trainee at Vestas Wind Systems A/S in Aarhus, Denmark. He joined Vestas Global Research in 2009 and focused on energy storage research and wind power grid code compliance projects in the Vestas Power Plant research and development department. Since May 2010, Hapke has focused mainly on the development of a 2 MW turbine development project for emerging Asian markets.

TERRY IRWIN, MFA, MS, is the head of the School of Design at Carnegie Mellon University, Pittsburgh. She has been a partner/creative director in the San Francisco office of MetaDesign, an international design firm with offices in London, Berlin, and Zurich. Since 1986 she has taught design and been on the faculty of Otis Parsons School of Design in Los Angeles, California College of Arts and Crafts, and Duncan of Jordanstone College of Art and Design, Dundee, Scotland. In 2003 she moved to the United Kingdom to earn a master's degree in holistic science at Schumacher College, an international center for ecological studies, and she later joined the faculty to teach design thinking to scientists. She is currently a PhD researcher in the Centre for the Study of Natural Design at the University of Dundee, Scotland.

ROBERT JOHNSON, BS, MBA, is senior vice president of global strategic alliances for IHS and founder of Environmental Support Solutions (ESS); he is a well-known entrepreneur, industry executive, and thought leader. He has more than 25 years experience building successful software companies that enable organizations to drive sustainability throughout an organization by minimizing risks and maximizing performance. Under Mr. Johnson's leadership at ESS, the company delivered innovative technology solutions and services that addressed urgent business challenges, including greenhouse gas and carbon management, health and safety management, product stewardship, environmental compliance, corporate responsibility reporting, and crisis management.

THOMAS E. KISER is chairman, CEO, and founder of Professional Supply Inc. (PSI), a pioneering energy system design firm headquartered in Fremont, Ohio. Through Kiser's creative vision, PSI has patented a revolutionary ductless method of providing energy for buildings of all types and combined it with the innovative application of time-tested technology to achieve significant energy and cost savings and carbon footprint reductions for manufacturers, commercial users, institutions, and municipalities across North America. PSI's green energy systems are achieving 20–60 percent savings on energy bills and reducing carbon footprints from 30 to 90 percent.

H. SCOTT MATTHEWS, PhD, is the research director of the Green Design Institute and a faculty member in the departments of Civil and Environmental Engineering and Engineering and Public Policy at Carnegie Mellon

University. The Green Design Institute is an interdisciplinary research consortium at Carnegie Mellon focused on identifying and assessing the environmental impacts of systems and helping businesses manage their use of resources and toxic materials. His research and consulting interests are in the areas of valuing the socioeconomic implications of environmental systems and infrastructure, and industrial ecology. Of particular interest are using the Internet to facilitate environmental life cycle assessment of products and processes, estimating and tracking carbon emissions across the supply chain, and the sustainability of infrastructure.

JAMES NIEMANN is senior director of Business Transformation Services, SAP America. This group is the management consulting arm of SAP that bridges business strategy and implementation by combining industry thought leadership with a strong knowledge of SAP solutions. They partner with customers to provide the strategies that will achieve the desired results. He has more than 25 years of business experience, including 15 years of executive management experience in the transportation and distribution industries. Mr. Niemann has significant national and international experience across the areas of operations improvement, business process transformation, corporate strategic planning, information technology strategic planning, financial analysis, cost management, and market research.

BRADLEY D. PARRISH, PhD, is a scholar-practitioner currently based in Bogor, Indonesia. He is a visiting research fellow in environmental social sciences at the School of Earth and Environment, University of Leeds, UK, and cofounder of an Indonesian-based start-up venture. His professional work in the area of humans and the natural environment seeks to put theory into practice, and practice into theory.

MELEA PRESS, PhD, is assistant professor of marketing and sustainable business practices at the University of Wyoming. Before receiving her PhD, she dedicated herself to printmaking and book arts, and spent time at Peacock Printmakers in Aberdeen, Scotland, and the Women's Studio Workshop in Rosendale, New York. Her interest in social science solidified in 1999 while she was doing volunteer work at The Hope Project in the Nizamuddin Basti in New Delhi, India. Her current work focuses on transformation, including strategies for building identification between constituents and organizations, strategies for organizations to engage with more sustainable business practices, and innovation in market channels. She is published in the *Journal of Public Policy and Marketing* and has presented work at numerous conferences.

DAN L. SHUNK, PhD, is the Avnet Professor of Supply Network Integration in Industrial Engineering at Arizona State University. He is currently pursuing research into collaborative commerce, global new product development, model-based enterprises, and global supply network integration. He won a Fulbright Award in 2002–2003, the 1996 SME International Award for Education, the 1991 and 1999 I&MSE Faculty of the Year award, the 1989 SME Region VII Educator of the Year award, and the 1982 SME Outstanding Young Engineer award. He has also chaired Auto-Fact in 1985. His primary area of expertise is supply network integration, collaborative commerce, and enterprise modeling.

BARBARA SUDICK, MFA, is associate professor in the department of communication and design at California State University, Chico. She teaches typographer and publication design. Her personal vision includes the relationship between print and digital media design, typographer and theatre, and the role of context in creating meaning. She continues to explore ways to embed responsible ethics of social, economic, and environmental sustainability in design practice and teaching. In 2008–2009 she was the Nierenberg Distinguished Professor of Design at Carnegie Mellon. She has more than 25 years of professional practice across disciplinary boundaries, and her clients have included such businesses and organizations as IBM Academic Information Systems, ITT Programming, the New York Public Library, and the Yale Repertory Theatre.

JOEL TICKNER, DS, is an associate professor in the department of community health and sustainability at the University of Massachusetts, Lowell, where he directs the chemicals policy and science initiative at the Lowell Center for Sustainable Production. He is a leading expert on chemicals regulation, regulatory science, and application of the precautionary principle and safer materials in science and policy. He has served as an advisor for governments, unions, nonprofit environmental groups, and international agencies. He is coeditor of *Protecting Public Health and the Environment: Implementing the Precautionary Principle* (Island Press, 1999) and editor of *Precaution, Environmental Science, and Preventive Public Policy* (Island Press, 2003).

FIONA TILLEY, PhD, seeks to be a practitioner of education for sustainability. Currently based in the United Kingdom, Fiona is a visiting research fellow in environmental social sciences at the School of Earth and Environment at the University of Leeds. Her interests include sustainability entrepreneurship, community building for sustainability, and holistic living.

ANDREAS VOGEL, PhD, recently returned to research when he joined SAP Research in October 2007, where he started the program Green2.0. Prior to joining SAP Research, Vogel held a variety of executive positions at SAP: as a member of the Corporate Consulting Team, he advised the chairman, the CEO, and executive board members on strategic topics; as vice president of product management, he led the initiative to service-enable (Enterprise SOA) SAP's core product ERP (financial and human resource enterprise software), managed the global roll-out of ERP 2005, helped with the creation of a new business unit, Governance, Risk and Compliance, and produced a business plan for SAP to become a leader in environmental management software.

CHRISTOPHER L. WEBER, PhD, is a research assistant professor of civil and environmental engineering and member of the Green Design Institute at Carnegie Mellon University. His doctoral research at Carnegie Mellon involved the connections between international trade, economic growth, and the environmental and climate impacts of household consumption in the United States and China. His current research interests involve climate change and the use of life cycle assessment and input–output analysis in business and government policy. His work includes, among other areas, environmental implications of globalization and international trade, life cycle assessment, and carbon footprinting and carbon labeling in environmental policy.

CHARLIE WILSON, PhD, is a lecturer in energy and climate change in the Tyndall Centre at the University of East Anglia, United Kingdom. His research interests focus on how people behave and make decisions with respect to energy and the environment. He had a previous career in the private sector working on renewable energy finance and energy policy.

ANDREW WINSTON, MBA, is a globally recognized expert on how business can profit from environmental thinking. He advises some of the world's leading companies, including Bank of America, HP, Boeing, Pepsi, and Bayer. He serves on the sustainability advisory board of the Kimberly-Clark Corporation. He is the coauthor of the bestseller *Green to Gold* (Yale, 2006) and author of *Green Recovery* (Harvard Business Press, 2009), a guide to surviving and thriving in an economic downturn. Winston is a highly respected and dynamic speaker, exploring the business benefits of going green with audiences around the world. His earlier career included corporate strategy at Boston Consulting Group and management positions in marketing and business development at Time Warner and MTV.

BRIAN K. YEOMAN has been the city director of the Clinton Climate Initiative since May 2007. He works closely with the leadership of the city of Houston to establish the priorities for developing and implementing projects that reduce energy use, use cleaner energy, and reduce greenhouse gas emissions. He also serves as the director of sustainable leadership for the National Association of Educational Procurement. He provides executive-level staff work for the chief executive officer and works with committees and board members on sustainability issues. He is the author of the first national Green Procurement Survey in higher education. He has developed curriculum for a sustainability institute, a diversity institute, e-commerce pro-cards, and strategic sourcing. He has written the "Roamin' with Yeoman" column for more than 17 years for the *NAEP Journal*.

ZHAOHUI WU, PhD, is an associate professor of supply chain management at the College of Business of Oregon State University. His research interests include supply networks and environmental decision-making strategy in supply chain operations. His research is published in *Journal of Operations Management*, *Journal of Supply Chain Management*, and *Journal of Cleaner Productions*, among others. Zhaohui worked as a buyer at Lord Corporation, a U.S. aerospace company, and as a project manager at CMEC, a Chinese international trade company.

Index